THE

HISTORY OF FREEMASONRY

Its Antiquities, Symbols, Constitutions, Customs, Etc.

*Embracing an Investigation of the Records of the Organisations of the
Fraternity in England, Scotland, Ireland, British Colonies,
France, Germany, and the United States.*

Derived from Official Sources.

By ROBERT FREKE GOULD, Barrister-at-Law,

Past Senior Grand Deacon of England;

Author of " The Four Old Lodges," " The Atholl Lodges," Etc.

VOLUME VI.

LONDON:

THOMAS C. JACK, 45 LUDGATE HILL.

1887.

CONTENTS.

LIST OF ILLUSTRATIONS.

IV. THE NATIONAL GRAND LODGE OF ALL GERMAN FREEMASONS AT BERLIN.[1]

The above title of this Grand Lodge is not now and never was justified. It is a barefaced usurpation. The Lodge never has been national in the way claimed, as embracing all Germany, and even at its birth was not so in the more restricted sense as applying to Prussia, where the National Grand Mother Lodge of the Three Globes already existed. That it assumed until quite recently to be the only legal Grand Lodge in Germany, that it to this day poses as infallible, the only true exponent of Freemasonry with the sole exception of Sweden, is, however, only in perfect keeping with the imperious temper of its founder. From its inception the Lodge has been dictatorial and oppressive towards its own daughters; scornful and even impertinent towards its equals; boastful of its own superior light, yet persistently shrouding itself in darkness; founded by a violation of all masonic legality, yet a stickler for legal forms when they suit its own convenience; revolutionary at its birth, and ever since most rigidly conservative. Nevertheless this Grand Lodge is the second largest in Germany, and has produced Masons of the highest culture, whose very names must always remain an honour to the Fraternity. Zinnendorff and his immediate friends and successors knew their own minds at a time when their German brethren were vacillating between Clermont degrees, Strict Observance Rites, Rosicrucianism, *et hoc genus omne*, and so knowing, carried out their views astutely, ruthlessly, and persistently—with the success that usually attends all well-directed efforts. No official history of this Grand Lodge has ever been published; its partisans speak with awe of its ancient documents, and hide them from the gaze of the student. Like holy relics they are only accessible to devout believers; nay, even a complete book of Constitutions has never been placed within reach of the public; and Worshipful Masters, in order to govern their Lodges, have been constrained to gather together the decisions pronounced at various times by the Grand Lodge, each thus forming for himself a species of digest of the common law as settled by decided cases. Such a collection has been made in Vol. xxvi. of the "Latomia," and will be used by me; my other facts I have had to collect from divers sources, but many gaps still remain to be filled up.

The early annals of this Grand Lodge are indissolubly connected with Zinnendorff, one of the most remarkable and perhaps unscrupulous Masons of whom we have any record. Ellenberger was his patronymic, and he was born August 11, 1731, at Halle; but, being adopted by his mother's brother, took his uncle's name of Zinnendorff. He followed the medical profession, and rose to be the chief of that department in the Prussian army, retiring in 1779. His initiation took place at Halle, March 13, 1757. When he joined a Berlin *Lodge*, or even which Lodge it was, are alike unknown; but he was one of the early members of the Berlin *Chapter* of Jerusalem. We have already seen how Schubart, the Deputy G.M. of the "Three Globes," was in November 1763 won over by Von Hund. Schubart's first step was to despatch a letter in Von Hund's interest to the "Three Globes," which was to be opened in the presence of 24 brethren, who were specified. On its arrival, Zinnendorff and three others being with Von Printzen, the G.M., Zinnendorff persuaded

---

[1] The literal translation of the German title is "Grand Lodge of the Country." I therefore reject as a barbarism the accepted designation "Grand Countries Lodge"—a phrase which proclaims either a contempt for, or an ignorance of, the structure of both the German and English tongues; it is not English, and it is not German, because *Landes* is not the plural of *Land*, which would be *Länder*, but its genitive singular.

them to open the letter then and there, and to extenuate their fault as an excess of zeal. Schubart being asked " for more light," insisted upon the letter being shown to the others, and as a result Zinnendorff and Krüger were selected to visit Von Hund. Probably from selfish motives, the former of these emissaries appeared alone, saying that the latter was ill, but this was afterwards denied by Krüger, who ultimately arrived on the scene. Zinnendorff signed the act of Strict Observance (*or* Unquestioning Obedience), August 24, 1764, was knighted by Von Hund October 30, and made Prefect of Templin, *i.e.*, Berlin, on the 6th.

In June 1765 Zinnendorff was elected G.M. of the Three Globes, possibly because the Lodge was already tending towards the Strict Observance sytem, of which he was the resident chief in Berlin. Scarcely was he installed before complaints arose of his arbitrary proceedings and haughty independence, not only from his Masonic, but also from his Templar subjects. Almost his first act was to despatch his friend Baumann to Stockholm in order to obtain information there respecting the Swedish rite. The requisite funds were taken from the treasury of the Three Globes, though the Lodge was not consulted either with regard to the mission or the appropriation of its money—and, worst of all, Zinnendorff kept for his own use the information so acquired, at a cost to the Lodge for travelling expenses of 1100 thalers. Baumann obtained from Dr Eckleff not only the rituals of the Swedish High Degrees, but a warrant of constitution; and Findel states that the latter was 220 ducats in pocket by the transaction.[1] It is a somewhat important point to decide whether Eckleff[2] was at this time G.M. of the Grand Lodge of Sweden, or merely, as the Swedish Grand Lodge subsequently affirmed, the Head-Master of the Scots Chapter at Stockholm. We have already seen that the Grand Lodge of Sweden was formed in 1759, and that on December 7, 1762, the King assumed the Protectorate, so that the probability is that *he* was virtually its G.M. But even if Eckleff were at the time G.M., it is obvious that if he acted in the matter without the knowledge of Grand Lodge, the step was equally *ultra vires*. Both these grounds were alleged when, in 1777, Sweden repudiated Zinnendorff; but on the other hand, it should be mentioned that as late as 1776, the Swedish authorities were in close and fraternal correspondence with him, and these intimate relations must be held to have condoned any irregularities in the initial stages.

In 1766 the Berlin Templars complained strongly of the impossibility of obtaining any financial statements from Zinnendorff, but Krüger, who was sent by them on a mission to Von Hund, advised the Prov. G.M. to treat him delicately, because he might become dangerous and create scandal—another testimony to the character of the man.

In June 1766 Zinnendorff was not re-elected G.M. of the Three Globes, but of course retained his office as Prefect of Templin (which was not elective), and on August 9 the Three Globes formally joined Von Hund's system. The financial dispute between Zinnendorff and the Three Globes now assumed a threatening aspect, so Schubart and Bode were deputed to arrange matters in July 1766. Zinnendorff being called to account, made up a statement on the spur of the moment, showing that, even admitting for argument's sake the debt of 1100 thalers, there still remained 800 thalers owing to him. In the interests of peace and quietness it was at length decided to let the matter drop on both sides. On November 16, 1766,

[1] Findel, Gesch. der Freim., 4th edit., p. 419. For the preceding facts concerning Zinnendorff, as well as for much that follows, see *Allgemeines Handbuch, s.v.*

[2] *Ante,* p. 196.

Zinnendorff wrote a formal letter to Von Hund renouncing the Strict Observance; and on May 6, 1767, he resigned the Three Globes. By the "Three Globes," however, as well as by the Provincial Chapter of Von Hund, a sentence of expulsion was passed upon him, and from that moment he became the bitter and confirmed enemy of the Strict Observance system.[1]

In 1768, "by virtue of his inherent power," *i.e.*, as a Scots Master, Zinnendorff erected his first Lodge on the Swedish system in Potsdam;[2] on August 10, 1769, his second, the Three Golden Keys, in Berlin—of which he became W.M.;[3] and—November 3, 1769—he instituted the Scots or St Andrew's Lodge "Indissoluble" in Berlin. His conversion of two clandestine Swedish Lodges at Hamburg in 1770 to his own rite has already been noticed,[4] in fact such was his energy and activity, that before midsummer 1770 he had already 12 Lodges at work.

Then began a series of attempts to obtain a patent enabling him to erect a Grand Lodge. He first of all applied to the High Chapter at Stockholm, but his request was refused on the ground that Sweden never constituted Lodges abroad, a statement tending to invalidate Eckleff's proceedings. Undaunted, Zinnendorff called his 12 Lodges together and proclaimed the "National Grand Lodge for all German Freemasons."[5] According to *his* view none but those of his own rite were entitled to be called Freemasons, and least of all, the brethren under the Strict Observance. I have been unable to glean any particulars of the primary organisation of this Grand Lodge, but from subsequent facts I believe it to have been (in theory) representative, and that all Masters (in office) were members. As the election of these Masters, however, was invalid unless approved by the Grand Lodge, the system of representation was defective and a sham, because the Grand Lodge practically became self elective. Now, although Zinnendorff always professed the greatest contempt for the Grand Lodge of England as being deficient in true knowledge—and possessing the shell only, of which he and the Swedish Masons held the kernel—yet his advances meeting with no encouragement from Sweden, he made application to London—March 29, 1771—requesting recognition as a Grand Lodge, partly on the ground of possessing superior degrees, and partly from the circumstance of his holding a Swedish patent. The petition, however, failed to elicit any response.[6]

Upon this followed the constitution of a second Berlin Lodge, "The Golden Ship," and the election of Martin Kronke as G.M. with Zinnendorff as Dep. G.M.

On October 29, 1771, he renewed his request, and on this occasion to De Vignolles[7] as Prov. G.M. for foreign Lodges. But De Vignolles at least understood the course affairs had taken, and answered that he could not even acknowledge him as a brother until he had proof that he was received in a legitimate Lodge. The only legitimate Lodge in Berlin was the "Royal York;" the Three Globes had never been warranted by England, and was now a Strict Observance Lodge, and all such were clandestine. That beyond this it would be most unseemly of England to subordinate such personages as the Duke of Brunswick[8] and other Provincial Grand Masters to unknown men like Zinnendorff and Kronke.[9] Zinnendorff's efforts were therefore turned to procuring a show of regularity—and a prince as G.M.

Accordingly, on January 8, 1772, he applied to the Royal York Lodge for permission to use their rooms for an initiation, and invited that Lodge to be present on the 10th. This was

[1] *Ante*, p. 104; and O'Etzel, Geschichte, etc., p. 55. [2] O'Etzel, etc., p. 55. [3] *Ibid.*, p. 17. [4] *Ante*, p. 226.
[5] Acta Latomorum, p. 96; and O'Etzel, p. 61. [6] Findel, p. 422. [7] Chap. XX., pp. 474, 495.
[8] Appointed Prov. G.M. of Brunswick in 1770, but who had already at this time joined the Strict Observance.
[9] Findel, p. 422; and Allgemeines Handbuch, *s.v.* Zinnendorff.

done, a sheet of paper was clandestinely inserted in the minute-book of Royal York, the proceedings taken down, signed by the Royal York members, and the sheet secretly abstracted and forwarded to England, in order to prove that Zinnendorff and his friends were acknowledged as regular Masons by a properly constituted English Lodge.[1]

On August 11 following he further induced the Landgrave Louis of Hesse Darmstadt to accept the office of G.M., and negotiations were resumed with England; this time with Grand Secretary Heseltine, and in spite of De Vignolles, who, writing to Du Bois[2] in Holland, states that matters were arranged behind his back, and accuses Heseltine of receiving a £50 bribe.[3] In the same year a third Berlin Lodge—" Pegasus "—was warranted, and the total of subordinate Lodges had risen to 18.

Zinnendorff's great argument of course was, that the Strict Observance had strangled pure Freemasonry in Germany, and that it was necessary to erect a powerful Grand Lodge as a counterpoise. That his own system was as great an innovation as any of the others he naturally concealed, as he did the fact that all he wanted was England's name to conjure with. In its lamentable ignorance the Grand Lodge of England fell into the trap—De Vignolles appears to have been the only one of its officers *au courant* of passing events—and in consequence acted most unjustly towards its faithful daughter the P.G.L. of Frankfort.

On November 19, 1773, "the Grand Secretary (Heseltine) informed the G.L. of England of a proposal for establishing a friendly union and correspondence with the G.L. of Germany, held at Berlin, under the patronage of His Serene Highness the Prince of Hesse and Darmstadt, which met with general approbation."[4]

The compact with Zinnendorff[5] was signed (on behalf of the G.L. of England) November 30, 1773. As it was executed in Berlin on October 20, it is evident that the terms had already been settled by Zinnendorff and Heseltine prior to the latter's motion in Grand Lodge. §§ 1 and 2 confirm in their offices Prince Ferdinand at Brunswick and Gogel at Frankfort for their respective lifetimes, protect their districts, and leave them free—in the future—to make terms with the Grand Lodge of Germany. § 3 deposes various other Prov. G.M.'s (who had gone over to the Strict Observance), among whom I need only mention Jaenisch of Hamburg. § 4 reserves Hanover as common ground for England and Berlin. By § 5 Berlin is to contribute to the charity according to its increase of power, but never less than £25 per annum. § 6 recognises the German Grand Lodge as the only constituent power in Germany, always excepting Brunswick and Frankfort, and these only for the term of the then existing personal patents. § 7 forbids the G.L. at Berlin to exercise its powers outside Germany. In clause 9 both parties bind themselves to combat *all innovations in Masonry*, especially the Strict Observance.

Zinnendorff had thus, although under false pretences, obtained his point, and was con-

---

[1] Hauptmomente der Geschichte der Grossen Loge von Preussen Royal York zur Freundschaft, p. 19.

[2] G. Sec. of G.L. of the Netherlands.

[3] Allgemeines Handbuch, *loc. cit.* The following excerpt from the minutes of the G.L. of England—April 23, 1773 —may possibly serve to explain De Vignolles' mistake, and clear the G. Secretary from an odious charge:—'' Bro. Charles Hanbury, of Hamburg, Esq., attended the G. Lodge, and on behalf of the G. Lodge of Germany, situated at Berlin, paid in the sum of £50 towards the fund for building a Hall, and received the thanks of the Grand Lodge thereupon."—But although Heseltine personally could not have benefited by this, yet the transaction does bear the appearance of at least a propitiatory gift to the G.L. The donation was made in April, and the contract with Zinnendorff in the following October and November at Berlin and London respectively.

[4] Constitutions, 1784, p. 305.   [5] For the text see Findel, pp. 822-824.

stituted the sole Masonic authority in Germany, by the Mother Grand Lodge of the Craft, and July 16, 1774, his own G.L. obtained the protection of Frederick the Great.[1] Prince Louis having served the end for which he was elected, was evidently treated with scant courtesy, for on September 20, 1774, the Landgrave resigned, alleging as his reason for so doing, that he was ignored in his own Grand Lodge.[2] Zinnendorff was elected G.M., but in the following year—June 30, 1775—made way for Duke Ernest II. of Saxe-Gotha-Altenburg.[3] This high-minded prince exerted all his efforts to heal the strife which raged between Zinnendorff's Lodges and the Strict Observance, and though he failed to accomplish a union, at least succeeded—July 1776—in effecting a pact of mutual recognition and tolerance. This, however, being at once broken by Zinnendorff, the Duke—unable to endure the petty quarrels any longer—resigned, and was succeeded by G.M. Golz[4]—December 21, 1776—and by Dr T. Munssen in 1777.[5] Meanwhile the system had increased considerably; in Berlin alone Lodge "Constancy" was erected in 1775, and Lodges "Pilgrim," "Golden Plough," and "Ram" in 1776, making a total of no less than 7 Lodges in that city.

At this period began the negotiations between the S.O. and the Duke of Sudermania, threatening to end in the withdrawal of Sweden's tacit support of the National Grand Lodge. The Strict Observance Masons may at this time be said to have had only one formidable rival, viz., Zinnendorff, whose party enjoyed the great advantage of knowing their own minds, whereas we have seen that Ferdinand and his friends did not. Such an opportunity of humiliating Zinnendorff could not be allowed to pass, but that able tactician, who probably saw the storm brewing, took measures to draw still closer the bonds between England and himself. In April 1777 he despatched his attached ally, Leonhardi,[6] to London, who in August 1779 obtained a warrant to establish there the Pilgrim Lodge, No. 516 (now No. 238), under a special dispensation to work in German and use their own ritual. Leonhardi was admitted to Grand Lodge—February 7, 1781—as the representative of the National Grand Lodge, and took rank immediately after the Grand Officers.[7] We have already seen how in 1782 Leonhardi frustrated the efforts made by the Frankfort brethren through Pascha, subsequently to Gogel's death.[8]

Meanwhile—April 27, 1777—the Swedish G.L., to please the S.O. members, drew up a document signed by Karl of Sudermania and others, declaring that Eckleff's patent to Zinnendorff had been granted without the knowledge or consent of the Chapter, and therefore—being illegal—was thereby cancelled and annulled.[9] In August the Swedish envoys, Oxenstierna and Plommenfeldt, arrived in Berlin, published this document, and formally repudiated Zinnendorff and all his doings. Zinnendorff's circular to his Lodges announcing the foregoing proceedings is a masterpiece,[10] and however we may disapprove of his conduct, it is quite impossible to withhold our respect for his singular ability. He clearly places the G.L. of Sweden in the wrong, and demonstrates its inconsistency; he also frankly avows, " moreover, we no longer require the help of the Swedish fraternity, and can well spare their recog-

---

[1] O'Etzel, p. 61.   [2] Allgemeines Handbuch, *loc. cit.*   [3] *Ibid.*; and Acta Lat., p. 117.

[4] Findel, p. 425.   [5] *Ibid.*, p. 429.   [6] See *ante* (Hamburg), p. 226.

[7] Chap. XX., p. 478; see further, Festgabe, London, 1879, being the Centennial History of the Pilgrim Lodge, 238, by Karl Bergmann, P.M.

[8] *Ante*, p. 233.   [9] For the text see Paul, Annales des Eclectischen Freimaurerbundes, p. 225.

[10] To be found in Findel, p. 426 *et seq.*

nition." Nor was this an idle boast, for at that time (1778) eight years only after its birth, the National Grand Lodge ruled over 34 Lodges, with Provincial Grand Lodges in Austria, Silesia, Pomerania, and Lower Saxony.[1]

In 1780—June 24—Zinnendorff replaced Mumssen as G.M., and two years later—June 6, 1782—this unscrupulous but eminently strong and masterful man was struck down by apoplexy, gavel in hand, at the very moment he was opening his Lodge "of the Three Keys." His death produced no ill effect on his life's work. Able and resolute brethren—trained up in his school—were ready to carry on the system where he left it. His immediate successor as G.M. was Castillon; and that the death of the founder had not destroyed the spirit implanted by him, may be gathered from the fact that in 1783, the "Three Globes" having made advances by permitting the visits of brethren of the Zinnendorff Rite, the National Grand Lodge replied by enacting—October 30, 1783—that only Lodges on the official list were to be considered legitimate, and no communication was to be held with others.[2]

One more heavy blow awaited the National Grand Lodge. That which De Vignolles had been unable to avert in 1773, Graefe was destined to undo in 1786. Count Graefe, a Brunswicker (to whom reference has already been made), was a captain in the English service in America. He had also been a Deputy P.G.M. of Canada, and returned to Brunswick in 1785, with an appointment as representative of the Grand Lodge of England at the National Grand Lodge, which, under the contract of Nov. 30, 1773, was of course tantamount to representative for all Germany. On August 15, 1785, he wrote from Brunswick to the National Grand Lodge that instead of harmony among the Fraternity in Germany he found only discord and antipathy, and called upon it to assist him in finding a remedy.[3] The National Grand Lodge —October 20—expressed a willingness to receive and aid him, but objected to the term "Supreme Grand Lodge" as applied to that at London, and expected that he would only visit such German Lodges as were recognised by their own body.[4] Graefe's eyes were soon opened to the state of affairs, and in the spring of 1786 he left for England. We find the results of his report in the minutes of the Grand Lodge of England, April 12, 1786, when the Grand Treasurer announced that the intolerant spirit of the Berlin Grand Lodge had evoked quarrels and scandals in Germany, and that many Lodges looked to London for redress. It was resolved that the proceedings of the Berlin Grand Lodge tended to divide the Fraternity, to limit its progress, and were in contravention of the treaty of 1773, and that steps should be taken to abrogate or alter that compact.[5] As we have already seen, this was followed by the re-inauguration of the Hamburg Provincial Grand Lodge under Graefe, by whom—August 17, 1786—a letter was despatched to Berlin inviting the presence of the National Grand Lodge at the ceremony. He added "that Berlin appeared to doubt the power of the Supreme Grand Lodge to make new arrangements, but he prayed them not to force him to take steps which old friendship had hitherto restrained."[6] Castillon replied by excluding all Hamburg Lodges and even Graefe himself, upon which the latter issued a circular inveighing against the intolerance and injustice of the National Grand Lodge, and declaring it to be his duty to pronounce that body and all its daughter Lodges illegitimate.[7] This action was approved in London, and Leonhardi, finding his presence no longer of any use, left that city—April 9, 1787—and betook

---

[1] Findel, p. 425.   [2] Latomia, vol. xxvi., 1868, p. 89.   [3] Nettelbladt, Gesch. Frei. Systeme, p. 575.
[4] *Ibid.*   [5] *Cf. ante,* p. 228 ; and Appendix, giving Grand Lodge Minutes, April 12, 1786.
[6] Nettelbladt, p. 575.   [7] Findel, p. 462.

himself to St Petersburg.[1]   In 1788—April 23—the Grand Lodge of England apprised the Berlin Lodge by letter of the abrogation of the treaty, and—November 26—the G.M. communicated to the Grand Lodge that he had acted on the resolution of April 12, 1786, and gave his reasons for so doing.[2]   They are very cogent, and show more knowledge than usual of Continental affairs, but are too long for even partial reproduction; suffice it to say, that the Berlin Lodges, although deprived of all supremacy, continued to be recognised by the Grand Lodge of England as legitimate.   But in spite of all difficulties the National Grand Lodge continued to prosper as before.

In 1789—June 24—the National Grand Lodge became wearied of its isolated position in Germany, and passed a decree whereby the legality of all Lodges constituted by any recognised authority was acknowledged, and mutual intercourse permitted, excepting, of course, in the case of brethren of the Hebrew faith.[3]   This Grand Lodge has from the first been so intensely Christian that the Jewish question has never been even mooted, and it is only of late years that, yielding to outside pressure, Jews are allowed to be present in Lodges as occasional visitors.

Castillon resigned June 24, 1790, and was succeeded as G.M. by C. A. von Beulewitz.   By the Royal Edict of October 20, 1798, the National Grand Lodge was included as one of the three Grand Lodges of the Prussian States, and in 1799—January 14—Beulewitz died, whereupon Castillon was re-elected G.M.   From 1807-9 the Grand Lodge was closed on account of the presence of the French Army of Occupation.   In 1814—January 27—the G.M., Castillon, died; and on December 27 ensuing the previous Dep. G.M., Joachim F. Neander von Petersheiden, was elected in his stead, who was followed in turn (1818) by J. H. O. von Schmidt.

Under G.M. Schmidt the quarrel with Sweden was made up, and a contract of mutual amity and support signed, April 6, 1819.[4]   On this occasion the Grand Lodge of Sweden furnished complete copies of its constitutions, ritual, etc.; and Nettelbladt, one of the foremost Masons of Zinnendorff's rite, and an ardent defender of his master's probity, was at once set to work to revise the ritual of the National Grand Lodge.[5]   A backward glance at my account of Freemasonry in Sweden will enable the reader to discern that at the time of the Eckleff transaction the Swedish rite was still incomplete, as the cope-stone of the highest degrees had not been placed on the structure.   In consequence the National Lodge had always been deficient of two degrees, and knew nothing of a Vicarius Salomonis.   These defects were now remedied, the ceremonies throughout brought into unison, and a Vicarius Salomonis under the title of "Master of the Order," elected.   In 1821 we first hear of Palmié under that title, but I have not met with the date of his election, which was probably in 1820.   The G.M.—Schmidt—took the title of First Assistant of the Master of the Order in 1821, and retained it so long as he remained G.M.   A decree of October 2, 1820,[6] affirms that

---

Karl Bergmann, Festgabe, etc., p. 4.

[2] Chap. XX., p. 481; O'Etzel, p. 91; and Appendix (*post*) giving Grand Lodge Minutes, November 26, 1788.

[3] Latomia, vol. xxvi., p. 91.   [4] O'Etzel, p. 140.

[5] Findel, p. 516.   Although Nettelbladt wrote a history of all the other Masonic systems and rites (including the English)—in which the ignorance and credulity of their votaries are pitilessly denounced—unfortunately he has not favoured us with one of the National Grand Lodge.   He always, however, maintains its infallibility in strong terms, which to the student of to-day are somewhat amusing.   *Cf. ante*, p. 187.

[6] Latomia, vol. xxvi., p. 95.

Masters of Lodges are elected for life, the triennial re-election being a concession on the Master's part, not a right of the Lodge. The election of the Master, according to a decree of March 2, 1824,[1] was to take place by casting the names of all those eligible into an urn; the youngest member drew a name, its owner had to leave the Lodge, and his merits were canvassed. A ballot was then taken for him, and required a two-thirds' majority in his favour. If unfavourable, a second ticket was drawn, and so on until the necessary majority was obtained. In 1825—December 5[2]—it was affirmed that the election must be approved by the Grand Lodge; in 1830—December 20—that Lodges which became dormant ceded their property and funds to the Grand Lodge;[3] and in 1837[4]—September 11—that the "Master of the Order shall be *eo ipso* also Grand Master, but he may appoint his First Assistant to this office for life."

In 1838 Count Henckel von Donnersmark was elected G.M. in succession to Schmidt, but in 1841 the "Master of the Order"—Palmié—dying, he was elected in his room, and conformably with the above last quoted law, retained both offices until his death.

In 1843 Constitutions were printed, but I have been unable to procure a complete copy. They were only issued to Masters of Lodges—who are not allowed to show them, or even give extracts, and are kept under three keys held by different Officers of the Lodge.[5] Keller, however, gives some excerpts,[6] and the chief points are naturally more or less well known. The Inner Orient is composed of members of the highest degrees only. It comprises, at its head, the M. of the Order, his two assistants, called Senior and Junior Architects, and nine Officers. These twelve represent the twelve Apostles, and to a certain extent, the M. of the O. is the Vicar of Christ. Their functions are to supervise everything, but especially the ritual and dogma. The members have the right to preside and vote in any Lodge, and can even stop the proceedings. The Grand Lodge, with the G.M. at its head, is divided into two bodies, the St John's and the St Andrew's Lodges, to rule respectively the degrees of pure Freemasonry and the Scots degrees. Grand Officers must at least be Scots Masters. The ritual is identical with that of Sweden and Denmark.

In 1849 — July 24 — Henckel von Donnersmark died, and — October 23 — K. F. von Selasinsky was elected "Master of the Order."

On November 5, 1853, an event of great importance to the present generation of Masons throughout Germany took place; this was the initiation of Frederick William, Prince, now Crown Prince, of Prussia. The ceremony took place in the palace of his father, the then heir to the throne, who presided in person, in the presence of the Grand Officers of the three Prussian Grand Lodges, and in the name—or as we should say in England, "under the banner"—of the National Grand Lodge, of which he became a member. The Master's gavel used on this occasion was that formerly belonging to Frederick the Great. The eighth and last of the Berlin Lodges under this system was constituted exactly two years afterwards—November 5, 1855—and named in his honour "Frederick William of the Dawn."

In 1860—April 26—Selasinsky died, and Prince Frederick William of Prussia accepted the office of Master of the Order on June 24 following.

Ten years later—June 24, 1870—the Grand Lodge celebrated its centenary, with the Prince in the chair. On this occasion a bombshell fell amongst the brethren. The G.M., in a

[1] Latomia, vol. xxvi., p. 95.   [2] *Ibid.*, p. 96.   [3] *Ibid.*   [4] *Ibid.*, p. 97.   [5] *Ibid.*, pp. 83 and 87.
[6] Gesch. der Freimaurerei in Deutschland, 1859, pp. 14-17 ; and Findel, p. 423 *et seq.*

long and able speech, alluded to the superior knowledge and greater purity of origin to which the National Grand Lodge had always laid claim—also to its persistence in requiring that those statements should be taken as articles of faith, whilst the documents on which they rested were jealously preserved from the vulgar ken. He showed how impossible it was to resist libellous misrepresentation from outside, except by frankly producing proofs to the contrary, and how the assumption of infallibility was not only untenable in the nineteenth century, but injurious to the best interests of the Grand Lodge; and concluded by calling upon all to aid him in ascertaining the historical truth of those supposed documents and traditions, and to freely give up whatever should be found unsupported.[1] The excitement caused throughout the Lodges of the system was intense, and two opposing parties—of light and leading, of mystery and conservatism—were at once formed. In 1873 twenty brethren at Hanover were suspended for advocating reform, whilst in 1871 six Lodges attempted to found an historical and archæological union—a crime almost amounting to treason under this Grand Lodge. Schiffmann of Stettin received the prince's commission to undertake researches, but was denied access to the archives. Wearied by this persistent opposition, the Crown Prince at length— March 1, 1874—resigned his office.[2] In his place Von Dachroden was elected, with Schiffmann as Senior Architect. The danger then became obvious that Schiffmann might at the next election be appointed "Master of the Order," and have the archives at his disposal. The Statutes were therefore arbitrarily altered, and the election placed in the hands of the highest degree only. It was also laid down that the G.M. should live in Berlin. As Schiffmann held an ecclesiastical appointment in Stettin, he was thus rendered ineligible for election, but he nevertheless proceeded with his researches, and made most damaging discoveries. For this the G.L suspended him—May 1, 1876—but his part was warmly taken by several Lodges, and many, especially of other systems, made him an honorary member. Two months later— July 1—Schiffmann was expelled, and several Lodges who supported him were erased; others transferred their allegiance.[3] Thus for the moment the movement was crushed, but with the increasing enlightenment of our age, I cannot but think that the latent volcano is merely crusted over for a time, and that the smothered fire will sooner or later break out afresh. The position and attitude of the National Grand Lodge of Germany is an anomaly in the nineteenth century, and can only be likened in many respects to the standpoint of the Church of Rome.

In 1872 G. A. von Ziegler had been appointed Grand Master, and succeeded the "Master of the Order"—Dachroden—on his retirement, in both capacities. He in turn was followed by F. R. A. Neuland, the present "Master of the Order" of the National Grand Lodge of all German Masons.

In May 1885 this Grand Lodge, with 3 Provincial Grand Lodges, ruled over 93 Lodges, with a membership of 10,276, or an average of 110 members per Lodge.[4]

---

[1] An English translation of this address was read before the St Mary's Lodge, No. 63, by Dr E. E. Wendt, Grand Secretary for German Correspondence—March 20, 1873—and will be found in the Centennial History of that Lodge, 1883, by George Kelly and Wilmer Hollingworth. *Cf. ante,* Chap. XVI., p. 257.

[2] This was the *third* Royal G.M. of the National G.L. who resigned the chair in disgust.

[3] Allgemeines Handbuch, etc., vol. iv., 1879, *s.v.* Schwedischer System; and Findel, Gesch., etc., p. 568 *et seq. Cf. ante,* pp. 79, 92 (note 4).

[4] Throughout Germany no Mason may be an active member of two Lodges at the same time.

The epoch-marking dates of this Grand Body are:—

1768.—Erection of Zinnen-dorff's first Lodge at Potsdam.	1772—August 11.—Land-grave of Hesse-Darmstadt, G.M.	1777—April 27.—Repu-diation by Sweden.	1819—April 6.—Contract of Amity with Sweden, and com-pletion of Rite.
1770—June 24.—Creation of the National Grand Lodge.	1773—November 30.—Compact with England.	1788—April 23.—Repu-diation by Eng-land.	1853—Nov. 5.—Initia-tion of the Crown Prince of Prussia.

1870—June 24.—Centenary festival, and Prince Frederick William's speech.

V. The Grand Lodge of Prussia, called Royal York of Friendship, at Berlin.[1]

On May 5, 1760, the Lodge of the Three Globes was informed that several resident French Masons—Frederick the Great had established a large colony of that nationality in Berlin—had petitioned for a warrant to enable them to meet as a Lodge—"Joy and Peace"—to initiate Frenchmen only, offering to pay all their income into the funds of the Mother-Lodge. In fact it was to be merely a distinctly French branch of the Three Globes. The request was granted, and in the same year—August 10—Von Printzen constituted the Lodge under the name of the "Three Doves." No reason is assigned why the title originally chosen was not adhered to. In 1761—March 13—the Mother-Lodge took into consideration a request to enlarge the powers of its daughter, as it was found impossible to recruit the Lodge solely from Frenchmen and to carry it on without funds. The petition was acceded to, and a fresh warrant granted—April 12—whereby the Lodge became an independent sister Lodge of the Three Globes. Its title had at this time been altered to "Friendship of the Three Doves." In the same year it joined with the "Three Globes" and "Concord" in forming the Masonic Tribunal of which Von Printzen was elected Grand Master.[2]

From the character and composition of the Lodge it was inevitable that degrees beyond that of Master Mason would be wrought. These appear as early as 1763 to have included some or all of the following:—"Elect of 9, of 15, and of Perpignan; Red Scots Degree and St Andrew's Scot; Knight of the East; Knight of the Eagle or Prince Sovereign Rose Croix: the members of this last and 7th degree forming a Sublime Council, which ruled all the others. To vest these degrees, it is possible, with an enhanced authority, the Lodge procured —March 6, 1764—a Scots patent from the Scots Lodge "Puritas," at Brunswick.

The work was, of course, conducted in French, but not without exceptions. Thus in 1764 we find an instance of a Lodge transacting its business in German, but the minutes record a resolve not to do so again. A most curious minute occurs in 1765, when a member proposed for initiation, "somebody"—having forgotten the candidate's name!

July 27, 1765, was a most important date for this Lodge. On that day it initiated into the Craft H.R.H. Edward Augustus, Duke of York, the brother of George III., and his com-panion, Colonel Henry St John. On August 2 the Prince signified his acceptance of the title of patron of the Lodge, and authorised it to assume the name of "Royal York of Friendship."

---

[1] The history of this Lodge has been very well, although somewhat too concisely, told in its official publication, "*Hauptmomente der Geschichte der Grossen Loge von Preussen genannt Royal York zur Freundschaft,*" Berlin, 1849. The following sketch is given in the main on the authority of that work. For biographical notices and dates I am indebted chiefly to the excellent "Allgemeines Handbuch." Other sources will be mentioned when made use of.

[2] *Ante*, p. 243.

The Lodge then applied to the Grand Lodge of England for a patent, and entrusted the petition to St John. To this circumstance may be due the fact that the Lodge never joined the Strict Observance system, but on the contrary always strenuously opposed it.

The next few years furnish two events which may be recorded. On September 6, 1765, the Lodge warranted its first daughter, at Rheims; and in 1767—June 6—it initiated a Jew. This is remarkable, because in 1779 it had so far modified its views as to refuse admission to two English Masons because they were of the Hebrew persuasion.[1] The latter position it retained until the revision of the Statutes in 1872; but the Jewish question does not appear to have evoked the same strife in this Lodge as in the Three Globes and in the Eclectic Union.

In 1767—June 24—it received a warrant from England as No. 417, successively altered by the closing up of numbers to 330, 260, and 219 (1770, 1781, 1792)—after 1813 it disappears from our lists.

Its next step was to apply for a patent as a *Grand Lodge*, but—February 14, 1769—De Vignolles wrote refusing the request as beyond England's power to grant—a Grand Lodge being the result of several Lodges combining for the purpose. He, however, authorised the Lodge to grant a three months' dispensation to brethren to act as a new Lodge, during which time they were expected to apply for a constitution from England.[2]

The "Royal York" formally seceded from the Three Globes in 1768. Zinnendorff's proceedings within its precincts in 1772 have already been narrated.[3] In 1772 it sent a cypher to London in which to conduct its correspondence, and the same year forwarded by this means the statutes and rituals of its Scots degrees for approval. The result is unknown to me. In the same year also it warranted a Lodge at Besançon. Of this and the former Lodge at Rheims no further notices appear. In 1773 the Lodge gradually ceased to work in French, and—August 13—constituted its first legitimate daughter at Cassel. This Lodge was registered in London, November 19, 1773, as No. 459.

Meanwhile the treaty—so often cited—had been contracted between Zinnendorff and the older or legitimate Grand Lodge in London, and by it the Lodge "Royal York" came under the jurisdiction of the National Grand Lodge. The Royal York succeeded in making terms by which it was to preserve its own ritual and in a great measure its former autonomy, and concluded a treaty of union May 19, 1774. Quarrels, however, ensued and appeals to London, and in the end the "Royal York" reasserted its independence in 1776, a course of action which was approved by England, April 11, 1778.

In 1778 the Royal York constituted its second Lodge—at Mannheim—and in 1779 one each at Munich and Potsdam. A proposal for union with the Three Globes fell through in this year, but a treaty of friendship was entered into, which is still in effect.

In 1779—November 24—Baron Heyking was commissioned by the Lodge to travel throughout Poland, and where he found Masons in sufficient numbers to erect Lodges. This resulted in the formation (1780) of no less than eight Lodges, and ultimately of an English Provincial Grand Lodge of Poland.[4] From 1782 to 1795 nothing of importance demands record beyond the constitution of seven Lodges, and the occasional use of the names Mother-

---

[1] It had meanwhile been for a few years in close alliance with Zinnendorff's National Grand Lodge, which always has been, and is now, intensely Christian, which may account for the change of views regarding the Jews.

[2] Nettelbladt, Geschichte Freim. Systeme, p. 624.   [3] *Ante*, p. 253.   [4] *Ante*, p. 221.

Lodge and Grand Lodge as applied to the Royal York, but without a specific assertion of either of these titles.

With 1796 there commenced a period of evolution and internal change in this Lodge, not unaccompanied by strife. The central figure of the movement was one of the most prominent Masons of that or any time, noteworthy not only as a Mason, but also as a theologian, politician, and author—Ignatius Aurelius Fessler. I regret that the exigencies of space forbid anything approaching a detailed biography of this remarkable man. The following few data must therefore suffice.

Fessler was born in Lower Hungary in 1756, his father being a retired soldier, and his mother a religious devotee. Educated by the Jesuits, but refused admission to their ranks, he took the Capuchin vows in 1773. In 1779 he was ordained priest, and was at that time of a most serious and earnest disposition, verging on bigotry. But above all things he was plain-spoken, and in 1781 called the Emperor's attention to the disgraceful morals of conventual life. No longer safe in the monasteries from papal vengeance, he was placed in professional chairs at the universities, and led from that time to his death a most eventful and kaleido-scopic life, pursued by the unrelenting hate of the Jesuits. In 1789 he embraced the Lutheran faith, and in 1796 came to Berlin. He entered the Craft at Lemberg in 1783, a period coeval with the fall of the Strict Observance, the founding of the Eclectic Union, and the commencement of the first serious attempts to study and appreciate Freemasonry. Throwing himself with his usual ardour into this new pursuit, he succeeded in a few years in making himself acquainted with the broad facts of Masonic history, and the whole series of fantastic theories and rites to which the original institution had nearly succumbed. Such a man could not fail to attract the attention of his Masonic fellows, and accordingly, we find that having joined the Royal York, May 12, 1796, he was much against his wish forced by the brethren—November 20—to become a member of the Sublime Council. The Three Globes, Frankfort, and Hamburg G.L. had all reformed their rites or were engaged in so doing, the Royal York felt it necessary to follow suit, and in Fessler lay their best hope. One other matter also loomed large on the horizon. In consequence of the French Revolution an edict against secret societies might be expected, and although the Lodges would probably be tolerated, yet it was to be feared that the Royal York would be called upon to submit to the jurisdiction of a Grand Lodge, unless its position as a Grand Lodge in itself could be satisfactorily settled. De Vignolles' letter, already referred to, had indicated the only legal means of attaining this object, and we shall see that Fessler was not the man to neglect such a hint.

Scarcely was Fessler a member of the Sublime Council than he received a commission to draft a constitution, and to revise the ritual and bring the various degrees into accord. He threw himself with almost superhuman energy into the work. His first inclination, as was natural to an enlightened Masonic student, was to abolish all high degrees, and he made this proposal, April 12, 1797.[1] His coadjutors were, however, not yet prepared for such a drastic remedy, so he contented himself with making each (so-called) high degree a separate course of philosophy, and with remoulding the Sublime Council, which became the Innermost Orient.[2] His new ritual and constitutions were rapturously approved and accepted, August 3, 1797. The constitution was to be subject to revision in three, six, and afterwards

[1] Findel, p. 485.　　　　[2] *I.e.*, "Innermost" for *Grand*, and "Inner" for *private*, Lodges.

every nine years.[1] In 1798—June 11—at Fessler's instance, the Lodge, Royal York of Berlin, was divided into four Lodges—Frederick William of Justice, Victorious Truth, Urania of Immortality (with Fessler as W.M.), and Pythagoras of the Flaming Star. These four Lodges remained in many respects one. Membership is still interchangeable. The officers of one Lodge may be chosen from the members of another. They also possess in common a general and a charity fund. These four Lodges then combined to erect from among themselves the "Grand Lodge of Prussia, called Royal York of Friendship," with 14 daughters, viz., 4 in Berlin, and 10 previously warranted elsewhere. The Grand Lodge was at once recognised by the Three Globes, and by the King; but the National Grand Lodge refused to do so, maintaining that a Grand Lodge could not be formed by a single Lodge divided *ad hoc*, nor could such a body be established in a kingdom where one already existed—though when Zinnendorff established *his* Grand Lodge for Germany, the Three Globes and others were already in existence.—But even in the Royal York itself the measure met with bitter opposition from shortsighted and undiscerning brethren. Fessler, a strong man, imperious, hasty, though wanting in conciliation, overbore all opposition, but his victory made him enemies.

De La Goannère was first Grand Master, and Fessler Dep. G.M.; but the Grand Master being called to Coruña as Consul, resigned, October 5, 1798, and was succeeded, October 28, by F. W. A. Von Sellentin.

In the same month—October 20—the Royal Edict appeared, wherein the Royal York is named as one of the three authorised Grand Lodges of Prussia.

On December 20, 1798, the Berlin Lodge, "Victorious Truth," initiated and admitted to active membership, H.R.H. Augustus Frederick, Duke of Sussex, sixth son of George III., and nephew to the Duke of York, initiated in 1765.[2] From 1813 to 1843 the Duke of Sussex was Grand Master of England. Some idea of Fessler's rite may be acquired from the following facts. The Duke of Sussex was passed to the degree of Fellow Craft, January 19, 1799; raised a Master Mason, February 4; received the degree of Perfect Scots Architect, March 6; of Master of Mount Heredom, March 10; of the Cross and Eagle, March 22; and became an Elect of the New Jerusalem, December 23. In 1839, being then G.M. of England, he renewed his permission to continue his name on the books of the Lodge as an active member. Long previously—April 5, 1799—the Duke had agreed to accept the position of representative of Grand Lodge, Royal York, at the G.L. of England.

In the same year (1799) three new Lodges were warranted, and in 1800 the period arrived for the first revision of the constitutions.

Fessler, meanwhile, had entered into very friendly relations with another reformer—F. L. Schroeder[3]—whose influence now began to act through him on the Royal York.

In August 1800 Fessler once more proposed to abolish high degrees, but the time for this salutary reform had not yet arrived. Something in the nature of an extrinsic degree was still

---

[1] It was revised accordingly in 1800, 1803, 1806, 1815, 1824, 1832, 1836, 1845, 1854, 1863, 1872, and probably in 1881, but of this I have no precise record.

[2] Almost every writer states that the Prince was made in the Royal York Lodge, which of course is incorrect, as the name then only applied to the Grand Lodge or Legislative Body. But the mistake is excusable—at least I hope so, having committed it myself (Chap. XX., p. 484)—as it is easy to confuse the four allied Lodges with the Grand Lodge. Even Mr G. W. Speth—I am somewhat relieved to find—in his recently issued "Royal Freemasons" has fallen into the same error.

[3] *Ante*, p. 227 *et seq.*

urgently in demand. A compromise was effected. In lieu of the high degrees Fessler elaborated a history of Freemasonry, its origin, revival in 1717, early progress and subsequent obliquities. This was communicated to Master Masons in five "Steps to Knowledge," *Erkenntniss-stufen*, and to satisfy all parties, each step was preceded by a ceremonial, designed to symbolically illustrate various phases in man's life on earth. The ritual of the three degrees was remodelled on the basis of that of Schroeder, and the constitutions altered in accordance therewith. The complete revision was accepted, December 31, 1800.[1]

In this year (1800) one new Lodge was warranted, and the Sun Lodge at Bayreuth—now the "Grand Lodge of the Sun"—was affiliated, and remained for a time a Provincial Grand Lodge under the "Royal York."

In 1801—June 5—the G.M. Von Sellentin resigned on account of ill health, and—September 13—Ern. Ferd. Klein was installed as G.M. The same year saw the birth of a Lodge at Charlottenburg, and of the Lodge Socrates at Frankfort.[2] The total of private Lodges had now risen to 16.[3] In 1802 one Lodge was warranted, and the closing scenes of Fessler's connection with the Lodge were enacted. For some time angry feelings had been at work on both sides, want of appreciation on the one produced bitterness on the other, and Fessler's own domineering temper added fuel to the flame. At length the G.M. himself went over to Fessler's enemies. According to the constitution the Dep. G.M. was the all-powerful prime minister—the G.M., a very limited monarch. But Klein—a man of character and determination—was little inclined to play the part of *Roi Faineant* to that of Fessler's *Maire du Palais*, and the position became too strained to continue.

On April 30, 1802, Fessler wrote that to facilitate a reconciliation he intended to lay down his offices *pro tem.*, and requested all complaints against him to be at once openly preferred. On May 7 the Grand Lodge agreed to consider this as a formal resignation, and Fessler, indignant, resigned his offices as Dep. G.M. and W.M. of Urania on the 9th. His Lodge was then ordered to exclude him from membership, and Fessler hearing of this order—August 15 —wrote—September 6—with haughty scorn, washing his hands once and for all of both Lodge and Grand Lodge.[4] After many troubles in private and public life, Fessler entered the service of the Czar Alexander in 1809, and died December 15, 1839, aged 83, being at the time President of the Russian Lutheran Consistory at Saratow.

In 1803 the Statutes underwent their periodical revision, the Innermost Orient was remodelled, and besides overlooking the dogma and ritual of the Fraternity, became the dispenser of the Steps to Knowledge, and its subordinate Inner Orients were charged with the same duties in the provinces. But these steps were reduced to a single one under the name of Scots Master, and the initiations were abolished, so that practically from henceforth we have a modification of the Hamburg *Engbund*, and the rite of the Royal York may be looked upon as in all essentials that of Schroeder. The irony of fate willed that Fessler's original plans should be adopted within a few months of his expulsion.

In 1806 the Grand Lodge was closed during the French occupation, but the presence of the enemy served to draw closer the rival German rites, and the National Grand Lodge entered into a pact of amity with the Royal York. In 1808 the G.L. resolved that the officers of private Lodges must be confirmed and approved by itself, thus somewhat, though possibly

[1] Nettelbladt, p. 636; and Findel, p. 487.   [2] *Ante*, p. 236.   [3] Findel, etc., p. 490.   [4] Nettelbladt, p. 641.

unintentionally, limiting its own representative character. And at the revision of the Statutes in 1872, the distinctively Christian requirements for initiation were modified, so that Jewish candidates are now accepted.

Little remains to be added except statistics. Lodges warranted :—in 1803, 1; 1812, 2; 1813, 1; 1816, 4; also the Provincial Grand Lodge of Silesia; 1817, 2; 1818, 2; 1820, 1821, 1823, 1824, 1826, 1827, 1828, 1836, 1840, 1843, 1846, 1 each. Later lists I have not been able to procure.

In 1810—March 18—G.M. Klein died, and—April 30—J. H. A. Hey was elected to the office. In 1832 Hey resigned from sickness and old age, and died December 17, 1838. He was succeeded by Prof. H. F. Link as G.M., who died in office—January 1, 1851. On June 2 ensuing, Dr C. von Kloeden was elected G.M., and also died in office—January 10, 1856. A similar fate befel the next G.M.—Dr C. W. F. Amelang—who died December 3, 1858; and on the following year—March 26—Prince Louis William Augustus of Baden, a brother of the Grand Duke, was installed as G.M. The G.M.'s tenure of office being terminable with the periodical revisions of the Constitutions, the Prince declined re-election at the revision of 1863, but was appointed Hon. G.M., a position which he still holds. In 1864 Dr J. F. Schnakenburg was installed Grand Master,[1] and in 1873 Professor Chr. Fr. L. Herrig, who was re-elected in 1882, and still holds the office.

In January 1885 the Grand Lodge "Royal York of Friendship" ruled over 62 Lodges with 6102 members, or an average of 99 members per Lodge. Of these Lodges 4 are outside the limits of Prussia, 3 in Alsace-Lorraine, and 1 in Bremen. It has 1 Provincial Grand Lodge —that of Silesia—and 8 Inner Orients.

VI. THE GRAND LODGE "SUN" AT BAYREUTH.

On January 21, 1741, the Margrave Frederick of Brandenburg-Kulmbach erected in his own castle at Bayreuth, the capital of his dominions, a Lodge under the name of the "Sun," of which he remained Master till his death in 1763. On December 5, 1741, this *Castle* "Sun" instituted in Bayreuth a *City* "Sun" with much pomp, the Margrave himself taking part in the procession. The Castle "Sun" soon grafted on itself a Directory of Scots Masters, which in some respects discharged the functions of a non-representative Grand Lodge.

In 1757—October 24—this Directory opened the Lodge "Lebanon of the Three Cedars," in Erlangen ; and in 1758—May 17—that of the "Three Stars," in Anspach, the capital of the Onolzbach or cadet line of Brandenburg.

In 1763 the Margrave was succeeded by his uncle, the Margrave Frederick Christian, both in his civil and Masonic capacity.

In 1769, the elder line being extinct, the Margrave Frederick Carl Alexander of Brandenburg-Onolzbach (the younger or Anspach line) united the two Principalities. The Anspach Lodge of 1758 being also possessed of a Scots Directory, the new ruler caused it in 1772 to amalgamate with the (*Castle*) Sun Directory, and removed the seat of this conjoint Directory to Anspach, granting it jurisdiction over the two Sun Lodges in Bayreuth, the Lebanon Lodge in Erlangen, and the Three Stars Lodge in Anspach. From 1774 therefore the Sun ceased to work as a Mother-Lodge. In 1776 the City Sun went over to the Strict Observance,

---

[1] Under him in 1872 the Statutes were altered to admit of Jews being initiated.

which the Margrave himself had joined in the same year, being the first reigning Prince who ever signed the act of Implicit (or Unquestioning) Obedience. He himself was the son of the Margrave Carl who had espoused the sister of Frederick the Great, and been initiated by that king in 1740 in Frederick's Royal Lodge.[1] The Margrave Frederick dying childless in 1799, the Brandenburg Principalities reverted to Prussia.

By the Royal Edict of October 20, 1798, all Prussian Lodges were required to hold from one of the three Berlin Grand Lodges. Accordingly, in 1799—November 19—the Anspach and Erlangen Lodges joined the "Three Globes;" whilst the two Suns joined the Royal York in 1800, the Castle Sun being made a Provincial Grand Lodge. It naturally accepted the Fessler Rite, and was granted an Inner Orient, April 1, 1802. The Lodge of Truth and Friendship at Fürth, warranted by the Royal York—March 4, 1803—was placed under its rule, and also the "Morning Star" at Hof, constituted June 9, 1799.

In 1806 Anspach fell to the new kingdom of Bavaria. It had meanwhile been raised to the rank of a Provincial Grand Lodge "Anacharsis," under the Three Globes, with several daughter Lodges, and at the time of these all becoming Bavarian, Freemasonry was under an interdict in that country by virtue of decrees issued March 2 and August 16, 1785;[2] renewed by the Elector—afterwards King of Bavaria—Maximilian Joseph, himself a Free-mason, November 4, 1799, and March 5, 1804. In 1807, however—May 8—the King issued an edict of toleration, to which were attached very stringent conditions. A list of all members was to be forwarded to the authorities every three months, all changes of officers or by-laws to be notified, correspondence with Berlin to cease, etc. A further edict was published January 17, 1808, forbidding all State servants to join the Craft. As this deprived the Lodges of all their best members, judges, notaries, professors, military officers, and even schoolmasters and clergymen, the blow was a severe one; but many of the Lodges nevertheless continued to struggle on as independent communities, until in better times they were able to join one of the Grand Lodges of Germany.[3]

In 1810—June 30—Bayreuth also was acquired by the kingdom of Bavaria, and the Lodges had to conform to the same rules, the Sun losing not less than fifty of its best members.

The Provincial Grand Masters meanwhile, under the Royal York Grand Lodge, were Count von Giech, Von Volderndorf, and Schunter.

In 1811—December 13—the Provincial Grand Lodge of the Sun declared itself an inde-pendent Grand Lodge, with four daughters, viz., the City Sun under a new name—Eleusis of Silence—the Truth and Friendship at Fürth, the Morning Star and the Golden Balance at Hof—which was warranted February 20, 1804, by the National Grand Lodge of Berlin. By slow degrees and in spite of difficulties, it added to this number. The ritual was naturally the so-called "Fessler," that is, as we have seen, the "Schroeder" slightly modified, and which does not differ materially from our own. The first G.M.—Schunter—was followed by Münch, Birner, and in 1844 by S. Kolb—under whom, in 1847, the constitutions were amended so as

---

[1] *Ante*, p. 242.   [2] *Ibid.*, p. 123.

[3] By an English patent—dated June 6, 1806—"Charles Alexander, Prince of Thurn and Taxis, Principal Com-missary to His Imperial Majesty in Germany," was appointed "Provincial Grand Master for Bavaria." This description, however, is vague and misleading, since with the exception of Ratisbon—which was not permanently incorporated with the new kingdom until 1810—Bavarian Masonry was extinct. *Cf. post*, pp. 277 (note 3), 279.

to admit Jews to the full benefits of the Fraternity. In 1849—August 25—Chr. K. Künzel was elected G.M., and in 1862, Friedrich Feustel. At this time the Grand Lodge Sun numbered ten daughters. New constitutions were drawn up in 1868, and accepted in 1869. They are among the most liberal in Germany. The Grand Lodge is thoroughly representative on the English system; its seat as an executive body is at Bayreuth, but it holds, in turn, an annual deliberative meeting and festival at the various towns where it possesses a Lodge.

In 1872 Bluntschli became G.M., and in 1878 Feustel once more—the present G.M. being Dr Löwe. In January 1885 the Grand Lodge ruled over 24 Lodges—chiefly in Bavaria and Baden, 1 each in Hamburg, Bremen, and Norway, and 2 in Würtemberg—where Masonry was forbidden in 1784, but has been again tolerated since 1835. The membership of these 24 Lodges was 2017, or an average of 84 per Lodge.[1] A second Norwegian Lodge has since been erected.

VII. THE NATIONAL GRAND LODGE OF SAXONY AT DRESDEN.

Many Provincial Grand Masters for the circle of Upper Saxony and for the Electorate of Saxony were appointed by England in the last century. For instance, in 1737, by Lord Darnley, H. W. von Marschall to the Circle of Upper Saxony;[2] in 1762, Major Aloys Peter D'Agdolo to the Electorate; and in 1766, Count von Werthern to Upper Saxony. There were possibly others, with whom we need not concern ourselves, for it cannot be shown that they ever warranted a single Lodge or exercised their office in any way. Of Marschall it is known that he joined and accepted office in the Lodge Absalom at Hamburg[4] and nothing more, whilst at that very time Rutowsky was active in his especial district; and of the two latter, we know that they were expressly relieved of their duties in the 1773 contract with Zinnendorff.[5] Werthern indeed went over to the Strict Observance immediately after his appointment.

Nevertheless a Grand Lodge of Saxony existed at a very early date. Count Rutowsky—initiated at Warsaw in 1735[6]—who had been a brigadier in the French service, entered that of the Elector of Saxony in 1731, and was a Field-Marshal and Governor of Dresden in 1741. He died March 16, 1764. In 1738 he erected a Lodge of the "Three Eagles" at Dresden. It increased so rapidly that in 1739 a new Lodge of the "Three Golden Swords" was formed also at Dresden, which two years afterwards numbered over fifty members. In 1741—February 15—a third Lodge—of the "Three Swans"—was founded. These three met together, June 24, 1741, raised the Three Swords to the rank of a Grand Lodge, and chose Rutowsky as G.M. It appears to have been taken for granted by German writers that Rutowsky held an English patent—which may possibly be true, although in the absence of anything like evidence to authenticate the belief, it must of necessity remain an open question.

---

[1] I know of no official or detailed history of this Grand Lodge. The above facts have been gleaned chiefly from the Allgemeines Handbuch, 1863-1879, *s.v.* Bayreuth, Brandenburg, Erlangen, Anspach, Friedrich II., Fürth, Hof, Baiern, Zweibrücken, Kolb, Feustel, Würtemberg, Deutschland, etc.

[2] Once more I am constrained to protest against the uncouth title in common use, Grand Countries Lodge of Saxony (*Grosse Landes Loge von Sachsen*). Masonic writers, even of high classical attainments, have adopted this barbarism, of whose paternity I am ignorant. Yet, although a knowledge of German in every case is not to be pre-supposed, I think we are entitled to expect at least an acquaintance with *English* grammar on the part of English authors. The following sketch is again chiefly based upon the excellent "*Allgemeines Handbuch*," *s.v.* Sachsen, Dresden, Leipzig, Altenburg, Rutowsky, Marschall, Deutschland, Warnatz, Wertheim, Agdolo, etc., etc.

[3] Constitutions, 1756, p. 333.   [4] *Ante*, p. 225.   [5] *Cf.* Findel, p. 822.   [6] W. Keller, Fr. in Deut., p. 80.

The Three Swans amalgamated with the Three Swords, July 2, 1741. Earlier in the same year—March 20—a Lodge was formed at Leipsic, which subsequently became "Minerva of the Compasses," and is now the independent Lodge "Minerva of the Three Palms."[1] If not warranted by Rutowsky in the first instance, it certainly owned his sway *circa* 1747.

In 1742—January 31—this Lodge Minerva inaugurated the Lodge at Altenburg, now "Archimedes of the Three Tracing Boards," one of the five independent Lodges of Germany.[2] This also joined the union.

Rutowsky further warranted—September 2, 1743—the "Three Roses" at Sachsenfels, which was one of the first to join the Strict Observance; and in 1744 the "Three Squares" in Nossen, which soon afterwards died out. There are also traces of one or two other Lodges. The existence of this flourishing body at so early a date is very remarkable.

In 1755 the first efforts of Von Hund's still undeveloped imaginings may be traced in a Lodge—" Of the Three Palms "—warranted by him in Dresden on September 5.

In 1760 the Three Globes also began to constitute a few Lodges in Saxony. But this part of Germany was the very centre of the Strict Observance—Von Hund possessed large estates in the neighbourhood, at Lausitz and elsewhere—and naturally the first to be overrun by the new rite. In 1762—September 5—the "Three Swords" accepted the Templar ritual and system, and every Lodge in the Electorate followed suit. The history of the Craft in Saxony for the ensuing half century is comprised in that of the Strict Observance, the three Grand Lodges at Berlin, and the Grand Lodge of Hanover, all of which bodies constituted Lodges in the country at various times.

In 1805 some of the Dresden Lodges began to moot the question of establishing a National Grand Lodge. The idea met with general favour, four Lodges only—those at Görlitz and Bautzen and the two at Leipsic—raising objections. But the project came to naught, the stern necessities of war occupying men's minds to the exclusion of other matters.

In 1811, however, the subject was revived, and a National Grand Lodge for Saxony erected. Twelve Lodges combined for the purpose. These had been constituted, in the years within brackets, as follows:—By Rutowsky—1, The Three Swords, Dresden, being the original Grand Lodge of 1742: By the Grand Lodge of the Three Globes—2, Golden Wall, Bautzen (1802); 3, Leopard, in Lübben (1809); 4, Golden Cross, in Merseburg (1805): By the National Grand Lodge of Prussia—5, The Desert Well, at Kottbus (1797); 6, Golden Apple, Dresden (1776); 7, the Three Hills, Freiberg (1798): By Von Hund—8, the Crowned Serpent, Görlitz (1751): By the Three Roses of 1743 under the Strict Observance—9, the Three Flames, Plauen (1788): By the Grand Lodge Royal York—10, Harmony, in Hohenstein (1799): By the Provincial Grand Lodge of Hamburg—11, the Three Pillars, in Triebel (1806): By Lodge Archimedes of Altenburg—12, Archimedes of the Saxon Union, Schneeberg (1806). It will be remarked that Nos. 1, 9, and 12 connect this new Grand Lodge historically with the extinct Grand Lodge of Rutowsky. From this date the Grand Lodge, in spite of a few losses, has gradually, but continuously, increased the number of its Lodges. Some, however, of these were lost in 1815, because a part of Saxony then passed under Prussian rule.

The Constitutions were accepted September 28, 1811, and signed by the Lodges of the Union. They are the most liberal in Germany. The Union does not forbid high degrees, but

---

[1] *Post*, p. 271.   [2] *Ibid.*, p. 272.

simply ignores them, and deals only with the Craft. It permits any ritual in the three degrees provided a copy is approved by Grand Lodge. The Grand Lodge consists of two bodies. A legislative, composed of the Master, Deputy Master, and Wardens of each Lodge, and of a Dresden brother specially appointed to represent each Lodge. These all have a deliberative voice, but each Lodge only has one vote. An executive, composed of the Grand Officers chosen from among the members of the legislative body. The ritual used by the Grand Lodge and recommended to its daughters is that of Schroeder.[1]

Of the earlier Grand Masters of this body I have been unable to procure a list. In 1866 G. H. Warnatz, M.D., was elected to the chair, and, dying in 1872, was succeeded— October 27—by Dr Eckstein, who gave place to Albert Wengler in 1881. Under Dr Eckstein the revision of the Statutes, begun in 1874, was completed October 18, 1876. The chief alteration was a declaration that Jews were eligible for initiation—they had already been admitted as *visitors* in 1837. The executive still remains at Dresden, but it was enacted that the annual meeting of Grand Lodge may be movable.

The number of Lodges on the roll in January 1885 was 20, with a membership of 3692, or an average of 185 per Lodge. Of these Lodges, two—at Meiningen and Greiz—are not in the kingdom of Saxony. On the other hand, two Lodges at Leipsic do not belong to the Union, but are independent. The ritual is Schroeder's, with the exception of the Bautzen Lodge, which has retained that of the Three Globes, and the Freiberg Lodge, which still adheres to Fessler's. Dr Bernhard Arthur Erdmann is the present G.M.

VIII. Grand Lodge "Concord" at Darmstadt.

When Louis X., Landgrave of Hesse-Darmstadt, commenced his reign in 1790, the only Lodge in his dominions was that at Giessen, of which he was a member, as well as its chief and patron. In 1785 it had joined the Eclectic Union. In 1793 the English Prov. G.L. at Frankfort commenced to warrant a series of Lodges in this principality; which in 1806 was made a Grand Duchy, Louis X. becoming the first Grand Duke Louis I. By the events of 1814 he acquired a considerable extension of territory, and in the new provinces of his state existed other Lodges. He died in 1830, protector of all these Lodges, and his successor, Louis II., who took an active part in Lodge work, also assumed the title and duties of protector. By 1839 all the still existing Hessian Lodges had joined the Eclectic Union.

It will now be necessary to recapitulate some facts already alluded to. In 1808 the Grand Orient of France had constituted the Lodge "Nascent Dawn" in Frankfort, which contained a large Jewish element. After various quarrels this Lodge split into two factions: the Landgrave Karl of Hesse-Cassel reconstituted the Christian members as "Karl of the Dawning Light," according to the rite of the rectified Strict Observance, whilst the Jewish brethren received in 1817 a warrant from London as the Lodge of the "Nascent Dawn" (No. 684).[2] In 1836 Prince Karl died; and in 1840—September 27—"Karl of the Dawning Light" joined the Eclectic Union. The Lodge, however, could not agree on all points with its new Grand Lodge, more especially in relation to the high degrees, and after many quarrels and bickerings, was excluded on July 2, 1844. Its part was taken up warmly by the "Friends of Concord" at Mayence and "St John the Evangelist of Concord" at Darmstadt, with the result that in 1845 these two Lodges retired from the Eclectic Union.

---

[1] For the text of these Constitutions see Keller, G. der Fr. in Deut., p. 24.   [2] *Ante*, pp. 236, 237.

The *three* Lodges, which had thus recovered their independence, petitioned the Grand Duke and Protector, Louis II., to form a new Eclectic Union; their prayer was granted, and nine prominent members—one of whom, Leykam, will be presently referred to—were deputed to frame a constitution. This act of foundation (*Grundvertrag*) emphasised the purely representative system of G.L. government, forbade all high degrees (Karl of the D.L. voluntarily dissolved its Scots Lodge, which had been the origin of the whole quarrel !), and had but one fault. It refused even the right of visiting to Jews. It was signed by the three Lodges—February 27, 1846; approved by the Grand Duke—March 22—and on the following day the three Lodges met, proclaimed the Grand Lodge " Concord," and elected J. H. Lotheissen, President of the Court of Appeal, as their first G.M.

Curiously enough the Lodge Karl, whose traditions were so purely Christian, was the first to protest against the intolerance of the new Grand Lodge, and this it did within fifteen months. On December 14, 1847, a majority in the Lodge repealed the by-law which debarred Jewish Masons from entering their doors, and the minority, headed by Leykam, resigned their member-ship. In 1849—March 15—nine of this minority petitioned the G.L. for a warrant for a new Lodge in Frankfort, to be called Karl of Lindenberg. The old Lodge desired to raise no objection, but as it felt that it could not meet the new one in perfect amity, sought permission —November 18—to leave the Darmstadt G.L. Both petitions were granted, and Karl of the Dawning Light rejoined the Eclectic Union June 30, 1850. Here it will be convenient if I slightly anticipate, though at the same time I also go over ground that we have already traversed,[1] by at once recording the fact that Karl of Lindenberg also seceded to the Eclectic Union in 1878.

The Grand Lodge Concord—consisting of three Lodges in all—elected Betz as G.M. in 1851, and in 1853 Lotheissen once more.

Meanwhile, Louis II., who died in 1848, had been succeeded by Louis III., who was not a Mason, nor did he appear to interest himself at all in Masonic matters. Great therefore was the astonishment produced by a Grand Ducal decree of 1859, expressing a *wish* to see all Hessian Lodges united under the authority of the Grand Lodge Concord at Darmstadt. This affected four Eclectic Lodges, one each at Alzey, Giessen, Offenbach, and Worms ; and a royal wish being equivalent to a command, non-compliance probably meant dissolution. On the other hand, submission was difficult, because the Eclectic Union having admitted Jews to initiation in 1848, whereas the Darmstadt Union would not even allow them to visit, the Lodges ran the risk of losing their Jewish brethren, who had become very dear to them ; Giessen especially was largely recruited from members of the Hebrew race. Grand Lodge, how-ever, passed a resolution to allow these four Lodges to violate the constitutions, provided they would consent to certain disabilities, viz., deprivation of the right to vote on matters of ritual, and inability of their members to fill offices in Grand Lodge. The four Lodges then joined, making seven in all.

In 1859—September 11—Lotheissen died, and Matthew Leykam, Doctor of Laws, was elected G.M. As the latter resided in Frankfort, the Grand Lodge was removed for nine years to that city.

A new Lodge (No. 8) was constituted at Friedberg on November 10, 1862, and in the

---

[1] *Ante*, p. 240.

same year the constitutions were revised. Intercourse with their Jewish brethren having removed many prejudices, the right of visiting was conceded to all Masons of that faith.

The ninth and last Lodge was warranted at Bingen July 7, 1867, and—a further sign of progress—its constitutions permitted it to initiate Jews, but it had to submit to the same restrictions as the other four Lodges.

In 1868 the Christian Lodges, "out of their exceeding love," voluntarily conceded full rights to the five mixed Lodges, merely debarring them from furnishing a G.M. from among their members. Leykam, who died on February 20 in this year, was succeeded as G.M. by the Postmaster-General, Pfaltz.

At the revision of the Statutes in 1872 the Jews were granted full rights; so that in all Germany there are now only two Grand Lodges, the National and Three Globes, both at Berlin, which insist upon a candidate for Freemasonry being a Christian.

In 1877 the Frankfort Lodge joined the Eclectic Union, reducing the number of Lodges to eight, the figure at which they still stand. In January 1885 they numbered 855 members, or an average of 107 per Lodge. The G.M. is Phillip Brand, and the Protector of the Brotherhood is the present Grand Duke, Louis IV., who succeeded his uncle, Louis III., in 1877, and like the latter, has not been enrolled as a member of the Fraternity.

INDEPENDENT LODGES.

I. Minerva of the Three Palms, Leipsic.[1]

In 1736 seven Masons who had been made abroad, were in the habit of meeting together in Leipsic, and on March 20, 1741, they formed themselves into a Lodge. This Lodge is usually accounted a member, from the commencement, of Rutowsky's Grand Lodge of Upper Saxony; but it is also possible that it only entered into friendly relations with the "Three Gold Swords."[2] The Lodge had no special name, but it prospered exceedingly, and at the end of the year already numbered 46 members. In 1742 its services were called into requisition to inaugurate the Lodge at Altenburg.[3] In 1745 it split up and divided into a French Lodge "of the Three Compasses," and a German-speaking Lodge, "Minerva." These reunited on June 5, 1747, as Minerva of the Three Compasses, which was confirmed by the G.M. Rutowsky. In 1747—November 20—a Scots Lodge, "Apollo," was grafted on the Lodge.

In 1766 a difference of opinion respecting the expediency of joining the Strict Observance caused a majority of the members to found a new Lodge, "Minerva of the Three Palms," under Von Hund, and in 1772 they finally severed themselves entirely from "Minerva of the Three Compasses," which gradually died out. The Knightly Chapter was erected March 16, 1767.

In 1773 the Lodge constituted "Minerva of the Three Lights" at Querfurt, and in the following year the Scots Lodge "Apollo" changed its name to "Karl of the Three Palms," in honour of Prince Karl of Courland, a member of the Lodge.[4]

The Lodge took an active part in all the affairs of the Strict Observance, but began to tire of the folly about 1776. It therefore sent no deputies to the Wilhelmsbad Convent in 1782, nor did it adopt the rectified system. On the contrary, it ceased in 1776 to create fresh

[1] Allgemeines Handbuch, *s. v.* Leipzig.　[2] *Ante*, p. 268.　[3] *Ibid.*; and *post*, p. 272.　[4] *Cf. ante*, p. 116.

knights, so that the Chapter gradually died out, until at last the Count Hohenthal alone was left—who, to keep the history of the Chapter alive, formed a so-called Inner Union of a few chosen members of the 4th or Scots grade. The exact scope of this institution has, however, eluded my researches.

In 1783 the Lodge for a time showed signs of an inclination to join the newly formed "Eclectic Union," but it ultimately decided to remain isolated, or rather independent.

The last of the Knights, Hohenthal, died in 1819, and the constitutions of the Lodge were remodelled, April 8, 1820. The old Scots Lodge "Karl" was formed into a Directoral Lodge, governing the affairs of the Lodge. It consists of twenty-seven Masters. On the death of a member the Lodge submits the names of three of its Master Masons, from whom the Directoral Lodge chooses one to complete its number. Seven members of this Directoral Lodge combine to form an Inner Union, who also complete their number from time to time in a similar manner. The duty and privilege of the Inner Union is to discuss all matters of importance before they are submitted to the Directoral Lodge, etc.

Mahlmann, W.M., 1813-26, revised the ritual which had suffered much during the Strict Observance times, and this version was accepted in 1829, three years after his death.

The Statutes underwent revision in 1832 and 1867. On the latter occasion Jews were freed from all disabilities. In 1863 the Lodge had 359 members, which in 1878 had increased to 414, and in 1885 to 447.

II. BALDWIN OF THE LINDEN, LEIPSIC.[1]

In 1776—February 7—several Masons, among them some of the Minerva members, founded a Lodge "Baldwin" under the Zinnendorff rite. The Lodge was constituted on February 23 by Duke Ernest of Saxe-Gotha-Altenburg, G.M. of the National Grand Lodge of Berlin. It suspended work July 24, 1781, but resumed on March 13, 1783, under the title of the Linden (lime-tree). In 1807—November 7—this Lodge threw off its allegiance and declared itself independent.

Beckmann, the English Prov. G.M. for Hamburg, granted it a new constitution—January 14, 1809—as an independent Lodge under its present title "Baldwin of the Linden." The Lodge adopted the Schroeder Ritual and new constitutions—which were revised in 1833 and 1854.

The Lodge joined the Grand Lodge of Saxony in 1815, but retired once more in 1824, since which date it has maintained its independence. Its members numbered in 1864, 302; in 1878, 424; and in 1885, 509. The strength of the Leipsic Lodges is remarkable. There are but three in the city: Minerva, independent, with 447 members; Baldwin, independent, with 509; and Apollo—under the Grand Lodge of Saxony—with 384.

III. ARCHIMEDES OF THE THREE TRACING-BOARDS IN ALTENBURG.[2]

In 1741 several Altenburg Masons applied to H. W. von Marschall, Prov. G.M. of Upper Saxony, for permission to erect a Lodge. Marschall granted the prayer, and forwarded a copy of the English Ritual, but advised them to apply elsewhere for a warrant. The brethren turned to the Minerva Lodge at Leipsic, and were constituted by a deputation from that

---

[1] Allgemeines Handbuch, s.v. Leipzig.   [2] Ibid., s.v. Altenburg.

body, January 31, 1742.[1] From the very first, Lodge Archimedes conducted its proceedings in the vernacular idiom, and was probably the earliest German Lodge that ever did so; in 1743 it published the first German Masonic song book. In 1751 Prince Louis Ernest of Saxe-Gotha-Altenburg was W.M. of the Lodge, and he procured from the "Three Globes" a warrant for a Scots Chapter, which, however, died out almost immediately afterwards. The Altenburg Fraternity, which has always adopted innovations with reluctance, worked pure English Masonry until 1775. We have already seen[2] that on June 30 of that year Duke Ernest II. of Saxe-Gotha-Altenburg was elected G.M. of Zinnendorff's Grand Lodge; and "Archimedes" very naturally joined the National Grand Lodge and accepted the Swedish Rite. Athough the Duke resigned in disgust the following year, the Lodge did not reassert its independence until 1785, and subsequently to that date continued to use the Ritual, to which it had become accustomed in the preceding ten years, even keeping up the practice after joining the Eclectic Union in 1788.

It seceded from the Eclectic Union, in anticipation of the threatening political troubles, in 1793; and the same reasons induced it to suspend its meetings on January 9, 1795, after having declared its officers "permanent" during the interim. In 1796 it reopened. At the beginning of the century it rejected the Zinnendorff Ritual, and accepted as a temporary measure that of the Eclectic Union. Pierer received orders to compile a new one, and after carefully comparing the rituals of England, Scotland, Ireland, the Royal York, and Hamburg, his version was accepted in 1803. In the same year Schneider published the constitutions of the Lodge, a work even now much sought after for its valuable contributions to Masonic archæology, and which show a wonderful power of just criticism considering the time at which they appeared. From this epoch may be dated the rise of the brilliant Altenburg school of Masonic historians and students, to whose labours we are all so much indebted. No less than three Masonic journals owe their birth to this school—the *Journal für Freimaurer*, the *Zeitschrift für Freimaurerei*, and the *Ziegeldecker*—which in later years became the *Bruderblätter*. The last-named publication continued to appear until 1854. Fallou, whose work has been so often alluded to in Chapter III. of this History, was a member of the Lodge.

In 1803—December 18—the Lodge opened a branch at Gera, but this was afterwards constituted by it an independent Lodge, October 25, 1804.[3] The Altenburg Lodge divided into two in 1803, and erected a Directoral Lodge to govern the Lodge at Gera and the two new divisions at Altenburg; but the whole arrangement was abrogated in 1805, and the old position resumed.

In 1809 the Lodge established a branch in Schneeberg, but this joined the Grand Lodge of Saxony in 1812.

In the election of its officers, etc., this Lodge follows the English plan; but it possesses a sort of permanent committee to sift matters before they come before the Lodge, consisting of the Master and Deputy Master, the Wardens, and all Past Masters and Wardens. Its library contains over 700 valuable works. In 1823 it opened a savings' bank, largely used by the surrounding population. In 1861 its members numbered 210; in 1878, over 250; and in 1885, 271.

[1] *Ante*, pp. 268, 271.   [2] *Ibid.*, p. 255.   [3] *Post*, p. 274.

IV. Archimedes of Eternal Union at Gera.[1]

On January 16, 1803, several resident Masons formed a Masonic club in Gera, and at the close of the same year—December 18—this club was declared a branch establishment or "Deputation Lodge" of Archimedes at Altenburg, under the name "Archimedes of Eternal Union." That is, it could only act under the directions of its parent, and in its name, much as an agent acts for his principal. This state of tutelage proving inconvenient, the Lodge petitioned for independence, and in the result was reconstituted by Lodge Archimedes (of Altenburg), October 25, 1804. The German Grand Lodges, however, refusing to acknowledge the right of one Lodge to constitute another, and declaring the Lodge at Gera to be clandestine, the subject of this sketch at last petitioned Schroeder in Hamburg to grant it an English charter. This was issued April 30, 1806. It then accepted, and has ever since worked, the Schroeder or Hamburg Ritual. Gera was not in the jurisdiction of Hamburg; but G.M. Beckmann granted the warrant by virtue of his right to do so outside his district in states where no Grand Lodge existed.[2] At Gera and Hamburg the Lodge was considered as directly dependent on London, whilst by the English authorities it seems to have been long regarded as subject to Hamburg. This may account for the fact, that it only received an English number (669) in 1815, five years after the Prov. G.L. of Hamburg had ceased to exist. Virtually, however, "Archimedes" retained its independence. The princes of Reuss have ever been members and patrons of this Lodge. Speth[3] gives as such Henry LIV. of Reuss-Lobenstein (1810), Henry LXXII. of Reuss-Ebersdorff and Lobenstein (1827), Henry LXXVI. of Reuss-Lobenstein (1852), and Henry LXVII. of Reuss-Schleiz (1852). In 1862 the membership of this Lodge was 121; in 1885, 187.

V. Karl of the Wreath of Rue, Hildburghausen.

Hildburghausen is a town in the small duchy of Saxe-Meiningen. According to the *Handbuch*, a Lodge, "Ernestus," was warranted here by England in 1755, which only lived a few years. No trace of it is to be found in our Lodge lists.

In 1787 a second Lodge[4] was warranted—also from London; this is the Lodge Charles of the Ruewreath,[5] but our Lodge lists call it Lodge of St Charles, No. 495. It has ever since worked independently under the immediate protection of its princes, and the number of its members in 1885 was 54.

In 1883—October 14—the five Independent Lodges (pp. 271-274) entered into a Treaty of Alliance and Bond of Union. Dr Victor Carus of Leipsic is the President of this League.

---

[1] Allgemeines Handbuch, *s.v.* Gera; Verfassungs Urkunde der F.L. Archimedes, 1841; Asträa, Sondershausen, 1853, p. 258 *et seq.* Gera is the capital of the principality of Reuss, junior line, one of the pigmy independent states of Germany. A good tale is told of a German Liberal who was ordered by a prince to leave his dominions. "If," said the former, "your Highness will deign to ascend to the attic of your palace, you shall see me cross the frontier in five minutes!" The story might well have applied to Reuss.

[2] See the *Freemason*, May 16, 1885 (N. and Q., No. 599), where this warrant is given at length by Mr G. W. Speth.

[3] Royal Freemasons, Philadelphia, 1885.

[4] Continued in our lists until the Union.

[5] The Wreath of Rue is part of the armorial bearings of the Dukes of Mecklenburg.

EXTINCT GRAND LODGES.

I. HANOVER.

Of all the extinct Grand Lodges of Germany this is by far the most important, and naturally of most interest to English readers. I shall therefore devote a few pages to describing its career with some amount of detail; its equally defunct sisters will, however, in each case, only be sketched in broader outline.

In 1743—July 26—Prov. G.M. Lüttmann of Hamburg deputed Simon as Prov. G.M. of Hanover, but no sign exists that he ever displayed any activity in that office.

The following year—January 19—Lieutenant, afterwards Captain, of Horse Grenadiers, Mehmet von Königstreu was initiated in Lodge "Absalom" at Hamburg.[1] In 1746—January 21—he obtained a warrant from Lüttmann, and on the 29th founded the Lodge Frederick in Hanover, so called in honour of Frederick, Prince of Wales. In 1753—June 27—Hinüber was elected W.M., and in 1755 in consequence of a slight difference of opinion with Hamburg, and of discovering that the Lodge had not been registered in England, he made use of his business relations with England to ascertain if there was any chance of obtaining a provincial warrant for Hanover. Being assured that if the Lodge would indicate some special brother, a patent would be forthcoming, the Lodge elected Hinüber as G.M.—June 25—and—November 28—he was appointed G.M. of all His Majesty's German dominions, "with a power [in the Province] to choose his successors." [2] The G. Lodge Frederick in Hanover was registered as No. 208, became No. 122 in 1792, and was "dropped out" at the Union (1813).[3]

On June 24, 1756, the Grand Lodge made a formal visitation to the Lodge Frederick, and the next year—January 31—"Frederick" accepted a warrant of confirmation from the new G.L. of Hanover. In 1760 a Scots Lodge, "Karl of the Purple Mantle," and in 1762—May 24—the Lodge "George" of Hanover, were founded.

In 1764 Hanover was formed by Von Hund into the "Prefectory Callenberg" under the S.O. system, which at first was vigorously opposed by the G.L. and its daughters, but gradually acquired preponderating influence. The last Craft meeting of the Lodge Frederick occurred January 12, 1765.

Schubart arrived in Hanover October 13, 1766, and commenced his propaganda on the 27th. Prince, afterwards Grand Duke, Karl of Mecklenberg-Strelitz joined the S.O. in Celle, and was appointed Protector of the district; on November 25 the Lodges George and Frederick dissolved in order to reconstitute themselves as the Strict Observance Lodge of the "White Horse," and thus the G.L. of Hanover ceased to exist. As a consequence we find that in 1773 Hanover was made a neutral territory, open alike to the G.L. of England and the National Grand Lodge of Prussia at Berlin.[4]

Zinnendorff, who immediately invaded the district, met with remarkable success. In 1774 he established a Lodge of the "Golden Compasses" at Gottingen; in the same year this

---

[1] His father, Mahomet, had been taken prisoner of war as a child in Candia during the Venetian Wars. Prince Maximilian of Hanover brought him home and had him baptized Louis Max. Mehmet. He was subsequently ennobled, appointed Gentleman of the Bedchamber to King George, and died at Kensington Palace, 1726.
[2] Constitutions, 1756, p. 333.   [3] *Post*, p. 277.   [4] *Ante*, p. 254.

Lodge warranted the " Black Bear " in Hanover, and the " Crocodile " in Harburg, and in 1775 a Lodge in Lüneburg; whilst in 1777 the National Grand Lodge constituted the " Cedar " in Hanover, and a Lodge in Stade, and in 1778 one in Hameln.

Meanwhile the Fraternity had found themselves disappointed in the Strict Observance, and took no interest in Lodge matters, so much so that the " White Horse " did not meet between 1775 and 1778. The Protector, Grand Duke Karl, to remedy this state of affairs, ceased working the S.O. Rite, gradually altered the ritual of the first three degrees, and without formally renouncing the Templar connection, practically revived the extinct Grand Lodge by converting the Scots Lodge " Karl of the Purple Mantle " into a Directoral Lodge over all Lodges of the Strict Observance in His Majesty's dominions in Brunswick, Lüneburg, and Hanover. After the Wilhelmsbad Convent of 1782 the Fraternity in these lands declined to accept the rectified system, and calmly continued in their own way. Some few of the Zinnendorff Lodges, more especially the " Black Bear," at this time entered into more or less intimate relations with the Lodges under the Grand Duke.[1]

In 1786 this Prince being in England, procured, with Col. Graefe's assistance, the reinstatement of the Prov. G.L. of the Electorate of Hanover and British Dominions in Germany,[2] together with a warrant under the No. 486 for the former Zinnendorff Lodge of the " Black Bear." The Lodge " White Horse " then prefixed its former name, and became " Frederick of the White Horse," and, November 28, this Lodge and the " Black Bear " joined in re-establishing the Provincial Grand Lodge. A Royal Arch Chapter was also added by Graefe, but was very short lived.[3]

The district was, however, invaded in 1786 by the Eclectic Union at Hoya, and in 1792 by the National Grand Lodge of Germany at Osterode.

In 1796 new statutes were enacted in consonance with the new arrangements, of which the chief fault was the non-admission of Jewish candidates.

In 1791 the Provincial Grand Lodge constituted new Lodges in Münden and Einbeck. In 1799 Fessler visited Hanover, and was enthusiastically received, as was Schroeder in 1800. The immediate result of these visits was a closer bond of union between the Grand Lodge Royal York and the Provincial Grand Lodges of Hanover and Hamburg.[4] But of still greater importance was the consequent adoption by Lodge " Frederick "—August 10, 1801— of the Schroeder Ritual, and the example was soon followed by the Provincial Grand Lodge and all its daughters. This opened the door to candidates of the Jewish persuasion.

A troublous time now awaited the Fraternity in Hanover: in 1803 the French troops entered into possession of the country, and in 1806 were replaced by the Prussians. Meanwhile the Lodges only met when absolutely necessary, but it is worthy of note that they yet managed secretly to celebrate the birthday of King George. In 1806 the Grand Lodge of the Three Globes constituted a Lodge at Osnabrück. In 1807 the Lodges summoned courage to resume work; in 1808 new statutes were promulgated; in 1809 the Provincial Grand Lodge warranted a Lodge in Lüneburg, and that of the Three Globes another in Goslar; and in 1810

---

[1] Governor of Hanover for King George III. *Cf. ante*, p. 105 *et seq.*

[2] The patent granted to " Prince Charles of Mecklenburg-Strelitz," bore date July 5, 1786 (G.L. Records).

[3] This degree appears never to have had any attractions for Germans, in spite of—or possibly owing to—its similitude to the French Scots Master degree.

[4] *Post*, p. 282.

Hanover became an integral part of the short-lived kingdom of Westphalia. The Grand Lodge of that kingdom[1] was, however, so tolerant that the Lodges were not compelled to give in their adhesion, and although some few Hanoverian Lodges joined it, the Provincial Grand Lodge retained its separate existence, as did most of its daughters.

In 1813—November 30—Ernest Augustus, Duke of Cumberland, fifth son of George III., visited the Lodge "Frederick of the White Horse," and at the ensuing banquet prayed admission as an active member. It is needless to say that the request was joyfully granted. The events of 1814-15 raised the Electorate of Hanover to the rank of a kingdom, besides considerably enlarging its boundaries. In 1815 the Provincial Grand Lodge constituted a Lodge in Nienburg, and affiliated the one warranted in Celle by Hamburg in the previous year. It also received the adhesion of a Lodge in Göttingen which had been erected by the Grand Lodge of Westphalia, and several of its daughters who had joined that body now returned to the national fold.

Karl, Grand Duke of Mecklenburg, died November 6, 1816, and was succeeded as Prov. G.M. by Count L. F. von Kilmansegge, whose appointment is first noticed in the *Freemasons' Calendar* for 1822. In the same publication, the Lodge, Frederick of the White Horse, *reappears* as No. 146*, and eleven other German Lodges—Nos. 734, Frankfort; 735, Nuremberg; 736-44, Hanover—are *added* to the roll.[2] Gradually, however, a feeling arose that the Grand Lodge should declare its independence. In consequence—November 1, 1828—the Duke of Cumberland proclaimed the autonomy of the Grand Lodge of the Kingdom of Hanover, and was himself elected its first G.M.

The year 1828 saw the accession of the Lodge at Hildesheim, Door to Virtue, No. 312, warranted by England, December 27, 1762; and new Lodges were constituted at Stade 1845, at Kassel 1849, and at Klauenthal 1851. New statutes had been passed January 22, 1839.

At the death of William IV. in 1837, Hanover became an independent kingdom, and the Duke of Cumberland, G.M., succeeded to the vacant throne. He died in 1851, and was followed by his son, George (V.). In 1852—March 19—although not a Mason, King George V. assumed the patronage of the Craft, and in 1857 caused himself to be initiated in the "Black Bear," as the representative of all the other Lodges in the kingdom, becoming thereby an active member of each one of them.

Von Hattorf had been elected G.M. in 1851, and at his death, July 29, 1854, was succeeded by Count Bentinck, February 1, 1855. In 1857, however, the King expressed his intention of assuming the Grand Mastership upon the condition that the Hanoverian Lodges under foreign jurisdictions should join the Grand Lodge of Hanover, and that the statutes should be so altered as to exclude Jews from initiation. The latter condition was sorrowfully complied with; the former was only opposed by the Zinnendorff Lodge erected at Stade in 1777, which preferred dissolution.

In the following years new Lodges were constituted—1857, at Verden; 1858, Harburg; 1859, Leer; 1860, Ulzen. In 1861 the number of Lodges was 22, with 2187 members. The last Lodge was warranted in 1863 at Hameln.

In the Austro-Prussian conflict of 1866 Hanover unfortunately espoused the losing side, and

---

[1] *Post*, p. 281.

[2] All under the year 1821. Nos. 662—the Three Mallets, Naumberg; 669—Archimedes, Gera; 671—the Three Arrows, Nuremberg—were placed on our roll in 1815: and 684—the Nascent Dawn, Frankfort—in 1817.

suffered by annexation to Prussia. Now, inasmuch as the edict of 1798 only acknowledges three Grand Lodges in Prussia, and no other Lodges but those dependent upon these three, extinction stared the Grand Lodge of Hanover in the face. Nevertheless had it at once applied for permission to rank as a fourth Grand Lodge, and had the G.M. himself resigned, there is reason to believe that the prayer might have been granted. Hamburg and Frankfort are now Prussian, but the edict of 1798 was not enforced in their case in 1870. But resignation formed no part of the late King's intentions; there is every cause to conjecture that, on the contrary, the position of G.M. entered into his political calculations. Let us not heedlessly stigmatise the action of Prussia as tyrannical and uncalled for, but rather let us try to imagine how—in our own country—the case would have been dealt with, had the young Pretender been at the head of a British Grand Lodge in 1746 ?

The Deputy G.M., Krüger, endeavoured to get Hanover constituted a fourth Grand Lodge. King George thereupon tried to impeach him in Grand Lodge—by which body resolutions were passed—December 8—approving the step taken by the Deputy, but setting a limit to his future activity. Krüger resigned, as did his successor, Bödeker. The King then appointed Bokelberg. On April 17, 1867, the Grand Lodge resolved to petition the King to retire, upon which his agent, the Deputy G.M. Bokelberg, resigned. The Grand Lodge then took matters into its own hands, and—June 6—17 Lodges elected Krüger G.M. But it was too late. On September 30 the Minister of Justice and of the Interior closed the Grand Lodge of Hanover by virtue of the edict of 1798, and nothing remained for the subordinate Lodges but to choose their new superiors. Velzen, Goslar, and Osnabrück joined the Three Globes; Bückeburg, the Grand Lodge of Hamburg; Walsrode dissolved; "Cedar," in Hanover, joined the National Grand Lodge; the other 17 Lodges affiliated with the Grand Lodge Royal York, and were of material weight in carrying the more liberal constitutions of that Grand Lodge in 1872.[1]

II. MOTHER-LODGE OF SILESIA IN GLOGAU.

This was a Grand Lodge under the Strict Observance. On May 20, 1765, Von Hund constituted a Mother-Lodge at Nistiz, with the name of "Celestial Sphere of Gold." It was removed in 1772 to Gross-Osten, and warranted in 1772 a Lodge at Glogau. In 1779 the Mother-Lodge removed to Glogau as the Grand Lodge of Silesia. It constituted some other Lodges, but both the Grand Lodge and its daughters closed on June 24, 1794, after the downfall of the Strict Observance and the death of Duke Ferdinand of Brunswick.

III. MOTHER-LODGE FOR THE PROVINCES OF EAST AND WEST PRUSSIA AND LITHUANIA AT KÖNIGSBERG.

This also was a Strict Observance Grand Lodge. The oldest Lodge in Königsberg, the "Three Anchors," was constituted September 12, 1746, dissolved in 1760, and immediately reconstituted by the "Three Globes," June 10, 1760, as the "Three Crowns." In 1769 it joined the Strict Observance, and was raised to the rank of a Provincial Grand Lodge, as above, in which capacity it warranted several Lodges. In consequence of the Prussian Edict of 1798

[1] Ante, p. 265. Authorities consulted :—For the general history—Neueste Zeitschrift fur Freimaurerei, R. R. Fischer, Altenburg, 1838, pp. 161 et seq.; Geschichte der G. and V. Fr. Loge Friedrich zum Weissenpferde, Fr. Voigts. Hanover, 1846; and Allgemeines Handbuch, s.v. Hannover, Mehmet, etc., etc. For the closing scenes—Latomia, vol. xxvi., 1868, p. 217 et seq.; and Mittheilungen aus dem Verein Deutscher Freimaurer, Findel, Leipsic, 1864.

recognising only three Grand Lodges in that kingdom, it subsided into its former position of a daughter Lodge of the "Three Globes" in 1799. The Lodge is still active. In 1863 it numbered 262, and in 1885, 312 members.

IV. GRAND LODGE "OF THE THREE KEYS" AT RATISBON.

This was in its time a most important Grand Lodge, and remarkable for having successfully resisted the blandishments of the Strict Observance. Its influence extended over a very large circle. In 1765 a Prince of Thurn and Taxis founded in Ratisbon a Lodge "St Charles of Constancy," which he himself dissolved in 1774. But during these nine years it had given birth to a second Lodge, "Crescent of the Three Keys," constituted May 1, 1767. The Master of that Lodge, Schkler, who had been initiated in Amsterdam, obtained—July 1, 1768—from G.M. Von Botzelaar of the Netherlands, a warrant of constitution, and immediately assumed for the Lodge the prerogatives of a Grand Lodge. It worked the degrees of the Craft, with those of a Scots Lodge superadded, in 1770; the latter were, however, suppressed in 1784, so that—considering the times—the Lodge kept itself remarkably pure. In 1771 it warranted its first daughter, "Hope," in Vienna, and during the next twenty years, Lodges in Marktseft on the Main, Munich, Passau, Ulm, Baitsch, Neusohl in Hungary, Hermannstadt in Siebenbürgen, (a second) in Vienna, Görlitz, Dresden, and Hanover—in all twelve. Schkler was G.M. from 1771 to 1777, when he resigned; and the second G.M., the Prince of Thurn and Taxis,[1] was elected in 1799. It is probable that this long interregnum was due to the ravages committed in every direction by the Strict Observance. From 1793 to 1799 the Lodge was perfectly dormant owing to the disturbing effects of the Revolution. But it resumed activity with the new G.M., who, June 6, 1806, obtained a patent from England.[2] In this he is styled "Provincial Grand Master for Bavaria," an excusable error, Ratisbon being one of the recent acquisitions of that State; and it is indeed surprising that the Grand Lodge did not take the place now occupied by the "Sun" of Bayreuth. The Lodge also changed its name to "Karl of the Three Keys," and constituted several Lodges, for instance, Leipsic and Heidelberg. In the first decade of this century the Grand Lodge had lost all her daughters through death or desertion, but was itself strong and much respected throughout the Continent; with Sweden especially it stood on the most intimate terms from 1801 to 1823. It gradually fell into decay, but once more, about 1830, flickered up under Von Stachelhausen. On his departure from Ratisbon the Lodge died out altogether, *circa* 1840.[3]

V. ENGLISH PROVINCIAL GRAND LODGE OF BRUNSWICK AT BRUNSWICK.

This Grand Lodge can hardly be said to have existed, but its short history exemplifies the unsettled state of the Craft at this period. In 1744 — February 12 — the Lodge "Jonathan" was founded and opened by the Grand Lodge of Hamburg; and on December 27 its founder, Kissleben, was appointed "Permanent Deputy G.M."[4] In 1762 the Lodge superadded the Rosa-Clermont Chapter; and in 1764, the Master, Von Lestwitz, was

---

[1] I do not know if this Prince is identical with the founder of the Lodge. *Cf. ante*, p. 266, note 3.

[2] Grand Lodge Records. Nuremberg became a Bavarian city in 1806. *Cf. ante*, p. 277.

[3] A detailed account of this Lodge will be found in "Latomia," vol. xxii., 1863, pp. 322-330.

[4] It will be remembered that Lüttmann, Provincial Grand Master for Hamburg, took upon himself to make a similar appointment in Hanover. *Cf. ante*, p. 275.

appointed by England Prov. G.M. of Brunswick.[1] But whilst the warrant was on the road, Lestwitz and the Lodge had both deserted to the Strict Observance, so that the Provincial Grand Lodge was never erected. A minority of the Lodge, however, continued the old Lodge "Jonathan;" and in the same year, Le Boeuf, in his quality of a Scots Master, established a French Lodge. These three quarrelled, so that the Duke Ferdinand of Brunswick closed them all and founded two new ones, one working in French as a Mother-Lodge, "St Charles of Concord," and a German Lodge "Jonathan." This he did by virtue of a Provincial patent granted to him by England, July 5, 1768. The Lodges were constituted on October 10 and 11, 1770. But before the end of the year Ferdinand had signed the Act of Strict Observance, and that was the end of the second Provincial Grand Lodge of Brunswick.[2] "St Charles of Concord" was granted a place in the English registry as No. 400 in 1770, and continued on the roll until 1813 (as No. 259)—one of many proofs that the Grand Lodge of England knew little and cared less concerning foreign affairs.

VI. BODE'S UNION OF GERMAN FREEMASONS.

In 1788—March 1—the Directoral Lodge of the Eclectic Union at Frankfort resumed its former position as a Prov. G.L. under England. This seems to have given umbrage to the "Compass" Lodge in Gotha, who feared or pretended to fear, that the perfect equality among the Eclectic Lodges would be violated. Their chief adviser was Bode. As he was a convert to the Illuminati, and Frankfort had declared itself adverse to that sect, this circumstance may have also contributed to the ensuing events. Certain it is that the Gotha Lodge issued a circular to all German Lodges—November 24, 1790—signed by nine Masters "acting under the advice of a highly instructed Mason"—Bode—calling upon all Lodges to aid in forming a general Union of German Lodges on the real Eclectic principles. The Gotha Lodge was erased, and that of the "Three Arrows" at Nuremberg[3] took its part so warmly as to provoke a like result. These were the only two Eclectic Lodges that joined Bode's Union, which in all never numbered more than ten Lodges. Bode died in 1793, and with him the projected union and Grand Lodge after a precarious existence of three years. The movement is of interest, as the last effort of a man who was made a Hamburg Mason in 1761, dubbed a Templar Knight in 1764, who in 1782 first took up the idea that the Jesuits were at the bottom of all the high degrees, and finished by joining the Illuminati.

VII. GRAND ORIENT OF BADEN AT MANNHEIM.

In 1778 Mannheim belonged to Bavaria, and the Lodge "Karl of Unity" was constituted in that city—November 28—by the G.L. Royal York. In 1783 it joined the Eclectic Union, and in 1785 was closed together with all other Bavarian Lodges.[4] In 1803 Mannheim was made over to the Grand Duchy of Baden, and in 1805 the Lodge reopened under Karl von Dalberg.[5] In 1806 it received a warrant from the G.O. of France, accepted the modern French

---

[1] Constitutions, 1767, p. 365; Preston, 1812, p. 261.

[2] It is not unlikely that England, or at least De Vignolles, contributed to this result! See the letter of December 28, 1770, from the Prov. G.M. for foreign Lodges (*ante*, Chap. XIX., p. 459, note 8).

[3] Became No. 671 *English*, in 1815; and again *Eclectic* in 1823 (*ante*, p. 277).

[4] *Ante*, pp. 123, 266.   [5] *Ibid.*, p. 236.

Rite, and changed its name to "Charles of Concord." Its Chapter then declared itself a Grand Orient for the Duchy of Baden, and was acknowledged as such by France on June 25, 1807.

In 1808 it was joined by the Lodge "Karl of Good Hope," Heidelberg, warranted in 1807 by the G.L. of Ratisbon—which it deserted, but rejoined, in the same year. In 1809 it constituted the Lodges "Temple of Patriotic Light" at Bruchsal, and Karl and Stephanie at Mannheim; so that in all the G.O. extended its jurisdiction over three Lodges. Its Grand Master was Karl, Prince of Ysenburg. The Grand Duke, Karl Friedrich, being dead, his successor, Karl Ludwig Friedrich, issued—February 16, 1813, and March 7, 1814— decrees suppressing secret societies, and with them Freemasonry throughout his dominions. All Lodges in Baden then closed, and the Craft was not allowed to reassert itself until 1845; but there is no longer a Grand Lodge for Baden, the Lodges being pretty equally divided between the "Sun" and the "Eclectic Union."

VIII. Grand National Union of Baden Lodges at Carlsruhe.

This Union was contemporary with the foregoing. The "Karl of Unity" at Carlsruhe was warranted by the Eclectic Union in 1786, closed during the Revolution from 1791 onwards, and reopened in 1808. The Lodge "Noble Prospect" at Freiburg was warranted by the Prov. G.L. of Austria at Vienna in 1784, joined the Eclectic Union in 1785, and was also dormant from 1793 to 1808. The "Karl of Good Hope" at Heidelberg was warranted by Ratisbon in 1807, joined the G.O. of Baden 1808, and rejoined Ratisbon the same year.

These three Lodges—May 23, 1809—erected the Grand National Union of Lodges, to be governed, not by a Grand, but by a Directoral Lodge, the Lodge exercising this function to change every three years. Lodges of each and every ritual were eligible for the Union, except those working the French Modern Rite—which was ceded to the Grand Orient of Baden. These two Grand Bodies subsisted side by side in perfect amity. The Heidelberg Lodge threw off a shoot in 1809, which was constituted by the Eclectic Union, and joined the Baden Union without apparently deserting Frankfort. In like manner the original Heidelberg Lodge appears to have belonged to the Ratisbon G.L. and the Baden Union. In 1809 the Bruchsal Lodge also joined it without deserting its Grand Orient, and there is a further though somewhat undefined allusion to a Minerva Lodge at Mannheim. Its Grand Masters were successively K. F. Schilling von Canstadt, and Hemeling. The directory remained at Carlsruhe until July 1, 1812, when it was removed to Freiburg, but in 1813-14 the same fate of course overtook this Union, which crushed the Grand Orient of Baden.[1]

IX. Grand Orient of Westphalia in Cassel.

An English Provincial Grand Master, described in the Constitutions[2] as "George Augustus, Baron of Hammerstein," was appointed by Earl Ferrers—1762-64—for Westphalia, but he does not appear to have exerted himself to any purpose, for nothing more is known of him.

In the electorate of Hesse-Cassel the first Lodge was constituted at Marburg in 1743, and

---

[1] The origin of these Baden Grand Lodges is well told by J. H. Burmann (Maurer Archiv., Mannheim, 1809), who was a high official of the Grand Orient of Baden.

[2] Edition 1767, p. 365. A marginal note (MS.) in the office copy preserved in the library of the G.L. of England, runs—"don't know of a Lodge."

others soon followed. The Strict Observance in due course swamped the Craft, and on its subsidence the preponderating influence was that of the G.L. Royal York. In 1794, however, the Elector suppressed all the Lodges in his dominions.

In 1807 the Electorate and the city of Cassel became the centre of Napoleon's kingdom of Westphalia, at the head of which he placed his brother Jérome.

The first Lodge to revive, Frederick of Friendship, took the name of "Jérome Napoleon of Fidelity," and in order to avoid falling under a French jurisdiction, erected a Grand Orient of the Kingdom of Westphalia, February 10, 1808. This was done at the instigation of Count Siméon, Jérome's chief minister, himself an assistant G.M. of the G.O. of France. The king was G.M., and Siméon his deputy; but all the other officers were Germans. The utmost toleration prevailed, as I have already had occasion to remark, and Lodges under other jurisdictions were not compelled to affiliate; any ritual was permitted, and Lodges enjoyed complete freedom from interference in their private affairs. Three new Lodges appear to have been constituted in Cassel (1808-13), and the following joined:—Münden, Alfeld, Hildesheim, Einbeck, Goslar, Osterode, Heiligenstadt, Eschwege, Göttingen, Nordhausen, Celle, Marburg, Hanover (a new French one), Helmstedt, Magdeburg, etc. In 1813 the kingdom of West-phalia disappeared, and with it the Grand Orient.

X. Grand Lodge of Hesse-Cassel in Cassel.

The Elector having been restored, the old edict of 1794 suppressing the Craft was revived. Von Bardeleben succeeded in obtaining a repeal of this obnoxious decree, but only on the condition that the Lodges would submit to the G.L. Royal York, under an intermediate Prov. G.L. of the Electorate, with Bardeleben as the Prov. G.M. Accordingly two Lodges at Cassel and one at Eschwege constituted—May 26, 1814—the Prov. G.L. desired by the Elector, and placed themselves under the Royal York of Berlin. In 1817, however, this Prov. G.L. declared its independence under the title of "Mother Grand Lodge of the Electorate of Hesse," and the Elector William II. on his accession promised it his protection. Besides the three already mentioned, the following at Marburg, Rinteln, Hanau, Ziegenhain, Hersfeld, Neuters-hausen; in all, nine Lodges formed part of this jurisdiction. But on July 19, 1824, an edict of the Elector once more suppressed and interdicted the Lodges, and in spite of all petitions to the contrary, they remained forbidden and closed until the events of 1866 caused the Electorate to be incorporated with Prussia.

OTHER MASONIC UNIONS NOT CLASSED AS GRAND LODGES.

I. Grand Union of Freemasons (Fessler's)

It will be remembered that in 1799 and 1800 both Fessler and Schroeder visited Hanover, and about the same time these two ardent reformers made each other's acquaintance. Early in 1801 Fessler attempted to strengthen the hands of the leading supporters of pure Freemasonry by drawing closer the bonds of union between the Provincial Grand Lodges of Hamburg and Hanover, and the Grand Lodge Royal York of Berlin. On August 20, 1801, a tripartite treaty was concluded between these bodies, entitled "*Magnum Foedus Latomorum*," providing for mutual representation, and communication of all minutes, and for a select circle

RIGHT HONOURABLE LORD BROOKE

PROVINCIAL GRAND MASTER OF ESSEX

Thomas C. lark London & Edinburgh

in each Grand Lodge for the free imparting to one another of all ritualistic and historic knowledge. Resolutions were adopted against the use of any of the old fashioned high degrees, and provision was made for the admission to the Union of other Grand Lodges.[1] Frankfort was invited to join the Union. But at this time the Prov. G.L. was dormant,[2] and wished to refer the matter to England before deciding. Deceived by this condition of affairs, the "Royal York" warranted a Lodge—"Socrates"—in Frankfort, December 4, 1801, and to the friction to which this gave rise, the absence of a reply from London, and the renewed dormancy of the P.G.L. of Frankfort in 1803-5, must be ascribed the failure on the latter's part to affiliate with the Union. Following this came the French occupation of Berlin and Hanover, and thus the Union gradually lost its hold on the Lodges, and is now confined to a mutual representation in Grand Lodge, which, however, has extended to all the other Grand Lodges of Germany.

II. THE CORRESPONDENCE BUREAU.

In most German Lodges two secretaries divide the work between them, one attending to the minutes and records, and the other conducting the correspondence, both with members and with the Lodges in fraternal alliance. It is usual for the latter to forward, in the summer, to every member and allied Lodge a so-called St John's letter, detailing the events of the past twelve months, and giving a list of present members. In some cases allied Lodges undertake a regular exchange of their respective minutes. As the parties to these arrangements increased in number, the work became more onerous, and Dr Lechner of the Baldwin Lodge, Leipsic, formed a plan to facilitate matters, which was communicated to the Lodges by circular in 1831. According to this scheme the Baldwin Lodge was to act as a central point under a special officer charged to receive proceedings from all quarters, and to distribute them to all corresponding members. Forty-two Lodges joined the association at the outset, and at present almost every German Lodge is affiliated, besides many in Switzerland, Denmark, and North America.

III. UNION OF THE THREE GRAND LODGES OF BERLIN.

A Union, composed of the Grand and Deputy Grand Masters of these three Grand Lodges, was founded in 1810 to deliberate on matters of common interest. It had been preceded by a joint monthly committee meeting, established in 1807. Unfortunately in 1823 the G.L. of Hamburg and the National G.L. quarrelled about the Lodge at Rostock. Hamburg brought its case before the Union through the good offices of the G.L. Royal York. This produced very strained relations, and the Union—by common consent—quietly came to an end.

IV. PRUSSIAN GRAND MASTERS' UNION.

About the year 1830 the three Berlin Grand Lodges had, in a great measure, forgotten their quarrels, and lived together in peace and amity. To ensure a continuance of this happy state of affairs, the Union of Prussian Grand Masters was established December 28, 1839. On that day the following officers met together—Von Donnersmark and Selapinsky, the G.M. and Dep. G.M. of the National G.L.; Link and Bever, the G.M. and Deputy of the

---

[1] For the full text of this treaty see W. Keller, Gesch., etc., pp. 225 *et seq.*   [2] *Ante*, p. 235.

Royal York; O'Etzel and Schmückert, filling similar offices in the Three Globes; and the three Grand Secretaries. The object of this Union was to take council in common on important Masonic matters, and to strengthen the bonds of friendship between the Grand Lodges. The Union might propose Masonic principles for acceptance, but was powerless to force their adoption on the individual Grand Lodges.

One of the first acts of this Union was an important one. At a meeting held May 18, 1840, at the premises of the Royal York, Von Donnersmark informed the Grand Masters that Prince William of Prussia (now the Emperor of Germany) had obtained his father's permission to join the Craft, provided he could be made in the name of all three Grand Lodges, and belong to them conjointly; further, that in that case he would assume the protectorate of the entire Craft in Prussia. For such a purpose the Union was exactly fitted, and—May 22, 1840—the Prince was initiated. Donnersmark, his old companion in arms, presided at a "Common Prussian G. Lodge," and on the right and left were the other Grand Masters. The Masters of the fifteen Berlin Lodges were also present. The National G.L. lent its premises for the occasion. The Prince swore "truth and silence" to all three Grand Masters, and then in his capacity of Protector received their vows of fealty in return. The Union still subsists, and has been of great service to the Fraternity in Prussia, as preparing the way for joint action in many matters.

V. Grand Masters' Diet.

This may be considered as an extension of the Grand Masters' Union, applied to all Germany. In 1868, Warnatz, G.M. of Saxony, invited the other G.M.'s of Germany with their Deputies to meet him in conference. The first meeting was held May 3, 1868, at Berlin. Every G.L., except the Sun of Bayreuth, was represented by its G.M.; and in some instances by the Deputy Grand Masters or their substitutes. An idea of the scope of this association may be gathered from the proceedings of the Third Annual Diet, held June 5, 1870, when it was agreed to accept the Old English Charges as the basis and landmarks of Freemasonry. At the fourth Diet at Frankfort in 1871, the formation of a "Union of German G. Lodges" was mooted, and G.M. Warnatz was deputed to draw up a draft code of by-laws for the same. These were duly approved, and as a consequence the fifth and last Diet of 1872 at Berlin became the first meeting of the

VI. German Grand Lodges' Union.

This Union has worked to great advantage for the Craft, and in the absence of an impossible General Grand Lodge, serves to maintain a close bond between every system in the Fatherland, and to preserve or inaugurate a common line of conduct in external affairs.

VII. Union of German Freemasons.

This is a purely deliberative and literary society, composed of individual Masons meeting yearly at various cities. It was founded in 1861, and at first met with strenuous opposition from some of the Grand Lodges, so that in 1867 it only numbered 309 members. It has however, formed a valuable library and museum at Leipsic, and its official organ is the Leipsic "Bauhütte." Its influence has grown yearly, and in 1878 it numbered 1509 active, and 31 corresponding, members. As a Literary Masonic Association, it takes high rank; as a Deliberative Assembly, there are signs of an unfortunate and regrettable tendency towards a mild form of socialism. Although politics are rigorously forbidden in the Lodge, it would appear that Germans do not include political economy under this head, and the boundary-line is easily overstepped.

Although the exigencies of space forbid more than a passing allusion to many subjects of deep interest to our antiquaries, but lying on the extreme border line of history, there is one upon which—at this stage of our inquiry—some general observations will not be out of place.

Germany (including Austria and Switzerland) excels all other countries, both in the affluence of its Masonic literature, and in the profundity of research which has characterised the labours of so many gifted historians of the Craft. The earliest efforts of German Masonic writers—translations of the English constitutions, orations, and didactic pieces—evince both diligence and accuracy. Thence, by a gradual transition—the publication of the constitutions of many other Grand (and private) Lodges, and of songs and poems remarkable for beauty of thought and diction—we are brought to a higher sphere of intellectual labour, and find in the literature of the Craft, the noblest moral teaching, accompanied by very learned and ingenious reflections on both the origin and objects of our Society.

Lessing—"the father of German criticism"—known to Masonic readers by his "Ernest and Falk," 1778, and "Nathan the Wise," 1779—a noble plea for toleration and a rational religion—was followed by Vogel, "Letters on Freemasonry," 1783-85; Albrecht, "Materials for a Critical History," 1792; Schroeder, "Materials for the *Engbund*," 1802; Schneider, "Constitutions of Archimedes," etc., 1803; Fessler, "Attempts at a Critical History," etc., 1801-7; Krause, "The Three Oldest Masonic Documents," 1810; Mossdorf, "Addresses to Thoughtful Masons," 1818; Heldmann, "The Three Oldest Historical Documents of German Masonry," 1819; Nettelbladt, "History of Masonic Systems," *circa* 1836; O'Etzel, "History of the Three Globes," 1840; Kloss, "Annals of the Eclectic Union," 1842—"Freemasonry in its True Significance," 1846—"Freemasonry in Great Britain," 1848—and "in France," 1852; Fallou, "The Mysteries of Freemasonry," 1848; Winzer, "The German Brotherhoods," 1859; Keller, "History of the Eclectic Union," 1857—"Of Masonry in Germany," 1859; Findel, "History of Freemasonry," 1861-62; and Paul, "History of the Eclectic Union," 1883. The list might be extended, but I shall merely add that both Herder and Goethe are to be classed among "writers of the Craft." [1]

---

[1] German periodical literature devoted to the Craft began in 1776-79 with Bode's "Almanach," and subsequently there appeared (*inter alia*) the "Freemasons' Library," 1778-1803; "Vienna Journal for Masons," 1784-86; "Kothener Annual," 1798-1805; Meissner's "Pocket-Book," 1801-17; "Altenburg Journal," 1804, continued as Fisher's *Zeitschrift* and *Neueste Zeitschrift;* Nettelbladt's "Calendars for the Prov. G. L. of Mecklenburg," 1821-46; but above all, the matchless "Latomia," commenced by Meissner and Merzdorf in 1842, and continued to 1873. The most prominent Masonic journal in Germany at the present date, is the *Bauhütte*, begun in 1858. Works of especial merit are Gädicke's "Lexicon," 1818, but chiefly on account of its being the first of its kind; Kloss' "Bibliography," 1844, a monument of research; and the "Handbook," 1863-79—or the second edition of Lenning's "Encyclopædia," edited by Mossdorf in 1822-28. No other Masonic work of a similar character can pretend to rival the *Handbuch der Freimaurerei* in the extent, variety, and accuracy of its information.

CHAPTER XXVIII.

FREEMASONRY IN SOUTHERN EUROPE.

AUSTRIA AND HUNGARY—SWITZERLAND—ITALY—PORTUGAL—SPAIN—GREECE—TURKEY—ROUMANIA—MALTA.

AUSTRIA AND HUNGARY.[1]

THE history of Freemasonry in Austria—its traces in the Austrian Netherlands have already been referred to in connection with Belgium [2]—may be said to commence with the initiation of the Duke of Lorraine.

Francis Stephen was born 1708, and succeeded his father as Duke of Lorraine in 1729. In 1731 a special Lodge was held at the Hague under Dr Desaguliers as W.M.; John Stanhope and John Holzendorff, Wardens; the Earl of Chesterfield, and others, in order to initiate and pass the Duke, who was afterwards made a Master Mason in England in the same year.[3] In 1736 he married Maria Theresa, the heiress to the throne of Austria, and, on the death of Gaston of Medici, in 1737, exchanged the crown of Lorraine for that of the Grand Duchy of Tuscany. To his influence with his father-in-law, the Emperor, may be probably ascribed the fact that Clement's Bull of 1738 was promulgated in the Austrian dominions. In 1740 Maria Theresa succeeded to the imperial diadem of Austria, and appointed her husband Co-Regent. Personally the Empress was averse to the Craft, but her consort was able to procure for it a certain amount of tolerance in the long run, although powerless to prevent occasional outbursts of persecution. In these early days Freemasons existed in the Austrian dominions in considerable numbers, but as yet there was no Lodge.

In 1742—September 17—the first Vienna Lodge, "The Three Firing Glasses," was constituted by the "Three Skulls" of Breslau, under its Master the Prince Bishop of that city; but on March 7, 1743, the Lodge was, without warning, closed by the military at the command of the Empress, and 18 members—chiefly of the nobility—taken prisoners. Tradition has it that Francis himself had considerable difficulty in escaping by the back stairs. On the 19th, however, the prisoners were released in honour of the *fête* of the young Crown Prince, and documentary evidence is forthcoming that the Lodge continued to meet in secret,

---

[1] The leading authority on the history of the Craft in these countries is Dr L. Lewis, "Geschichte der Freimaurerei in Oesterreich," etc., Vienna, 1861. The information contained in that work may be supplemented by reference to Beigel, "Verfassung der Provincial und Gr. Loge von Oesterreich, 1784," Vienna, 1877; and Allgemeines Handbuch, *s.v.* Oesterreich, Ungarn, Wien, Boehmen, Prag, Pest, Mailand, Innspruck, etc., etc.

[2] *Ante*, p. 209 *et seq.*   [3] Chap. XVII., pp. 353, 388.

relying doubtless on the protection of the Prince, who in 1745 was elected Emperor of Germany as Francis I.

According to Lawrie, Freemasonry was introduced into the province of Bohemia (Prague) in 1749.[1] He speaks of the members as "*Scotish Masons*," and the probability is that they were "Scots degree" Masons. Subsequent writers have, however, stated on the strength of this passage that the Grand Lodge of Scotland warranted a Lodge at Prague, a conclusion which is not supported by any evidence which has come under my notice.[2]

The Bull of Benedict XIV. in 1751 gave fresh courage to the clergy surrounding the Austrian throne, and renewed efforts to suppress Freemasonry were made. The Empress, however, held her hand, and (*it is said*) visited the Lodge in company with one of her ladies, both disguised as men, in order to assure herself that none of the *beau sexe* were admitted to the mysteries. Having satisfied herself on this point she retired. As this legend, however, derives no support from "inherent probability," not even can the Italian maxim, "*Se non è vero, è ben trovato,*" be applied to it.

In 1751—May 22—the Lodge Frederick at Hanover warranted a branch Lodge, Frederick, at Vienna; in 1764 the Strict Observance began to constitute Lodges in the Austrian dominions; and in the same year a decree was issued suppressing Freemasonry altogether. But Francis, the Emperor, was himself at that time Master of "The Three Firing Glasses," and we need therefore not be surprised to find that it remained inoperative.

Francis died at Innsbruck, August 18, 1765, and his son, Joseph II., was elected Emperor. The Empress Maria Theresa also made him Co-Regent (with herself) of Austria. Although not a Mason, on more than one occasion he expressed a favourable opinion of the Craft. At this period the Jesuits were straining every nerve to avert their own extinction, and the Fraternity of Masons therefore obtained a little breathing time. Lodges began to multiply. In 1771 the Strict Observance founded one—the Three Eagles—in Vienna; and Zinnendorff followed the lead by erecting two others in the same city, 1771 and 1775. In 1776 Prague already possessed four Lodges, and in 1777 Zinnendorff's National Grand Lodge at Berlin established a Provincial Grand Lodge of Austria at Vienna.

By the death of Maria Theresa—November 19, 1780—the Emperor Joseph II., became Emperor of Austria also, and the Craft continued to prosper. The greater part of the new Lodges were constituted by Zinnendorff or by the Provincial Grand Lodge at Vienna of the same system; and in 1784 there were no less than 45 Lodges in the various provinces of the Austrian Empire (8 being in Vienna alone) under the following Provincial Grand Lodges: —Austria proper (Vienna), 17; Bohemia, 7; Hungary, 12; Siebenburgen, 3; Galicia, 4; and Lombardy, 2.

On April 22, 1784, the Provincial Grand Lodges of Bohemia, Hungary, Siebenburgen, and Austria met and formed a National Grand Lodge of the Austrian States, with Count Dietrichstein as Grand Master. Their intention was to declare themselves independent, but they met with such opposition from Berlin, that Dietrichstein was obliged to content himself with the position of a Prov. G.M. under the National—*i.e.*, Zinnendorff—Grand Lodge. In 1785, however, the Emperor ordered the latent Grand Lodge to assert its independence, and Berlin was naturally obliged to give way. The other Provincial Grand Lodges

---

[1] Edit. 1804, p. 181.   [2] *Cf. ante*, p. 196.

appear to have joined the Union. Each Lodge had by its delegate one vote in the Provincial Lodges, which met every three months, and each Provincial Grand Lodge had one vote at the half-yearly meeting of the National Grand Lodge (of the Austrian States), thus forming a perfect representative system.

Unfortunately at this time the Emperor interfered in the internal arrangements of the Craft, apparently at the instigation of Dietrichstein, the G.M. The desire to suppress the Asiatic Brothers—at work in Austria since 1780—was not unconnected with these proceedings. An edict appeared on December 1, 1785, restricting the number of Lodges in any city to three, and ordering all those established in towns where there was no imperial court to close altogether. On the strength of this edict Dietrichstein caused the eight Vienna Lodges to reduce their number by amalgamation to two, and to greatly curtail their membership. Each member had to submit to a fresh ballot, and many were thereby prevented from taking any further part in the proceedings of the Craft. Several of the best Masons in Austria retired in disgust, numerous Lodges were closed by virtue of the edict, the spirit and independence of the Craft had flown, and its best days vanished.

Joseph died in 1790, and Leopold II. expressed himself as not unfriendly to the Fraternity; but his successor in 1792, Francis II., tried at the Ratisbon Diet to induce the German Princes to suppress Freemasonry throughout the Empire. In this he failed, but the Vienna Lodges, taking the cue, voluntarily closed in 1794 "until better times;" and in 1795 an imperial edict suppressed the Craft and all secret societies throughout the States of Austria. A further edict of 1801 required all State officials to sign a paper affirming that they did not belong to any such society. Freemasonry thus died out in Austria, and has not since revived. During the French occupation, 1805-9, some ephemeral Lodges arose, and even a short-lived Grand Orient under French jurisdiction; and again in 1848 a former Vienna Lodge reopened October 5, but was closed on the 6th. All subsequent attempts have proved fruitless as far as Austria is concerned, but Hungary rejoices in a better fate.

In 1861 Dr Lewis made an attempt to revive the Craft in Hungary, and founded a Lodge in Pesth, but it was quickly closed by the police. The political division of 1867, however, by which Austria and Hungary became separate kingdoms under one crown, opened the door to Hungarian Freemasonry, no Hungarian law existing to the contrary. The Government approved in October 1868 the statutes of Lewis' Lodge "Unity," and in 1869 two other Lodges arose in Temesvar and Oedenburg. The "Unity" threw off shoots in Baja, Pressburg, and Buda-Pesth, and the Temesvar Lodge one in Arad. On January 30, 1870, these seven formed a Grand Lodge of Hungary, and were strengthened in the same year by a new Lodge in Szegedin. These eight increased in 1871 to twelve. In 1872 the members already mustered 800 strong. The G.M. was, and still is, Franz Pulszky. But although prosperous in numbers, the organisation, ritual, and spirit of the new body left much to be desired, and the Craft seemed destined to wreck on the lee-shore of its own unworthiness, when a judicious change of *personnel* in 1875 enabled it to make a good offing. The new Constitutions were approved February 24, 1876, providing a representative system of government, and the new ritual came into force on July 1. The immediate consequence of this was the formation of four new Lodges before the end of the year, since which date the National Grand Lodge of Hungary has proceeded on its way without much of importance to relate.

Returning to 1869, we find that in this year several Masons who had been initiated abroad opened a Lodge (the proceedings being conducted in the Hungarian tongue) according to the A. and A.S.R. 33°, under the auspices of the Grand Orient of France. This was soon followed by a second, working in German. As one of the prime movers in this matter, the celebrated Hungarian patriot Klapka should be mentioned. In 1870, these two Lodges made honourable overtures to the Grand Lodge for a fusion of government combined with freedom of ritual. Unfortunately, as we have seen in the History of French Freemasonry, such a fusion is difficult, and it failed on this as on so many previous occasions. Thrown upon their own resources, the two Lodges constituted—on the part of the Grand Orient of France—further Scots Lodges in Kaschau, Werschetz, Oravicza, Arad, Beregszasz, and other towns; and having instituted the necessary High Chapters, these Lodges in 1872 formed a Grand Orient of Hungary for the A. and A.S.R. 33°, under Grand Master George Joannovics. In 1875 this Grand Orient exercised jurisdiction over some 20 Lodges with 1000 members. It has since lost much in importance. The two Grand bodies are on a perfectly friendly footing. The statistics of 1885 are as follows:—Grand Lodge in Buda-Pesth, founded January 30, 1870, 26 Lodges and 1268 members; Grand Orient of Buda-Pesth, founded 1872, 12 Lodges and about 502 members.

In Austria proper there are many Masonic clubs, that is, merely social clubs composed exclusively of Freemasons; as Lodges they are forbidden to meet. But Vienna itself is so near the Hungarian frontier, that many of these clubs are really Lodges which take a short railway trip in order to meet as such. In Pressburg and Oedenburg there are several Lodges whose members are all resident in Vienna. The other large towns of the Empire are, however, not so fortunately situated, and the Fraternity in each of such cities has to content itself with meeting as a social club.

SWITZERLAND.

The early history of the Craft in the Swiss Confederation is so involved, that unless my readers will kindly bear a few historical data in mind, I can hardly expect to make myself clear.

When Freemasonry first appeared in the valleys of Switzerland the Confederacy consisted of fourteen autonomous and confederated Cantons. Beyond these were a few districts, now Cantons with full rights, but then subject to individual Cantons by right of conquest, such as the Pays de Vaud—dependent on Berne. Further we have to deal with certain of the present Cantons which at that time were independent Republics in alliance with the Confederacy, such as St Gall and Geneva; and lastly, the present Canton of Neufchatel was at that time Prussian (1707-1806), from 1806-14 French, and since 1815 has been a member of the Confederation, but under Prussian suzerainty. At first we need chiefly concern ourselves with Zurich, Basle, and Berne, belonging to Switzerland proper; with Vaud, the dependency of Berne; with the Allied Republic of Geneva; and with the then Prussian State of Neufchatel.

The first distinct period may be taken as extending to the reign of terror in 1792-93.

GENEVA.—In 1736 some English gentlemen established a Lodge in the city of Geneva, a resident and naturalised Scotsman, George Hamilton, being the Master. On March 5 of the same year he was forbidden by the Republic to initiate native citizens—a decree which appears to have been systematically violated—and in 1737 he was appointed by the G.L. of England Prov. G.M. for all Lodges in the state.[1] Even in these few months many had been established. To attempt to follow their history would be impossible. Throughout Switzerland Lodges were like mushrooms, they sprang up in a night and disappeared as quickly, leaving, in most cases, nothing but a name behind. In 1744 the Archives of the Town Council make mention of three Lodges only. These—February 13—the Fathers placed under a ban, which, however, did not prevent the Prov. G.L., under Lord Malpas, from holding a public festival on June 24. In 1745—when six Lodges are mentioned—the Council renewed its edict, which, however, was allowed to lapse. This was the last obstacle thrown in the way of the Craft in this territory. For the next fifteen years little is known of Geneva Freemasonry, except that Lodges were formed, existed for a time, and died out. The history of this period is involved in much confusion. In 1768—February 7—the "Union of Hearts" was established. This is the first Lodge which kept minutes, and its so-called "Golden Book" is full of interesting notes on Swiss Masonry. At this time Alexander Gerard returned from England, and set to work to reduce the existing chaos to order. At his instigation ten Geneva Lodges met on June 1, 1769, and on the 24th erected the Independent Grand Lodge of Geneva —working pure English Masonry. In the same year eight other Lodges united with this body, some being in France, and comprised of members averse to the high degrees (so-called). There was also one in Zurich and another in Constantinople. Before 1773 ten more had joined. This Grand Lodge was therefore of some importance, but towards 1782 the political ferment in France had extended to Geneva, and the state was put under military government. For the next four years the Craft was almost extinct.

In 1786 it re-awoke, and many Lodges joined the Grand Orient of France; but on March 22, eight Lodges reconstituted the Grand Lodge under the new title of Grand Orient of Geneva. It had much success—in the same year ten Lodges joined the original eight—and warranted a Lodge at Smyrna in 1787. The G.O. of France also extended its operations, and a Zurich paper of 1787 alludes to there being seventy-two Lodges (!) in Geneva. The Lodges were, however, continually shifting their allegiance from one Grand Orient to the other.

In 1790—February 10—the Lodge "Union of Hearts" initiated H.R.H. the late Duke of Kent, father of H.M. Queen Victoria.[2]

In 1792-93, during the reign of terror, the Grand Orient barely existed, almost all the Lodges dissolved or declared themselves dormant, and very few indeed professed to work on undismayed.

VAUD.—In 1739—February 2—some English noblemen in Lausanne were warranted as the "Perfect Union of Strangers," No. 187, on the roll of England,[3] and declared themselves a Directing or *quasi* Grand Lodge under the name National Grand Directory of French Helvetia. Other Lodges were formed, but—March 3, 1745—the authorities at Berne issued most stringent decrees against the Craft,[4] and the Lodges were closed. Although the Swiss Fraternity published a strong protest in Frankfort and Leipsic, Freemasonry became obliterated throughout Switzerland proper (as it then was) for quite fifteen years.

BERNE.—The State Archives mention a Lodge as existing here prior to the year 1745, which, however, must have succumbed to the above edict.

---

[1] Constitutions, 1756, p. 333.
[2] Chap. XX., p. 484.
[3] Engraved Lists. *Cf.* "The Four Old Lodges," p. 55.
[4] Printed in the "Pocket Companion," 1754.

VAUD.—In 1761 the Perfect Union reopened. It had gone over to the Strict Observance, and now called itself the Scots Directory for French Helvetia; it belonged to the Vth. Province, Burgundy. Other Lodges also reopened; and in 1772 the Lodges even appeared in a public manner, throwing open their halls to the large influx of foreign Masons attracted to Lausanne by the wedding of the Princess Carignan. When the guests, however, had left, the authorities requested the Scots Directory to close its doors, and were obeyed. In 1775 for some unknown reasons Berne suddenly withdrew all its edicts against Freemasonry, several new Lodges were warranted in 1776-78, and the Directory reconstituted.

ZURICH.—In 1740 a Lodge, Concordia, was warranted by a Swiss regiment in the Dutch service, but was closed by the authorities. Again in 1769 a Lodge, "Discretion," was formed by Geneva residents, and warranted by the Grand Lodge of Geneva, but appears to have died out almost immediately. In 1771—August 13—some officers who had seen foreign service opened a second Lodge "Discretion," according to the French Rite, but this was won over to the Strict Observance by Diethelm Lavater in 1772. Helvetia was a sub-priory of the Vth. Province, and a Chapter was established with Lavater as sub-prior.

BASLE.—In 1744 a Lodge is mentioned, and disappears in 1745. In 1765 the Strict Observance Lodge "Libertas" was opened, and in 1769 a second.

FRIBURG.—Gottreau de Trefaje opened a Lodge in 1761, but in 1763 the Lodge was closed, and Gottreau handed over to justice. In 1764 he was condemned to be burned, a punishment at that time reserved for sorcerers, but escaped with exile owing to the influence of his relatives.

In 1778 therefore we have Strict Observance Lodges in Vaud, Zurich, and Basle, and no others in Switzerland proper. In that year Lausanne and Zurich agreed to divide the country between them accordingly as the cantons spoke German or French. The French Scots Directory at Lausanne, and the German Scots Directory at Zurich, under their respective Grand Masters to be subordinate to Lavater as Sub-Prior. These two Directories attended the Convent de Gaules at Lyons in 1778, where the S.O. system was modified. Both were then raised to the rank of Sub-Priories, and Helvetia to that of a Priory of the Vth. Province, with Lavater as Grand Prior.

VAUD.—In 1782, on account of some students' follies, Berne renewed its decrees, and the Lodges closed. As, however, fourteen Lodges in Piedmont and Savoy were dependent on Lausanne, three directors were appointed to control external affairs. Gradually the state authorities relaxed their severity, and the Lodges resumed work; new ones even were constituted in 1786. In 1787 the number of Vaud Lodges was stated at twenty-four. 1788 witnessed two fresh Lodges, 1789 an alliance with England. Then came the French troubles, and in 1792-93 the Directors resigned their functions, and all the Lodges closed.

ZURICH.—The Lodges closed in 1786, and the Scots Directory in 1792.

BASLE.—A congress of the Vth. Province Burgundy was held here in 1779, but the Lodges were closed by superior authority in 1785.

NEUFCHATEL.—The G.L. of the Three Globes (Berlin) warranted the "Three Flaming Stars" here on June 6, 1743; the Lodge is known to have existed in 1750, and must have died out soon afterwards. Another Lodge was warranted by the G.L. of France at Locle—May 22,

1770—of which nothing more is known.[1]   Also, in 1791—December 27—the "Three Globes" constituted the "Frederick William of Good Harmony" at Neufchatel.

This brings us to the close of the first period of Swiss Freemasonry. In Switzerland the Craft was extinct, in Geneva languishing, and in Neufchatel scarcely founded. The second period will carry us to 1814-16.

GENEVA.—In 1795—June 21—the G.O. reopened under G.M. Louis Rivale, and for the next few years both the French and the native Grand Orients were fully employed in constituting and resuscitating Lodges. In 1798 Geneva was annexed to France, and the Paris G.O. began to obtain the upper hand. English Freemasonry also lost ground, and the French Rites were substituted. In 1801 the G.O. of France revised its statutes, and the G.O. of Geneva lost its independence, being made a Prov. G.L. under Paris. In this capacity it ruled twelve Lodges in 1802, at which time there also existed a Geneva Lodge under the Supreme Council of the A. and A.S.R. 33° at Paris. In 1809 the Prov. G.L. was dissolved in conformity with the centralising policy of the G.O., and the Geneva Lodges came under the immediate rule of Paris.

NEUFCHATEL was annexed to France in 1806, and the Lodge there reconstituted by the Grand Orient of France.

VAUD.—Several Lodges reopened in 1795, but no Grand Lodge; and in 1798 the Grand Orient at Paris commenced to constitute Lodges. In 1803 Napoleon reconstructed the Swiss Confederation, and absolved Vaud from its subjection to Berne, creating it an independent Canton. For the next few years French influence and French ritual were uppermost. In 1810 Maurice Glaire, a former minister of King Stanislaus of Poland, revived the Scots Directory in Lausanne, called seven Lodges together—October 15, 1810—and erected a National Grand Orient of French Helvetia, with Bergier as *ad interim* G.M. The Scots Directory was superior to this G.O. in matters of Ritual and Dogma only. Existing Lodges might use their own ritual, new ones were to accept Glaire's own version of the rectified system of the Strict Observance. Having thus made several innovations it ceased to be a part of the Vth. Province, and formed a system of its own known as the Helvetic Rite. In 1811—March 1—these statutes were approved, and Glaire—then 67 years old—elected G.M.; in 1813 he was reappointed for life. The G.O. prospered fairly well, but after the battle of Leipsic and the entry of the allies into Switzerland, Glaire closed the Lodges *pro tem.*

BASLE.—In 1807 a Lodge under the G.O. of France was opened here. In 1809 Burkhard reintroduced the former rectified Strict Observance, won over the Lodge, re-erected the Priory, and applied to Cambacères, at that time head of all the various rites in France, for a patent. Having given the assurance that the former Grand Prior, Lavater, had resigned, he was appointed to the office, and the Archives, closed in 1793, were transferred from Zurich to Basle. We have thus once more a Scots Templar Directory of the Vth. Province at Basle, but this time for all Switzerland—that at Lausanne having struck out a path of its own.

SOLEURE.—In 1809 this Canton was first opened to the Craft by the constitution of a Lodge under the Grand Orient of France.

ZURICH.—In 1810—March 4—a former Strict Observance Lodge was reopened by the Directory at Basle.

---

[1] It was revived later on, and will be mentioned again.

AARGAU.—In this newly emancipated Canton the first signs of improvement may be seen. Heldmann,[1] Zschokke,[2] and others opened a Lodge in 1810 at Aarau. They were obliged to apply to Basle for a constitution, as they did not wish to become subservient to a foreign jurisdiction, but they firmly rejected, from the outset, high degrees, Templarism, and Unknown Superiors, together with other innovations of a like character, and worked in the three degrees only according to Schroeder's Ritual.

BERNE.—In 1802—September 14—the Lodge Hope was warranted by the Grand Orient of France, and in 1804 a Rose Croix Chapter was added, of which Tavel was the Master. From its earliest days this Lodge was devoted to the task of forming one sole Masonic authority for Switzerland which should be independent, the Scots Directories being of course only partly so, as they were subordinated to the Prov. G.M. of the Vth. Province, *i.e.*, Cambacères. It even received encouragement from the G.O. of France to assume itself this *rôle*, but refused the offer from a fear lest its intentions might be misconstrued as a usurpation. This Lodge has ever since been one of the first in the Confederation, and in 1813 had the honour of initiating Prince Leopold of Saxe-Coburg Gotha, subsequently the first King of the Belgians.

From 1795 to 1813 we thus see Switzerland divided between the G.O. of France and the Scots Directories of the Vth. Province. The German Cantons possessed only a few Lodges, which were more numerous in the French provinces and at Geneva. There was much confusion, the most hopeful signs being the existence of the two new Lodges in Aarau and Berne.

With Napoleon's fall and the Congress of Vienna the Confederation was remodelled. Vaud and Aargau were confirmed as independent Cantons, and Neufchatel and Geneva were added in the same capacity. This was not accomplished without much internal friction, and during the troubled years, 1813-16, Masonry may be looked upon as once more dormant in Switzerland.

With the resumption of Masonic activity in 1816 we may cease to consider the subject under the heading of the different Cantons, but confine our attention to the fortunes of the various systems, that is, the Grand Orients of France, and of the Helvetic Rite in Lausanne, the Directory of the Rectified Strict Observance, and the Lodge of Hope at Berne.

THE GRAND ORIENT OF FRANCE may be soon dismissed. It gradually lost its Lodges throughout the country, chiefly through its own unworthiness. Those that still remained true to it were practically left to their own devices; of the others, some joined the Directory and others the G.O. of Lausanne. Many died out altogether.

THE DIRECTORY OF THE RECTIFIED RITE (S.O.).—This fell into a state of decay, and in 1817 the G.M., Burkhard, dying, was replaced by Kaspar Ott of Zurich. As a consequence the archives and Directory were transferred from Basle to Zurich. The system was strengthened by the adhesion of some Geneva Lodges in 1816, and by two new Lodges in St Gall and Chur (Brisons), thus opening up two fresh Cantons to the Craft. In 1820 G.M. Ott died at a time when Freemasonry was undergoing a series of virulent attacks, and it was thought advisable not to attract attention by a new election. A namesake, though not a relative, of the last G.M., one Hans Caspar Ott, was therefore entrusted with the direction of affairs. In 1821 a

---

[1] *Cf.* Chapter III., *passim.*   [2] To whose work I am indebted for much information. *Cf. post*, p. 297, note.

new Lodge at Winterthur, in the Canton of Zurich, was warranted, and in 1823 the Lodges in Locle and Neufchatel, under the G.O. of France, joined the Rectified Rite. This made nine Lodges of this system, which had now reached its culminating point, but still persisted in its refusal to aid in forming a National Grand Lodge otherwise than by absorbing all others within itself. It was, however, virtually the National G. Lodge for the German Cantons, but unfortunately its conduct of affairs did not equal its strength in Lodges.

GRAND ORIENT OF THE HELVETIC RITE.—This body reopened on March 9, 1816, with nine Lodges. G.M. Glaire resigned on account of old age (died March 26, 1820), and was replaced by Verdeil. The system was strengthened by some Geneva Lodges and a few new ones, and in 1820 Bergier d'Illens succeeded Verdeil as G.M. Various proposals from Berne to join the "Hope" Lodge, in forming a National Grand Lodge, had been refused by the Committee of Grand Officers; but the idea was taking root gradually among the rank and file of the private Lodges.

BERNE.—In 1817 the Hope, finding itself severed from its mother, the Grand Orient of France, made proposals to Ott, the G.M. of the Directory, but without results. In search of a new parent, and having fully made up its mind to dispense in future with all high degrees, it applied in 1818 to the Grand Lodge of England for a constitution. The Duke of Sussex not only granted this request, but raised the Lodge (No. 706) to the position of a Provincial Grand Lodge, under Tavel, G.M. This unlooked-for favour was hardly welcome, as it scarcely allowed the Lodge to take up its former independent position in proposing a National Grand Lodge. However, the Lodge accepted the patent, based its constitutions on the work of Dr Anderson (1723), and, unable to obtain a written ritual from London, adopted that of Schroeder. The Provincial Grand Lodge was inaugurated June 24, 1819, and all the nineteen Lodges of Switzerland, without regard to divergence of ritual and procedure, were invited to attend. In 1821 it constituted its first daughter in Neufchatel, and asked the Lausanne Grand Orient to unite with it in forming a National Grand Lodge—but the time for this had not yet arrived.

LAUSANNE.—Events within this Grand body brought about the desired result. The brothers Bedarride arrived in Switzerland to establish their Rite of Misraim. After much ill success they formed two Lodges at Lausanne, and won over the G.M. Bergier to their cause. It was arranged that the Lodges should submit to the Grand Lodge so far as concerned the first three degrees, but the high degrees were to be wrought under Bedarride. Bergier attempted to carry out this project at a Grand Lodge held in 1821, but was opposed by the majority at the meeting and by his Deputy, Mieville. He finally resigned and left the Lodge. Mieville's party then agreed to effect a fusion with the English Provincial Grand Lodge at Berne. On October 23, 1821, the Sublime Chapter met under Bergier and dissolved the Grand Lodge, which held from them, resolving to resume sole control of affairs. The Chapter, however, did not follow up this step, and became practically dormant. The members of the defunct Grand Orient entrusted their power of attorney to the former College of Grand Officers. The Provincial Grand Lodge of Berne addressed a circular to each of the private Lodges, and not, as formerly, to the Grand Lodge. The Committee of Grand Officers replied on behalf of the Lodges to these overtures, and a meeting was held at Berne—April 29, 1822 —between the deputies of the two Berne and of five Vaud Lodges. It was decided to form a Grand Lodge on the English system; to *recognise* three degrees only, but to *tolerate* any others as a refuge for the play of fancy; to allow the constituent Lodges to preserve their own rituals, but to require new Lodges to use the Schroeder version. The Lausanne Grand Lodge dissolved, May 18, 1822, and exactly a week later the English Provincial Grand Lodge followed suit. A National Grand Lodge of Switzerland was then constituted by the Masters and Wardens of the seven Lodges. The Hope Lodge resumed its place as a private Lodge under this Grand Lodge; and an eighth Lodge at Geneva immediately proffered its allegiance. The Grand Lodge was inaugurated June 24, when Tavel was elected G.M., and two more Geneva Lodges joined. The Grand Lodge entered upon a prosperous career, receiving adhesions from all parts, and in the course of a few years its daughter Lodges had ceased to work any high degrees, and had all adopted the Schroeder Ritual.

RECTIFIED RITE.—Left face to face with a single rival, this body bethought itself to put its house in order. The first step was to fill the vacant Grand Mastership, and Sarasin, of Basle, was elected to that office. All the Lodges of the system were invited to his installation (1823)—nine in all; and various attempts were made to bring the system and rite more into harmony with the spirit of the times. But the close of this, the third period of Swiss Masonry, presents to us two Grand Bodies, one—on the wane—the antiquated Templar system, and the other—older still—an offshoot of the pure English Craft, lusty as a young giant, prepared to run his race—and confident of victory.

The fourth period therefore opens with the National Grand Lodge of Berne and the Grand Directory of the Rectified Rite at Basle only in the field; for the Helvetic Rite, which still pretended to exist, for very many years resembled a general without an army, or a head without a body.

In 1828 the Rectified Grand Lodge was so dull and lifeless that Sarasin resigned, and it was not until 1829 that Von Escher, of Zurich, was elected in his stead. The Lodges themselves were induced to take part in festivals and meetings of the National Grand Lodge, and individually were not averse to a fusion, though unprepared to take active steps from an honourable feeling of loyalty towards their Grand Officers. Only one Lodge, that at Locle, deserted to the National Grand Lodge.

In 1830—June 19—Tavel, G.M. of the National Grand Lodge, died. The new election was delayed in order to make a further attempt at a fusion. The Lodge of Hope once more took the matter in hand. But the July revolution in Paris had raised an echo in the Cantons where the still somewhat patrician style of government was in course of being overthrown. Under these circumstances the Grand Directory—Rectified Rite—thought the moment not a propitious one for attracting public attention to the Fraternity, but admitted its inability to cope with the spirit of the times, and declared it would not attempt to prevent its daughters seceding, nor feel hurt at their desertion. As already related, a sentimental feeling prevented this, and as the effort was evidently not destined to succeed, the National Grand Lodge contented itself with quietly making friends in all directions. Shortly afterwards the Duke Charles of Hesse Cassel, G.M. of the Rectified system, died; the Provinces of the Order had all ceased to exist except Burgundy, represented by the Directory in Switzerland, and half a Lodge in Besançon, which professed to be the Provincial Chapter, and thus in 1844 it became possible, with the tacit consent of the almost defunct Directory, to appoint a commission to draw up the constitutions of the proposed Sole Grand Lodge. This constitution was finally approved at Zurich, July 22, 1844, by 14 Lodges present on the occasion. The following day

Hottinger was elected Grand Master, the *two* Grand Lodges previously existing made over to him all their rights and duties and dissolved, new Grand Officers were appointed, and—July 24, 1844—the Grand Lodge "Alpina," of Switzerland, met for the first time. Only six Lodges refused to join; one of these was dormant, the others were in Geneva; one persisted in retaining the Rectified system, and hung on to the shadow of a Chapter at Besançon; three still owned the sway of the Grand Orient of France, and one that of the Supreme Council 33° of the same country. So that the close of the fourth period leaves us with practically a united Craft in Switzerland under the Grand Lodge Alpina. There is no necessity to describe its constitutions at length; they were almost identical with those of England both in spirit and machinery.

The fifth period extends to the present time. The constitution had enacted six years as the term of office for the G.M. Hottinger therefore retired in 1850, and was succeeded by Jung. The last Provincial Grand Chapter of the Rectified Rite at Besançon having died out in 1845, the only remaining Lodge of this system (Geneva) joined the Grand Lodge Alpina in 1851; and the same course was pursued by the Geneva Lodge working under the A. and A.S.R. 33° at Paris. Two of the three Geneva Lodges under the G.O. of France also affiliated in course of time, thus leaving only one foreign Lodge in the Confederation.

But the extinct or rather dormant Supreme Chapter of the old Helvetic Rite at Lausanne made periodical efforts to recover control of the Lodges, though it only so far succeeded as to graft Rose Croix Chapters on some few French Lodges, and to sow dissension in the French Cantons. On the other hand, some old high degree Masons of the Rectified Rite followed a similar plan in the German Cantons, and these knightly degrees were worked until 1862, and possibly later. The system is, I believe, now quite extinct. But into the history of these and other "Masonic Aberrations" space forbids me to enter any further than is absolutely necessary to a due comprehension of the annals of the Craft.

The National Grand Lodge continued to prosper, resuscitating old Lodges and warranting new. The Annual Festival is movable, being held at various towns. At the Grand Lodge of 1853, 18 Lodges were represented; in 1856, 19 and 4 not. The periodical election of G.M. brought Maistre to the head of the Fraternity. In 1862 he was succeeded as G.M. by Dr Gelpke, the number of Lodges having increased to 25, with 1730 members. In 1866 the Lodges were 28. In 1868 Ruegg was elected G.M.

In 1869 the long extinct or dormant Helvetic Directory at Lausanne transformed itself into a Supreme Council of the A. and A.S.R. 33° for Switzerland, and began to pose as a Grand Lodge. The consequence was, that at the Grand Lodge in 1871 its members were excluded. Ruegg resigned, and was followed as G.M. by Humbert. The periodical election in 1874 placed Tscharner at the head of the Craft, who was in turn succeeded by John Cuinoud.

The exclusion of the A. and A.S.R. Masons produced great irritation, and the Supreme Council revenged itself by warranting Craft Lodges to the number of six. After many years of strife an arrangement was come to in 1876, whereby the excluded brethren were reinstated, and the Supreme Council undertook to leave the Lodges alone, confining its attention to the additional degrees. Its fate therefore interests us no more, but it still exists on friendly terms with the Grand Lodge. Five of its six Lodges joined the "Alpina," and the sixth amalgamated with a neighbouring Lodge.

The following table may serve to present the chief of the above facts in a concise form:

GENEVA.	VAUD.	GERMAN CANTONS.
1787. **Eng. Prov. Grand Lodge.** (Date of decay unknown.)	1739. **National Grand Directory** for French Helvetia. (Closed by civil authorities, 1745.)	1771. **Lodge of Discretion** at Zurich.
1769. **Grand Lodge**—Independent. (Closed by state of Siege, 1782.)	1761. **Scots Directory**, Strict Observance, Vth. Province, Burgundy.	1772. Embraced Strict Observance system, and became SUB-PRIORY OF VTH. PROVINCE.
1786. **Grand Orient** (A revival of the Grand Lodge.)	(Closed by authorities, 1773; reopened, 1776.)	1778. Adopted Rectified Rite, and became SCOTS DIRECTORY.
	1778. Adopted Rectified Rite.	

1792-1793. All Freemasonry ceased during the Reign of Terror.

1795. **Grand Orient.** (Revived.)	1809. **Scots Directory.** (Revived.)	1809. **Scots Directory of Vth. Province.** (Transferred from Zurich to Basle.)
1801. Transformed to PROV. GRAND LODGE OF GENEVA (under Grand Orient of France; abolished by G. Orient in 1809).	1810. Transformed to **Nat. Grand Orient of French Helvetia** (Glaire's Helvetic Rite).	

1813-1816. All Freemasonry ceased during political reconstitution.

BERNE.		
1818. **English Prov. Grand Lodge.**	1816. **Grand Orient of Helvetic Rite.** (Revived.)	1816. **Scots Directory.** (Revived at Zurich.)
		1823. Transferred to Basle.

1822. National Grand Lodge of Switzerland at Berne.

1869. **Sup. Council for Switzerland of Ancient and Accepted Scottish Rite 33°, at Lausanne.**	1844. **National Grand Lodge " Alpina."**

1876.
" Alpina," Sole Grand Lodge for the Craft.

The latest statistics before me refer to May 1885. The number of Lodges was 34, with 2451 members, an average of 72 per Lodge. Of these 11 are in Vaud, 6 in Geneva (all in the city itself), 4 in Neufchatel, 4 in Berne, 2 in Zurich, and 1 each in Freiburg, Basle, Schaffhausen, St Gall, Grisons, Aargau, and Ticino. 10 of the Cantons possess no Lodge; 7 of these are strictly Roman Catholic; the other 3, although Protestant—Glarus, Appenzell, and Thurgau—contain no town large enough to support a Lodge. As regards dialect, the result is curious. Only one-fifth of the Confederation speak the French tongue, yet here we find 22 Lodges; whereas the German four-fifths only contain 11. In Ticino the language is Italian. The present G.M. is E. C. Jung of Winterthur (Zurich). In Geneva there is still one Lodge under the Grand Orient of France—a "Memphis" Lodge, under the A. and P. Rite, England (*ante*, p. 135), established there in 1856, joined the National G.L. "Alpina" in 1865.[1]

[1] Authorities consulted :—Fr. Heldmann, Die 3 ältesten Geschichtliche Denkmäle, etc., Aarau, 1819, pp. 520-540 —Asträa, 1849, Sondershausen (a magazine). Article by Th. Zschokke, "Umrisse der Gesch. der Freim. in der Schweiz," pp. 226-240 ; J. G. Findel, Gesch. der Freim., fourth edit., pp. 623-640 ; Allgemeines Handbuch der Freim., 1863-79, *s.v.* Schweiz, Genf., etc. (by far the fullest article known to me—117 columns of data, very little of which is devoted to description) ; Nettelbladt, Gesch. Freim. Systeme, p. 748 (a mere sketch). Notices of the chief events may also be found in Thory, Acta Latomorum, and Em. Rebold, Histoire Générale de la Franc-Maçonnerie, Paris, 1851, but in both cases a want of accuracy makes itself felt. Heldmann and Zschokke mentioned above in this note were the founders of the Lodge in Aarau, which was the first in Switzerland to return to the practice of pure English Freemasonry.

ITALY.

Until 1859-60 Italy was merely a geographical expression, so that to obtain any amount of clearness in a description of the Craft in that district, it becomes essential, as in the case of Switzerland, to treat the various states separately.

THE TWO SICILIES (Naples and Sicily) 1717-1860.—In 1717 the kingdom was a portion of the Austrian Empire; in 1733 it was ceded to Spain; in 1759 under Ferdinand IV. it passed as an independent kingdom to the younger branch of the Royal House of Spain; in 1805 Naples—but not Sicily—was annexed to France; in 1806 Joseph Buonaparte was made King of Naples, and was followed in 1808 by Joachim Murat; in 1815 the two Sicilies were reunited under Ferdinand; and in 1860 Garibaldi incorporated them with the recently formed kingdom of Italy.

It would appear that about 1750 a Greek established a Lodge in Naples, and that on July 10, 1751, Charles III., influenced by the Bull of Benedict IV., prohibited Freemasonry throughout his dominions, but so soon changed his views, that in the following year he entrusted his son's education to a Mason and priest, whom he also appointed his own confessor. In 1754 we hear of another Lodge working under the Mother-Lodge at Marseilles, which in 1760 placed itself under the Grand Lodge of Holland, and in 1762 transferred its allegiance to England. Our Lodge Lists show no evidence of this transaction, but perhaps the appointment of Don Nicholas Manuzzi by Lord Blaney (1764-67), as Prov. G.M. for Italy,[1] may tend to support the assertion.

In 1764—February 27—a National Grand Lodge was erected, with four daughters in Naples itself, and an equal number distributed throughout the other cities of the kingdom. Besides these there existed in Naples in 1775, according to a report signed by the Grand Master of the Lodge, Prince Di Caramanica, a Lodge working under the Grand Orient of France, and two under the G.L. of England, pronounced clandestine by the National G.L. The latter are evidently those which appear in the Engraved List for 1769 as No. 433, "in his Sicilian Majesty's regiment of Foot," and No. 444,[2] "Well Chosen Lodge." Prince Caramanica's leaning to the Strict Observance, and the isolated position of the two English Lodges, probably led to the appointment by Lord Beaufort, G.M., in 1770, of a Prov. G.M. for Naples and Sicily.[3] The Craft at this period made great progress in the two Sicilies.

Meanwhile, in 1767, Ferdinand IV. assumed the government at the close of his minority, and his minister, Tanucci—an unscrupulous and inveterate enemy of the Craft—at last induced him—September 12, 1775—to suppress Freemasonry. The Lodges closed, but Tanucci, by means of *agents provocateurs*, induced some Masons to meet, who were duly arrested. Again, on the day of St Januarius, 1776, the saint's blood refused to liquify in the customary manner, which the agents of Tanucci attributed to the machinations of the Masons, and a regular persecution ensued. But Ferdinand's wife, Queen Caroline—daughter of the Emperor Francis of Lorraine—"loved Masons well." Owing to her advocacy the edict was revoked and Tanucci dismissed. In June 1776 Diego Naselli was elected G.M.

---

[1] Constitutions, 1767, p. 365 *et seq.*

[2] The warrant of this Lodge—granted to Prince Caramanica and others at Naples—is dated April 26, 1769.

[3] "The most noble Cæsar Pignatelli, Duke di la Rocca, [appointed Prov. G.M.] for the kingdom of Naples and Sicily" (G.L. Minutes, April 25, 1770).

in succession to Caramanica, four new Lodges were warranted, and the two English Lodges affiliated with the National G.L.

In 1777 Weiler came to Naples. This emissary of the Strict Observance had succeeded in erecting Italy into the VIIIth. Province, with a Provincial Grand Chapter at Turin, and as the National G.L. of Sicily had from its earliest days been on cordial terms with the German Lodges of Prince Ferdinand, he experienced no difficulty in converting it into a Chapter and Sub-Priory of the S.O., with Naselli as Sub-Prior. That this perversion displeased some of the Fraternity, and caused them to apply to England for relief, cannot be positively affirmed; but it is at least certain that the following Lodges were constituted almost immediately afterwards under English Charters [1]—No. 510 at Messina (May 12, 1778), No. 525 at Naples (March 6, 1780), No. 440 at Naples (1781). [2]

In 1781 Ferdinand IV. once more placed the Craft under an interdict; in 1783 he cancelled all former inhibitions, but subjected the meetings to strict judicial control. [3] Their independence and privacy being thus endangered the Lodges gradually dwindled and died out, and Masonry ceased to exist in the two kingdoms.

In 1804 the French entered Naples, and the Royal Family took refuge in Sicily under the protection of Nelson and the Fleet. I can discover no trace of the Craft in the island during this period; but in Naples a Grand Orient was established in 1804 by the French army of Italy, with General Lechi as G.M., [4] which in 1805 amalgamated with the G.O. of Italy at Milan. [5]

In 1809—June 11—Murat being King of Naples, a Supreme Council 33° was established in that city, and on June 24 of the same year a Grand Orient, [6] of which Murat allowed himself to be proclaimed G.M. In October 1812 he was appointed Sovereign Grand Commander of the 33°. But on the fall of Napoleon in 1815 Murat was driven out, and a law of 1816—August 8—prohibited Freemasonry under pain of the galleys. Nevertheless it dragged on a fitful existence, and the G.O. of France, in its list for 1820, still makes mention of three Lodges and one Chapter at Messina. This was followed by a new decree in 1821, upon which the Grand Orient for the two Sicilies declared itself dissolved. In the revolutionary year 1848 a Lodge existed—but for a few months only—in Palermo. This was the last effort of the Craft in the *kingdom* of the two Sicilies.

STATES OF THE CHURCH.—Freemasonry was early introduced into Rome. On August 16, 1735, a Lodge was opened there under J. Colton. It worked in English, but under the Earl of Wintoun in 1737, the Inquisition seized its serving brothers, and on August 20, it closed. [7] The Bull of Clement XII. was published in 1738, and confirmed—January 14, 1739—by a further edict forbidding Freemasonry throughout the Papal States under pain of death and confiscation of worldly goods. The burning by the public executioner in the same year— February 25—of the "*Relation Apologétique,*" wrongly attributed to Ramsay, has already been mentioned. [8] Nevertheless there is evidence to show that the foreign Masons then residing at Rome continued to meet from time to time. In 1742 they even issued a medal in honour of Martin Folkes, D.G.M. of England, 1724-25. [9] A Lodge was again established at Rome in

---

[1] The name of the Duke de Sandemetrio Pignatelli appears as Prov. G.M. for Naples and Sicily in the "Freemasons' Calendar" for 1779, and only disappears in the edition for 1888!

[2] Engraved Lists; and Four Old Lodges, pp. 67-72.   [3] Acta Latomorum, pp. 150, 158.

[4] *Ibid.*, p. 223.   [5] *Ibid.*, p. 229.   [6] *Ibid.*, p. 243.

[7] Freemasons' Quarterly Review, 1842, p. 393 *et seq.*   [8] *Ante,* p. 90.   [9] Merzdorf, Denkmünze, p 118, No. 8.

1787, but was surprised by the Inquisition, December 27, 1789; the brethren escaped, though the property and archives were seized. On the same day the Inquisition captured the charlatan Cagliostro, whose evil repute had acted most prejudicially upon Freemasonry. The Lodges in Lombardy issued a manifesto—which was brought up by the college[1] of Cardinals—disclaiming all connection with him, and defending the Craft from papal aspersions.

In 1809 the Papal States were incorporated with France, and Rome was declared the second capital of the empire. Under French rule several Lodges were established, but on the return of Pope Pius VII. in 1814 the Craft was once more effectually suppressed.[2] It was not until 1861 that a new Lodge opened, in which year one was formed under the Grand Orient of Turin. We may now leave these states until 1870, when the Franco-Prussian war permitted Victor Emmanuel to unite the ancient capital to his kingdom of Italy.

TUSCANY—FLORENCE.—On the extinction of the Medici family in 1737, Francis of Lorraine[3] received this Grand Duchy in exchange for Lorraine, which had been conquered by Louis XIV. of France and presented to his father-in-law, Stanislaus, ex-King of Poland. When Francis was elected German Emperor in 1745, the Duchy was vested in the junior branch of the Austrian family, but in 1790 reverted to the imperial crown under Leopold when his elder brother Joseph II. died childless. As Francis of Lorraine was Grand Duke from 1737 to 1765, it is somewhat surprising the Craft should have prospered so little in Tuscany during that period; for the only Lodge of which we hear, *supposed* to have been founded in 1733 by Lord Sackville, and closed under the persecutions of the Inquisition in 1739, probably never existed at all. Its existence has only been inferred on the authority of a medal by Natter dated 1733, which medal is almost certainly a fraud perpetrated at a much later date in the interests of the Strict Observance.[4] From this supposititious Lodge, however, both the Swedish system and the Strict Observance have professed to receive that light denied to England in 1717; but whether this legendary transmission inspired the medal, or whether the medal gave rise to the legend, I am unable to say, nor would it profit us much to inquire. Beyond this apocryphal Lodge we have only general accounts of Freemasonry in Tuscany[5] until June 24, 1763, when a Lodge—No. 117—was established at Leghorn[6] by the Schismatic G.L. of England (*Ancients*). This was followed by a second—No. 138—in 1765 (under the same sanction), also at Leghorn, where, in 1771, two further Lodges—of "Perfect Union," No. 410; and of "Sincere Brotherly Love," No. 412—were constituted by the older (or legitimate) Grand Lodge of England.

Troops were quartered in the Duchy by the French in 1796-97, and we again hear of

---

[1] Acta Latomorum, pp. 183-187.   [2] Chap. XX., pp. 477, 478.   [3] *Ante*, p. 286.

[4] See an interesting discussion extending from January to November 1883, in the "London Freemason," between disputants who wrote under the signatures of G.B.A. and Dryasdust.

[5] *E.g.*, *St James Evening Post*, letter from Florence dated May 24, 1738.—"The Freemasons' Lodges which had been interdicted here during the life of the great Duke are now held again with all the liberty and freedom imaginable, and without any dread of the Inquisition, which has no right to attack a society of which the new sovereign [Francis of Lorraine] is a member. The Freemasons of Leghorn have also reopened their Lodges" (Mas. Mag., vol. iv., July 1876, p. 421).

[6] Under the beneficent sway of the Medici, religious toleration was established at Leghorn, and merchants of all nations flocked there. We learn from Boswell that there was a British factory in that city, to which the Rev. Mr Burnaby was chaplain, in 1765 (Account of Corsica, 1768, preface, p. xiv.).

Lodges at Leghorn, which, however, were closed by the Grand Duke in 1800. But he was himself driven out by the French, and his Duchy transformed into an Etruscan Republic, then into a kingdom of Tuscany, and finally annexed to France, with Napoleon's sister, the Duchess of Lucca, as Grand Duchess. Consequently, from 1807 to 1809, we find Lodges erected both at Florence and Leghorn, hailing either from the Grand Orients of France or of Italy [at Milan].[1] But with the return of the (Austrian) Grand Duke Ferdinand in 1814 all Masonry once more died out, and was not revived until, in 1859, Tuscany became a part of the kingdom of Italy.

GENOA.—The old British and Ligurian Lodge, No. 444, was warranted here by the Grand Lodge of England in 1782. As Thory relates[2] that several Masons were imprisoned here in consequence of the Senate's edict of March 26, 1803, it is possible that this Lodge was then still in existence. This was under Napoleon's Ligurian Republic, finally established in 1802 after the Austrians had held the town for two years. In 1805 the State was annexed to France, and two Lodges were established under the Grand Orient of France, 1805-1807; a third but earlier one is also mentioned. In 1814 Genoa was handed over to Sardinia, and Freemasonry there ceased to exist.

LOMBARDY, MILAN.—We have already seen that in 1784, when the National Grand Lodge of Austria was formed, a Provincial Grand Lodge existed in this province of the Austrian dominions, with two daughters, at Cremona and Milan respectively.[3] It is not clear whether these Lodges expired before 1794 of their own want of vitality, or whether they survived long enough to be closed by the imperial edict of 1795. In 1797 this province formed part of Napoleon's Cisalpine Republic, to which I shall again allude.

VENETIA.—The Grand Lodge of England granted warrants on November 27, 1772, to the Union Lodge, No. 438, at Venice; and on the 28th to a Lodge, No. 439, at Verona. Nothing further is known of their history, but they are supposed to have continued in existence till 1785. In Padua, in 1781, there existed a Prefectory and Chapter of the Strict Observance under the Grand Priory of the VIIIth. Province, in Turin, which, after 1782, was changed to the IVth.; and this Chapter presided over a S.O. Lodge in Vicenza, of which there were notices in 1784-85. All these Lodges and any others which may have existed were suppressed by a decree of the Venetian Senate in May 1785.

By the peace of Campo-Formio in 1797, Venetia was divided, part going to Austria—where Freemasonry was already under a ban—and part to the Cisalpine Republic.

CISALPINE REPUBLIC.—This, formed in 1797 of Milan, Modena, Mantua, Bologna, Ferrara, Romagno, part of Venetia, etc., was called, in 1801, the Italian Republic, with Napoleon as President, and in 1805 became the kingdom of Italy, with Buonaparte as King, and Eugene Beauharnais as Viceroy.

On December 26, 1801, the French Grand Orient erected at Milan the first Lodge in this new State. In 1805—the A. and A.S.R. founded a Supreme Council 33° at Milan, which constituted a Grand Orient for the kingdom of Italy, with Beauharnais as G.M. The recently formed G.O. at Naples amalgamated with it,[4] and in 1808 it was recognised as an independent Grand Orient by the G.O. at Paris. Many Lodges were constituted in the kingdom, two at Milan itself, 1807-10, but the whole system was suppressed, when in 1814 the kingdom was broken up, Parma and Modena becoming separate States, and the greater part of the remainder

[1] *See* below.   [2] Acta Latomorum, p. 217.   [3] *Ante*, p. 287.   [4] *Ibid.*, p. 299.

falling to Austria, forming, with the previously acquired portion of Venetia, the Austrian Lombardo-Venetian kingdom. Freemasonry therefore ceased to exist here until in 1860 Lombardy, and in 1866 Venetia, were incorporated with the present kingdom of Italy.

SARDINIA (PIEDMONT AND SAVOY).—The first notice of the Craft in this kingdom is the appointment by Lord Raymond, G.M., of the Marquis des Marches as Prov. G.M. for Savoy and Piedmont in 1739.[1] Beyond this bare record nothing is known.

The next notice is the existence in Piedmont (Turin), in 1774, of a Grand Lodge called "La Mystérieuse," working a rite of its own, consisting of the three degrees and of 4° Elect Grand Master, 5° Perfect Irish Master, 6° Grand Scot, 7° Knight of the East, 8° Holy Kadosch, and 9° Rose Croix. This was transformed by Weiler in 1775 into the Great Priory of Italy (VIIIth. Province) or Bailiwick of Lombardy at Turin, with Weiler himself as Grand Prior, and after him Count Bernez.[2] It had three subordinate Prefectories—at Naples, Turin, and Padua—and a score or more of Lodges. In the same year—March 25, 1775—an English Lodge, St Jean de Nouvelle Espérance, No. 479, was constituted at Turin, of whose subsequent history nothing appears to be known.

Savoy, in 1778, joined the Rectified Scots Rite of the Strict Observance, with a Directory —"La Sincérité"—of the IInd. Province (Auvergne), at Chambery. The Grand Orient of France had, however, also constituted Lodges there from 1770 onwards, of which one—"The Three Mortars"—claimed to be a Grand Orient of Sardinia—a claim rejected by the G.O. of France in 1790—and even warranted a Lodge as far off as Dresden. In 1782 also, as we have already seen, no less than 14 Lodges existed in Piedmont and Savoy dependent upon the Scots Directory for French Helvetia in Lausanne.[3]

In 1788 the King of Sardinia, Victor Amadeus III., ordered the Strict Observance Grand Priory in Turin to dissolve, and transfer its powers to the Scots Directory at Chambery, which thus became the recognised Grand Lodge of the kingdom.

But on January 11, 1790, this Grand Lodge was also dissolved by the King (though *Freemasonry* was not otherwise interfered with), and the Lodges transferred their allegiance—as the Craft itself was not placed under an interdict—to the Grand Orients of France and Geneva, or to the Directory at Lausanne.

In 1792 Savoy was ceded to France, and the Craft there revived under the G.O. of the latter country. Two years later—May 20, 1794—Victor Amadeus III. issued an edict totally suppressing Masonry throughout the remainder of his dominions. In 1798, however, his sovereignty was restricted to the Island of Sardinia. The French occupied Piedmont, lost it temporarily in 1799, converted it into a Republic in 1802, and annexed it to France a few months later. Under French rule a Lodge was warranted in Turin, and probably others under the Grand Orient of Italy at Milan,[4] but they were all short-lived, for in 1814 the King of Sardinia re-obtained possession of Piedmont (enlarged) and of Savoy, besides acquiring Genoa, and in 1814—May 20—renewed the edict of 1794 rigidly suppressing Freemasonry.

---

[1] Constitutions, 1756, p. 333.

[2] In the Engraved List for 1773, and subsequently in the "Freemasons' Calendar" until 1804, Count de Bernez appears as English Prov. G.M. for Piedmont in Italy. I am not aware whether he was the G.M. of the "Mystérieuse," but even if so, it would not be the sole example of an English Prov. G.M. presiding over assemblies where degrees were wrought other than those of the Craft.

[3] *Ante*, p. 291.   [4] *Ibid.*, p. 301.

This edict remained in force until shortly before the dawn of Italian freedom in 1859, so that from 1821 (see under The Two Sicilies, *ante*, p. 299) until 1856, not a Lodge existed in any part of what is now the kingdom of Italy.[1]

THE KINGDOM OF ITALY.—In 1859, Victor Emmanuel of Sardinia acquired all northern Italy except Venetia, but lost Savoy, which was ceded to France; in 1860 Naples and Sicily were gained for him by Garibaldi; in 1866 he obtained Venetia by treaty, and in 1870 the city of Rome. The year 1859 forms therefore a perfectly fresh starting point for us, although the Grand Orient of France had warranted a Lodge at Genoa in 1856.

In 1859 several Masons constituted themselves into a Lodge at Turin working the so-called modern Italian rite of three degrees—in other words, pure English Masonry. Their example was soon followed by the erection of numerous other Lodges in Genoa, Milan, Pisa, Florence, Leghorn, Rome, and other places. These Lodges adopted measures to form a Grand Lodge, and by general correspondence agreed upon a provisional constitution, ritual, etc. The Chevalier Nigra, Ambassador at Paris, was elected G.M. provisionally. To this there was no opposition, but some few Lodges having given a *silent* vote, Nigra declined the nomination—November 22, 1861—in order to allow the proposed constituent assembly perfect liberty. This assembly met at Turin December 26, 1861, and sat daily until January 1, 1862. Twenty-two Lodges in all were represented. On January 1, 1862, the Grand Orient of Italy at Turin was proclaimed, with Nigra as G.M., and Garibaldi as Hon. Past G.M. The yearly assembly was declared movable from city to city. The Lodges not only restricted themselves to the three degrees, but agreed to refuse fellowship to those working any others. In most respects the organisation of the Grand Lodge followed the arrangements of the Grand Lodge of England. This was not accomplished without protest, which to understand, it will be necessary in some degree to retrace our steps.

In 1860 some Masons established a Supreme Council A. and A.S.R. 33° for Naples and Sicily, and professed to consider themselves a revival of the Supreme Council 33° established at Naples in 1809 and suppressed in 1821. Many Lodges sprang up and adhered to this organisation.

About the same time other Lodges in Sicily also working the A. and A.S.R. 33° met and established a Grand Orient of that Rite at Palermo, with Garibaldi as G.M.

Also at Turin there existed a Consistory of the 32°, likewise warranting Lodges, and assuming all the rights of a Supreme Council until the time arrived when they might be strong enough to form a Grand Orient of the Scots Rite in the capital of Italy—at that time Turin.

Further, about 1861, it would appear as if a similar Consistory existed at Leghorn for Tuscany.

The chief protests against the Grand Orient of Italy at Turin came from the Supreme Council at Naples. We thus see that not only was Italy divided in its views as to Masonic ceremonial, but also that the old territorial divisions showed a tendency to assert themselves

---

[1] Authorities consulted up to this point :—Engraved Lists ; Freemasons' Calendars ; Acta Latomorum ; Astræa, 1849, p. 237 *et seq.* ; Findel, Geschichte, etc., pp. 640-651 ; Allgemeines Handbuch, *s.v.* Mailand, Verona, Padua, Vicenza, Venedig, Rom, Neapel, Turin, Piedmont, Livorno, Florenz, Sardinien, Savoyen, Italien, etc., etc.

in spite of Italian unity. The Grand Orient was not only opposed by these four Scots Councils, but unfortunately failed to secure any external support beyond that of Belgium and France, because it very openly interfered in the politics of the day, domestic and foreign. Under these circumstances Nigra resigned—March 1, 1863—and Cordova was elected by the small majority of 15 to 13 over Garibaldi. Matters, however, did not improve under the new G.M.; England especially withheld its recognition. The Grand Orient in 1862 unwisely adopted very strong measures with regard to a Turin Lodge addicted to the high degrees, and general discontent prevailed. Nevertheless in July 1863 the G.O. had no less than 68 Lodges on its roll, including daughters at Alexandria, Cairo, Constantinople, Lima, and elsewhere.

On August 1, 1863, at a general assembly held in Florence, the troubles reached a climax. The Grand Officers, with one exception, resigned; and an *interim* committee of five was appointed to draw up a new constitution. These were all Scots, *i.e.*, A. and A.S.R. Masons.

This committee having concluded its labours, called a meeting at Florence, May 21-24, 1864. "Latomia" of the same year states that only some thirty Lodges of the Italian (*i.e.*, English) rite and a few of the Scots were represented, whilst the "Handbuch" of 1867 speaks of seventy Lodges and five Grand Lodges being present. This shows the difficulty of advancing anything of a positive character respecting this troubled period of Italian Free-masonry. On May 22 a new Grand Orient of Italy, consisting of forty members, was pro-claimed. The chief seat of this body was Turin, but sections were appointed for Florence, Naples, and Palermo. The Lodges were allowed to work in either rite; but it is evident that the A. and A.S.R. 33° had gained a victory. On the 23d Garibaldi was elected G.M., and Luca President of the Grand Council 33°. The Supreme Councils of Naples, Leghorn, and Turin appear to have concurred, for of these we hear nothing more; that of Palermo under Garibaldi stood out from the arrangement; Garibaldi himself speedily resigned; and on September 15, 1864, Luca was elected in his stead. But Garibaldi's S.C. had also to contend with a rival in Palermo itself, a so-called Central Supreme Council under Prince Sant' Elia. I must candidly confess that I have been unable to discover whether this was an offshoot from Garibaldi's Council, or whether it had spontaneously sprung up some few years previously. A further complication arose from the action of eleven Lodges working the Italian Rite of three degrees, who, dissatisfied with the May meeting at Florence and its results, met at Milan July 1-5, 1864, and erected a Grand Lodge, under the name of a Grand Council, to sit at Turin, with Franchi as President or Grand Master. In 1865 the Grand Orient of Italy (mixed rites) was transferred to the new capital, Florence, and the Grand Council (Craft only) from Turin to Milan. From 1864 to 1867 we have thus four Grand Bodies in Italy, whose strength in 1867 was about as follows :—

    I. Grand Orient of Italy at Florence (Composite), about 150 Lodges ; Luca, G.M.

    II. Supreme Council at Palermo (A. and A.S.R.), about 39 Lodges ; Garibaldi, G.M.

    III. Grand Council at Milan (Craft), 7-8 Lodges ; Franchi, G.M., who on July 15, 1867, was succeeded by Guastalla.

    IV. Supreme Central Council at Palermo (A. and A.S.R.), number of Lodges unknown; Sant' Elia, G.M.

Garibaldi himself was the first to take steps to put an end to this disastrous conflict of jurisdictions. He issued invitations to a congress of all Italian Lodges, which resulted in a meeting at Naples of deputies from his own Lodges and those under the Florence Grand Orient on June 21, 1867. Luca presided. The Supreme Council of Palermo became merged in the Grand Orient, the four sections of the G.O. at Florence, Turin, Naples, and Palermo were abolished, Cordova was elected G.M., Garibaldi Hon. G.M. for life, and Luca Hon. G.M. for a year. Cordova soon resigned on account of bad health, and was succeeded by Frapolli. Garibaldi's Supreme Council did not approve of the fusion, but elected Campanella as Grand Master, and essayed to maintain its position. It became even more careless than before in its choice of candidates, and warranted sixteen Lodges (one at Smyrna) in 1868. But this was an expiring effort. Its Lodges died out or joined the Grand Orient, and towards the end of the year the Supreme Council was practically extinct.

At this time the Grand Lodge at Milan, finding itself unable to make any progress, so far modified its views as to acknowledge that Lodges under the Scots Rite might be legitimate, and thus a fusion was easily arranged on March 4, 1868, at Milan, between the Grand Orient of Italy at Florence and the Grand (Craft) Lodge at Milan. The amalgamation was affected April 1. This left only the Grand Orient of Italy—the title adopted by the parties to the fusion last referred to—and the Central Supreme Council of Palermo, in the field. In the next year or two Grand Master Frapolli succeeded in great measure in banishing religion and politics from Lodge discussions, and at the annual meeting in Florence in 1869 no less than 150 Lodges were represented. But as a general rule there is little stability amongst Italian Lodges, they spring up in a night and die at noontide. In June 1870 Frapolli retired and Mazzoni was elected, and towards the end of the year the Grand Orient was transferred to the newly acquired capital, Rome.

In 1872—April 25—new constitutions were accepted, and at last in 1873 the Supreme Council at Palermo amalgamated with the Grand Orient, which has ever since been the sole Grand, or Governing Masonic Body in Italy. Under Mazzoni the quality of Italian Masonry has improved, at the expense of its quantity. Unworthy members and disreputable Lodges have been relentlessly weeded out. As we have seen, in 1869 there were over 150 Lodges, but in 1877 there remained only 134, and in 1878 only 109—with a membership of 12,053, or an average of 110 per Lodge—whilst in 1885 the number had once more increased to 146. Besides these there are 57 Lodges scattered throughout Roumania, Egypt—one, at Alexandria, is composed of Germans only—the Levant, and South America. The cities containing the greatest number of Lodges are Naples, with 10; Leghorn and Genoa, 5; Palermo and Rome, 4; Messina, Milan, and Florence, 3; and Venice, 2 each.

The seat of the Grand Orient is at Rome, the G.M. being Adriano Lemmi. It is divided into Three Chambers—for the Scots Rite 33°, a Supreme Council, under Giorgio Tomajo, as Sov. G. Com., with 174 Lodges, of which 54 are abroad—for the Craft, a Symbolic Grand Lodge, under a President, Perro Aporti, with 25 Lodges, of which 3 are abroad—and for the Rite of Memphis, a Supreme Council in Catania, under Gaetano Mondino, as President, with 4 Lodges only. The accompanying table of the Grand Bodies which have existed in Italy may be acceptable as an *aide-mémoire.*[1]

---

[1] Authorities consulted for the latter portion (kingdom of Italy):—Latomia, 1863, vol. xxii., pp. 104-129, 165-170, 200-205; vol. xxiii., 1864, pp. 266-270, 371-373; vol. xxvi., 1868, pp. 223-228; vol. xxvii., 1869, pp. 207-214: Allgemeines Handbuch, s.v. Italian, 1868-79: Findel, Geschichte, etc., pp. 640-651.

TABLE OF ITALIAN GRAND LODGES.

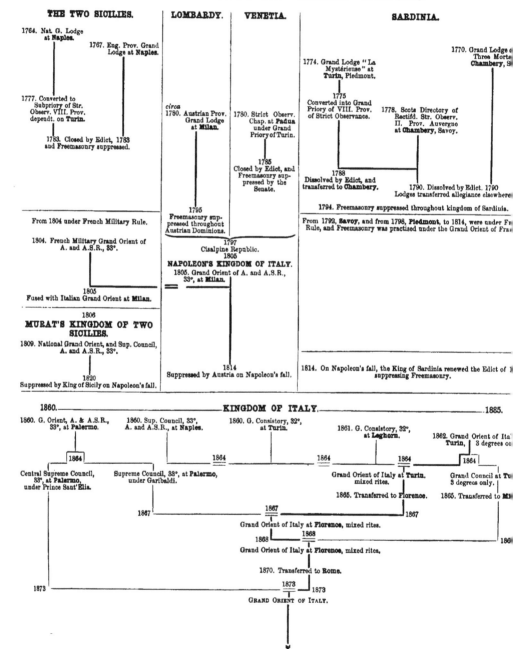

THE TWO SICILIES. | **LOMBARDY.** | **VENETIA.** | **SARDINIA.**

1764. Nat. G. Lodge at **Naples**.

1767. Eng. Prov. Grand Lodge at **Naples**.

1770. Grand Lodge of Three Morts Chambery, S...

1774. Grand Lodge "La Mystérieuse" at **Turin**, Piedmont.

1777. Converted to Subpriory of Str. Observ. VIII. Prov. dependt. on **Turin**.

circa 1780. Austrian Prov. Grand Lodge at **Milan**.

1780. Strict Observ. Chap. at **Padua** under Grand Priory of Turin.

1775 Converted into Grand Priory of VIII. Prov. of Strict Observance.

1778. Scots Directory of Rectifd. Str. Observ. II. Prov. Auvergne at **Chambery**, Savoy.

1783. Closed by Edict, 1783 and Freemasonry suppressed.

1785 Closed by Edict, and Freemasonry suppressed by the Senate.

1788 Dissolved by Edict, and transferred to **Chambery**.

1790. Dissolved by Edict. 1790 Lodges transferred allegiance elsewhere...

1794. Freemasonry suppressed throughout kingdom of Sardinia.

1795 Freemasonry suppressed throughout Austrian Dominions.

From 1804 under French Military Rule.

From 1792, **Savoy**, and from 1798, **Piedmont**, to 1814, were under Fr... Rule, and Freemasonry was practised under the Grand Orient of Fra...

1804. French Military Grand Orient of A. and A.S.R., 33°.

1797 Cisalpine Republic.
1805.
NAPOLEON'S KINGDOM OF ITALY.
1805. Grand Orient of A. and A.S.R., 33°, at **Milan**.

1805 Fused with Italian Grand Orient at **Milan**.

1806
MURAT'S KINGDOM OF TWO SICILIES.

1809. National Grand Orient, and Sup. Council, A. and A.S.R., 33°.

1820 Suppressed by King of Sicily on Napoleon's fall.

1814 Suppressed by Austria on Napoleon's fall.

1814. On Napoleon's fall, the King of Sardinia renewed the Edict of ... suppressing Freemasonry.

1860. ———————————— **KINGDOM OF ITALY.** ———————————— 1885.

1860. G. Orient, A. & A.S.R., 33°, at **Palermo**.

1860. Sup. Council, 33°, A. and A.S.R., at **Naples**.

1860. G. Consistory, 32°, at **Turin**.

1861. G. Consistory, 32°, at **Leghorn**.

1862. Grand Orient of Ita... **Turin**, 3 degrees on...

1864 | 1864 | 1864 | 1864 | 1864

Central Supreme Council, 33°, at **Palermo**, under Prince Sant'Elia.

Supreme Council, 33°, at **Palermo**, under Garibaldi.

Grand Orient of Italy at **Turin**. mixed rites.

Grand Council at **Tu**... 3 degrees only.

1865. Transferred to **Florence**.

1865. Transferred to **M**...

1867 ———————— 1867 ———————— 1867

Grand Orient of Italy at **Florence**, mixed rites.

1868 1868 186...

Grand Orient of Italy at **Florence**, mixed rites.

1870. Transferred to **Rome**.

1873 | 1873 | 1873

GRAND ORIENT OF ITALY.

PORTUGAL.

It is a well-known axiom with Freemasons, that their duty requires them to close their Lodges in the presence of a prohibition by the government of the day. We have seen this duty cheerfully submitted to in various countries, but Portugal forms an exception to the ordinary rule. In no country has the Craft been more persecuted—both by the Government and the Church—but it would appear as if the Fraternity had obstinately determined not to yield to any pressure from without. Once it had taken root, neither decrees of state nor tortures of the Inquisition ever succeeded in extirpating Freemasonry in Portugal, and at no time did Lodges cease to exist in more or less secrecy. Whilst as a law-abiding Fraternity, we must needs lament this disobedience of our Portuguese brethren—as admirers of devotion and courage, we may be permitted to appreciate their resolution and endurance.

Clavel[1] asserts that French deputies founded Lodges in Portugal in 1727, but this uncorroborated statement fails to inspire me with the confidence I should wish to attach to it. We touch solid ground, however, in the minutes of the G.L. of England, April 17, 1735.—"A petition from several brethren now residing in or about the City of Lisbon in Portugal, humbly praying that a Deputation may be granted to Mr George Gordon for constituting them into a regular Lodge—the prayer of which petition was granted;" and in the *St James' Evening Post*—letter from Lisbon, June 3, 1736—"by authority of the Right Honorable the Earl of Weymouth, the then G. Master of all Mason's Lodges, Mr George Gordon, Mathematician, has constituted a Lodge of Free and Accepted Masons in that City; and a great many merchants of the Factory and other people of distinction have been received and regularly made Freemasons. Lord George Graham, Lord Forrester, and a great many gentlemen belonging to the English Fleet, being brethren, were present at constituting the Lodge, and it is expected that in a short time it will be one of the greatest abroad." This early mention of the Fleet is notable, because in after times, during the Craft's darkest hour, foreign vessels in port were extensively used as safe meeting-places for the persecuted Lodges.

Freemasonry, however, from the very first, met with a determined enemy in the Church, and the opposition of the Roman prelacy became more pronounced, after the issue of the famous Bull of Clement XII., April 27, 1738.[2] At last, in 1743, King John V. (1707-50) was persuaded by his *entourage* that the Freemasons were heretics and rebels, and issued an edict of death against them. An era of persecution and torture at the hands of the Inquisition followed; the best known case being that of Coustos.

Coustos—the son of a Swiss surgeon—was born at Berne, but emigrated, in 1716, with his father to England, where he followed the trade of a gem-cutter, and was admitted into the Fraternity. After spending twenty-two years in London he went to Lisbon with the intention of shipping for Brazil, but failing to obtain a permit from the government, settled down to his trade in the Portuguese capital. There, with two French jewellers —Mouton and Braslé—he founded a Lodge, where they were surprised—March 14, 1743— by the familiars of the Inquisition. In order to wrest from him the secrets of a Freemason, and a renunciation of his religion, Coustos was within the space of three months subjected nine times to the rack, scourged, branded, and otherwise tortured, and—June 21, 1743—he

---

[1] *Histoire Pittoresque de la Franc-Maçonnerie.*

[2] *Cj.* Chap. XX., p. 477, note 3.

figured as a principal personage at an *auto-da-fé* in the Church of the Dominicans. He was sentenced to four years at the galleys as a Protestant and *Freemason*—but his two companions, being Catholics, to five years exile only. Mouton and Braslé were also tortured, and the latter died in consequence of his sufferings. Coustos was claimed by the British Embassy as an English subject, and with Mouton arrived in London December 14, 1744, where they were well received and cared for by the Fraternity.[1]

John V. was succeeded by his son Joseph II. (1750-77). Under this liberal prince and his celebrated minister, the Marquis de Pombal, the clergy lost much of their influence, and the Jesuits were banished from the kingdom in 1761. Freemasonry recovered, and only once—in 1776—did the Inquisition attempt to suppress the Craft. This tribunal, however, was constrained to release its victims, Major D'Alincourt and Dom Ayres de Orvellas Peraçao, after fourteen months' detention.[2]

Joseph was succeeded by his daughter Maria, married to her uncle, Dom Pedro. Pombal was dismissed, and the clergy once more gained the upper hand. The most talented men of the kingdom, being Freemasons, only saved their lives by flight, and the celebrated mathematician, Da Cunha, lay in the dungeons of the Inquisition from 1778 to 1780. In 1792 the Queen was attacked by incurable melancholia, and her son John was made Prince Regent. Matters then became worse, and in the same year the Governor of Madeira was ordered to deliver over all Freemasons to the Inquisition. A few only, escaped to America, their vessel on entering New York harbour flying a white flag with the inscription " *Asylum Quaerimus.*" Nevertheless the Fraternity was not exterminated. Lodges are known to have existed at Coimbra, 1793-94; at Oporto, 1795; and others were held in 1796-97 on board various ships in port. The frigate " Phœnix " is especially mentioned in this connection, and there soon arose five or six Lodges in Lisbon as well as elsewhere. Three at the capital—Nos. 315, 319, and 330—are shown on the roll of the (Atholl) Grand Lodge of England, under the years 1798, 1799, and 1807-13 respectively. Numerous others doubtless penetrated into the kingdom with the British regiments to which they were attached. Brethren of the Sea and Land services appear to have worked together in great harmony, and the records of the Grand Lodge last referred to, show that many seafaring men became members of Lodge, No. 332, held in the 58th Foot, whilst that regiment was quartered at Lisbon in 1811.

A committee of six was appointed to act as a Grand Lodge, and other Lodges were established. Great secrecy was observed; the places of meeting were continually changed, and often whilst some members worked in the upper story of a house, the remainder, with their wives and daughters, danced on the lower in order to deceive the police.[3] Although this persecution lasted until 1806, it is during this very period that some remarkable Masonic manifestations occurred. The first Grand Lodge for Portugal was erected, and the first G.M., Dom Sebastian José de Sampajo e Mello de Castro e Luziguano (brother of the Marquis de Pombal),

---

[1] A description of these horrors was published in a book, entitled "The Sufferings of John Coustos for Freemasonry," etc., 1746 ; 400 pages—of which an abridgment has been frequently reprinted.

[2] Thory, Acta Latomorum, vol. i., p. 123.

[3] Mr G. W. Speth remembers taking part in Lodge work under exactly similar circumstances and surroundings (Lodge above, ball below) in 1870-71 in Havana, Cuba. In his case, however, although the consequences of detection would have inevitably been serious, at least no Inquisition was to be feared. He pleads as an excuse for infringing the law that he was *very young*, both as a man and a Mason.

a counsellor of the High Court (or, according to Thory, Egaz-Moniz), was appointed in 1800 (or 1802). This new Grand Lodge, acting through four Lodges, " empowered Dom Hypolite Joseph da Costa to act as their representative at the Grand Lodge of England, and in their name to solicit a regular authority to practise the rites of the Order under the English banner and protection. After mature deliberation it was determined that every encouragement should be given to the brethren in Portugal ; and a treaty was immediately entered into and signed by Da Costa and Heseltine—then Treasurer of the Grand Lodge, and approved by the Grand Master, whereby it was agreed that as long as the Portuguese Lodges should conform to the ancient constitutions of the Order they should be empowered to have a representative in the Grand Lodge of England, and that the Grand Lodge of England should have a representative in the Grand Lodge of Portugal, and that the brethren belonging to each Grand Lodge should be equally entitled to the privileges of the other." [1]

In 1807 war broke out between France and Portugal, because the ports were not closed to the British fleet. On November 29 Prince John, the Regent, left for Brazil, and the next day the French entered Lisbon under General Junot. With the presence of the French troops Freemasonry of course showed itself openly ; but in order to counteract the evident desire of the French to bring the National Grand Lodge under the control of the Grand Orient at Paris, the G.M. closed the Grand Lodge *pro tem.* in 1808. The Junto, or Provisional Government, does not appear to have been inimical to Freemasonry after Junot's forced evacuation, and the presence of the English troops could not fail to have been beneficial. Marshal Soult's invasion in 1809 was of too short duration to produce any effect, but after his departure a deplorable, though ridiculous, incident occurred. The English Masons assembled publicly, and walked in procession with banners and emblems of the Society. This remarkable spectacle the Portuguese troops mistook—not unnaturally—for one of the pageants of the Romish Church, and therefore turned out in order to render the usual military honours; but on discovering their error the soldiers—aided by the populace—maltreated the itinerant Craftsmen, which resulted in a fresh series of persecutions at the hands of the Inquisition. At Massena's arrival in 1810 the Craft was re-established, but his retreat was followed by renewed persecutions, thirty at least of the foremost Freemasons of Lisbon being deported to the Azores in September of that year. But the Fraternity still persevered, and in 1812 there were no less than thirteen Lodges in Lisbon alone. Meanwhile, in 1809, the G.M., Dom Sebastian—whose other names may with convenience be omitted—had been succeeded by Dom Fernando Romão d'Alaide Teive, and the latter was followed in 1816 by General Gomez Freire d'Andrade. This Grand Master's fate was untoward; he lived at enmity with Lord Beresford, and having been accused of inciting a revolt against the English commander, was, with eleven co-conspirators, sentenced to death October 15, 1817. This was followed—March 30, 1818—by an edict of John VI.—whose mother, the Queen Maria, had died March 20, 1816—dated from Rio de Janeiro, threatening the Freemasons once more with death and divers other but minor terrors, which produced no effect whatever except a return to the most inviolable secrecy.

Beresford having left, there are to chronicle, a popular revolt in 1820; a Provisional Regency, the arrival from Brazil of the King, and his acceptance of a constitution abolishing the Inquisition, establishing trial by jury, etc., in 1821. Naturally enough Freemasonry

[1] Chap. XX., p. 489; Grand Lodge Minutes; and Preston, edit. 1812, p. 375, *ut supra.*

again emerged from concealment, and in 1822 the King's eldest son, Dom Pedro, having accepted the Grand Mastership of Brazil, the Lisbon Lodges, eight in number, elected Ioão da Cunha Souto Major, G.M. for Portugal.

In 1823, however, a counter-revolution of Royalists triumphed, and re-instated John VI. in all his autocratic privileges, Freemasons were once more persecuted—by an edict of June 20, 1823—and his second son, Dom Miguel, headed a proclamation of April 30, 1824, with these words, "Long live the King! Long live Roman Catholicism! Death and Destruction to the sacrilegious Freemasons!"

A proclamation by the Cardinal Archbishop Souza, published the same evening, so inflamed the minds of the rabble, that many people were murdered on the mere suspicion of being Freemasons.[1]

In 1826 King John died, and his eldest son Pedro disjoined the crowns of Brazil and Portugal—conferring the latter on his daughter Maria da Gloria, a minor, married to her uncle Dom Miguel. With the aid of the ultra Royalists, Miguel proclaimed himself king, so that in 1831 Dom Pedro abdicated Brazil, returned to Portugal, and in 1834 defeated and banished the usurper, his brother and son-in-law. Pedro himself died in September 1834, and the Cortes declared his daughter of full age. During all this troubled time the Lodges had been under a ban, and the brothers dispersed in all parts of Europe and Brazil. Under these circumstances some had elected Da Silva Carvalho, and others the Marquis Saldanha, as G.M., so that on the return of the exiles in 1834 two Grand Lodges existed in Lisbon. To add to the confusion the brethren in Oporto elected a third G.M., Manuel da Silva Passos. Carvalho left Portugal in 1836, and although his Lodges, with the exception of those in the Azores, lay dormant for a while, yet the Grand Lodge was revived a few years afterwards in the person of Manuel Gonzalves da Miranda as Grand Master (1839-41). An attempt at fusion in 1837 failed, and unfortunately politics were not kept out of sight in Craft matters. For unmasonic conduct of this kind the G.M. Saldanha was deposed in 1837, and his place filled by Baron Vialla Nova da Foz-Côa in 1839; the Oporto G.L. also elected a new G.M., Da Costa Cabal, in 1841. All these three Grand Lodges followed the modern French Rite of seven degrees.[2]

About this time a Rose Croix Chapter was established at Lisbon under the Grand Chapter of Prince Masons of Ireland. This, although not constituted as a Provincial Grand Orient, Chapter, or Lodge, apparently assumed, in some degree, the functions of such a body, since, by the authority last cited, Dom F. G. da Silva Pereira is described as having been its *Grand Master.*

In 1840, Carvalho—*ci-devant* G.M.—returned from Brazil with a patent from the Supreme Council 33° in that empire; erected a Lodge and a consistory 32°, which by a Brazilian patent of June 20, 1841, was—December 27—transformed into a Provincial Supreme Council of the 33° dependent on Brazil. This took the name of Grand Orient of Lusitania. It published its statutes in 1843, and in 1845 numbered no less than 17 Lodges.

To add to this multiplicity of jurisdictions we find the G.L. of Ireland warranting Lodges

---

[1] These persecutions—of which interesting details will be found in "Latomia," vol. viii.—were put an end to by the constitutional government established in 1834.

[2] Boletim Official do Gr. Oriente Lusitano Unido, 188 , pp. 93, 113, 130, 143, 163, 178, 193.

at Lisbon; Nos. 338, in 1839; and 339, 341, and 344,[1] in 1842-44; and ultimately a Provincial Grand Lodge was established (1856-72), making the fifth ruling body in Portugal. In 1848 we hear of a second Grand Orient of Lusitania asking for, but not obtaining recognition at Paris. Omitting this latter as an ephemeral appearance, we have in that year—I. A Grand Lodge at Lisbon (French Rite), under Carvalho in the first instance, and afterwards Miranda as Grand Masters. II. A Grand Lodge also at Lisbon (French Rite), under Saldanha and Foz-Côa successively. III. A Grand Lodge at Oporto (French Rite), under Passos and Costa Cabal. IV. A Grand Orient of Lusitania (A. and A.S.R. 33°) at Lisbon, under Carvalho, G.M., dependent upon Brazil. V. An Irish Provincial Grand Lodge—*de facto*, if not as yet *de jure*—under Frederico Guilheime da Silva Pereira at Lisbon.

In 1849 all these governing bodies, except that controlled by Pereira, united to form a Grand Orient of Portugal at Lisbon, with D'Oliveira as G.M. His successor, Alves de Mauro Contucho, unfortunately created dissatisfaction by his despotic rule, and the Scots Grand Orient of Lusitania was revived—January 31, 1859—under Count Paraty, G.M. This Grand Orient proved itself very active, even beyond the borders, many of the Spanish Lodges owning its sway. In 1869, however, the two Grand Orients amalgamated under Paraty as the G.O. of Lusitania. In 1872 they were joined by the Irish Lodges, leaving thus only one Grand Body in Portugal. In 1873 this G.O. ruled over 48 Lodges (12 in Lisbon and 15 in Spain); in 1885, 70 Lodges, of which 22 were in Portugal, 7 in Portuguese colonies; 32 in Spain, and 9 in Spanish colonies. Of the 22 Portuguese Lodges, 14 were in Lisbon. The present G.M. of the United Grand Lusitanian Orient is Dom Antonio Augusto D'Aguiar, and the brethren number 2800. The President or acting G.M. is Dom João Eusebio D'Oliveira. The Grand Orient comprises four subsections—a Symbolic Grand Lodge, under a President, for Lodges working Masonry only; a Supreme Council of the 33° for the A. and A.S. Rite; a Supreme Rose Croix Chapter for the French Rite, and—*Mirabile dictu*—a Grand Chapter of Royal Arch Masons, the only one except in Spain and Roumania outside of Anglo-Saxon Masonry.[2]

In 1881 occurred a movement of much significance. Five Lodges, possibly tired of the control, direct or indirect, exerted by the high degrees, combined to erect a Grand Lodge of the Craft, totally independent of all other degrees beyond the *three* of ancient Freemasonry. Count Paraty, the head of the Grand Orient, was called to preside also over the Grand Lodge of Ancient Free and Accepted Masons, which was formed on the English model. The movement does not appear to have been of English origin—because in the first list of Grand Office-Bearers only one English name is to be found, and that in a very subordinate position—but to have been purely national. Under Paraty's guidance, this Grand Lodge was brought back into the fold of the Grand Orient, which was subdivided into three Grand Bodies or Chambers, each having sole control over its own rite—a Supreme Council 33° for the Scots, a Supreme Chapter Rose Croix for the French, and a Sublime Chamber or Grand Lodge for the Craft. For matters of general interest these three Chambers

---

[1] It is possible that these warrants merely *legitimated* four Lodges which already existed—though irregularly—under the Rose Croix Chapter, of which Pereira was the "Grand Master"! This influential personage, who was Minister of Justice 1853-56, died in 1871. In the following year the Irish Prov. Grand Lodge joined the United Grand Orient, and the Rose Croix Chapter returned its warrant.

[2] For these statistics I am indebted to Dom Ferreira Gomes, G. Sec., U.G. Lusitanian Orient.

were united in one assembly, of which the Presidency was confided to Mig. Bapt. Maciel, who, on Paraty's death, was appointed his successor as head of all three Chambers and G.M. of the Grand Orient *ad interim*. An official bulletin informs us, that on December 6, 1883, at a convention of thirteen Lodges—all, with two exceptions, meeting at Lisbon—a Grand Lodge, totally distinct from, and independent of the Grand Orient, was organised, and the following officers elected :—Dr Jose Dias Ferreira, G.M.; J. d'A. de Franco Netto, D.G.M.; and Cæsar de Castello Bianco, Grand Secretary. There are thus in existence two Grand Lodges, one siding with and forming a Chamber of the Grand Orient, and the other bearing the former title of " G. Lodge of A. F. and A. Masons, founded 1737, re-established 1881." The latter has an apparent following of 24 Lodges. Why claim is laid to the earlier of these dates I am unable to conjecture, but although spoiling the unity which the Craft had so recently attained, it is impossible not to wish this body success. It has struck the right keynote in bidding its high degree friends go their ways in peace, to add as many degrees as their humour may suggest, but to cease from troubling the Craft.

SPAIN.

Spain disputes with Portugal the sad distinction of having most persistently and relent-lessly persecuted its own children on account of their attachment to the Craft ; and, like Portugal, it is somewhat remarkable for still practising Royal Arch Masonry. But unlike its sister kingdom, it has not yet succeeded in bringing its Lodges under one single juris-diction, and presents at the present day a picture of confusion in Craft matters unequalled elsewhere. It is much to be deplored that the partisans of these various Grand Lodges should have allowed their predilections to colour their historical statements. Indeed, to such a length has this been carried, that the later history of the Craft in Spain is more difficult to unravel than the earlier one; and although no source of information has been overlooked, I am unable to place on record the events of the last twenty years without entertaining some misgivings as to the accuracy of my own narrative. Masonic news from the Peninsula reaches us but rarely—in small and unsatisfactory quantities—and no two accounts are reconcilable with each other. I must therefore beg my readers to regard the description of this period (1868-85) as a conscientious attempt to lay some few facts before them, but by no means to pin their faith upon my narrative. Having confessed my inability to cope with the difficulties before me, I trust any errors that may be discovered will be leniently dealt with.

Before proceeding with our main subject it will be well to advert to two small territories, which, though forming a part of Spain—one geographically, the other politically—yet require separate mention. I allude to Gibraltar and Minorca.

A Lodge—" of St John of Jerusalem," No. 51—was constituted at Gibraltar by the Grand Lodge of England in 1728 ;[1] and three years later, Captain James Commerford was appointed Prov. G.M. for Audalusia, which, as we learn from the terms of subsequent patents, comprised the Rock or fortress, "and places adjacent." Commerford was succeeded by Colonel J. G. Montrèsor, 1752-53, Chief Engineer, one of the founders of No. 51—St John—but who embarked in 1754 for America. Further Lodges were established under the same sanction, in 1762—Inhabitants ; 1786—Hiram's ; 1789—Calpean ; and in 1791—Friendship. The first Lodge under the Schismatic Grand Lodge of England—No. 58—was formed in 1756, but was

[1] Chap. XVII., p. 384.

short-lived, and after this we meet, in 1773, with the same quarrels between the so-called "Moderns" and "Ancients," as prevailed in the mother country of Freemasonry.[1] The latter, however, were triumphant in the struggle which ensued,[2] and they established at Gibraltar Nos. 148—originally constituted in the Royal Artillery in 1767 (*now* St John's); 202 (*now* Inhabitants), in 1777; and a Prov. Grand Lodge in 1786. The Lodges under the earlier sanction continued to be shown on the lists until 1813, but only one—apparently a union of the Calpean and Friendship—was carried forward at the Union. Prince Edward—afterwards Duke of Kent—was appointed Prov. G.M. in 1790.[3] In 1792 there were no less than eleven[4] Military Lodges at Gibraltar, and the records from which I quote, mention three Lodges of the same character, as having recently left the garrison, besides a warrant, "No. 61 (*Irish*) held by the Officers of the 32d Foot, but for neglect erased." Many Lodges were locally constituted by the Atholl Provincial Grand Lodge, of which no record has been preserved, but in 1804 there were at least nine holding Provincial warrants.

Two English Lodges—now both extinct—"Ordnance" and "Calpean," were established in 1819 and 1822; and there are at present in existence three Lodges—St John's, Inhabitants, and Friendship—under the Grand Lodge of England; two under Scotland—St Thomas (1876), and "Al Moghreb al Aksa" (1882); and one—No. 325 (1826)—under the Grand Lodge of Ireland.

The Masonic annals of Minorca afford an interesting study owing to the vicissitudes of warfare. In 1708 England took the island from Spain, and held it until 1758, when it was taken by the French. We regained possession in 1763, but in 1782 once more lost it—on this occasion to Spain. Again, from 1798 until the peace of Amiens, 1802, the English flag floated over the island. During the first of these three periods Lord Byron—G.M. 1747-51— appointed Lieut.-Col. James Adolphus Oughton[5] Prov. G.M. for Minorca,[6] and the following four Lodges were constituted :—Nos. 213-215 in 1750, and No. 216 in 1751.[7] These Lodges were carried forward at the renumbering in 1756,[8] but dropping out in 1766, the *places* of original Nos. 213-215 (*then* 141-143) were assigned to three American Lodges in 1768.[9] Again during the third British occupation, a "Lodge in the Island of Minorca," No. 586, was established in 1800. Turning to the Atholl Register, we find that Lodges Nos. 141 and 117, were erected on the island in 1766 and 1770, and a Provincial Grand Lodge in 1772. Even in our own times Minorca seems to have been regarded as "unoccupied country," for French Lodges were formed at Mahon by the A. and A.S.R. 33° in 1860, and 1870.

The first Lodge in Spain was founded by the Duke of Wharton in his own apartments in a French hotel at Madrid, in February 15, 1728. Two months later—April 17—this Lodge, through its Worshipful Master, Mr Ch. Labelle (or Labelye), informed the Grand Lodge of the fact, but applied nevertheless to the same body—March 29, 1729—to be properly constituted, and the request was acceded to.[10] The Lodge received the number 50 on the list of Lodges, and *was the first Lodge warranted in foreign lands by the Grand Lodge of England*. It was erased in 1768, in company with the first Paris Lodge "Louis d'Argent,

[1] *Cf.* The Atholl Lodges, p. 29.   [2] Chap. XIX., p. 449.   [3] *Ibid.*, p. 454, note 1.
[4] One Scotch—32d Regiment ; six Irish—1st, 11th, 18th, 46th, 51st, and 68th Regiments ; three English (*ancient*) —50th Regiment, Royal Artillery, and Garrison ; and one Provincial—in the Company of Artificers.
[5] *Cf.* Chaps. XIX., p. 447; XXIII., pp. 61, 62, 76.   [6] Constit., 1756, p. 333.   [7] Engraved Lists.
[8] *Ibid.*   [9] Engraved Lists. *Cf. ante*, Chap. XX., p. 467.   [10] Chaps. XVI., p. 289; XVII., pp. 378, 384.

and the Duke of Richmond's Lodge at Aubigny [1] (a notable trio), either for having ceased to meet or neglected to conform to the laws of the Society.[2]

The next step introduces the first of the persecutions which, until quite recently, Spanish Freemasons have suffered, and like their Portuguese brethren, doggedly withstood. In 1740 King Philip V. approved the Papal Bull of 1738, and issued a confirmatory edict for his possessions. The Inquisition discovered a Lodge, and eight of its members were condemned to the galleys.[3]

But the Fraternity persisted in meeting, and we have proofs that at Barcelona a German chaplain visited a Lodge in 1743. Indeed the Lodges increased in spite of all difficulties, and —July 2, 1751—Father Joseph Torrubia, a member of the Inquisition, obtained from Ferdinand VI. a further decree condemning Masons to death without the benefit of a trial of any kind. It is affirmed that Torrubia traitorously caused himself to be initiated in order to betray every member's name to the Inquisitors, and his report mentions at that date 97 (!) Lodges in Spain. Meetings nevertheless continued to be held, even at the house of the British Ambassador (1753) in Madrid, and the "Freemasons' Calendar" of 1776 alludes to an independent Lodge in Spain. According to Don Rafael Sunyé, Spanish Freemasonry declared itself independent of England in 1767, and elected as Grand Master the Prime Minister of Charles III., Count d'Aranda, who had in the spring of the year procured the banishment of the Jesuits. This would provide a reason for the Madrid Lodge being struck off the roll in 1768 as mentioned above. In 1780 this Grand Lodge became permeated with French ideas, and took the name of Grand Orient. In 1795 Count d'Aranda having lost his liberty, his nominee, the Count de Montijo, was elected G.M. French ideas made further strides, and in 1806 the Royal Order of Scotland at Rouen was enabled to found a Spanish Grand Lodge of the Order at Xeres,[4] of which little more is known. This appears to have been followed by the erection of a real *Scottish* (not *Scots*) Lodge in 1807, the "Desired Re-Union," No. 276, on the roll of the Grand Lodge of Scotland;[5] and in the same year, James Gordon was appointed Prov. G.M. "over all the Lodges under that jurisdiction," "east of Balbos in Andalusia."[6] About this time appeared on the scene the Count de Tilly, brother of De Grasse-Tilly,[7] a bitter enemy of Buonaparte, who made himself famous in the south of Spain under the name of Gusman. Like his brother, Tilly was a stanch adherent of the A. and A.S.R., and—December 17, 1808—assembled several brothers at Aranjuez, where he constituted a Supreme Council of the 33° for Spain. At this time Freemasonry was openly practised in Spain without fear of persecution, for on the one hand the Craft was protected by the French armies who had invaded the country, whilst on the other hand it enjoyed the goodwill of the British troops who were assisting the legitimate sovereign, Ferdinand VII. On June 6, 1808, Joseph Napoleon was made King of Spain, and Spanish Lodges under the Grand Orient of France increased daily. The first of these was established as early as January 22, 1807, at Cadiz.

In October 1809 a Grand Orient of Spain, dependent upon the G.O. at Paris, was erected in the very dungeons of the Inquisition itself at Madrid, under the auspices of King Joseph, to which was attached a Grand Tribunal of the 31°. The Grand Master was Azanza, a former

---

[1] *Ante*, p. 138.   [2] G.L. Min.   [3] Acta Latomorum, vol. i., p. 47.   [4] *Ibid.*, p. 229.
[5] Erased in 1843.   [6] Laurie, 1859, p. 408.   [7] *Ante*, p. 124 *et seq.*

THOMAS FREDERICK HALSEY ESQ.

PROVINCIAL GRAND MASTER OF HERTFORDSHIRE

Minister of State. Two years later—July 4, 1811—the Count de Grasse-Tilly founded a Supreme Council of the A. and A.S.R. 33° in opposition to that of his brother, and in alliance with the last formed Grand Orient, whose G.M., Azanza, also became Sov. G. Com. of the new rite. At this epoch, therefore, we have four Grand Bodies : 1st, The Grand Lodge of 1767, converted in 1780 into a Grand Orient under Montijo : 2d, the Supreme Council of 1808, under the younger Tilly ; 3d, the Grand Orient of 1809 ; and 4th, the Supreme Council of 1811, both under Azanza—who was succeeded as the head of the last two bodies by the celebrated patriot Arguëlles.

The return to power of Ferdinand VII. inaugurated a fresh persecution of the Craft. In 1814—May 4—he abolished the constitution, re-established the Inquisition, and declared Free-masons guilty of treason. This was followed in September by the arrest and imprisonment of twenty-five members of the Craft in Madrid, amongst whom may be mentioned General Alava, Wellington's Aide-de-Camp.[1] Although the plan followed of handing suspected persons over to the barbarous Inquisition is of course indefensible, the attempted suppression of the Craft was only too well justified in those troublous times on account of its unhappy interference with Spanish politics. To this admixture of politics and Freemasonry I am induced to ascribe the obstinacy with which the Fraternity resisted all attempts to stamp it out. Far from succumbing, it consolidated its position, and at its head were always the liberal leaders of the day. Thus in 1818 Arguëlles, Riego, the brothers San Miguel, and others took part in important deliberations in Madrid, resulting in a fusion between the two Supreme Councils, Riego becoming G.M. This was followed by the popular movement in 1820, headed by Riego, which compelled the king—July 9—to regrant the liberal constitution, abolish the Inquisition, and expel the Jesuits.

For three years Masonry flourished ;[2] then followed a curious state of affairs. Foreign intervention was sought by Ferdinand, and with the assistance of French troops—formerly such enthusiastic propagators of the Craft—the Brotherhood was suppressed. French bayonets re-established Ferdinand in his old prerogatives, Riego was shot, and—August 1, 1824—the king issued a new edict, by which all Freemasons who failed to deliver up their papers and renounce the Society in thirty days, were to be, on discovery, hanged in the ensuing twenty-four hours—without trial of any kind. In pursuance thereof—September 9, 1825—a Lodge having been surprised at Granada, seven of its members were given a short shrift and gibbeted accordingly, whilst the candidate for admission was let off with eight years of forced labour. In 1828 the French troops evacuated Spain, but without having "stamped out" Freemasonry, for in 1829, fresh signs of its existence having been observed in Barcelona, Lieut.-Col. Galvez was hanged, and two other members of the Craft were condemned to the galleys for life.

In spite of all this, however, the Craft continued to consolidate itself, although compelled to exercise the greatest secrecy in all its proceedings.[3] One of the members of the United

---

[1] Acta Lat., vol. i., p. 265.

[2] A Lodge —No. 750—at Lanzarote, in the Canary Islands, was warranted by the G.L. of England in 1822.

[3] Much which precedes and follows rests on the sole authority of Don Rafael Sunyé, 33°, whose sketch of Spanish Masonry in the Monde Maçonique has been reprinted with more or less exactitude by other journals of the Craft. Either the writer has had access to archives hitherto preserved from public ken, or he has most ingeniously dovetailed his account with the known facts. As I have been unable to find any palpable discrepancies, as these facts—if such

Supreme Council at this time was no less a personage than Don Francisco de Bourbon. We may also mention General San Miguel, the minister Lopez, Magnan, and others. In 1829 Don Francisco having been elected G.M. of the Grand Orient, and Sov. Com. of the A. and A.S.R. 33°—the earliest Grand Orient (1767) united with the one under his leadership, and thus for a time formed one sole jurisdiction in Spain, working the English, French, and—so-called— Scottish Rites. The accession of Queen Isabella II. in 1833 did not suffice to relieve the Craft from the necessity of secrecy, but we hear nothing more of active persecution. An *anonymous* Grand Orient of Spain announced its existence to the G.O. of France, and sent in its statutes—signed April 20, 1843 [1]—with a list of members all designated by pseudonyms. In 1848 it called itself the Grand Orient of Hesperia. The G.O. of France refused recognition on account of the secrecy in which it had shrouded itself, and even founded a Lodge of its own at Barcelona.[2] At the head of this Grand Lodge was Don Ramon Maria Calatrava.[3]

Meanwhile, in 1848 fresh persecutions had broken out during the administration of Marshal Narvaez. Don Francisco, excommunicated by the Pope, fled the country, delegating his authority to Charles Magnan. Under this administration the Lodges were neither more nor less than secret political associations, until *circa* 1854, when the Craft once more obtained toleration. This is ascribed to the alleged fact that Don Francisco d'Assissi, the queen's consort, was the W.M. of a Lodge held in the palace itself. Of the succeeding period but little is really known, though there are notices on record of Lodges in various cities, and of one founded by France in Minorca (1860), also of a Lodge composed exclusively of Englishmen in Madrid.[4] But the Grand Orients under Magnan and Calatrava respectively, if not absolutely dormant, exhibited few signs of life. It would almost appear as if toleration were only to be attained at the price of a total absence of self-assertion.

The revolution of September 28, 1868, which expelled Queen Isabella, opened the country to the free exercise of the rites of Masonry, but in removing the necessity for union, has had the effect of dividing the Society into more cliques than can be distinctly described. The statements respecting the rise of these parties, their subsequent history, and their present state are so contradictory and vague that the student loses all feeling of certainty.[5] One fact alone stands out clearly, that the Grand Orient of Lusitania (Portugal) commenced to warrant ·

they be—were naturally kept secret at the time, and as they are well within the memory of the present generation, and therefore susceptible of revelation when secrecy is no longer demanded, I incline to credit them. Moreover, it should not escape our recollection that the position of the writer—33°—would—not improbably—give him access to much valuable evidence, dispersed throughout the documentary waifs and strays preserved in the jealously guarded *Chancelleries* of the (so-called) high degrees. *Cf.* The Freemason, April 3, May 8, and June 19, 1880 ; and the Freemasons' Chronicle, August 30, and September 6, 1884.

[1] A Lodge was established at Algesiras, under the Grand Lodge of Ireland—No. 347—in the above year, and cancelled in 1858.

[2] October 15, 1848 ; resumed work 1870 ; and is shown in the *Annuaire* of the G.O. for 1886. Another Lodge was erected by the same authority, at Carthagena in 1869, but is now extinct.

[3] Findel, pp. 654-656 ; Calatrava—an opponent of Napoleon—lived in exile in London until 1836, was chosen G.M. in 1847, and filled the office until his death, February 28, 1876.

[4] Handbuch, *s.v.* Spanien. A Lodge—No. 1024, "Morality and Philanthropy"—was formed at Cadiz under the Grand Lodge of England in 1857, the warrant of which was returned in 1875.

[5] As late as July 30, 1879, the United Grand Orient of the sister kingdom (Portugal) declared itself incapable of unravelling the tangled web of Spanish Freemasonry, or of discovering the most legitimate Grand Lodge, or the one likely to prove so in the long run (Boletim Official, 1880, p. 76).

Lodges in Spain, and at this day numbers almost as large a following as any other of the rival Grand Bodies.

The first step of importance appears to have been the revival of Calatrava's National Grand Orient of Spain in 1869. Contemporaneous with this was the revival under Magnan of his Grand Orient and Supreme Council. In 1870 he left for Santander, and his office was therefore transferred to Ruiz Zorilla. For this purpose Zorilla had in four days been passed from the humble position of a candidate for initiation through all the 33 degrees, one step— Knight of the East—having been conferred in the Iberian Grand Orient, a body which had been recently established in Spain by the G.O. of Portugal, a rival of the G.O. of Lusitania. G.M. Zorilla was prime minister during the short reign of Amadeus of Savoy, and during his tenure of office a treaty was entered into between the Grand Orients of Spain and Lusitania, granting a reciprocity of jurisdiction to the two contracting parties, February 12, 1872.[1] On the abdication of Amadeus, Ruiz Zorilla voluntarily resigned, and placed his powers at the disposal of the Craft, January 1, 1874. It was then agreed by some of the " Puissant " and " Illustrious " members of the 33° that Zorilla's reign should be considered as *non avenu*, null and void, and that Magnan should resume command as though his rule had never suffered interruption. Magnan appointed Carvajal as Lieut. G. Com., and immediately resigned in his favour. Carvajal was succeeded in turn as Sov. G. Com. by Ferrer, Conder, Avalos, Oriero, and Panzano y Almirall.

Some of the brethren, however, objecting to this resumption by Magnan as *ultra vires*, seceded and elected as Sov. G. Com., General La Somera in succession to Zorilla. Somera resigned after a twelvemonth in favour of Sagasta, afterwards Prime Minister, and the latter was followed by Antonio Romero Ortez, Governor of the Bank of Spain, who, dying early in 1884, was succeeded by Don Manuel Becerra. Under Somera, 1874-75, this Grand Lodge (it has dropped the title Orient) absorbed the Iberian Grand Orient mentioned above.

Besides these two Grand Orients there exists at present a National G.O. of Spain under the Marquis de Seoane. This National G.O. is Calatrava's Grand Orient of Hisperia, which is first heard of *circa* 1840-43. Calatrava must have considered himself at that date legitimately descended from the original Grand Lodge and the English Prov. G.L., for the official documents bear the following dates :—Grand Lodge, 1728 ;[2] Grand Orient, 1780; Supreme Council, 1808. Calatrava continued to be G.M. until his death, February 28, 1876.

But these three bodies not being sufficient for our Spanish brethren, a fresh schism arose in 1875. When Somera resigned—December 27, 1875—a certain Juan Antonio Perez, 30°, disapproving of Sagasta's election, induced a friend to pass him to the 33°, and erected a Grand Orient—comprising a Supreme Council and Grand Lodge—of his own. By dint of self-assertion this Grand Orient would appear to have prospered fairly well, judging from observations in the *Boletim Official* of the U.G. Lusitanian Orient for 1880, and the recognition of its Grand Lodge by several governing Craft bodies in America. I am unable to say whether it still exists, or has submitted to the authority of some other Grand Body in Spain. Perez is left unnoticed by the current Masonic journals, nor does his name appear in any of the numerous Calendars of the Craft—native and foreign—which I have consulted.

---

[1] Cosmopolitan Calendar, 1875, p. 217.
[2] The year in which the Duke of Wharton founded the first Lodge in Madrid.

On December 28, 1879, two Lodges withdrew from the Grand Lusitanian Orient in a perfectly legal manner, and formed themselves into a Grand Central Masonic Consistory 32° at Malaga, with the professed intention of remaining independent for a time, and eventually joining the Grand Orient which should ultimately succeed in being universally recognised.

With a similar intention 13 Lodges of this same Grand Orient withdrew from its jurisdiction at about the same time, and formed themselves into a Masonic Confederation of the Congress of Seville, extending their sway also to the 32° only. The modesty with which these two bodies refrain from establishing a Supreme Council 33° proves at least the sincerity of their protestations. At the head of this Confederation is J. L. Padilla, 33°.

A further proof of the good intentions of this Confederation may be hailed with hope and rejoicing, although it has had the effect of still further increasing the number of governing bodies. On February 7, 1881, it divested itself of all control over Freemasonry, and now declares in its very title that it has jurisdiction "over the 4th and 32nd degrees" only. This at least was a wise step, in which it followed the example set in many other countries by bodies assuming the title of Supreme Council, A. and A.S.R. 33°.

As a result, on the same date, February 7, the members of the Craft erected a Grand Spanish Independent Symbolic Lodge, "with jurisdiction over the first three degrees," at Seville, under Grand Master Castro, who has since been succeeded by Branlio Ruiz. In a circular of July 29, 1883, the number of subordinate Lodges under this Grand Body is stated to be twenty-one.

I think it quite possible that one more Grand Lodge exists—for when the Iberian Grand Orient was absorbed in 1874 by Somera, some Lodges, nine in all, increased to twelve by three seceders from Somera's Grand Lodge, were dissatisfied with the arrangement, and dissenting from the majority, revived or continued the Iberian G.O. In 1876 it reduced the 33 degrees to 7, condensing the pith of all the others, thus forming the Spanish reformed rite.[1] On the other hand it may be long since extinct.

All these Grand Bodies, with the exception of the one at Seville, work the A. and A.S.R. 33°; that of Perez superadds the modern French Rite of 7 degrees. Of their strength it is impossible to present any statistics, Spanish Lodges being most ephemeral in their nature. The official lists as given in the various Masonic Calendars of current date are of little avail, for they comprise Lodges which long since became extinct. Thus Becerra's Grand Lodge has an *apparent* following of 299 subordinate Lodges, and according to an official bulletin issued eighty-two new charters in 1882. But the *Freemason* of August 7, 1880, gives a list of the active Lodges under this G.M., and although the last number is 142, the total of Lodges only mounts up to 45, or about a third. If we apply this scale of proportion—where necessary—to the last lists at my disposal, we obtain (approximately)—Grand National Orient, 1885, 60 Lodges; Grand Lodge, 1885, 100; G.O. of Perez, 1881, 60; G.O. of Portugal, 1885, Lodges in Spain, 41; G.O. of France, 1886, 1; Supreme Council 33° of France, 1885, 5; G.O. of Italy, 1885, 1; and the Grand Lodge of Seville, 1885, 25. The accompanying table of Spanish Grand Lodges may help to make the subject a little less confused; but I have omitted as beside the question non-Spanish Grand Lodges which possess daughter Lodges in the Peninsula.

---

[1] Handbuch, *s.v.* Spanien.

PORTUGUESE GRAND LODGES.

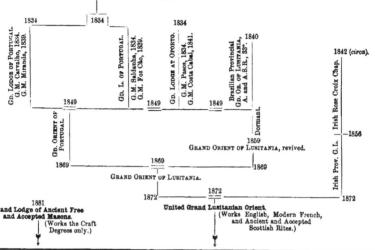

1797. A Directing Committee of six, transformed in 1800 into NATIONAL GRAND LODGE OF PORTUGAL.

SPANISH GRAND LODGES.

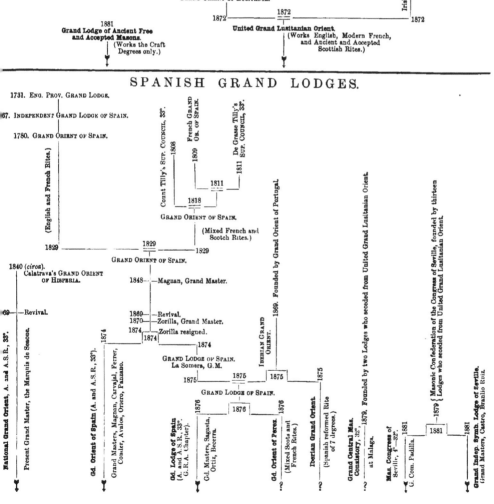

1731. ENG. PROV. GRAND LODGE.

1767. INDEPENDENT GRAND LODGE OF SPAIN.

1780. GRAND ORIENT OF SPAIN.

GREECE.

Freemasonry was late in obtaining a footing on the mainland of this kingdom, but somewhat earlier accounts come to us from what is now an integral part of the territory of Greece, viz., the Ionian Islands. These islands, in early days the prey of Naples, Genoa, and Venice, were ceded to France in 1797. They were next successively taken possession of by Russia and Turkey in 1800, by France in 1807, and by England in 1809. The G.O. of France founded a Lodge at Corfu—St Napoleon—in 1809, and a second in 1810. In 1815 the islands were formed into the Ionian Republic under the protection of England, and a Lodge, No. 654, "Pythagoras" (to which a Royal Arch Chapter was subsequently attached), was erected at Corfu in 1837. About 1840 we hear also of a Grand Lodge of Greece at Corfu,[1] with Angelo Calichiopulo as G.M. He died November 13, 1842, and further information respecting this Grand Lodge is altogether wanting. Another English Lodge—No. 1182, Star of the East—was established at Zante in 1861. This and Lodge Pythagoras are still active. The Lodges under the G.O. of France (1809-10) are extinct, but two others were constituted by the same authority at Corfu—Phœnix, 1843—and at Zante— Star, 1859,—the former of which survives at this day.

On the mainland there was in existence in 1866 a Provincial Grand Lodge or Directory under the Grand Orient of Italy, with eight subordinate Lodges—at Syra, Athens, Piræus, Chalkis, Corfu, Patras, Lamia, and Argos—dating from 1860-1866. In 1867, these eight Lodges, with the consent of the G.O. of Italy, formed themselves into an independent Grand Lodge of Greece. A council of nine members to direct the Grand Lodge was appointed by the representatives of the Lodges, July 9, 1872. By this council—July 11—Prince Rhodocanakis of Scio was elected G.M., and retained the office until 1881, when he was succeeded by Nicholas Damaschino. The Grand Lodge shook off the fetters of the high degrees, but otherwise retains much of an Italian impress. A Supreme Council 33° was, however, formed at a later period for the degrees of the A. and A.S.R., with the same individuals as office-bearers as in the Grand Lodge, but without any control over or influence in the latter. Of the subordinate Lodges, six are in a flourishing condition—at Athens, 3; Piræus, Corfu, and Zante, 1 each—but the others can hardly be said to exist.

TURKEY.

Turkey can hardly be said to enter into the family of Grand Lodges at all, and possesses no independent or National Grand Lodge. Lodges, however, exist at Constantinople, Smyrna, Damascus, Beyrout, and Ephesus, hailing from England, Scotland, France, Italy, and Ireland. A warrant was also *granted* for a Lodge—the Royal Solomon—at Jerusalem, by the Grand Lodge of Canada in 1873! The earliest allusion to Masonry in Turkey that I have met with occurs in the *St James' Evening Post* of 1738, where, in a letter from Florence, dated May 24 of that year—which has been already referred to[2]—there appears:—" We hear

---

[1] *Latomia*, iv., p. 158.   [2] *Ante*, p. 300, note 5.

from Constantinople that the Lodges of Smyrna and Aleppo are greatly increased, and that several Turks of distinction have been admitted into them."

No Lodge, however, seems to have been erected in Turkey by virtue of any warrant or patent from a legitimate governing body until February 3, 1748, when, as related at an earlier page, a Lodge was constituted at Aleppo, either by, or under the auspices of, Alexander Drummond. This worthy, however, before receiving a "provincial commission" from the Grand Lodge of Scotland, "had taken up his residence at Alexandretta in Turkey, and erected several Mason Lodges in that part of the country." [1]

The curious manner in which the grant of an early Scottish charter was sometimes recorded, will be seen in the note below,[2] which evidently refers to a later Lodge established by Drummond at Aleppo, though singular to state—no corresponding entry is to be found in the books of the Grand Lodge.

Dr Dionysius Manasse was appointed English Prov. G.M. "for all Armenia in the East Indies," by Earl Ferrers, 1762-64, and his name only disappears from the official lists in 1805! Of this personage nothing further is known. Lodges came into existence, as we have already seen, under the Grand Lodge (and G.O.) of Geneva, in 1769 and 1787, at Constantinople and Smyrna respectively.[3]

After this period there is nothing to record until we approach our own times. Lodges were established at Constantinople (Pera) by the Grand Lodge of England—Oriental, No. 988 —1856; by the Grand Orient of France—L'Étoile Du Bosphore—1858; and by the Grand Lodge of Ireland—No. 166—1865. The Grand Lodge of Scotland has been represented in Turkey (Syria) since 1861 by the Palestine Lodge, No. 415, at Beyrout. The Lodges under the G.O. of Italy have been previously referred to.[4]

In 1859—June 1—the Grand Lodge of England was informed by the Board of General Purposes that a communication had been received from the Oriental Lodge, No. 988, at Constantinople, respecting the existence of irregular Lodges at Smyrna. The Board expressed their belief that the Lodges in question—named Ionic, Anatolia, and Benzenzia—were irregular assemblies, and that the so-called Grand Lodge of Turkey, formed of those three Lodges, was also an irregular body until the same date.

At the next meeting of Grand Lodge—June 23—the President of the Board again called attention "to what was called 'The Grand Lodge of Turkey,' and explained that it had been formed by a brother who was at Smyrna at the end of the Crimean war, and who, it was stated—but no proof had been brought forward on the subject—was in possession of an Irish warrant. That this brother made about twenty Masons, and divided them into three Lodges, which afterwards called themselves 'The Grand Lodge of Turkey.' He therefore moved—'That the W. Masters of all regular Lodges be cautioned against

---

[1] *Ante*, p. 53 ; Lawrie, 1804, p. 165.

[2] The following extracts from the Minutes of Lodge Canongate Kilwinning, Edinburgh, have been supplied to me by Mr A. Mackenzie :—April 8, 1752, "The Lodge being mett according to adjournment .·. .·. at the same time a charter for constituting a Lodge at Alleppo was signed by the Most Worshipful Master and the other proper office-bearers of the Grand Lodge, and also by the office-bearers of this Lodge." June 24, 1760, "the R.W. Master Desired leave to resign that office, and having accordingly declared the Chair vacant, he proposed for his successor our R.W. Brother, Alexander Drummond, Esq., late His Majesty's Consul at Aleppo."

[3] *Ante*, p. 290.   [4] *Ibid.*, p. 304.

receiving persons claiming admission (either as Visitors or joining Members) on the ground of their having been initiated by such irregular Lodges in Smyrna'—which was ordered accordingly." [1]

In 1861 the English Lodges were united in a District Grand Lodge under the British Ambassador, Sir Henry Bulwer, as D.G.M., who was followed in 1869 by John Porter Brown, and in 1873 by Stephen Scouloudi. The number of English Lodges within what for convenience sake may be termed the jurisdiction—for there is at present no District Grand Lodge—is ten—at Smyrna, 6; Constantinople, 3; and Ephesus, 1—an eleventh, composed of Germans, having been unable to maintain its existence. The Grand Orient of France owns 4 Lodges—Constantinople, 3; Beyrout, 1; that of Italy 3—Constantinople, 2; Damascus, 1; and the Grand Lodges of Ireland and Scotland 1 each—at Constantinople and Beyrout respectively.

The Turks, however, are said to have always had secret societies of their own, that of the Begtaschi—it is alleged—numbering many thousands of Mussulmans in its ranks, and in which brotherhood none but a true Moslem can be admitted. The Begtaschi possess certain signs and passwords by which they are enabled to distinguish "true brethren" from vagabond impostors.

The Ancient and Accepted Scots Rite is represented by a Supreme Council 33° of Turkey, founded about 1869, with J. P. Brown as Sovereign Grand Commander. In 1872 he was succeeded by His Highness Prince Halim Pasha, the present head of the Turkish branch of the rite. The operations of this body are, however, confined to the so-called high degrees, so that Turkey can hardly be said to boast of an independent national Masonry.

ROUMANIA.

Prior to 1859 we hear nothing of Freemasonry in this principality. In that year, however, the G.O. of France warranted a Lodge in Bucharest, and the example was followed by others, so that in 1880 Lodges existed as follows:—Under the G.O. of France, 9; G.O. of Italy, 10; and the Grand Lodge of Hungary, 1. On September 8, 1880, the National Grand Lodge of Roumania was formed, and the official list of 1882 shows 19 Lodges, while that of 1884 presents us with the names of 23. But it may be observed that if Roumania began late, it lost no time in acquiring every possible grade and rite that Masonic inventors could supply. On June 24, 1881, the Supreme Council of the Rite of Memphis 95° was erected; on September 8, 1881, the Supreme Council 33° of the A. and A.S.R.; in 1882 the Supreme Grand Chapter of Royal Arch Masons; and finally—March 10, 1883—the Supreme Grand Lodge and Temple of the Swedenborgian Rite of Roumania. The Grand Lodge follows the Memphis or Ancient and Primitive Rite, with 23 Lodges as already stated, besides 9 Rose Croix Chapters, 1 Senate of Kadosch, 1 Grand Tribunal, and the Supreme Council. The Supreme R.A. Chapter has only 1 subordinate Chapter. The A. and A.S.R. 33° possesses 4 Lodges and 3 Chapters, and the Swedenborgians, 2 Lodges. The Grand Master of one and all these bodies is C. Moroin, Captain of infantry.

Roumania is a small province, but the wide world itself could scarcely offer a more choice selection of pretended Masonic wares.

[1] Proc. G.L. of England, June 1 and 23, 1859.

SERVIA.

In Belgrade, the capital, there are two Lodges under the Grand Orient of Italy.

MALTA.

This small link in England's chain around the globe has never possessed a Grand Lodge of its own, but deserves mention, because at the time of the revival, and until the close of the last century, it was an independent state governed by the military order of the Knights of Malta. It has been repeated *ad nauseam* by foreign writers that the Knights were inimical to the Craft, but so far from this being the case, it has been clearly shown by a recent writer[1] that as individuals they were in many instances stanch supporters of it, and that only officially, and under papal pressure, did the Grand Masters of the Order reluctantly interfere. Acting under this compulsion the G.M. in "1740 caused the Bull of Clement XII. to be published in that island, and forbade the meetings of the Freemasons." "In 1741 the Inquisition pursued the Freemasons at Malta. The G.M. proscribed their assemblies under severe penalties, and six Knights were banished from the island in perpetuity for having assisted at a meeting."[2]

But shortly afterwards Masonry was practised without any great effort at concealment, for an unchartered (or independent) Lodge which dissolved in 1771, reassembled July 2, 1788, under its old title of Secrecy and Harmony. The Master and Deputy Master were Tommasi and De Lovas, both Grand Crosses of the Order, and all the other officers were Knights. A letter of this Lodge is extant, and has been reprinted.[3] In 1789—March 30—the Lodge was constituted by the Grand Lodge of England as No. 539.

The more recent history of Freemasonry in Malta may be very shortly summed up. In 1815 Waller Rodwell Wright was appointed Prov. G.M., and his district was subsequently enlarged so as to embrace the whole of the Mediterranean. Under his successor, Dr Burrows, Gibraltar and Malta became a linked province, but each at the present day possesses its own District G.M. Tunis was incorporated with the Malta district in 1869.

In Malta itself there are six Lodges, five English—Nos. 349, 407, 515, 1923, and 1926—and one Irish—No. 387, formed in 1851—whilst at Tunis there are two—Nos. 1717 and 1835—both of which are on the roll of the G.L. of England. In the island itself, or rather at Valetta, the capital, where all the Maltese Lodges assemble, the membership, as a matter of course, shows a large military element.

---

[1] A. M. Broadley, The History of Freemasonry in Malta, 1880, pp. 3-8.

[2] Political state of Great Britain, vol. lix., 1740, p. 427; Acta Lat., pp. 47-49; and Broadley, *loc. cit.* The authorities quoted record the occurrence in almost, if not quite, identical terms.

[3] Rapp, Freimaurer in Tyrol, pp. 134, 135; see also the "Handbuch," vol. iii., *s. v.* Malta.

CHAPTER XXIX.

FREEMASONRY IN ASIA—AFRICA—WEST INDIES—MEXICO— CENTRAL AMERICA—SOUTH AMERICA—AUSTRALASIA— OCEANIA.

FREEMASONRY IN ASIA.

T has been the practice of Masonic writers to pass very lightly over the history of Freemasonry in non-European countries, and to exclude almost from mention the condition or progress of the Craft in even the largest Colonies or Dependencies within the sovereignty of an Old World power. Thus we are told by Findel that " the Lodges existing in these quarters of the globe were one and all under the Grand Lodges of England, Scotland, Holland, or France, and therefore their history forms an inseparable part of that of the countries in question."[1] With all deference, however, the position here laid down must be respectfully demurred to. In the East and West Indies— and elsewhere—the natives of many countries commingled, Lodges existed under a variety of jurisdictions, and if an intelligent appreciation of Freemasonry is best attained by comparing one Masonic system with another, the brethren at a distance from Europe enjoyed in many cases opportunities denied to those residing in London, Paris, or Berlin. The most popular and extensively diffused of the Masonic Innovations which either claim an equality with, or a superiority over, the Grand Authority of the Craft, was cradled in the Greater Antilles;[2] whilst in the Lesser Antilles—as in the East Indies—British, French, and Dutch Lodges existed side by side. Indeed, in some of these islands, there were, as will shortly appear, Lodges under still other jurisdictions than those already enumerated, and the reader desirous of studying the Masonic history of the West Indies, would, in the absence of any further materials to facilitate his inquiry, be left very much in the position of an astronomer without a telescope, who might seek to compute the path of a planet by conjecture.

I shall therefore do my best, in all cases where there has been a conflict of jurisdictions, to enable those of my readers who are especially interested in the department of inquiry we are now pursuing, to take what I may venture to term " a bird's-eye view " of Freemasonry —both in a general and contemporaneous aspect—as existing at any time in the various portions of the earth's surface which fall within the purview of the present chapter.

According to Rebold, " After Holland had become incorporated with the French Empire (July 1810), the Grand Orient of France assumed the control of all the Dutch Lodges which

---

[1] P. 614. [2] *Cf. ante*, pp. 59, 124, and *post*, p. 353.

then existed, with the exception of those of the Indies, which remained under the obedience which had created them, and which carried on the title of Grand Lodge of the United Provinces of the Low Countries." [1]

Thus, for a time, and during the temporary obliteration of Holland as a kingdom, what had been the Colonial Lodges of that monarchy, became, in strictness, the only component members of the Grand Lodge.

In another way, as will be presently narrated, the Provincial Grand Lodge of Bengal, in British India, became, on more than one occasion, in everything but name, a Grand Lodge, independent of the mother country, and unless its proceedings formed the subject of a separate inquiry, the student who in all good faith accepted the assurance of Findel, that the history of Masonry in Hindostan was inseparable from that of England, would vainly search the archives of the Premier Grand Lodge of the World, for the names of Lodges that never appeared on her roll, or for an account of transactions that were never entered in her records.

INDIA.

BENGAL.—In 1728 a deputation was granted by the Grand Lodge of England to George Pomfret, Esq., authorising him " to open a new Lodge in Bengal." Of this personage nothing further is known; but under Captain Ralph Farwinter, who in the following year succeeded him as " Provincial Grand Master of India," a Lodge was duly established in 1730, which in the Engraved Lists is distinguished by the arms of the Company, and is described as No. 72, at Bengal, in the East Indies.

The next P.G.M.'s were James Dawson, *temp. incert.*, and Zech. Gee, who held the office in 1740; after whom came the Honourable Roger Drake, appointed April 10, 1755. The last named was Governor of Calcutta at the time of the attack made on the settlement by Surajah Dowlah in 1756. Drake escaped the horrors of the Black Hole by deserting his post and flying to the shipping; but though present at the re-taking of Calcutta in January 1757 by the forces under Clive and Watson, it is improbable—after the calamity which befel he Settlemen t—that he resumed the duties of his Masonic office.

The minutes of Grand Lodge inform us that William Mackett, Prov. G.M. of Calcutta, was present at a meeting of that body, November 17, 1760; and we learn on the same authority, that at the request of the Lodges in the East Indies, " Culling Smith, Esq.," was appointed P.G.M. in 1762. At the period in question it was the custom in Bengal " to elect the Prov. G.M. annually, by the majority of the voices of the members then present, from among those who had passed through the different offices of the [Prov.] Grand Lodge, and who had served as Dep. Prov. G.M." This annual election, as soon as notified to the Grand Lodge of England, was confirmed by the G.M. without its being thought an infringement of his prerogative.

In accordance with this practice Samuel Middleton was elected P.G.M. (*circa*) 1767; but in passing I may briefly observe, that a few years previously a kind of roving commission had been granted by Earl Ferrers—1762-64—to " John Bluvitt, commander of the Admiral Watson, Indiaman, for East India, where no other Provincial is to be found."

---

[1] Hist. des Trois Grandes Loges, p. 119. *Cf. ante*, p. 205.

Middleton's election was confirmed—October 31, 1768—and as the Dispensation forwarded by the Grand Secretary was looked upon as abrogating the practice of annual elections, he accordingly held the office of Prov. G.M. until his death in 1775.[1]

The records of the Provincial Grand Lodge only reach back to 1774, and it will therefore be convenient if, before leaning on their authority, I give a preliminary outline of the progress of Masonry in Bengal from the erection of the first Lodge in 1730.

A second Lodge soon after sprang into existence, which, becoming too numerous, seven of its members were constituted—April 16, 1740—by the Prov. Grand Lodge into a new and regular Lodge. Of the former nothing further is known; but the Grand Lodge of England, on the petition of the latter, ordered "the said Lodge to be enrolled (as requested) in the list of regular Lodges, agreeable to the date of their Constitution." [2]

A Lodge—No. 221—was formed at "Chandernagore, ye chief French Settlement," in 1752.[3] Others sprang up at Calcutta, 1761—No. 275, *now* Lodge of Industry and Perseverance, No. 109; and at Patna and Burdwan, 1768—Nos. 354 and 363, erased in 1790. As the last named, however, were styled respectively the 8th, 9th, and 10th Lodges, some others of local constitution must have been erected.

Five Lodges—Nos. 441-445—were warranted in 1772, the 5th, 6th, 7th, 8th, and 9th Lodges of Bengal. These were at Dacca, Calcutta, and with the 1st, 3d, and 2d Brigades respectively. All, however, with the exception of the 6th Lodge, No. 442, Calcutta—afterwards "Unanimity"—were erased in 1790.[4]

The 10th and 11th Lodges of Bengal—Nos. 452 and 453—were added to the roll in 1773, and the 12th—No. 482—in 1775. The former were at Moorshedabad and Calcutta respectively; whilst the latter was "with the 3d Brigade." No. 453, which underwent many vicissitudes, appears later as Lodge Humility with Fortitude; whilst No. 482 is described in 1793 as the Lodge of St George in the East, and in the following year—having then become No. 316—as the Lodge of True Friendship, with the 3d Brigade.

Returning to the year 1774, there appear, from the records of the Prov. Grand Lodge, to have been at that time only three Lodges in Calcutta, viz., (*local*) Nos. 1, Star in the East—constituted in 1740 as the *third*, but which became the *first*, Lodge of Bengal on its predecessor of 1730 dropping out in 1770; 2, Industry and Perseverance; and 3, Humility with Fortitude. Besides these, however, there were Lodges at Chandernagore, Patna, Burdwan, Dacca, and Moorshedabad, and also at some of the military stations or with the army brigades. The Provincial Grand Lodge under England seems to have worked in perfect harmony with a similar body under Holland,[5] "The Grand Lodge of Solomon at Chinsura;" and the officers and members of the two Societies exchanged visits and walked together in processions.

In 1775—February 15—the Prov. Grand Lodge, "taking into consideration the propriety

[1] According to the terms of the Patent, in the absence of Middleton, Thomas Burdell might act until a new Provincial was appointed. It appears, also, that one John Graham was *elected* P.G.M. in 1769 to succeed in like manner.

[2] G.L. Min., April 3, and December 16, 1747. *Cf.* The Four Old Lodges, p. 53.

[3] Dormant in 1788; erased in 1790.

[4] Became No. 292 in 1792, but lapsing in the following year, its place was assigned to Lodge Anchor and Hope, Calcutta, on the *Provincial* establishment.

[5] Constitutions were granted by the Grand Lodge of Holland to the following Lodges in Bengal:—Solomon, 1759; Perseverance, 1771; and Constancy (Houghly), 1773.

of preserving concord and unanimity, recommend it to the Brethren who call themselves 'Scott and Elect,' that they do lay aside the wearing of red ribbons, or any other marks of distinction but such as are proper to the Three Degrees, or to the Grand Lodge as such "—a request, we are told, which was cheerfully complied with.

In the same year Middleton died, and in 1776 Charles Stafford Pleydell was elected in his room; but the confirmation of the Grand Lodge of England was withheld until 1778. The latter was succeeded by Philip Milner Dacres, under whose presidency the Prov. Grand Lodge of Bengal had a very brief existence. It assembled for the last time January 25, 1781. Doubtless, the war in the Carnatic, which broke out about that time, had much to do with its dissolution, and Masonry in India was very nearly swept away by it. Every Lodge in Calcutta, where alone in Bengal, Masonry may be said to have existed, was extinguished, with the exception of "Industry and Perseverance," and even there the light glimmered feebly. But the members of that Lodge nobly determined that the light should not go out.

The Provincial Grand Lodge was reopened July 18, 1785 under the presidency of George Williamson, a former Deputy P.G.M., who, on the same date, produced a patent from England, appointing him Acting P.G.M., and directed that a meeting of the Prov. Grand Lodge should be held a fortnight later for the express purpose of electing a Grand Master.[1]

The election, however, did not take place until November 14, when *four* votes were cast for Williamson, and *six* for Edward Fenwick, a former Grand Warden.

The new Prov. G.M. was installed March 17, 1786, although the patent granted to Williamson clearly indicated that he was to retain his *acting* appointment until the confirmation from London of the person who might be *elected* to the office. This led to serious disagreements, which harassed the Fraternity for some years. Williamson was supported by the Grand Lodge of England, but the Prov. Grand Lodge stoutly refused to yield to its mandate;[2] and in spite of repeated protests by the Prov. G.M. *de jure*, Fenwick continued to exercise all the duties of that office, until his election was confirmed, May 5, 1788.[3]

An interesting account of the state of Masonry in Bengal appears in a letter of February 6, 1788, from the Prov. Grand Lodge to Grand Secretary White, from which I extract the following :—

"We earnestly wish to see the whole number of Lodges which existed in 1773 or 1774 re-established. But Country Lodges. the Subordinates at Patna, Burdwan, Dacca, and Moorshedabad now consist of such small societies, and these so liable to change, that we must confess it rather to be our wish than our hope to see Lodges established at any of these places.

"With respect to the Brigades, they have been divided into six of Infantry and three of Artillery. This Military Lodges. regulation has lessened the number of officers in each, and they will be more liable to removals than formerly. The first circumstance must be a great discouragement to the formation of

[1] At this assembly, the Wardens of Lodge "Star in the East" said their meetings had been interrupted, because, in the absence of the Prov. Grand Lodge, no new Master could be installed. Williamson, however, ordered them to proceed with the election of a new Master, and engaged to convene a Prov. Grand Lodge for his installation.

[2] A letter from G. Sec. White, dated March 24, 1787—continuing to Williamson the powers specified in his patent of 1784—was read in the Prov. Grand Lodge on August 27 of that year. In the discussion which ensued, the Master of Lodge Star in the East observed :—". ∙. Mr Williamson, whose affairs have long been in a most anxious situation—who has been obliged, for a long time past, to live under a foreign jurisdiction—who now cannot come to Calcutta, but on a Sunday, or, if he comes on any other day, is obliged to conceal himself during the day time, and to be extremely cautious how he goes out even when it is dark " !

[3] The patent, however, did not arrive in India until March 4, 1789.

Lodges in the Brigades, and the second would sometimes expose such Lodges to the risk of being annihilated. However, we shall give all encouragement to the making of applications, and all the support we possibly can to such Lodges as may be constituted."

A grand ball and supper was given by the Prov. Grand Lodge, January 14, 1789, to which invitations were sent, not only to residents in Calcutta, but also to "Bro. Titsingh, Governor of Chinsurah, and other Masons of that Colony; to Bro. Bretel, and the other Masons of Chandernagore; and also to the Masons of Serampore, and to the Sisters of these Colonies, according to what has been customary on such occasions formerly." [1]

In 1790—December 27—Fenwick resigned; and on the same day the Hon. Charles Stuart was elected and installed as his successor. The latter, however—owing to the government of the country devolving upon him in consequence of the absence of Lord Cornwallis from Calcutta—appointed Richard Comyns Birch "Acting Prov. G.M. of Bengal."

The Lodges in the Presidency are thus described in the *Freemasons' Calendar* for 1794:—

Nos.			Nos.		
70.	Star in the East, Calcutta, 1st L. of Bengal,	1740	316.[5]	Lodge of True Friendship, with the 3d Brigade, 4th Lodge of Bengal, . .	1775
143.	Lodge of Industry and Perseverance, Calcutta, 2d Lodge of Bengal, . . .	1761	390.[6]	At Futty Ghur, Bengal, ...	1786
288.[3]	Lodge of Unanimity, Calcutta, 3d Lodge of Bengal, ...	1772	464.	Lodge of the North Star,[7] Fredericksnagore, 7th Lodge of Bengal, .	1789
292.[3]	Anchor and Hope, Calcutta, 6th Lodge of Bengal, ...	1773	528.[8]	At Chunar, in the East Indies, 8th Lodge of Bengal, ...	1793
293.[4]	Lodge of Humility with Fortitude, Calcutta, 5th Lodge of Bengal, . .	1773	529.	Lodge of Mars, Cawnpore, 9th Lodge of Bengal, ...	1793

There was also in existence about this time the "Marine Lodge," [9] Calcutta, which, however, only obtained a local number; and a Stewards' Lodge—established June 24, 1786—with privileges akin to those of its prototype under the Grand Lodge of England.

It unfortunately happened, that the officers of the Prov. Grand Lodge had always been selected from the first two Lodges on the above list, and this circumstance led to no slight dissatisfaction on the part of the other Lodges, who, feeling themselves aggrieved, were not slow to resent the treatment. This it was which mainly conduced to the almost general

---

[1] Chinsurah, Chandernagore, and Serampore were Dutch, French, and Danish settlements respectively.

[2] Constituted 1771; revived—then consisting of handicraftsmen in Calcutta—1787.

[3] According to the Grand Lodge Records, the Lodge was placed at this *vacant* No. in 1793.

[4] Constituted 1774, but became dormant. Constituted anew by Acting P.G.M. Williamson as No. 14, and given the local No. 11 in 1787.

[5] 1773, constituted by Middleton; 1787, composed of non-commissioned officers and privates belonging to the 3d Brigade, and called No. 10; 1788, the 3d Brigade moving to Berhampore, a new warrant—No. 12—granted to seven members remaining in Calcutta. Whether Nos. 10 or 12 survived in the Lodge above is uncertain; but the latter supposition is the more probable.

[6] Constituted by Williamson; dormant in 1788; erased 1794.

[7] The Danish Factory in Bengal. Constituted —as Lodge No. 13 of Bengal—by the Prov. G.M., March 8, 1789.

[8] Lodge of Sincere Friendship. Dormant 1796-1812. Erased from the *English* roll 1813, though, according to the records of the Prov. Grand Lodge, "doing well, and their members daily increasing," Nov. 23, 1814.

[9] Originally formed by persons employed in the marine service of the Government.

defection, about the close of the century, from the Prov. Grand Lodge of Bengal, and consequently from the older or legitimate Grand Lodge of England. A Lodge—No. 146—under the Atholl (or *Ancient*) Grand Lodge, was established at Calcutta in 1767, but it took no root, and it does not appear that any further Lodges were erected by the same authority until the secession I am now about to describe. The Lodges "True Friendship" and "Humility with Fortitude" were the first who transferred their allegiance, the former becoming No. 315,[1] or No. 1 of Bengal—Dec. 27, 1797, and the latter, No. 317,[2] or No. 2 of Bengal—April 11, 1798. The "Marine Lodge" followed their example, and obtained a similar warrant—No. 323[3]— March 4, 1801. Meanwhile, Lodge "Star in the East" fell into abeyance, and "Industry and Perseverance" was on the point of closing also. *One* meeting only was held in each of the years 1802, 1803, and 1804, after which, for a long period, there were no more. Lodge "Anchor and Hope" obtained an Atholl warrant as No. 325[4]—Oct. 1, 1801. Little is known of Lodge "Unanimity," which, though carried forward at the Union (1813), must have died out at least several years before.

During the ten or eleven years that intervened between the obliteration of the Prov. Grand Lodge and its re-establishment in 1813, Masonry in Calcutta was represented almost exclusively by the Lodges which had seceded from the (older) Grand Lodge of England.

On St John's Day (in Christmas) 1809, the Lodges, True Friendship, Humility with Fortitude, Marine, No. 338 (*Ancients*) in the 14th Foot, and the "Dispensation Lodge," working under a warrant granted by No. 338, walked in procession to St John's Church, where a Masonic sermon was delivered by the Rev. Dr James Ward.

Happily, Lodges Star in the East, and Industry and Perseverance, were revived in 1812, and on December 22 of that year, accompanied by the "Officers' Lodge,"[5] No. 347 in the 14th Foot, and Humility with Fortitude, also walked in procession to the same church, and benefited by a like sermon from Dr Ward.

On October 4, 1813, the Earl of Moira—who had been appointed Acting Grand Master of India—arrived in Calcutta. The first Masonic act of the Governor-General was to constitute a new Lodge in that city—the Moira, Freedom and Fidelity—November 8, and his second, to re-establish the Prov. Grand Lodge of Bengal under the Hon. Archibald Seton.

As soon as the union of the two Grand Lodges of England became known in India, the "Atholl" Lodges at Calcutta tendered their allegiance to the Prov. Grand Lodge. These were, True Friendship, Humility with Fortitude, and Marine. The Anchor and Hope—which also seceded from the legitimate Grand Lodge of England—is not mentioned in the records of the Province 1814-40.

At the period of this fusion, there were the following Lodges under the older sanction: The Stewards,[6] Star in the East, Industry and Perseverance, and Sincere Friendship (Chunar). Of these Lodges, the first never held a London warrant, and the last was struck off the roll inadvertently at the Union. There were also then in existence the Moira Lodge, and three others constituted since the revival of the Prov. Grand Lodge, the names of which head the following table of Lodges erected during the period 1813-26 :—

---

[1] Now No. 218.   [2] Now No. 229.   [3] Now No. 232.   [4] Now No. 234.
[5] Possibly the "Dispensation Lodge" before alluded to.   [6] Abolished December 27, 1819.

1. Moira,[1] Calcutta, November 13, 1813.
2. Oriental Star,[2] Noscollee, April 21, 1814.
3. Aurora,[3] Calcutta, June 23, 1814.
4. Courage with Humanity,[4] Dum Dum, July 12, 1814.
5. Northern Star, Barrackpore, July 18, 1816.
6. Sincerity, Cawnpore, January 8, 1819.
7. Hastings Lodge of Amity and Independence, Allahabad, April 9, 1821.
8. United Lodge of Friendship, Cawnpore, June 13, 1821.
9. Humanity with Courage, Prince of Wales' Island, July 1822.
10. Amity, St John's, Poona (Deccan), Jan. 30, 1824.
11. Kilwinning in the West, Nusseerabad, October 20, 1824.
12. Larkins' Lodge of Union and Brotherly Love, Dinapore, October 20, 1824.
13. Independence with Philanthropy, Allahabad, October 26, 1825.
14. South-Eastern Star of Light[5] and Victory, Arracan, October 26, 1825.
15. Tuscan, Malacca, October 26, 1825.
16. Royal George, Bombay, December 9, 1825.
17. Union and Perseverance, Agra, October 23, 1826.
18. Kilwinning in the East, Calcutta, Dec. 23, 1826.

Out of these *eighteen* Lodges, however, only *seven*—Nos. 2, 3, 4, 6, 7, 13, and 18 above—secured a footing on the roll of the Grand Lodge of England,[6] and it is not a little curious that of the two now alone surviving, Courage with Humanity (1814), and Independence with Philanthropy (1825), which were placed on the general list in the same year (1828) in juxtaposition, the latter bears the earlier *number*, and has the higher precedence!

The sway of Earl Moira extended over the whole of India, and he was empowered by the Duke of Sussex to appoint Provincial Grand Masters for Districts, with rank and authority equal to those appointed by the Grand Master himself.

The Acting Prov. G.M.—Seton—left India in 1817, and the Governor-General—then Marquis of Hastings—intimated to the Prov. Grand Lodge that he had selected the Hon. C. Stuart to succeed him. The latter does not appear, however, to have entered upon the duties of his office; and in the following year—January 17—the Hon. C. R. Lindsay was successively appointed, by warrants of Lord Hastings, Prov. G.M. of Bengal, January 17, 1818, and Deputy G.M. of India, January 13, 1819.

On November 30, 1818, an application was made to the Grand Master of India, by eight brethren residing at Poona, in the Deccan, praying for authority to meet as Lodge "St Andrew" at that station, and also for "a dispensation for holding a Provincial Lodge, for the purpose of making the Hon. Mountstuart Elphinstone a Mason, he having expressed a wish to that effect." The petitioners further requested "that his name might be inserted in the body of the warrant, authorising them to install him, after being duly passed and raised, a Deputy G.M. of the Deccan." Of the reply made to this application, no record has been preserved.

---

[1] Of this Lodge—the only one in India warranted by Earl Moira—the first Master was Major-General Sir W. G. Keir, and the first Wardens Col. C. J. Doyle and Commodore Hayes. It numbered thirty-eight members within a month of its constitution, but had ceased to work in 1821.

[2] Sent £100 to the English charities, 1816; warrant surrendered 1821.

[3] Amalgamated with Lodge True Friendship, 1830.

[4] Composed for many years of non-commissioned officers of the Bengal Artillery. It threw off a shoot in Penang—Humanity with Courage—in 1822, which took the place of the Neptune Lodge (*Atholl*), No. 344, established in 1809.

[5] Owing to the dispersion of the petitioners, never actually established.

[6] Nos. 685, Oriental Star, 1817; 816, Aurora, 1827; 822, Independence with Philanthropy; and 823, Courage with Humanity, 1828; 824, Sincerity; 825, Hastings; and 845, Kilwinning in the East, 1829.

Lindsay was succeeded as Deputy G.M. of India, and Prov. G.M. of Bengal, by John Pascal Larkins, December 24, 1819. In 1822—December 20—an address was presented to Lord Hastings on his approaching departure; and a week later, on the Festival of St John, that nobleman was present at the Cathedral Church—whither the Lodges had walked in procession —in his capacity of Grand Master.

Larkins returned to Europe in 1826, from which date until 1840 the Craft in Bengal was (nominally) ruled by a Prov. G.M. in England, with a Deputy at Calcutta. This resulted in the extinction of the Prov. Grand Lodge, and the annihilation of all order and constituted authority for a time. In 1827—November 22—Lodge Independence with Philanthropy, at Allahabad, so resented the conduct of the P.G.L. as to return its warrant, intimating that its future meetings would be held under a dispensation obtained from Lodge Union, No. 432 (Irish Register), in the 14th Foot,[1] until a warrant could be obtained from England, for which application had been made direct.[2]

The Lodges in Bengal made their returns regularly, and forwarded their dues punctually, to the Prov. Grand Lodge; but as no steps were taken for the transmission of these returns and dues to their destination, the Grand Lodge of England ceased to notice or regard the tributary Lodges of Bengal. On the submission of a motion for inquiry—March 22, 1828— the Deputy Prov. G.M. "felt himself constrained to resign his chair on the spot, and the Grand Wardens also tendered their resignations."

This led, at the instance of Lodge Aurora—to the formation of a representative body, styled the LODGE OF DELEGATES, who were charged with the duty of preparing a memorial to the Grand Lodge of England, which, bearing date August 28, 1828, was sent to the Duke of Sussex, signed by the Masters and Wardens of the following Lodges:—True Friendship, Humility with Fortitude, Marine, Aurora, Courage with Humanity, and Kilwinning in the East.

To this no reply was vouchsafed. The letters of the Lodges in Bengal remained unanswered, and their requests unheeded. The usual certificates for brethren made in the country were withheld, notwithstanding that the established dues were regularly remitted; and applications for warrants were also unnoticed, though they were accompanied by the proper fees. This state of affairs continued until 1834, when the question of separation from the Grand Lodge of England was gravely and formally mooted in the Lodges. Overtures for a reconciliation at length came in the shape of certificates for brethren who had by this time grown grey in Masonry. Answers to letters written long ago were also received; but the most important

---

[1] In 1834, some Masons at Delhi applied to their brethren at Meerut for an acting constitution of this kind, which might serve their purpose until the receipt of a warrant from the Grand Lodge of *England*. At the latter station there were two Lodges, one of which, however, was itself working under dispensation, and could not therefore dispense grace to another. The other belonged to the 26th Foot, No. 26, under the Grand Lodge of *Ireland*. This Lodge declined giving a dispensation, for the somewhat Irish reason that the Cameronian Lodge had already granted one to another Lodge, *of the propriety of which act they had great doubt;* and that until an answer had been received from Ireland, they could not commit a second act of doubtful legality! The custom, however, was a very old one. In 1759, Lodge No. 74, I.R., in the 1st Foot (2d Batt.), granted an exact copy of its warrant—dated October 26, 1787—to some brethren at Albany, to work under until they received a separate charter from *Ireland*. This was changed—February 21, 1765—for a warrant from George Harrison, *English* Prov. G.M. of New York; and the Lodge—Mount Vernon— is now No. 3 on the roll of the Grand Lodge of that State. *Cf.* Barker, Early Hist. of the G.L. of New York, preface, p. xviii.

[2] The request appears to have been granted, as the Lodge was placed on the English roll—as No. 822—in 1828. *Cf. ante*, p. 330, note 6.

concession made by the Grand Lodge of England was the constitution of the first District Grand Lodge of Bengal—under Dr John Grant—which held its first meeting, February 28, 1840.[1]

During the decade immediately preceding this epoch eight new Lodges had been erected in Bengal; and from 1840 down to the present year there has been an addition of 81 under the English and 11 under the Scottish registers respectively.

Although the Masonic jurisdiction of the Grand Lodge of Ireland has always been a favourite one with the rank and file of the British army, and the number of military Lodges under it has ever been vastly in excess of those owning allegiance to any other authority, only a single Irish warrant for a stationary Lodge in India appears to have been issued. This was granted in 1837 to some brethren at Kurnaul, but its activity seems not to have outlasted the year of its constitution. An attempt was made in 1862 to establish an Irish Lodge in Bombay, but on the representation of the Grand Secretary of England to the Deputy Grand Secretary of Ireland that it would be objectionable " to create a third Masonic independent jurisdiction in the province, there being already two, viz., English and Scotch," the Grand Lodge of Ireland declined to grant the warrant.[2]

In the decennial periods 1840-50 and 1850-60 there were in each instance 12 additions to the roll. In 1860-70 the new Lodges amounted to 19, and in 1870-85 to 38. These figures are confined to the English Lodges, but extend over the area now occupied in part by the District Grand Lodges of Burma and the Punjaub, both of which were carved out of the territory previously comprised within the Province of Bengal, in 1868. The following statistics show the number of Lodges existing—January 1, 1886—in the various states and districts which until 1868 were subject to the Masonic government of Bengal : under the Grand Lodge of England—Bengal (D.G.L.), 39; British Burma (D.G.L.), 7; and Punjab (D.G.L.), 24. Under the Grand Lodge of Scotland, 11—the earliest of which, St David (originally Kilwinning) in the East, No. 371, Calcutta, was constituted February 5, 1849.

The Dutch Lodges in Hindostan have passed out of existence, but with regard to these, and also to certain other Lodges established by the Grand Lodge of Holland in various places beyond the seas, the materials for an exhaustive list are not available to the historian.

MADRAS.—The earliest Lodge in Southern India—No. 222—was established at Madras in 1752. Three others—Nos. 353-355—were formed at the same station in 1765. Shortly afterwards, about 1766, Captain Edmond Pascal was appointed Provincial Grand Master for Madras and its Dependencies ; and in the following year a fifth Lodge, No. 323, was erected at Fort St George. It is worthy of recollection that for a short period this Presidency was predominant over all the other English settlements in India ; and during the latter half of the eighteenth century the continuous wars with the French, and afterwards with Hyder Ali and his son, cause the Carnatic to figure largely in Indian history.

[1] Authorities up to this point :—G. L. Records ; Constitutions ; Masonic Calendars—England, Scotland, Ireland, Holland, France, and Bengal ; A. D'Cruz, "Freemasonry in Bengal," 1866 ; Communications from the Grand Secretaries of Scotland, Ireland, and Holland, and from Mr H. D. Sandeman—Prov. G.M. of Bengal, 1862-75 ; F. Q. Rev., 1838, p. 465 et seq.; 1845, p. 377. For what follows in the text—in addition to the above—I have consulted Laurie, pp. 219, 256, 271, 276, 395 ; Constitutions, Grand Lodge of Scotland, 1881, pp. 154, 160 ; Preston, edit. 1821, p. 258 ; Freemasons' Magazine, 1863, pt. i., p. 442 ; Freemasons' Chronicle, vol. v., 1877, pp. 274, 290 ; and am indebted somewhat to my own personal recollections.

[2] Grand Lodge Minutes, June 4, 1862.

In 1768, a Lodge—No. 152—was established by the Atholl (or *Ancient*) Grand Lodge of England at Fort St George; and in 1773 one by the Grand Lodge of Holland at Negapatam. The next event of importance was the initiation, in 1776, of Umdat-ul-Umará,[1] eldest son of the Nabob of Arcot, at Trichinopoly—who, in his reply to the congratulations of the Grand Lodge of England, stated " he considered the title of an English Mason as one of the most honourable he possessed."

A Provincial Grand Lodge under the Atholl sanction was established at Fort St George in 1781, " but the dissensions in the settlements had so rent asunder every link of social life, that even the fraternal bond of Masonry had been annihilated in the general wreck." [2]

In 1786—February 20—Brigadier-General Horne was appointed (by the Duke of Cumberland) " Prov. G.M. for the Coast of Coromandel, the Presidency of Madras, and parts adjacent," and under this able officer a union of the brethren in Southern India was effected.

At this period all the Lodges under the older Grand Lodge of England seem to have been extinct; but in 1786 the Carnatic Military Lodge, No. 488, was established at Arcot; and in the following year the Lodge No. 152 tendered its allegiance to General Horne, and surrendering its warrant, joined one of the Lodges under that officer. Of these, four were *added* to the roll in 1787, Nos. 510-513—Perfect Harmony, St Thomas Mount; Social Friendship, Madras; Trichinopoly; and Social Friendship, St Thomas Mount—and styled Nos. 3, 4, 5, and 6, Coast of Coromandel.[3] Two other Lodges were also *established* in the same year, the Stewards and Perfect Unanimity, which, according to the loose practice of those days, were given the *places* on the list of the two earliest Madras Lodges, and became (in 1790) Nos. 102 and 233 [4] respectively.

A Lodge of happy nomenclature—La Fraternité Cosmopolite—was constituted at Pondicherry in 1786 by the Grand Orient of France, and a second—Les Navigateurs Réunis—in 1790.

In the latter year—July 5—John Chamier received a similar patent—as Prov. G.M.—to that previously held by General Horne, and was succeeded by Terence Gahagan, 1806; and Herbert Compton,[5] 1812. During this period four Lodges were added to the roll—Solid Friendship, Trichinopoly, 1790; Unity, Peace, and Concord, 1798; St Andrew's Union 19th Foot, 1802; and Philanthropists, in the Scotch Brigade [94th Foot], 1802, at Madras. These Lodges were numbered 572, 574, 590, and 591 on the *general*, and 7, 9, 10, and 11 (Coast of Coromandel) on the *local* lists respectively.[6]

After the Union, the province was ruled by Dr Richard Jebb, 1814; George Lys, 1820;

---

[1] The last reigning Nabob of Arcot (1795-1801). The dignity was abolished in 1855, but that of Prince of Arcot was granted by letters patent to Azím Jáh (uncle of the last titular Nabob), in 1865.

[2] Letter from Sir John Day, Advocate-General, Bengal, to Umdat-ul-Umará, 1778, accompanying an Apron and Book of Constitutions, entrusted by the Grand Lodge of England to the former for presentation to the latter (Freemasons' Calendar, 1781, p. 43).

[3] Nos. 488, 510, and 512 were " dropped out " at the Union (1813), and 511 and 513 were erased March 5, 1862; 511, however, was subsequently restored to the roll, and is *now* Lodge of the Rock, Trichinopoly, No. 260.

[4] The numbers allotted to the Nos. 222 and 353 of 1752 and 1765 respectively at the closing up of numbers in 1782. Perfect Unanimity still exists (No. 150), but the Stewards Lodge is extinct.

[5] S.G.W. of England, 1809.

[6] None were carried forward at the Union (1813) except No. 574, which about 1826-27 was attached to the 1st Foot (the Royal Regiment), and still exists.

and in 1825 by Compton once more. The name of this worthy only disappears from the *Freemasons' Calendar* in 1842, and with it the provincial title, "Coast of Coromandel" —exchanged for "Madras," over which Lord Elphinstone had been appointed Prov. G.M. in 1840.

Within this period—1814-42—numerous Lodges were warranted locally, as in Bengal; but 13 only—of which 7 were in Madras itself—secured places on the London register. Eighteen English Lodges have since been established in the Presidency, and there are at present in existence 20 Lodges on the register of England and two on that of Scotland—both erected in 1875—but the introduction of Scottish Lodges into India will be referred to in the ensuing section.

The French Lodge at Pondicherry—La Fraternité Cosmopolite—was revived (or a new one established under the old title) in 1821. Another—L'Union Indienne—was erected at the same station in 1851. At the present date, however, there exist throughout India and its dependencies no other Lodges than those under the Grand Lodges of England and Scotland respectively.

BOMBAY.—Two Lodges were established in this Presidency during the last century—Nos. 234, Bombay, in 1758, and 569, Surat, in 1798, both of which were carried on in the lists until 1813, but disappear at the Union. A Provincial Grand Master—James Todd—was appointed in 1763, whose name only drops out of the *Freemasons' Calendar* in 1799. In 1801, an Atholl warrant, No. 322, was granted to the 78th Foot, which regiment was engaged in the Mahratta war under Sir Arthur Wellesley, and took part in the decisive victory of Assaye (1803). In 1818, as we have already seen,[1] Lord Moira was asked to constitute a Lodge at Poona. But none were again established in the Presidency until 1822, in which year the Benevolent Lodge, No. 746, Bombay, was placed on our lists.[2] In 1823, a Military Lodge— Orion in the West—was formed in the Bombay Artillery, and "installed" at Poona as No. 15, Coast of Coromandel, November 15. According to the early proceedings of this Lodge, members "were examined in the Third Degree, and passed into the chair of the Fourth Degree" —for which a fee of three gold mohurs was exacted. In the following year, a second Lodge at Poona was established by the Prov. Grand Lodge of Bengal,[3] which, however, has left no trace of its existence. In 1825, the civilian element of Orion seceded, and formed the Lodge of Hope, also at Poona, No. 802. Here, Orion, unrecognised at home, aided in the secession of

---

[1] *Ante*, p. 330.

[2] Among the Masons about this time in Bombay were thirteen non-commissioned officers who were too poor to establish a Lodge of their own, and too modest to seek admittance in what was considered an aristocratic Lodge. They met, however, monthly in the guard-room over the Apollo Gate, for mutual instruction in Masonry. This coming to the knowledge of the Benevolent Lodge, the thirteen were elected honorary members of No. 746, for which they returned heartfelt thanks. At their first attendance, when the Lodge work was over, and the brethren adjourned to the banquet, the thirteen were informed that refreshments awaited them *downstairs*. Revolting at the distinction thus made among Masons, they one and all left the place. The next morning they were sent for by their commanding officer, who was also one of the officers of the Lodge, and asked to explain their conduct. One of the party—Mr W. Willis (by whom this anecdote was first related to me), told him that as Masons they were bound to meet on the Level and part on the Square; but as this fundamental principle was not practised in No. 746, of which they had been elected honorary members, they could not partake of their hospitality. The astonished colonel uttered not a word, but waved his hand for them to retire. Ever after this, the Benevolent Lodge—including the thirteen—met on the Level, both in Lodge and at the banquet-table.

[3] *Ante*, p. 330.

some of its members, who obtained a warrant, on the recommendation of the parent Lodge, from the Grand Lodge of England. A Lodge was erected at Bombay—Perseverance, No. 818—in 1828. Two years later it was discovered that no notification of the existence of Orion in the West had reached the Grand Lodge of England, nor had any fees been received, though these, including the quarterages, had been regularly paid to the Prov. Grand Lodge of the Coast of Coromandel. It was further ascertained that in granting a warrant for a Bombay Lodge, the Prov. G.M. of the Coast of Coromandel had exceeded his powers. Ultimately, a new warrant, No. 598, was granted from England, July 19, 1833.

Up to this time the jurisdiction of the Grand Lodge of England had not been invaded; but in 1836 Dr James Burnes [1] was appointed by the Grand Lodge of Scotland, Provincial G.M. of Western India and its dependencies. No Prov. Grand Lodge, however, was formed until January 1, 1838. A second Scottish Province—of Eastern India—was subsequently erected, which, on the retirement of the Marquis of Tweeddale,[2] was absorbed within the jurisdiction of Dr Burnes, who, in 1846, became Prov. G.M. for all India (including Aden), but with the proviso, that this appointment was not to act in restraint of any future subdivision of the Presidencies.

Burnes, in 1836, may be best described, in ecclesiastical phrase, as a Prov. G.M. "*in partibus infidelium,*" for whatever Lodges then existed throughout the length and breadth of India were strangers to Scottish Masonry. But the times were propitious. There was no English Provincial Grand Lodge of Bombay; and under the Chevalier Burnes, whom nature had bountifully endowed with all the qualities requisite for Masonic administration, Scottish Masonry presented such attractions, that the strange sight was witnessed of English Masons deserting their mother Lodges to such an extent that these fell into abeyance, in order that they might give their support to Lodges newly constituted by the Grand Lodge of Scotland. In one case, indeed, a Lodge—Perseverance—under England went over bodily to the enemy, with its name, jewels, furniture, and belongings, and the charge was accepted by Scotland.

From this period, therefore, Scottish Masonry flourished, and English Masonry declined, the latter finally becoming quite dormant until the year 1848, when a Lodge, St George—No. 807 on the roll of the Grand Lodge of England—was again formed at Bombay, and for some years was the solitary representative of English Masonry in the Province.

In 1844, Burnes established a Lodge, No. 413, "Rising Star," at Bombay, for the admission of natives—by whom a beautiful medal, cut by Wyon, was struck in consequence [3]—and No. 414, St Andrew in the East, at Poona. These were followed by Nos. 421—Hope, Kurrachee—and 422—Perseverance, Bombay—in 1847.[4]

Scottish Lodges were next erected in Bengal—No. 353, *now* 371, Kilwinning in the East, Calcutta, 1849; and in Arabia—No. 355, Felix, Aden, 1850. At the close of 1885, 33 Lodges

---

[1] *Ante,* p. 68; and see Chap. XI., p. 504.

[2] So far Laurie (edit. 1859, p. 395); but I am informed by Lyon (on whose authority is given what follows in the text) that though Lord Tweeddale was Governor and Commander-in-Chief of Madras from April 1842 to September 1848, his name does not occur in any records of the Grand Lodge of Scotland of that period, nor indeed of any other, as Prov. G.M. of Eastern India. It may be added that the first Scottish Lodge constituted in any other Presidency than Bombay was No. 353, "Kilwinning (*now* St David) in the East," Calcutta, erected February 5, 1849.

[3] *Cf. ante,* p. 68, note 7.

[4] The dates here given merely represent when the charters granted by Burnes were confirmed by the Grand Lodge of Scotland. As Nos. 421 and 422 enjoy precedence from 1842, they were probably locally constituted in that year.

in all—or under Bombay, 19; Bengal, 11; Madras, 2; and in Afghanistan, 1—had received Charters from the Grand Lodge of Scotland. With a single exception—which reduces the Bombay Lodges to 18—these are all in existence.

Burnes left India in 1849, and was succeeded by a Prov. G.M. of Western India only. In 1874, however, Captain Henry Morland became Prov. G.M. of Hindostan, and was subsequently commissioned as Grand Master of All Scottish Freemasonry in India.

Returning to the Lodges under the Grand Lodge of England. St George—No. 807—constituted in 1848, was for ten years the only representative of its class. In 1858, however, Lodges "Concord"—No. 1059—and "Union"—No. 1069—were established at Bombay and Kurrachee respectively. A year later, "Orion in the West" awoke from its dormancy.[1] In 1861, a Provincial Grand Lodge was established, and since that date 18 Lodges have been chartered in the district, 15 of which survive, and, together with Orion, St George, Concord, and Union, form a grand total of 19 Lodges under the District G.M. of Bombay.

Until of late years, it cannot be said that Freemasonry has taken any real root among the native population of India. Umdat-ul-Umará, son of the Nabob of Arcot, was admitted a member of the Society, as we have already seen, in 1776. The princes Keyralla Khan (of the Mysore family) and Shadad Khan (ex-Ameer of Scinde) joined, or were made Masons in, the Lodge of "True Friendship" in 1842 and 1850 respectively; and in 1861 the Maharajahs Duleep and Rundeer Sing were initiated in Lodges "Star of the East" and "Hope and Perseverance"—the last-named personage at Lahore, and the other three in Calcutta.

A by-law of the Prov. Grand Lodge of Bengal, forbidding the entry of Asiatics without the permission of the P.G.M., was in force until May 12, 1871; and there was at least a popular belief in existence so late as 1860,[2] that Hindus were ineligible for initiation. The Parsees of Western India were the first of the native races who evinced any real interest in the institution, and are to be congratulated on the recent election (1886) of one of their number—Mr Cama—to the high position of Treasurer of the Grand Lodge of England.

In 1876, a Scottish Lodge, No. 587, "Islam"—presumably for the association of Mohammedans—was erected at Bombay. The extent to which Freemasonry is now practised by the Hindus—who form 73½ per cent. of the total population of India—I am unable to determine. The first of this class of religionists to fill the chair of a Lodge was Mr Dutt, whose election in 1874 may not have been without influence in the diffusion of Masonic light.

The *Indian Freemasons' Friend*, a publication of rare merit, was set on foot at Calcutta in 1855, but was short-lived. A new or second series was commenced in May 1861, and lasted

---

[1] It was at my instance that this Lodge was revived, and I had the pleasure—being then W.M. of No. 1045, attached to the 31st Foot—of installing the Master—Colonel Forster, R.A., an old P.M. of the Lodge—on the occasion.

[2] An assistant military apothecary was initiated in the Meridian Lodge, 31st Foot, in that year. The legality of this act—on the score of the intrant being a Brahmin—was demurred to in the Masonic press; and the 31st Regiment being with the Expeditionary Force in China, Mr G. W. Ingram, P.M., No. 345, took up the cudgels on behalf of the Lodge, pointing out, in an elaborate argument, "that the very ground-work of the Brahmin faith is the belief in one Grand Superintending Being." The journal in which these letters appeared ultimately reached the Lodge—then at Tien-Tsin—when I addressed to it a final letter, deposing that, having filled the chair on the occasion alluded to, the individual whose admission had been called in question was, "by his own statement, delivered to me in person, a Christian." *Cf.* Freemasons' Magazine, April 21, September 8, and October 13, 1860; and May 18, 1861; and for some startling assertions respecting Freemasonry forming a portion of the Brahminical knowledge, see Higgins, Anacalypsis, 1836, vol. i., pp. 767-69; and H. Melville, Revelation of Mysteries, etc., 1876, p. 17.

to the end of 1867. In Bombay, the *Masonic Record of Western India* enjoys an extensive circulation, and is very ably conducted.

EAST INDIA ISLANDS.

CEYLON.—Masonry was established in this island—which I here group with all those which in former days were conveniently included in the expression "East Indies"—by the Grand Lodge of Holland. Lodges were erected at Colombo—Fidelity—1771; Point de Galle —Sincerity—1773; and at Colombo again—Union—1794. In 1795 the British took possession of the Dutch settlements on the island, and annexed them to the Presidency of Madras; but six years after, in 1801, Ceylon was formed into a separate Crown colony.

At this period—February 9, 1801—a charter from the Grand Lodge of Scotland was granted to the officers of the 51st Regiment, stationed at Colombo, for the Orange Lodge, No. 274. Lodges under the Atholl (or *Ancient*) sanction were also formed on the island— Nos. 329—in the 6th Battalion R.A.—1802; and 340—in the 34th Foot—1807.

Under the older Grand Lodge of England, a Provincial Grand Master—Sir Alexander Johnston—was appointed in 1810, whose name, however, disappears from the lists before the establishment of the first stationary English Lodge—St John's, No. 665—in 1838. But in the meantime greater activity was displayed under other jurisdictions. An Irish Lodge— No. 62—sprang up at Colombo in 1821, and a French one—Union, under the G.O.—in 1822. The latter of these was revived, or a new Lodge formed with the same name, in 1832.

At the present time there are six Lodges on the island, four Irish—Nos. 107, 112, 115, and 298, dating from 1861, 1863, 1868, and 1874, respectively; one English—St John's above, *now* No. 454; and one Scottish—No. 611, dating from 1877; an earlier Lodge—No. 446, erected at Kandy in 1865—having ceased to exist. The Irish Lodges are subject to a Prov. G.M. appointed in 1877, and No. 611 to the G.M. of All Scottish Freemasonry in India.

The Dutch Lodges, though now extinct, evinced great tenacity of existence. The two named above survived until within recent memory, and others were constituted, not only in Ceylon, but also in the East and West Indies, of which a very imperfect record has been preserved.[1]

SUMATRA.—An English Lodge—No. 356—was established at Bencoolen in 1765, and two others—Nos. 424 and 559—at Fort Marlborough in 1772 and 1796 respectively. These continued to appear in the lists until 1813; but only one, the "Marlboro" (afterwards "Rising Sun") Lodge (1772), was carried forward at the Union, which ultimately became No. 242, and having omitted to make any returns for several years, was erased March 5, 1862.

Sumatra was erected into an English province in 1793 under John Macdonald, who was succeeded as Prov. G.M.—December 10, 1821—by H. R. Lewis, and the latter continued to hold office until his death in 1877, there having been *one* Lodge in existence at the time of his original appointment, and none at all for fifteen years preceding his decease.

At the present date there are two Lodges on the island, one—No. 41, Mata Hari, at

---

[1] An exhaustive list of the Lodges chartered *out of Holland* by the Grand Lodge of that country is a *desideratum* in Masonic literature. The accounts of the *earliest* Dutch Lodges in the East and West Indies are derived from the (English) " Freemasons' Calendar," 1776 and 1778, and the (German) " Handbuch," which are substantially in accord. For a list of the Dutch Colonial Lodges at the present date I am indebted to Mr J. P. Vaillant.

Padang; the other—No. 75, Prince Frederick, at Kotta Raja (Atchin). These were constituted by the Grand Lodge of Holland in 1858 and 1880 respectively.

JAVA.—Masonry was introduced into this island in 1769, and a Lodge—Star in the East —constituted by the Grand Lodge of Holland at Batavia, which still exists. Others soon after sprang up in the capital and the larger towns, of which, however, no precise record is obtainable. A second Lodge was erected at Batavia in 1771, and charters were granted to brethren at Samarang in 1801, and at Sourabaya in 1809. At the present time (1886) there are eight Lodges in Java—at Batavia, Samarang, Sourabaya, Djokdjokarta, Rambang, Sura-karta, Salatiga, and Problingo. These are governed by Mr T. H. Dei Kinderen, Deputy National Grand Master for the East Indies of the Netherlands.

CELEBES.—A Lodge—Arbeid Adelt (*Labour ennobles*), No. 79—under the Grand Lodge of Holland, was erected at Macassar in 1883.

BORNEO.—On this, the largest island of the world—if we regard Australia as continental— an English Lodge was established in 1885, No. 2106, Elopura, at the station of the same name in North Borneo.

THE PHILIPPINES.—Masonry in these islands is of recent introduction, but at Manilla, the capital, there are now (1886) four Lodges in existence; one—No. 39—under the National Grand Orient, and three—Nos. 179, 204, and 208—under the Grand Lodge of Spain. The latter form a Province, and are subject to a Provincial Superintendent.

PERSIA.

Thory informs us that Askeri-Khan, ambassador of the Shah at Paris, and who was him-self admitted into Masonry in that city—November 24, 1808—took counsel with his French brethren respecting the foundation of a Lodge at Ispahan.[1] Whether this project was ever carried into effect it is impossible to say, but two years later we find another Persian— also an ambassador—figuring in Masonic history. On June 15, 1810, " His Excellency Mirza Abul Hassan Khan" was granted the rank of Past Grand Master of the Grand Lodge of England.[2] This personage—the Minister accredited from the Court of Persia to that of Great Britain—in addition to having been a great traveller both in Hindostan and Arabia, had also performed his devotions at Mecca. In the course of his journey from Teheran he passed through Georgia, Armenia, and Anatolia. At Constantinople he embarked in a British man-of-war, and reached England in December 1809. Sir Gore Ousely, Bart., who was selected to attend upon the Mirza " as Mehmander—an officer of distinction, whose duty it is to receive and entertain foreign princes and other illustrious personages "[3]—in the following year (1810) received the appointment of ambassador to the Shah of Persia, and was also granted an English patent as Provincial G.M. for that country. No Lodges, however, were established in Persia at any time by the Grand Lodge of England, nor,—so far as the evidence extends—by any other external authority. The Mirza Abul Hassan Khan was made a Mason by Lord Moira in 1810.[4] The extent of his services to the Craft we must leave undecided; but it was stated somewhat recently in the Masonic journals, on the authority of a Persian

[1] Acta Lat., vol. i., p. 237 ; cf. ante, p. 119.   [2] Grand Lodge Records.

[3] European Magazine, vol. lvii., 1810, p. 408.   [4] Freemasons' Magazine, Jan. 2, 1864.

GENERAL J. S. BROWNRIGG, C.B.

PROVINCIAL GRAND MASTER, SURREY

Thomas C. Jack London & Edinburgh

military officer [1] then pursuing his studies in Berlin, that nearly all the members of the Court of Teheran are brethren of our Society.

THE STRAITS SETTLEMENTS.

The Neptune Lodge, No. 344, was established at Penang (or Prince of Wales Island) by warrant of the Duke of Atholl, September 6, 1809, but became extinct in 1819. Three years later, a Military Lodge—Humanity with Courage—was warranted from Bengal.[2] The proceedings of this body, however, becoming irregular by the initiation of civilians, the Duke of Sussex renewed the charter of the Atholl Lodge, which flourished for a time, but eventually fell into decay, and was erased, together with another Lodge, "Neptune"—also at Penang, erected in 1850—No. 846 on the English roll, March 5, 1862. The only Lodge now existing in this settlement is No. 1555, warranted by the Grand Lodge of England in 1875.[3]

Passing over Malacca—where a Lodge was formed under the Prov. Grand Lodge of Bengal in 1825, but which never secured a place on the general list—we next come to Singapore, where English Lodges were established in 1845, 1858, and 1867, named Zetland in the East, Fidelity, and St George, Nos. 748, 1042, and 1152 respectively. Of these the first and last survive, and, together with the Lodge at Penang, compose the province of the Eastern Archipelago, of which Mr W. H. Read was appointed the first Prov. G.M. in 1858.

COCHIN-CHINA.

In this French dependency, a Lodge—Le Réveil de l'Orient—was established by warrant of the Grand Orient of France, October 22, 1868.

CHINA.

During the last century, two Lodges of foreign origin were constituted in the Celestial Empire—the Lodge of "Amity," No. 407, under an English, and "Elizabeth" under a Swedish, warrant. The former was erected in 1767, the latter in 1788; and in each case the place of assembly was Canton. The English Lodge was not carried forward at the Union (1813), and "Elizabeth," as I am informed by the Grand Secretary of Sweden, came to an end in 1812.

The next Lodge erected on Chinese soil was the Royal Sussex, No. 735, at Canton, for which a warrant was granted by the United G.L. of England in 1844. A second—Zetland, No. 768—was established at Hong-Kong under the same sanction, in 1846; and a third— Northern Lodge of China—at Shanghai, in 1849. No further increase of Lodges took place until 1864, in which year two were added to the English roll, at Hong-Kong and Shanghai respectively; and one each at the latter port under the Grand Lodges of Scotland and Massachusetts.[4] The progress of the Craft in the "Middle Kingdom" has since been marked, but uneventful, though as yet Freemasonry has failed to diffuse its light beyond the British colony

---

[1] A Mussulman, admitted (after examination) into a Berlin Lodge. *Cf.* Freemason, June 28, 1873.
[2] *Ante*, p. 330.   [3] *Cf.* F. Q. Rev., 1835, p. 460; 1846, p. 375; and Atholl Lodges, p. 62.
[4] At the time this occurred, I was W.M. of the Northern Lodge of China, *now* No. 570, and can therefore bear witness to the unity and concord which pervaded all the Lodges in Shanghai at that period. In the following year (1865), a few days before my departure from the Settlement, by desire of the associated Lodges—English, Scottish, and American—I laid the foundation-stone of a Masonic Hall, which is not the least of the pleasing recollections connected with my sojourn in the East.

of Hong-Kong, and the various ports on the mainland opened up by treaty to the merchants of foreign powers. Mr Samuel Rawson was appointed by Lord Zetland Prov. G.M. for China in 1847; and a second Province was carved out of the old one in 1877, by the appointment of Mr Cornelius Thorne as District G.M. for Northern China.

At the present time (1886) there are in existence at Victoria (Hong-Kong), and the Chinese treaty-ports, 13 English, 1 American, and 4 Scottish Lodges; and with a solitary exception—No. 1217, at Ningpo, formed in 1868, under the Grand Lodge of England, but now extinct—all the Lodges erected in China or Hong-Kong since the revival of Masonry in the Far East (1844), are still active, and can therefore be traced in the calendars of current date, by those desirous of further information respecting them.

Many secret societies exist in China, which, under slightly varied names (and spellings), will be found alluded to in the note below.[1]

The best known of these is the Triad Society, which has its headquarters in the Straits Settlements, no longer daring to show itself as an institution within the limits of the Middle Kingdom, though not a few of its members are to be found at and about Amoy. It took its rise some hundred and fifty years ago. The term "Triad" here alludes to a conjunction of the three great powers in nature—Heaven, Earth, and Man; hence it is sometimes called the Heaven and Earth Society. It admits members with ceremonies very similar to our own.[2]

JAPAN.

English Lodges bearing the following numbers were erected at Yokohama—1092 and 1263 —in 1866 and 1869; at Yedo (now extinct)—1344—in 1870; at Kobe—1401—in 1872; and at Tôkiô—2015—in 1883. These are subject to a Prov. G.M., who was appointed in 1873.

There are also three Lodges under the Grand Lodge of Scotland—Nos. 498, 640, and 710— at Kobe, Yokohama, and Nagasaki, established in 1870, 1879, and 1884 respectively.

There are numerous stories by the Japanese, during the latter part of the seventeenth and beginning of the eighteenth century, of mysterious documents carefully preserved in secret by the natives—precious heirlooms. Several of these are matters of history; and a theory has been advanced that the documents in question were the more important vouchers of Masonic Lodges, warrants, lists of affiliated brethren, etc., and in some instances the certificates of ancestors.[3] A noted Secret Society of Japan, that of the *Komosô*, now extinct or in abeyance, has been referred to at a previous page.[4]

NORTH AFRICA.

EGYPT.—Masonry, according to the "Official Bulletin" of the National Grand Orient at present existing in the valley of the Nile—in the form of a Memphis Lodge—was introduced into the country by Napoleon, Kleber, and other French officers in 1798 (?). Lodges of the Craft, however, practising pure and ancient Freemasonry, are not heard of until 1802,

---

[1] Thory, Ann. Or., 1813, pp. 233, 235; Gustave Schlegel, Thian ti hwi, the Hung-League, or Heaven-Earth-League, a Secret Society with the Chinese in China and India, Batavia, 1866; L. de Rosny, La Franc-Maçonnerie chez les Chinois, 1844; K. R. H. Mackenzie, Royal Mas. Cycl., p. 679, and Mas. Mag., vol. ix., 1881, pp. 89, 133; Notes and Queries, 1st ser., vol. xii., p. 233; and H. A. Giles, Freemasonry in China, 1880.

[2] Giles, *op. cit.*, p. 27, *ut supra.*

[3] Outlines of a Lecture on Masonry in Japan in the Seventeenth Century (Mas. Mag., vol. vii., 1880, p. 318).

[4] Chap. I., p. 30, note 4.

when *La Bienfaisance* was established at Alexandria; which was followed by a second, *Les Amis de Napoleon le Grand*, at the same city, in 1806. Both Lodges were under the Grand Orient of France. Others have since been constituted by the same authority, at Alexandria, 1847 and 1863; Cairo, 1868; and Mansourah, 1882; the first and last of these are still active. Under the rival French jurisdiction—Supreme Council 33°—a Lodge was constituted at Alexandria in 1862, and others at Ismailia, Port Said, and Suez in 1867—all of which (except the last named) are on the roll for 1886. Still another Lodge of French ancestry—under the newly formed Grand Independent Symbolic Lodge[1]—appears to have been in existence in 1879. Under the Grand Lodge of England Lodges have been formed at Alexandria, Nos. 1221 in 1862, 1082 in 1865, 1154 and 1157 in 1867; at Cairo, Nos. 1068 in 1865, 1105 in 1866, 1156 in 1867, 1226 in 1868, and 1855 in 1871; and at Ramleh, No. 1419 in 1872. Of these No. 1157, at Alexandria, and all the Cairo Lodges, with the solitary exception of No. 1156, are still active. Two Lodges—Nos. 472 and 707—were erected by the Grand Lodge of Scotland, at Suez and Alexandria, in 1867 and 1884 respectively. Under the G.O. of Italy there are now four Lodges each at Cairo and Alexandria, besides one at Mansourah, but the dates of their introduction I am unable to give.

The Rite of Memphis has been referred to in previous chapters,[2] and it again at this point crosses the path of Freemasonry. It will be recollected that in 1862 J. E. Marconis abdicated his position as Grand Universal Hierophant in favour of the Grand Orient of France. According, however, to the "Official Bulletin" already quoted, "long before Marconis treated for the transmission of the Rite to the G.O. of France, he constituted in Cairo the Lodge Menes, and in Alexandria founded a Supreme Council of the Order, with the distinctive title of Grand Orient of Egypt, with authority to confer from the *first* to the *ninetieth* degree, and to found Lodges, Chapters, Areopagi, Senates, and Consistories."

Upon these (and other) premises, therefore, it is laid down in the same publication, that the course adopted by Marconis was illegal, that he could not cede a Rite which was entrusted to him only as a sacred deposit to be preserved, etc. We next learn that the Grand Orient of Egypt, in accordance with powers which are duly set forth, convoked all the Patriarchs—of whom 95, created such by Marconis, resided in Egypt—and founded the first Sanctuary of Memphis in Egypt, in substitution of the demolished Sanctuary in Paris.

This occurred in 1867, and Prince Halim Pasha, son of the famous Mehemet Ali, was elected Grand Master of the Order, which prospered greatly until 1868, when the G.M. was exiled, and the Lodges and Councils ceased to work. In 1869 the Sanctuary, which worked for a time in secret with a limited number of Patriarchs, also fell into abeyance; but the Rite of Memphis—which at that time had not resigned its pretensions to control the three degrees of the Craft—revived December 21, 1872, when, with the sanction of the Khedive, S. A. Zola was elected and proclaimed G.M. of the Sanctuary of Memphis—Grand National Orient of Egypt; and in 1874 was further authorised to assume the title of Grand Hierophant—97°—the supreme office of the Rite. In the following year two treaties were concluded between the Grand Orient of Egypt—*i.e.*, the Rite of Memphis working 96 degrees—and the A. and A.S.R., working the 33d and some other (so-called) lower degrees. By these treaties, which recited that the A. and A.S.R. (in Egypt) was established in 1864 by charter from the G.O

---

[1] *Ante*, p. 193.   [2] *Ibid*, pp. 134, 189, 194.

of Naples—which in like manner had derived its authority from a Spanish source—and that the Order of Memphis (in Egypt) held under a charter from Paris, dated 1864, it was agreed: —That a Body should be formed like the Grand Council of Rites in Ireland; that the jurisdiction " of the G.O. of Egypt should be limited to the first three symbolic grades, and that the Rites of Memphis, and of the A. and A.S.R., should work the remainder."

In 1876—May 8—the Grand Orient was reorganised, and constituted a Federal Diet of Egyptian Masonry. It was resolved that there should be three Grand Masonic Bodies in the Valley of the Nile, each of which should be different, distinct, and separate from the others :—I. The National Grand Lodge of Egypt; II., The Supreme Council of the A. and A.S.R. 33°; and III. The Sov. Grand Council of the 96° of the Memphis Rite. The two latter bodies were to work from the 4° and upwards, never interfering with the three first or symbolical degrees, which were to wholly belong to the National Grand Lodge of Egypt.

It has been asserted that in the formation of an Independent Grand Lodge, the initiative was taken some years previously by a few French and Italian Lodges, but even if this was the case, the earlier movement certainly merged into the proceedings of 1876. At this period the number of subordinate Lodges had risen from 8 to 15. In 1878 the Grand Lodge of Egypt was included in the family of European Grand Lodges noticed in the official calendar of the Grand Lodge af England.

Down to 1879 Zola was at the head of each of the three divisions of the Diet; but in that year, in order if possible to bring the English Lodges within the fold, Ralph Borg was elected to the chair of the Grand Lodge, which soon after separated from the other divisions, and proclaimed itself free, sovereign, and wholly independent of the Federal Diet. In the same year the National Grand Lodge entered into a concordat with the National Grand Orient —under Zola—whereby the Memphis Rite, " out of courtesy and goodwill towards its offspring, the Grand Lodge of Egypt," agreed to waive its right to work the three first degrees of Masonry.

Zola resigned the position of Grand Hierophant—97°—April 6, 1883, in favour of Professor Oddi.

Under the National Grand Lodge of Egypt there are now (1886) 25 Lodges, with a total membership of about 400. The G.M. is Dr Iconomopulo.[1]

TUNIS.—In this Regency, as in many other parts of the world where the exercise of " concurrent jurisdiction " by competing Grand Bodies is indulged in, the Craft is represented by a variety of Lodges, which reflect pretty clearly the national instincts of the brethren who compose them. The French Lodges are three in number, the English two, and there is one under the G.O. of Italy. Of the French Lodges, two hail from the Grand Orient—Perseverance (1860) and New Carthage (1885), and one from the S.C. 33°—Secrecy (1862). The dates of formation of the English Lodges have been already given ;[2] that of the Italian Lodge—Resurrection—I am unable to supply.

Besides the above, a Grand Lodge of Tunis held its first session July 17, 1879, under a Signor Cassanello as G.M., and claimed at that date to have eight Lodges under its jurisdic-

---

[1] Authorities :—Masonic Calendars ; Bolletino Officiale del Grande Oriente Nazionale Egiziano, April 1883, and December 1875 ; the Kneph ; and Letters from Professor F. F. Oddi and Mr John Yarker.

[2] *Ante,* p. 323.

tion. Two years later—May 2, 1881—this apparently became a Grand *Orient* under an authority from the Supreme Council—A. and A.S.R. 33°—of Italy.

It remains to be stated that according to the leading journal of this country there is in existence a widely spread system of "Moslem Political Freemasonry." This has five sub-divisions, one of which—the powerful confraternity of Sidi Abdel Kader el Chiliani—possesses a college at Kairwan.[1]

ALGERIA.—In this French province there are at the present time ten Lodges under the G.O. and five under the S.C. 33° of France. The earliest—Belisarius—which still exists, was founded by the former, January 1, 1832. It may be added that throughout Africa the native race taking the most intelligent interest in Freemasonry are the Arabs of Algeria, of whom the late heroic Emir, Abd-el-Kadr, may be cited as the most prominent example.

MOROCCO.—A Lodge was formed at Tangier—Union, No. 194—under the S.C. of France in 1867, and one also exists—or at least did so, until quite recently—under the G.O. of Spain at Ceuta.

In 1882, the number of competing jurisdictions in the Sultanate was increased by the action of the Grand Lodge of Manitoba, which in that year proceeded to throw off a shoot in Morocco. This, however, was effected in a somewhat singular manner, as the "Special Deputy" entrusted with a warrant for the establishment of a Lodge at Tangier, granted the founders permission to assemble temporarily at Gibraltar—and subsequently at St Roque, in Andalusia. The course thus pursued was disavowed, and the commission of the Special Deputy revoked, but the Lodge—Al-Moghreb-Al-Aksa—is now at work in Tangier, which is the seat of government of the "Masonic District of Morocco," under the Grand Lodge of Manitoba.

WEST COAST OF AFRICA.

Richard Hull was appointed Provincial G.M. for Gambay, West Africa, in 1735; David Creighton, M.D., was similarly commissioned for Cape Coast in 1736; and William Douglas for the African Coast and American Islands in 1737. Notwithstanding these appointments by the (older) Grand Lodge of England, the earliest Lodge in the western portion of the Continent established by that body, seems to have been No. 586, at Bulam, constituted in 1792. After this came the Torridzonian Lodge, No. 621, at Cape Coast Castle, in 1810. The former of these disappeared at the Union (1813), but the latter was only erased March 5, 1862, though doubtless inactive for a long time previously, as three Lodges of much later constitution—Nos. 721, Sierra Leone, 1820; 599, Cape Coast, 1833; and 867, Bathurst, River Gambia, 1851—were likewise struck off the roll on the same occasion. Two further English Lodges were established in the district—Nos. 1075, Cape Coast Castle, 1859; and 1171, Lagos, West Coast, 1867—both of which are still shown in the list.

At Senegal, the name given to the French possessions in Senegambia, there are two Lodges, one—Union, 1874—under the G.O. of France; the other—Misa—under that of Italy.

LIBERIA.—This remarkable State, colonised in 1821 by a handful of freed slaves from the United States, recruited ever since by emigrants of the same class and by the wretched cargoes of captured slave vessels, acknowledged in 1847 as an independent Republic, governed, and

---

[1] *The Times*, September 27, 1881. Kairwan, long the capital of Moslem Africa, and formerly a place of great literary eminence, is still considered a sacred town.

well governed too, on the American model, by the elsewhere despised negro race, with a navy of one vessel (a present from England), a college with professorial chairs all filled by negroes, —this successful outcome of a daringly humane experiment, which has partly civilised countless hordes of natives on its borders, possesses an independent Grand Lodge of its own, with a seat at Monrovia, the capital. I can well imagine that its Masonic history, properly told, would prove both interesting and instructive, but unfortunately nothing beyond the barest statistics are at my command. A Grand Lodge was established in 1867, of which the first G.M. was Amos, an ex-Pennsylvanian slave. In 1870 he died, and was followed by Joseph Roberts, an ex-President of the Republic. According to the Masonic Calendars, in 1876 C. B. Dunbar was the Grand Master, with five Lodges; in 1877, Reginald A. Sherman; and in 1881, William M. Davis, with six Lodges and 125 members. No enlargement of the jurisdiction has since occurred, the same G.M. is in office, and the Rite practised is the pure one of the English Craft.

THE AZORES.—In these, which form a province, and not a dependency, of Portugal, there is a Lodge under the United Grand Lusitanian Orient. That jurisdiction is a favourite one in the islands of the North Atlantic, as we find in MADEIRA three, and in the CANARIES [1] nine, Lodges holding warrants from the same G.O.

ST HELENA.—An (Atholl) Lodge—No. 132—was established in this island in 1764, and another—No. 568—under the (older) Grand Lodge of England in 1798. The former became extinct in 1766, but the latter was carried forward at the Union (1813), though it did not survive the renumbering of 1832. Lieut.-Colonel Francis Robson was appointed Prov. G.M. in 1801, and David Kay, M.D., in 1803, both holding office under the senior of the two Grand Lodges. The latter continued for several years to preside over a Province in which there was no Lodge; but a revival took place in 1843, when No. 718 was erected, and a second Lodge— No. 1214—came into existence in 1862. Both of these meet at James Town, and are still active.

The 20th Foot—to which the famous "Minden Lodge," No. 63, was attached by the Grand Lodge of Ireland in 1748—formed the guard over Napoleon in 1819-21; but the historian of the Lodge informs us, "the political and peculiar state of the island during our station at St Helena, the severity of duty, the want of a building, all operated to prevent the best intentions .˙. .˙. to assemble for Masonic purposes." [2]

In the only other British island on the coast of Africa lying south of the Equator— ASCENSION—a Lodge, No. 1029 on the English roll, was erected in 1864, but has ceased to exist.

SOUTH AFRICA.

The Cape Settlement was taken by a British naval force in 1795, restored to Holland in 1802, retaken in 1806, and permanently ceded to Britain at the Congress of Vienna.

Dutch Lodges—"Of Good Hope," and "Of Good Trust"—were erected at Cape Town in 1772 and 1802 respectively. These, happily, survive; but several Lodges, at least, in South Africa under the same jurisdiction appear to have passed away without leaving any trace of their existence.

After the final cession of the colony, Lodges under the rival Grand Lodges of England were

---

[1] *Cf. ante*, p. 315.   [2] Sergeant-Major J. Clarke, Hist. of the Minden Lodge, 1849, p. 18.

established at the capital in 1811 and 1812 respectively—in the former year, the "British," No. 629, under the older sanction; and in the latter, No. 354, the "Cape of Good Hope" Lodge, in the 10th Battalion of the Royal Artillery, under an Atholl warrant.

The first band of English settlers arrived in 1820, and in the following year a second stationary Lodge, under the United Grand Lodge of England—Hope, No. 727—was erected at Cape Town—where, also, a Lodge bearing the same name, under the G.O. of France, sprang up, November 10, 1824. A third English Lodge—Albany, No. 817—was established at Grahamstown in 1828. "The Dutch Lodges received the English brethren with open arms, and with great satisfaction. When English Masonry had increased, and it was considered right to form a Provincial Grand Lodge, the brother selected for the office of Prov. G.M. was the Deputy G.M. of the Netherlands, who continued till his death to hold the two appointments."[1] This must have been Sir John Truter, who received an English patent in 1829; for although an earlier Prov. G.M. under England—Richard Blake—had been appointed in 1801, the words quoted above will not apply to the latter. Between 1828 and 1850 there was no augmentation of the Lodges; but in the latter year a revival set in, and during the decade immediately ensuing—1851-60—six[2] were warranted by the Grand Lodge of England.

In 1860, to the jurisdictions already existing (those of Holland and England) was added that of Scotland, under the Grand Lodge of which country a Lodge—Southern Cross, No. 398—was erected at Cape Town. Shortly afterwards, in a single year (1863) two Dutch Lodges were established in Cape Colony, and one at Bloemfontein, in the Orange Free State. This period coincides with the appointment—after an *interregnum*—of the Hon. Richard Southey as Prov. G.M. under the G.L. of England; and it will be convenient if I here proceed to describe *seriatim* the progress of Masonry under the three competing jurisdictions. Commencing with that of England, between the date to which the statistics were last given (1860) down to the close of 1885, 62 Lodges were added to the roll. The number at present existing in South Africa, as shown by the official calendar of current date, is 54, viz.: Eastern Division, 24; Western Division, 8; Natal, 11; and 11 not subject to any provincial authority, some of which were formerly under the District Grand Lodge of Griqualand (*now* abolished), and two—Nos. 1022, at Bloemfontein (Orange Free State), and 1747, at Pretoria (Transvaal)—are situate in foreign territory. Within the same period—1860-85—12 Lodges have been established under the Grand Lodge of Scotland, and now compose a Masonic District (or Province). The Dutch Masonic Calendar for 1886 shows 23 Lodges as existing in South Africa. Of these, as already related, two were erected before 1803, and three in 1863. The latest on the present list dates from 1884. These Lodges are distributed throughout the British possessions and the different Boer Republics as follows, viz.: In British South Africa, 16;[3] in the Orange Free State, 4; and in the Transvaal, 3; and at the head of all is a Deputy National G.M.—Mr J. H. Hofmeijr—at Cape Town.

The relations between the English and Dutch Masons at the Cape have always been of the

---

[1] Proceedings, Grand Lodge of England, June 5, 1867.

[2] Nos. 871, 884, 987, 1013, 1040, and 1130—in the Sovereignty, Fort Beaufort, King William's Town, Port Elizabeth, Durban, and Grahamstown respectively.

[3] The date of constitution of one of these—the "Union," No. 50, at Graaf Reinet—is given as ¹⁸³⁴⁄₁₈₆₆ in the Official Calendar. From this may be inferred, that it was originally formed in 1834, and revived in 1866; also, that other Dutch Lodges were constituted in South Africa between 1802 and 1860, which have ceased to exist!

most friendly character. When the D.G.L. under England was re-erected (1863), the Deputy G.M. under the Grand Lodge of the Netherlands assisted at its re-inauguration, and placed at the disposal of the English brethren, the Masonic Hall belonging to the Dutch Fraternity. At the celebration of the festival of St John, it has long been customary for the English and Dutch Masons to assemble at different hours of the day, in order that the brethren under each jurisdiction might be present at both meetings.

At a quarterly communication of the Grand Lodge of England, held June 5, 1867, it was stated, "recently an objection has been raised by some of the younger English Masons against the establishment of some new Lodges lately formed by the Dutch, on the ground that the Convention of 1770 [1] prohibits their doing so, the Cape now being an English possession, and having been so since the early part of the present century. In this view, the District Grand Lodge does not seem to participate. That body is anxious that the amicable relations that have so long subsisted between the English and Dutch Masons should continue. .·. .·. After setting the foregoing facts before the Grand Lodge, the Grand Registrar expressed an opinion that whatever might have been the intention of the Convention of 1770, it had not been acted on in the Cape Colony, but that the G.M. of England, by appointing the Deputy G.M. of the Netherlands to be his Prov. G.M. over English Lodges, virtually recognised the Dutch Lodges. It must be taken for granted that both the contracting parties have tacitly consented that it should not apply to the Cape. .·. He was of opinion that as both parties seem to have considered that the Cape was neutral ground, and the existence of two Grand Lodges having been allowed to continue side by side, it would be for the benefit of the Brethren in that Colony, that as they have gone on working as friends and brothers, they should still continue to do so." [2] A resolution embodying the foregoing was then put and unanimously adopted.

SOUTH AFRICAN ISLANDS.

RÉUNION, or BOURBON.—Masonry appears to have been established with some success in this island, under the sanction of the Grand Orient of France. Lodges "Perfect Harmony," "Happy Reunion," and "Triple Union" were erected in 1775, 1777, and 1784; the second in order at St Pierre, and the others at St Denis, the capital—where also there was a Provincial Grand Lodge (taking rank from 1781), presided over in 1787 by De Beurnonville,[3] afterwards Marshal of France. Other Lodges sprang into existence—under the same authority— "Friendship," 1816 (revived 1859); "Happy Union," 1819; and "Beneficence," 1862. With the exception of Lodge "Friendship," however—which is also a Chapter and Areopagus—all the bodies enumerated above have ceased to exist.

MAURITIUS, or ISLE OF FRANCE.—Lodges—under the G.O. of France—were established at Port Louis, "Triple Hope," 1778; "The Twenty-One," 1785; "The Fifteen Articles," 1786; and "Peace," 1790. In 1810 the island was captured by Britain, to whom the seizure was confirmed at the peace of 1814. The Earl of Moira, on his way to India, stayed a short time at the Mauritius, and—August 19, 1813—"at the head of all the Masons of the island, laid in Masonic form, the first stone of the (Catholick) Cathedral of Port Louis." [4] Lodge "Peace,"

---

[1] Chaps. XX., p. 474; XXVI., p. 204.   [2] Proceedings G.L. of England.   [3] Chap. XXV., pp. 169, 174.
[4] Daruty, *op. cit.*, p. 65.

after a slumber, resumed its labours in 1857, but is again dormant or extinct, and the only Lodges at present active under the Grand Orient of France are "Triple Hope" (1778), and "Beneficence"—constituted in 1881.

In 1811 R. T. Farquhar was appointed Prov. G.M. "of the Isle of France" under the Grand Lodge of England, but no Lodge was formed in the jurisdiction until 1816, when No. 676—Faith and Loyalty—came into existence. This was short-lived, becoming extinct before 1832, and the next English Lodge on the island was the British—No. 1038—erected in 1858. After which came the Lodge of Harmony—No. 1143—in 1860 (*now* extinct), followed by one bearing the same title—No. 1535—(possibly a revival), in 1875; and Friendship—No. 1696 —in 1877.

An Irish Lodge—No. 235—was established at Port Louis in 1858, the warrant of which was surrendered in 1873, but a later one—Independent, No. 236—erected in 1878, still holds its ground.

Scotland is represented by a single Lodge, the "Friendship"—No. 439—chartered in 1864. The fifth and last Masonic jurisdiction which remains to be noticed is that of the Supreme Council of France, under which *L'Amitie*, No. 245, was added to the roll of Lodges on the island, March 30, 1877.[1]

A resolution, expressing sympathy with the brethren in the Mauritius under the persecutions they had experienced at the hands of the Roman Catholic authorities in that island, was adopted unanimously by the Grand Lodge of England, December 5, 1855.

SEYCHELLES.—In these dependencies of the Mauritius a Lodge—Sincere Reunion—was erected at Mahé, the largest island of the group, under the G.O. of France in 1869.

MOZAMBIQUE.—This island and town forms the capital of the Portuguese possessions in S.E. Africa. It possesses two Lodges, both of which hold their warrants from the United Grand Lusitanian Orient.

THE WEST INDIES.

By the expression "West Indies," is understood the large group of islands lying east of Central, and north of South America. Of these the northernmost are the Bahamas or Lucayos—a long archipelago. South-west of them stretches the vast island of Cuba, the most important of the whole group, as well as the principal member of the Greater Antilles, within which are also comprised Jamaica, Hayti, Porto Rico, and several smaller islands.

East of Porto Rico begin the Lesser Antilles, also known as the Caribbee Islands, by navigators again sub-divided into the two groups of the Windward and Leeward Islands, so-called in accordance with the direction in which they lie with regard to the prevailing easterly trade wind. With a single important exception all these islands belong to European nations, being shared between Great Britain, Holland, Sweden, Denmark, France, and Spain. The solitary exception is Hayti, which is divided into two independent native states. Some few also of the Leeward group belong to the South American Republic of Venezuela.

Much confusion has arisen from the same name being given to different islands, and from the same island having different names. Thus, there is Barbadoes and Barbudo, whilst the

---

[1] Throughout this Chapter the Lodges under the G.O. and S.C. of France are taken from the calendars of those bodies, and from the lists given by Rebold (Hist. des Trois G.L.) and Daruty (Recherches, etc.).

Saintes[1] were at one time called Barbata. St Christopher is commonly termed St Kitts, Porto Rico was formerly known as San Juan—the proximity of the latter to St John naturally introducing a new element of uncertainty. Then we have Cariacou, one of the Grenadines, and Curaçoa. The Bahamas, as observed above, were likewise the Lucayos. Hispaniola, St Domingo, and Hayti are all appellations for one island, and St Domingo is also the name of the principal city in the Spanish part of it. Two islands are called Anguila; there is a *New* as well as an *Old* Providence—and the latter was also known as St Catherine. The *island* of Samana occasionally comes in conflict with the peninsula of the same name in Hispaniola. Three islands in the West Indies were called Santa Cruz, and the same name is borne by a group in the South Pacific, and by the capital of the Canaries. There is Tortuga and the Tortugas, and the following very puzzling names of towns :—Basseterre, the capital both of Guadaloupe and St Kitts; St Pierre, a town in Martinique, and also in Réunion (or Bourbon) ; St Louis, common to Guadaloupe and Senegal; St Denis, a town in France, as well as the capital of Réunion ; Port Louis, a seaport of France, and the capital of the Mauritius; St George, the name of towns in Grenada and Bermuda; and lastly, Santiago, the most familiar title of all, which occurs not only in Old and New Spain (Hispaniola), the Cape Verde islands, Cuba, and Jamaica, but is also met with both in Central and South America.

It will be seen, therefore, that a study of the Masonic history of the West Indies is beset with a new class of difficulties, differing materially from those which have been already encountered in our previous researches. A great part of the information upon which I am obliged to rely, is contained in old calendars where the name of a town or an island is, as often as not, given without any real approach to exactitude. Less uncertainty prevails, as we gradually sail down the river of time, but even when approaching our own times, the references to Lodges in foreign parts (*en pays étrangers*) under continental jurisdictions, by the most discursive of writers, are in too many instances both vague and misleading. In every case, however, I have carefully compared all the authorities at my disposal, and to the extent that the particulars I am about to give fall short of being absolutely exhaustive, I hope some readers may be found who, with greater opportunities than myself, will be able to supply the deficiency.

I. The Greater Antilles.

CUBA.—*Le Temple des Vertus Theologales*, No. 103—with the notorious Joseph Cerneau as first Master—was chartered at Havana by the Grand Lodge of Pennsylvania, December 17, 1804.[2] Other Lodges were erected under the same sanction—Nos. 157, 161 in 1818; 166, 167 in 1819; and (at Santiago de Cuba) 175 in 1820, and 181 in 1822. All, however, but the last two had died out by 1822, and in 1826 the charters of Nos. 175 and 181 were revoked, because the Lodges had failed to meet for more than a year. The privilege of warranting Lodges on

---

[1] This denotes three of the Caribbee Islands, and is also the name of a town in France.

[2] During the progress of the negro revolution, three Lodges originally constituted in Hispaniola—Réunion des Cœurs (*French*), Concorde, and Persévérance (*Pennsylvanian*)—were reorganised at Santiago de Cuba in 1805-6. Again dispersed in 1808, many of the members removed to New Orleans in 1809, where—October 7, 1810—the two Lodges first named amalgamated, as No. 117 (Concord), under the G. L. of Pennsylvania, by which body a Charter—No. 118, Perseverance—was also granted the same day to certain petitioners, "chiefly refugees from San Domingo and Cuba."

the island was next assumed by the Grand Lodges of Louisiana and South Carolina, under the former of which bodies sprang up Nos. 7, 1815, 11 and 14, 1818 ; and under the latter Nos. 50—*La Constancia*, 1818, and 52—*La Amenidad*, 1819. Then followed the Grand Orient of France with a Lodge and consistory (32°), 1819; and two further Lodges—*La Constante Sophie* and *L'Humanité*,[1] 1821. In the year last named a circular was received by the G.L. of South Carolina from the G.L. of Ancient Freemasons in Havana, stating that a Grand Lodge had been organised there, to which the Lodge *La Amenidad* requested permission to transfer its allegiance. A favourable answer was of course returned, but the G.L. of South Carolina retained on its roll *La Constancia* for a few years, when the warrant was surrendered by the members "in consequence of the religious and political persecutions to which they were subjected."

For many years Masonry languished in the "Pearl of the Antilles," its votaries practising their rites in secret, but not daring to indulge in any overt acts, which might entail not only expulsion from the country, but also confiscation of their property. At length, however, a faint revival set in, and a warrant was granted, November 17, 1859, by the Grand Lodge of South Carolina to St Andrew's Lodge, No. 93, "for the purpose of establishing, with two other Lodges [2] already existing on the island, a Grand Lodge," which was accomplished on December 5 of the same year.

An independent "Grand Lodge of Colon" was thus established at Santiago de Cuba, and —December 27, 1859—a Supreme Council of the A. and A.S.R. 33° was founded in the same city by Andres Cassard.[3]

At this time, it must be recollected, the practice of assembling as Freemasons was forbidden by the Spanish laws, which laws, moreover, though destined to become—after the dethronement of Queen Isabella (1868)—innocuous in the Peninsula, remained for a long time in full force in Cuba.

Several, indeed, of the Captains General and other officers who ruled the island were Masons, and therefore from time to time the Craft was tolerated, but its members being always compelled to work to a great extent in the dark, found it necessary to observe the most inviolable secrecy, and even to shield themselves under "Masonic names,"[4] lest by the discovery of their own, they might incur the most grievous penalties.

For the same reason the Supreme Council and the Grand Lodge, which soon after united in forming a Grand Orient, found a convenient title for the amalgamated body in the name of Colon—the Spanish for Columbus—it being desired above all things to conceal from the public ken the seat of the "Grand East" of the Society.

At the formation of the Grand Orient of Colon, a constitution published at Naples in

---

[1] At *Saint-Yago*, which I take to be *Santiago de Cuba* ?

[2] Two excellent authorities, Messrs Albert Pike and Josiah H. Drummond, concur in the belief that these were *Spanish* Lodges—*i.e.*, holding warrants from some Peninsular authority. The state of Masonic anarchy, however, at that time prevailing in Spain, wholly forbids an investigation of this interesting point. *Cf. ante*, p. 316.

[3] Under the sanction of the S.C. 33° for the Southern Jurisdiction (Charleston) U.S.A., for the Masonic jurisdiction of Cuba, and other "unoccupied" West India Islands.

[4] *Cf. ante*, pp. 308, 316. Among the names given in an official report dated August 6, 1873, of the officers of the S.C. of Colon are "Bismark" and "Josaphat," but a paragraph states—"the real names of the officers you will find in the enclosed slip, and are not stated here, to prevent their being divulged should this communication come to print" (New England Freemason, February 1874, p. 80).

1820,[1] was adopted as that of the new organisation. By this the Supreme Council necessarily became a section of the Grand Orient. In 1865 a new constitution was promulgated. The Sov. G. Com. of the Supreme Council became—*ex officio*—G.M. of the Grand Orient, but the G.M. of the Grand Lodge was still required to submit himself for election. All charters for Lodges were issued by the Grand Lodge, but had to be confirmed and *viséd* by the Supreme Council.

In 1867 the Grand Lodge promulgated a constitution of its own, in which, while recognising its continued membership of the Grand Orient, it claimed the *exclusive* power to enact its own by-laws, issue charters, constitute and regulate Lodges. Their right to do this was denied by the Supreme Council. In 1868—September 30—the Grand Lodge *suspended*[2] its constitution until a meeting took place of the Grand Orient, convoked for November 30. But before that time the revolution broke out, and Freemasons being regarded by the Spanish government as revolutionists,[3] the G.O. could not meet. The Grand Lodge, so far as it was possible, resumed labour. But the times were unpropitious. In the winter of 1869, at Santiago de Cuba, by order of Gonzales Bret, an officer of the government, eighteen persons were seized without warrant, and immediately shot, without a trial, for being Freemasons— one of them the M.W.G.M. of Colon—and many others were arrested and committed to prison for the same offence.

The number of Cuban Lodges, which in 1868 amounted to about thirty, had fallen in 1870 to about seven, and in the latter year the S.C. organised a Provincial Mother Lodge at Havana, against which the Grand Lodge very naturally protested. The warrant to this "Mother Lodge" was soon after recalled, but the dispute between the S.C. and the Grand Lodge continued. In 1873—April 11—the Grand Lodge resumed work openly, and in the following year entered into a compact with the Supreme Council, whereby it was agreed that the former should have exclusive jurisdiction over Symbolic Masonry, with the sole right of chartering Lodges, and that it should establish a Provincial Mother Lodge[4] in the western section of the island to govern the Lodges there, but in submission to the laws of the Grand Lodge. After this compact it is contended that the Grand Lodge, though still nominally a section in the Grand Orient, had full jurisdiction over Symbolical Masonry. Nevertheless, it is quite clear that there was a divided authority, and apparently great Masonic confusion on the island.

The Grand Lodge of Colon held five meetings in August 1876, on the last of which—

---

[1] According to M. Lecerff, however—"in Naples a Grand Orient was founded, which in 1830 [*not* 1820] enacted its constitution and by-laws, entitling the book '*General Statutes of the Scottish Rite;*' these came to America, and happened to come to hand of (*sic*) Brother Andres Cassard, the propagator of Masonry in South and Central America; in establishing Masonry in those countries, he gave the *General Statutes* as the universal laws of Masonry, and the Grand Orient system with the allegiance of all to the thirty-third degree was provided for therein" (Proc. Grand Lodge of *Cuba*, 1879).

[2] This, by the rival Grand Lodge of *Cuba*, the proceedings of which will shortly enter into the narrative, was most erroneously styled a *dissolution* of the Grand Lodge of *Colon*. The Lodges under the latter were in consequence deemed to have become "orphaned" by the former, who straightway constituted itself the foster-parent of a number of them!

[3] I am told by Mr G. W. Speth, who resided on the island at the time, that the sympathies of the Freemasons were undoubtedly ranged on what the government regarded—not unnaturally—as the *wrong side*.

[4] Instituted in April and dissolved in July 1875.

August 26—it declared itself free from all other authority, a sovereign body, with full and unlimited powers over its subordinates.

This action, however, was accelerated by an event which had taken place on August 1, when the representatives of nine chartered Lodges, and of four under dispensation,[1] met at Havana, and formed the Grand Lodge of Cuba. This body from the very first kept itself free from the blighting influence of the (so-called) high degrees,[2] which it willingly consented— December 31, 1876—should be ruled in Cuba by the Grand Orient of Spain. In a circular of September 4, 1876, the Grand Lodge of Colon claimed to have on its register 36 Lodges and 8000 members; whilst its newly-formed rival, the Grand Lodge of Cuba, in 1877, possessed an apparent following of 17 Lodges. In the latter year—June 3—a second Grand Lodge of Colon (or Columbus) at Havana was added to the two existing Craft Grand bodies.

Thus we find three organisations, each claiming to be the regular Grand Lodge. From a circular of the Grand Lodge of Cuba, we learn that in 1879 the three Lodges which formed the Grand Lodge of Colon at Santiago de Cuba in 1859, and four others, adhered to that body; but that the remaining Lodges—excepting those under the Grand Lodge of Cuba—were subject to the control of the Grand Lodge of Colon at Havana. To local jealousies must be attributed this multiplication of Grand Lodges. The representatives of some of the Havana Lodges seceded from the old (or *original*) Grand Lodge of Colon at Santiago de Cuba, met *as the Grand Lodge*, and decreed its removal to Havana.

Eventually, however, the Grand Lodges of Colon (at Havana) and Cuba formally united, and—March 28, 1880—the G.M. of one body became Grand Master, and the G.M. of the other body Deputy Grand Master. The title assumed by the new organisation was the United Grand Lodge of Colon and the Island of Cuba, and it entered upon its career with a roll of 57 Lodges, and between 5000 and 6000 Masons. The Lodges under the original Grand Lodge of Colon at Santiago de Cuba, I believe, remained true to their allegiance.[3]

In 1885, the number of Lodges under the "United Grand Lodge" had apparently increased to 82, with Provincial Grand Lodges at Santiago de Cuba and Porto Rico; but from the official List,[4] which has just reached me, I find there are now only 58 Lodges in all upon the roll. Of these, 30 are at the capital, or in its vicinity, and 28 in other parts. It is possible that further schisms may have disturbed the peace of Cuban Masonry; and it strikes me as somewhat remarkable, that the Provincial Grand Lodge of Porto Rico—with the fourteen subordinate Lodges on that island, shown in sundry Calendars for 1886—have wholly disappeared in the official list of current date.[5]

It only remains to be stated, that from the statistics before me, there would appear to be in existence on the island 13 Lodges under the National Grand Orient, and 27 under the

---

[1] Of these Lodges, six were chartered by the Grand Lodge of Colon *before*, and three *after*, 1868. The remaining four acted under dispensations from the *two* Provincial Mother Lodges.

[2] In a printed circular of the Grand Lodge of Cuba, dated April 30, 1879, the following is assigned as one of the reasons for the formation of that body:—"IX.—The majority of the Lodges working in the western part of the Island (then the full majority of the Lodges in the whole country) now resolved not to suffer any more the arbitrary and irregular authority of the Supreme Council and its subordinates, the 'Grand Symbolical Lodge' and the 'Provincial Mother-Lodge of the West.'"

[3] *Cf. post*, pp. 372, 373.

[4] In a letter from Sr. Manuel N. Ocego, of Havana, dated May 8, 1886.   [5] *Cf. post*, p. 360.

Grand Lodge of Spain. The latter are subject to a Prov. G.M., whose jurisdiction also extends to Porto Rico.[1]

HISPANIOLA.—This island is divided into the republics of Hayti in the west, and St (*or* Santo) Domingo in the east. It was originally a Spanish possession, but the western portion was ceded in 1697 to the French, under whom it prospered rapidly, and in 1789 contained 793 sugar plantations, 3117 coffee plantations, 789 cotton plantations, and 182 establishments for making rum, besides other minor factories and workshops.

But the conflicting diversity of race, and monopoly of political power by the whites, led to a rupture on the outbreak of the revolution in the mother country. After fierce revolts of the mulattoes and negroes, and inroads of the English and Spanish, all the inhabitants of the colony were declared free and equal in 1793, and the command of the army was given to Toussaint l'Ouverture, who expelled the hostile intruders, and restored peace to the island.

English troops arrived in Hayti from Jamaica in 1793, and afterwards were poured into the country; but they came to die. The 82d Foot, numbering 880 men, lost all but 50 in ten weeks. Another regiment, in the same time, lost 700 men out of 1000; and it is stated that the 96th Foot perished to a man.[2] Major-General Sir Adam Williamson,[3] who succeeded the Earl of Effingham[4] as Governor of Jamaica, ultimately followed the troops sent from that island, with the title of Governor-General of St Domingo. At the close of 1798, however, when the colony was evacuated, millions of treasure had been wasted, twenty thousand soldiers and sailors had perished, whilst there never had been any reasonable prospect of conquering the island.[5]

The Spanish territory was ceded to France in 1795, but Napoleon attempted to re-establish slavery in 1801, and the inhabitants shook off the French yoke in 1803, St Domingo in that year declaring itself an independent republic. A period of confusion then ensued, there being no less than five distinctive governments upon the island in 1810. The whole of it passed again under a single republic, that of Hayti, in 1822, but in 1844 the Dominicans reasserted their independency, and the two districts have since remained separate. The territory comprised within the republic of St Domingo was ceded to Spain in 1861, but again declared free by an act of the Cortes, March 3, 1865.

Of the present condition of St Domingo, Mr Hazard, a recent traveller, gives a deplorable account. The fertile plains lie untilled; the rich mines are unworked. There is not a plough in the whole island; and the only steam engine ever set up was destroyed by the Spaniards in 1865.

[1] Authorities:—J. B. Scot, Freemasonry in Louisiana, 1873; Early Hist. G.L. of Pennsylvania, vol. i., 1877-84; New England Freemason, Feb. 1874, p. 75; Proceedings, Committees on Correspondence, Grand Lodges of Indiana, 1870; Canada, 1871; New Brunswick, 1877, 1878, 1880; *Cuba,* 1879 [by E. E. Lecerff, *now* Ch. Com. For. Cor. United Grand Lodge of Colon and Cuba]; Maine [containing the masterly report of Josiah H. Drummond, presented May 1879]; and Connecticut, 1880; Letters from Mr Ch. Inglesby and Sr. D. José F. Pellón, G. Secretaries, South Carolina, and Cuba (*United* Grand Lodge), dated April 6 and May 25, 1886, respectively.

[2] Bryan Edwards, Hist. of the West Indies, vol. iii., p. 411.

[3] Prov. G.M. of Jamaica under the original Grand Lodge of England, 1793-98.

[4] Acting Grand Master of England—under the Duke of Cumberland, G.M.—1782-89.

[5] The loss of the English has been estimated by a recent writer at 45,000 men, and twenty millions sterling. *Cf.* Hazard, p. 131.

In the republic of Hayti, on the western side of this beautiful island, the state of things is even worse than in the eastern or Dominican part. All traces of the old French civilisation have vanished. There are no manufactures, and the government is bankrupt; the towns are in ruins, and the men spend their time in idleness, living on the industry of the women.[1]

Two Lodges—*St Jean de Jérusalem Écossaise* and *Concorde*—were formed on the island, under the *Grande Loge Anglaise de France*[2] in 1749. Others soon followed—*Frères Réunis*, 1763; *Amitié Indissoluble*, 1765; *Verité*, 1767; *Frères Choisis*, 1772;[3] and a Provincial Grand Lodge—under the Grand Orient—October 1, 1778. These were doubtless established on French territory, in the district now known as "Hayti," though the term "St Domingo" is alone used in the lists.

The remaining Lodges, constituted under French authority prior to the Revolution were—*L'Unanimité*, Petit Goave,[4] 1774; *Les Frères Zélés*, Cavaillon, 1775; *Raison Perfectionnée*, Petit Tron, 1779; *Réunion désirée*,[5] Port au Prince, 1783; *Choix des Hommes*, Jacmel, 1784; and *Frères Discrets*, Cayes, 1785 (Nos. 292, 291, 456, 466, 521, and 591).

Besides the degrees of the Craft, the rite of Perfection, as we have already seen,[6] had been introduced into the island by Stephen Morin in 1761, and doubtless continued to be worked until swept away—like all other vestiges of French domination—by the great political cataclysm, in which that remarkable personage is himself believed to have perished. We have seen that during the closing years of the eighteenth century Hispaniola had become the headquarters of the newly invented American rite, called—but without any valid reason—the A. and A.S.R. 33°, and that on the expulsion of the French colonists the rite in question had been introduced into France.[7]

The Dominican, or to speak with precision, the Haytian Lodges, which had served as the basis of the rite, in most cases closed their doors during the political troubles, and Freemasonry, which was strictly confined to the white inhabitants, became almost, if not quite, extinct.

A warrant was granted from Pennsylvania, in 1786, on the application of "a *Lodge* held at Cape François, directed to General Washington as Grand Master of all America." A second Lodge, under the same jurisdiction, was established at Port au Prince in 1789, which

---

[1] Bates, pp. 170, 172.

[2] *Ante*, p. 142. Down to 1787, where the *numbers* of French Lodges are given, these are taken from Daruty's lists, two of which are shown in his work, and begin at pp. 90 and 142 respectively. As a rule, Lodges constituted down to the year 1772, will be found in the earlier, and those erected after the formation of the Grand Orient, in the later lists. The numbers attached to Lodges under the S.C. 33° are the official ones.

[3] Nos. 39, 41, 107, 144, 187, and 255.

[4] A Lodge—*L'Humanité*, No. 27—was constituted at this place by the "Mother Lodge of the Scots Philosophic Rite" or "Social Contract," April 26, 1784. Several of the Lodges named above were also *re*-constituted by the same authority, but I am unable to record each transfer of allegiance—and shall content myself with naming the Lodges in the order of their first appearance. *Cf. ante*, p. 117.

[5] Removed to New Orleans for the second time, 1803. Duplicate Charter granted 1806. Lapsed, 1808.

[6] Chaps. XXIII., p. 59; XXIV., p. 125.

[7] Chaps. XXIV., p. 124; XXV., p. 164. Both De Grasse-Tilly and Hacquet—who so far anticipated him as to be first in the field with the revived Rite of Perfection—the former a planter and the latter a notary, were residents in the French (or western) side of St Domingo, *i.e.*, the part *now* known as Hayti.

continued to meet regularly throughout the political convulsions of 1791, and at the close of 1798 (as related in the Proceedings of the G.L. of Pennsylvania), "after having been obliged by reason of the disturbances in the island, their Lodge being burnt, etc., to suspend their Masonic operations, had again begun, and were carrying on their works."

In 1793—December 4—sundry French brethren, "driven from the island of St Domingo," were granted a dispensation by the Grand Lodge of New York to meet as a Lodge in that city for the period of six months. This, which was named La Tendre Amitié Franco-Americaine, surrendered its acting warrant, June 4, 1794; but the money and papers of the Lodge were delivered—by order of the Grand Lodge—to L'Unité Americaine, which took its place, May 19, 1795. The latter received a regular charter in 1797, becoming No. 12 on the roll, and in the same year was concerned in a series of irregularities which are not without interest in our present inquiry. From internal bickerings dissensions had arisen in the Lodge, and it decided to return the New York warrant, and revert " to the authority of their natural Grand Lodge of France." Accordingly, a French Lodge, L'Union Française, was established in New York, December 6, by Huet Lachelle, a Deputy G.M. under the jurisdiction of the G.O. of France, and Prov. G.M. for St Domingo. L'Unité Americaine after this made submission, was accorded grace, but split into two parts, one remaining the old Lodge, and the other becoming L'Union Française, No. 14 on the roll of New York. With the subsequent history of these bodies, we are not concerned; it will suffice to have learnt from the authority upon which I have relied for the foregoing details, that a large number of Haytian brethren found an asylum in New York; also, that the Prov. G.M. of "St Domingo" and four of his Grand Officers were included in the number of these refugees.[1]

In 1802, owing to the arrival of 30,000 veteran French troops, the negro forces of Toussaint l'Ouverture were compelled to retire to the mountains, and the survivors of the colonists who had fled to different countries returned in great numbers, but in 1803 were for the second time expelled. Meanwhile, however, the Grand Lodge of Pennsylvania had extended its jurisdiction in Hayti. Several Lodges were erected, a list of which will be found below;[2] and a Provincial Grand Lodge of St Domingo was established January 9, 1802. This was vacated (apparently in error) April 7, but reinstated September 15, 1806, and the jurisdiction extended to the island of Cuba—whither, with two of his Lodges, the Prov. G.M. had retired.

In 1806, in the portion of Hayti ruled by President Pèthion, some of the French Lodges revived, and negotiations were set on foot by one Trichet, which resulted in the erection of

[1] Barker, p. 227. L'Union Française, No. 14, consisted of twenty-eight charter (or *original*) members. The proceedings of these brethren are highly commended in one of the communications addressed to the G.L. of New York (1797) by Chalon Dayral, De Olior, Verdier, Courbe, and Huet Lachelle—who subscribe as "the administrator and officers of the R.W. Provincial Grand Lodge of San Domingo."

[2] Nos. 46 [ ], Cape François, February 3, 1786 ; 47, Union of Franco-American Hearts, Port au Prince, December 18, 1789; 87, Frères Ré-unis, the Cape, December 15, 1800 ; 88, Concorde, St Marc, May 4, 1801—reinstated September 15, 1806—surrendered September 4, 1809 ; 89, Frères Sincèrement Réunis, Cayes, May 4, 1801 ; 95, Humilité, Lusé à Veau, December 6, 1802; 97, Parfaite Harmonie, St Domingo, September 5, 1803 ; 98, Persévérance, Abricots, September 5, 1803—reinstated March 21, 1808—finally vacated October 27, 1810 ; 99, Temple du Bonheur, Arcapays, December 5, 1803. *All* the above, except No. 46 (extinct in 1790), were erased (or "vacated") April 7, 1806, and those only "reinstated" which are specifically mentioned. Nos. 95 and 97-99 were established in the first instance by the Prov. G.L. of St Domingo.

two Lodges under the (older) Grand Lodge of England in 1809.[1] This was followed up by the appointment of a Prov. G.M.—John Goff—in 1811,[2] and by the formation of two further English Lodges in 1817.[3] Meanwhile the efforts of the G.O. of France to obtain the upper hand were frustrated by the action of the Government.

About the same time—1810—in that part of the island under the sway of the Emperor Henry I., there was also a revival, and a vast number of so-called degrees, with pompous and unmeaning titles, were introduced by a charlatan named D'Obernay, which were accepted with avidity at the Imperial Court. After this came a pause, owing to the political convulsions which disturbed the peace of the island. In both of the existing Republics—mulatto and black—one revolution seems to have followed another, the only variation being the wars that from time to time broke out between the two States. But after the establishment of a single Government (1822) the English Prov. Grand Lodge was transformed—May 23, 1823—into an independent Grand Lodge of Hayti, with President Boyer as patron, and his Prime Minister, General Ingignac, as G.M. The constitutions were settled January 24, 1824, and the Grand Lodge was established on precisely the same basis as the United Grand Lodge of England. For many years the Craft prospered and pursued the even tenor of its way, until about 1830, when a certain St Lambert, an envoy of the Supreme Council of France (or A. and A.S.R. 33°), began to stir up strife by again attempting to propagate the high degrees.

Five Lodges in all, the two earliest of which are still in existence, were erected under the authority of the A. and A.S.R. ;[4] whilst the rival French jurisdiction, that of the Grand Orient, has only warranted a single Lodge on the island during the present century. This, " Les Mages du Tropique," was established at Cayes in 1831, and has long since disappeared from the roll of the G.O., though as an *Areopagus* distinguished by an identical title, and meeting at the same place, is shown in the *Tableau Des Ateliers*, Supreme Council of France, from which an extract will be found below,[5] it is natural to suppose that there must have been a transfer of allegiance.

In 1836 the Grand Lodge, with a view to terminating the confusion which prevailed, transformed itself into a Grand Orient. This alteration, of course, involved the institution of a Supreme Council 33°, which duly claimed the allegiance of all fluctuating bodies under the obedience of any branch of the Ancient and Accepted Scottish Rite.

In 1843, owing to an insurrection of the blacks, Boyer—the mulatto President—was displaced. A few years of turmoil then ensued, and the Craft once more languished. In 1845 a new envoy of the French Supreme Council, Fresnel, having obtained the protection of President Santana, almost overthrew the National G.O., but was himself ultimately expelled for political intrigue. After his departure the G.O. of Hayti revived, entered into a compact with

[1] Nos. 603 and 604—L'Amitié des Frères Réunis, Port au Prince, and L'Heureuse Réunion, Aux Cayes.

[2] A Royal Arch Chapter—Philanthropy—was established by the Grand Chapter of England (Moderns) in 1810.

[3] Nos. 699 and 700—Réunion des Cœurs réunis, Jeremie ; and Parfaite Sincerité des Cœurs réunis, Jacmel.

[4] Nos. 10, Élèves de la Nature, Cayes, 1822 ; 59, Philadelphes, Jacmel, 1837 ; 62, Vraie Gloire, St Marc, 1837 ; 97, Philalèthes, Port au Prince, 1845 ; 105, Constante Union, St Domingo, 1846.

[5] AREOPAGUS (30°)—No. 52, Les Mages du Tropique, Cayes, 1834. CHAPTERS (18°)—Nos. 49, La Constance Eprouvée, Cayes, 1832 ; 69, *Les Elus de la Vérité*, St Marc, 1839 ; 73, La Croix du Sud, Jacmel, 1840 ; and 106, *Les Croisés Dominicains*, St Domingo, 1846. LODGES—Nos. 10, Les Élèves de la Nature, Cayes, 1822 ; 59, Les Philadelphes, Jacmel, 1837 ; 62, *La Vraie Gloire*, St Marc, 1837 ; 97, *Les Philalèthes*, Port au Prince, 1845 ; and 105, *La Constante Union*, St Domingo, 1846. The italics denote bodies which are dormant or extinct.

the G.O. of France, and in 1851 ruled over no less than 31 Lodges, besides 49 associations of Masons which met under varied titles for the communication of the so-called high degrees.

The seat of the G.O. is at Port au Prince, and the Grand Masters, as far as I have been able to trace them, were (*circa*) 1860, J. de Paul, President of the Council; 1865, Dubois, Ambassador at London; 1871-80, A. T. Bouchereau, Senator; and since 1881, F. F. Duplessis, President of the Council of Instruction.

In 1844—February 27—total separation from Hayti was declared by the Dominicans, and the eastern (or Spanish) portion of the island formed itself into the republic of Santo Domingo. In 1861, as already related, it once more placed itself under the government of Spain. A revolt, however, broke out in 1863, and Spain finally relinquished its changeful child.

A Grand Orient of St Domingo was organised at the capital of the same name December 11, 1858. The Lodges taking part in this proceeding were originally warranted, 1830-34, by the G.O. of Hayti (Port au Prince), at the time when the whole island was under an undivided rule. Falling, however, into a state of somnolency during the wars, 1844-47, they were suppressed (or erased) in 1849. The G.O. of St Domingo, thus formed by these resuscitated Lodges, appears never to have had more than some half dozen daughters on its roll.

During the reunion with Spain, 1861-65, Masonry either died out or was practised in secret, but a Grand Lodge of the Dominican republic was organised—January 26, 1865—under Benito Perez as G.M. This was followed—October 22—by a Supreme Council for the High Degrees, and the two bodies united—January 1, 1866—in re-establishing a National Grand Orient.

In January 1867 Thomas Bobadilla presided over the G.O., with Castro as D.G.M.; whilst the Lodges were ten in number, with a total membership of about 2000.

The sequence of Grand Masters of the Grand *Lodge* has been as follows :—1858-59, Bobadilla; 1860, Antonio Abad Alfan; 1861, Jacinto de Castro; 1861-64, Grand Lodge *dormant;* 1865, Benito Perez; 1866, Manuel Echenique; 1867, Peter A. Delgado; 1869, Noël Henriquez; 1870, Sully du Breil. From 1871 the presidents of Grand Lodge are no longer given in the official lists, and whilst Bobadilla has ever since been G.M. of the G.O., the Grand Lodge and Supreme Council have evidently been relegated to the position of subordinate chambers, as indeed is generally more or less the custom in all Grand Orient systems.

In bringing this sketch to a close, it is only necessary to add that a solitary Lodge—Alianza, No. 251—appears to have been erected at "Santo Domingo" by the Grand Lodge of Spain, or in other words, by the governing Masonic body of which Don Manuel Becerra is the G.M.[1]

JAMAICA.—Lodges owning fealty to the Mother Grand Lodge of the world were of early introduction in this British dependency. The first was established at Kingston in 1739, and the second at Port Royal in 1742. But it is probable that the number of Masons in Jamaica

---

[1] Authorities :—S. Hazard, Santo Domingo, with a glance at Hayti, 1873 ; Dr J. R. Beard, Life of Toussaint l'Ouverture, 1853 ; H. W. Bates, Central America, the West Indies, and South America, 1878 ; Masonic Calendars ; Rebold, Histoire des trois Grandes Loges, pp. 150, 452 ; Daruty, p. 168 ; Findel, p. 698 ; Latomia, vol. xxvi., pp. 118, 119 ; Barker, Early History Grand Lodge of New York, pp. 144, 166, 215, 229 ; and Early History Grand Lodge of Pennsylvania. For some interesting remarks on the characteristics of a Grand *Orient* as contrasted with those of a Grand *Lodge* system, the curious reader is referred to the report on Foreign Correspondence already cited (*ante*, p. 352, note 1) of Mr Josiah H. Drummond of Maine.

at that period was much larger than would be inferred from these statistics, as there were ten thousand resident whites on the island in 1741; and in the same year the harbour of Port Royal was crowded with twenty-nine line-of-battle ships, and a large number of frigates, sloops, and transports, containing in all, fifteen thousand sailors and twelve thousand soldiers.[1]

Ballard Beckford, George Hynde, and Alexander Crawford were appointed Provincial Grand Masters for Jamaica by Lord Ward in 1742-44,[2] but the exact dates of their respective appointments there are no means of determining.

A third Lodge was erected on the island in 1746, but as we now approach a conflict of jurisdictions, it will be convenient if the statistics first in order are separately grouped, so that the proceedings of the *two* Grand Lodges of England in this distant possession may be distinguishable.[3] Before, however, passing away from our immediate subject, the appointments of Thomas Marriot Perkins,[4] 1762-64; William Winter, 1768-69; Jasper Hall, 1772; Sir Peter Parker,[5] 1778; and Major-Gen. (afterwards Sir Adam) Williamson,[6] 1793, as Prov. G.M.'s under the older Grand Lodge, may be briefly recorded.

Although Lodges under the Schismatic (or *Ancient*) sanction were established at Old Harbour and Green Island in 1763 and 1772 respectively, the two Grand Lodges of England appear to have kept out of collision—at least in the Greater Antilles—until 1775, by warranting Lodges in different parts of the island. In the year named, however, a Lodge was erected at Green Island by the older of these bodies. This, being viewed as an invasion of jurisdiction, led to reprisals, which in the first instance took the form of a counter demonstration at Kingston—hitherto a virgin fortress of the original Grand Lodge—where an "Atholl" Lodge was established in 1786.[7]

After 1775 no further Lodges under the original Grand Lodge of England came into existence on the island until 1812, when a warrant—No. 638—was granted to some French refugees from Hayti. This Lodge, however, soon died out.

In 1806 Dr (afterwards Sir) Michael Benignus Clare was appointed (Atholl) Prov. G.M. The formation of this Prov. Grand Lodge sealed the fate of the Lodges under the rival sanction. Many of them ceased to work, whilst others accepted provincial numbers at the hands of the enemy. But besides absorbing Lodges already in being, the new Prov. Grand Lodge was instrumental in ushering into existence many others, some of which obtained places on the

---

[1] Of a previous expedition sent out under Admiral Hozier—it is related that in a couple of years two admirals, ten captains, fifty lieutenants, and four thousand men had perished.

[2] Constitutions, 1756, p. 333.

[3] The following Lodges were constituted by the original Grand Lodge of England:—Nos. 182, Kingston, 1739; 193, Port Royal, 1742; 208, Spanish Town, 1746; 219, St Mary's Parish, 1757; 418, 419, Kingston,—420, Montego Bay, and 421, St James' Parish, 1771; 446, 447, Kingston, 1773; 483, Green Island,—485, Hanover Parish,—486, Spanish Town, and 487, Savannah la Mer, 1775; and 638 (La Loge, Frères Réunis), Kingston, 1812. Of these fifteen Lodges, all but five—Nos. 193, 208, 446, 447, and 486 above—were carried forward in the lists until the Union, when they disappear, with the solitary exception of No. 638, which survived for a few years longer.

[4] Prov. G.M. for the Mosquito Shore, 1758-62.   [5] Chap. XX., pp. 481, 490.   [6] *Ante*, p. 352.

[7] The undermentioned Lodges were constituted by the Atholl Grand Lodge:—Nos. 121, Old Harbour, 1763; 177, Green Island, 1772; 233, Kingston, 1786; 257, [   ], 1789; 262, Royal Artillery, Port Royal, 1790; 281, Port Royal, 1793; 283, Kingston, 1794; 288, Kingston, 1795; 301, Kingston, 1796—became the Prov. Grand Lodge, 1806; and 342, Kingston, 1809. Of these Lodges Nos. 121, 177, 233, 262, and 301 were *not* carried forward at the Union; Nos. 257, 281, and 288 died out before 1832; whilst Nos. 283 and 342 survive as the "Royal" and "Friendly" Lodges, *present* Nos. 207 and 239.

London roll. Nineteen Lodges, and probably more, if we could trace them, were ranged under the Provincial banner a few years after 1806.

A Lodge, St Andrew, No. 102, was established on the island by the Grand Lodge of Scotland in 1760, which remained on the roll, though probably inactive for many years, until 1816. Jamaica has also been the seat of a Scottish province from at least 1771, in which year it is first alluded to in the records of the G.L. of Scotland.

Three Jamaica Lodges were constituted by the Grand Lodge of Ireland during the last century, and a fourth sprang into existence in 1814.[1] At the present time, however, that jurisdiction is unrepresented on the island.

In 1782, of all our former possessions in the West Indies, Jamaica, Barbadoes, and Antigua only remained. Jamaica would have next fallen—in which case its later Masonic history might have formed a part of that of the Grand Orient of France—had it not been for the victory of Lord Rodney over the Count de Grasse on April 12 of that year. The whole of the battering cannon and artillery intended for the attack on the island was on board the ships then captured.

The Earl of Effingham, who only resigned the office of Acting G.M. of the (older) Grand Lodge of England, on his appointment as Governor of Jamaica, arrived in the colony in 1790, but died November 19 of the same year.[2]

As we have already seen, six British Lodges, which, with a single exception,[3] worked under Atholl warrants, were brought forward at the Union (1813) on the roll of the United Grand Lodge of England. In 1816 Sir Michael Clare—former Prov. G.M. under the junior society—received what may be termed a patent of confirmation, and until the departure of this worthy for England, June 9, 1831,[4] when the Prov. Grand Lodge came to an untimely end, Freemasonry on the whole made satisfactory progress on the island.

During the period last reviewed, 1813-31, some Lodges under other jurisdictions were formed in the colony, to which it becomes necessary to refer. One—as we have seen—sprang up under an Irish warrant in 1814,[5] and two years later the first of a series of Lodges was established by the Grand Orient of France.[6]

---

[1] Nos. 456, Kingston, 1767 ; 699, Kingston, 1789 ; 738, [ ], 1790-99 ; and 85, Kingston, 1814.

[2] The mortality among all ranks was most frightful. From Commissary Sayers' regimental returns, we learn that of 19,676 European soldiers sent by England to the West Indies in 1796, before March 1802, 17,173 died of complaints incidental to the climate.

[3] No. 645—*former* No. 638. The others were Nos. 324, 355, 357, 364, and 438—*former* Nos. 257, 281, 283, 288, and 342.

[4] During this period nine new Lodges, Nos. 686, Phœnix, Port Royal ; 691-97, Sussex, Kingston—Clare, Spanish Town—Atholl, Lucca Bay—Seville, St Ann's Bay—Duke of York, Falmouth—Concord, Spanish Town—and Cornwall, Montego Bay—all in 1817 ; and 810, Montego Bay, 1826, were added to the English roll.

[5] Dec. 9, 1818 :—The Board of General Purposes (Grand Lodge of England) having received letters from the Grand Lodge of Ireland and the Prov. G.M. of Jamaica relative to some proceedings in that island, recommend that a deputation from the two Grand Lodges should be appointed to confer on the subject [that certain regulations common to the Grand Lodge of England and Ireland should be established for the government of the Lodges abroad and in military corps], and that the Grand Lodge of Scotland should be invited to join in the conference. March 3, 1819.—The Board report the receipt of a letter from the Grand Lodge of Ireland, and the matter was left in the hands of the Duke of Sussex, G.M. (Proceedings, Grand Lodge of England).

[6] Lodges erected by this body :—Fidélité, Port Royal, 1816 ; Réunion des Arts (Lodge and Chapter), Port Royal ; and Bénignité, "*Ile de la Jamaique*," 1819 ; Trigonométrie, 1831 ; and Les Anciens Frères Réunis, 1832, both at Port Royal (Rebold, Histoire des trois Grandes Loges, pp. 127, 132, 150).

According to a local historian,[1] the G.O. in 1817 issued charters to some French refugees at Kingston, empowering them to erect three several chapters or consistories—the Sublime Lodge, for conferring the so-called " Ineffable Degrees "—the second, for a Council of Princes of Jerusalem—and the third, for a Grand Council of thirty-three degrees. The same writer adds, that becoming "wearied of these diversions, and desirous of working legitimate Masonry," the members of the bodies aforesaid applied in 1818 to the Grand Lodge of England for a warrant to open the Lodge *La Bénignité,* which, however, drew its last breath in 1829. Here there is manifest confusion with regard to dates, which is heightened by some evidence from another source, which informs us, that in 1811, a charter for Lodge *Bienfaisance,* No. 1, was granted by the Grand Consistory of Jamaica, to a number of St Domingo Masons at New Orleans—late residents on the island. Also, unless *Bénignité* was held at Kingston, none of the French Lodges met at the capital. The Lodge in question, moreover, never obtained an English warrant, *one* alone having been issued to Jamaica between 1817 and 1840, *viz.,* to the Friendly Lodge, Montego Bay, No. 810, in 1826—which at the present time is still in existence. Nevertheless there is no reason to doubt that the various French rites were extensively worked in the colony. This was apparently the case from very early times, and if those writers are correct by whom Stephen Morin is alleged to have been a Jew,[2] the fact that there has always been a large Hebrew element in Jamaica, coupled with the circumstance that in no other island of the group under examination were either Jews or Freemasons so safe from persecution, will in a great measure account for the causes which have led to its figuring so largely in the history of the A. and A.S.R. 33°.[3]

On the passing of the act for the abolition of slavery—1833—many Lodges closed their doors, nor did any general reaction set in until about the end of 1844, when two new Lodges were erected, one a representative of the Scottish jurisdiction, whilst the other was opened under a charter from the Grand Lodge of Carthagena by a number of Columbian patriots who had taken refuge in Kingston. The latter ultimately became No. 754—Union et Concordia—under the Grand Lodge of England [4] in 1845.

The Rev. W. P. Burton had been appointed Prov. G.M. for Jamaica by the Grand Lodge of Scotland in 1843, who, however, as in the parallel cases of Colonel Young in the West and Dr Burnes in the East Indies, at first held office *in partibus infidelium.*[5] But Scottish Masonry soon secured a firm footing on the island, where there are now ten Lodges, which with No. 357, Greytown, Mosquito, form the present province of Jamaica and Greytown, No. 33.[6]

This resolute action on the part of Scotland threatened to be fraught with the same evil consequences to the English Lodges in the colony as befell those in the Bombay Presidency on the appointment as Scottish Prov. G.M. of Dr Burnes. It was soon felt that the brethren under the Grand Lodge of Scotland enjoyed a precedence over the others, and the English Lodges at last mustered up courage to petition for the appointment of Dr Robert Hamilton

[1] Burger, *op. cit.*   [2] Ragon, Thory, Clavel, Rebold, etc.   [3] *Ante,* pp. 59, 60, 128.

[4] English Lodges warranted *after* 1826:—Nos. 686, Falmouth, 1840 ; 746, Savanna La Mar, and 747, Lucia, 1844 ; 754, Kingston, 1845 ; 1107, Spanish Town, 1860 ; 1216, Port Royal, 1862 ; 1377, Savanna La Mar, 1871 ; 1440, Spanish Town, 1873 ; 1771, 1836, 1873, 1933, all at Kingston, in the years 1878, 1879, 1880, and 1881 respectively.

[5] *Ante,* pp. 58, 59, 335.

[6] Scottish Lodges erected *after* 1760 :—Nos. 415, Kingston, 1844 ; 417, Kingston, 1845 ; 359, Black River, 1851 ; 367, Falmouth, 1853 ; 369, St Andrew, 1855 ; 402, Spanish Town, 1860 ; 530, St Anne's Bay, 1873 ; 550, Spanish Town, 1874 ; 554, Port Maria, 1874 ; and 623, Kingston, 1878.

as their Provincial ruler.   Their request was granted, and the Doctor commissioned in the first instance—November 5, 1858—as Prov. G.M. for East Jamaica, a jurisdiction which was subsequently extended over the whole island.   Dr Hamilton died in 1880, and no successor was appointed until 1886.   The English Lodges in Jamaica are now eleven in number.   Seven of these meet at Kingston, and one each at Port Royal, Savanna La Mar, Spanish Town, and Montego Bay.[1]

PORTO RICO.—The last of the Greater Antilles is this Spanish possession, which alone of the group is entirely colonised, cultivated, and peopled.   The climate is healthy, and more favourable for Europeans than that of any other of the West Indian islands.   The number of inhabitants (1877) is 635,000, rather more than half of whom are whites ; yet though twelve times smaller in extent than Cuba, it contains half the population of that island.   Under the numerous Spanish and Cuban Grand Bodies, Porto Rico has generally occupied the position of a separate district under a Provincial Superintendent.   Upon its early Masonic history, however, I shall not dwell, inasmuch as it would be only pursuing still further the vein of conjecture in which it has been necessary to indulge whilst attempting to deal with the difficult problem of Spanish Masonry.   A Lodge—Le Restauracion—under the G.O. of Colon, was in existence at Mayaguez in 1860, and the fluctuations of which Cuba was the scene during the struggle for existence of the Grand Lodges there, made their influence felt throughout the Spanish Antilles.

In the lists before me Don Manuel Romeno is shown as the Provincial Superintendent of Cuba and Porto Rico under the Grand Lodge of Spain (of which Becerra is the G.M.).   No Lodges are enumerated, but we find five on the roll of the Grand Orient of Spain, though in this case without a Provincial Superintendent.   The S.C. of France is represented by a single Lodge—Le Phénix, No. 230, constituted 1874.   Until quite recently there were fourteen Lodges on the island in subjection to the United Grand Lodge of Colon and Cuba. These, however, formed themselves into an independent Grand Lodge, September 20, 1885. The ports of San Juan, Ponce, and Mayaguez are the greatest centres of Masonic activity ; and the last-named town, besides supporting two Lodges, possesses a Consistory 32°, a Council 30°, and a Chapter 18°.   It is a little singular that whilst the *Lodges* at Porto Rico have severed their connection with the " *United Grand Lodge* of Colon and the Island of Cuba," the *Chapters* and other associations of Masons in the lesser Spanish dependency are still dutiful in their allegiance to the *Supreme Council* of the same title.

Upon this a little light is thrown by the action of Don Antonio Romero Ortiz (at the time presiding over the Grand Lodge of Spain), who, in a decree, dated March 13, 1883, " denounced the Grand Lodge of Colon and Cuba and the Masons of its obedience as traitors to the Government and to the Mother Country," simply because they declined to recognise his authority to govern or interfere in the affairs of " Symbolical Masonry " in Cuba.   In the same year the United Grand Lodge of Colon and Cuba announced by circular that there being in all three Supreme Councils and three Grand Lodges in Spain, it had recognised the Grand
. Lodge of Seville as being " the only really independent organisation of Craft Masonry " then

---

[1] Authorities :—W. J. Gardner, Hist. of Jamaica, 1873, pp. 123, 214, 222 ; Bryan Edwards, Hist. of the West Indies, 3d edit., 1801, vol. iii., p. 411 ; T. Southey, Chron. Hist. of the West Indies, 1827, vol. ii., p. 284, vol. iii., p. 227 ; H. J. Burger, Hist. of Freemasonry in Jamaica—printed in the Handbook for the Colony, 1881 ; Freemason, August 6, 1881 ; Laurie, 1859, p. 403 ; Scot, 1873, p. 14 ; and lists kindly supplied by D. M. Lyon, G. Sec., Scotland, and S. B. Oldham, Dep. G. Sec., Ireland.

existing in that country. This, of course, was dealing very summarily with the pretensions of the Grand Lodge (or Orient) under Ortiz, which Mr Albert Pike pronounced to be the only Grand Body in Spain legitimately entitled to recognition as a regular Masonic body. The name I have last quoted being, as many will be aware, that of the Sov. G. Com. of the S.C. 33° for the U.S.A., Southern Jurisdiction—the body of which he is the head being to other Supreme Councils what the Grand Lodge of England is to other Grand Lodges, and his own personal authority perhaps ranking higher than that of any other Mason either in the Old World or the New.

The Grand Lodge and Supreme Council of Colon and Cuba have therefore followed different roads, the latter treading in the beaten track traversed by Supreme Councils in amity with that presided over by the patriarch and law-giver of the rite,[1] and the former boldly striking out a path of its own.

Owing to the state of political affairs in the island, and from the influential position held by Ortiz in Spain,[2] the charges he made were calculated to subject the Cuban Masons both to surveillance and persecution on the part of the authorities. At Porto Rico the circumstances were somewhat different. Out of Cuba itself the S.C. of Colon was long regarded—and not alone by votaries of the A. and A.S.R. 33°—as a more stable institution than any other of the numerous Grand Bodies which sprang up like mushrooms in the island. When, therefore, the two governing Masonic bodies at Havannah, each in its own way, attempted to solve the problem of Craft sovereignty in Spain, it is not to be wondered at that the confusion existing in the Peninsula was reproduced with more or less fidelity in the Spanish Antilles. In Porto Rico there are no less than five Chapters 18°, besides a Council 30°, and a Consistory 32°. These, as already related, adhered to their allegiance; but the *Lodges* on the island set up a Grand Lodge of Porto Rico at the city of Mayaguez in 1885, and it is satisfactory to state that the Grand Lodge of Colon and Cuba has since established fraternal relations with the new body.

II. The Virgin Islands.

This name is given to an extensive group of small islands lying between Porto Rico and the Lesser Antilles. The islands are divided between Great Britain, Denmark, and Spain; Tortola and Virgin Gorda (or Spanish Town) being the most important of those under British rule; St Thomas, St John, and Santa Cruz (or Sainte Croix), of those belonging to Denmark; whilst the largest of the Spanish islets—Culebra—has an area of only ten square miles. The islands changed hands very frequently up to 1815, when their present political position was defined. The British islands are under the governor of St Kitts, the Spanish are dependencies of Porto Rico, and the Danish governor has his seat at Christianstadt, the capital of Santa Cruz. This island, which, though politically united with the Virgin group, is geographically distinct, has attained to a higher degree of prosperity than any other in the archipelago. English is generally spoken throughout the entire group, with the exception of St Thomas and St John, in which the language of their first possessors—Dutch—has been retained.[3]

---

[1] The Rose-Croix Chapter, No. 25 on the roll of the S.C. of Colon, is named after Mr Pike.

[2] *Ante*, p. 317.

[3] The works and references cited in connection with the Greater Antilles are also to a great extent my authorities for the remaining sections relating to the West Indies.

TORTOLA AND VIRGIN GORDA.—Lodges were established in these islands by the Schismatics or "Ancients" in 1760 and 1763, and by the rival organisation—the original or legitimate Grand Lodge of England—in 1765. Each of the three Lodges was continued in the lists until the Union (1813), when they one and all disappear.[1]

SANTA CRUZ, or ST CROIX.—A Lodge at this island, dating from 1756, obtained a temporary footing on the English roll in the Engraved List for 1758, as No. 224, and ten years *later* was advanced to a higher niche corresponding with its actual seniority, as No. 216. This was afterwards described as the Lodge of St George, and is shown in our lists until 1814, but it apparently became subject to Danish jurisdiction in 1776, and died out in 1788. John Ryan was appointed Prov. G.M. under England in 1777, but no English charter has since been granted to the Masons in Santa Cruz, though a Scottish Lodge—Eureka, No. 605—was erected at Christianstadt in 1877.

ST THOMAS.—A dispensation "to hold a Lodge for six months" was granted for this island, by the G.M. of Pennsylvania, in 1792. Next comes "La Concorde," borne on the register of the Grand Lodge of Denmark, 1798-1823, but whether of "Danish or English origin" there is no evidence to show. The Harmonic Lodge, No. 708, which still exists, was founded by the Grand Lodge of England in 1818. After this, in the year 1855, came Les Cœurs Sincères, No. 141, under the S.C. for France. Not content, however, with these two jurisdictions, some Masons on the island requested Andrew Cassard of New York to procure them a warrant from the S.C. for the United States S.J., but at his suggestion they eventually applied to the Grand Lodge of Colon—at Santiago de Cuba—and were constituted as a Lodge—Star in the East—under the authority of that body by Cassard in 1871. But the S.C. for Colon claimed that as the Grand *Orient* had not met, the Grand *Lodge* was still "in recess,"[2] and in 1872 passed a formal decree censuring Cassard for his action at St Thomas. In the same year the members of Star in the East applied, though without success, to the G.M. of South Carolina for a *Dispensation* to enable them to continue their labours, alleging that the other Lodges on the island would not recognise them, on the pretext that the Grand Lodge of Colon was not known to be in existence. In 1873, however, they were more fortunate, as a charter and not merely a temporary dispensation was granted them by the Grand Lodge of Louisiana—from which body the circumstance of a prior application having been made to the G.M. of South Carolina had been carefully withheld. But the petitioners were in no better position than before, for they were neither recognised nor allowed to visit by the other Lodges of St Thomas, and the warrant which had been so imprudently granted by the Grand Lodge of Louisiana was at once withdrawn when the actual circumstances of the case were brought to the notice of that body.[3]

---

[1] Lodges constituted :—*Ancients*—Nos. 82, Virgin Gorda, 1760 ; 108, Road Island of Tortola, 1763. *Grand Lodge of England*—No. 351, Tortola and Beef Island, 1765.

[2] *Cf. ante*, p. 350.

[3] Authorities (Santa Cruz and St Thomas) :—Proceedings, Grand Lodges of South Carolina, 1872 ; Louisiana, 1874 ; [according to the Grand Master's address, the Grand Orient of Colon was in full communication with other Masonic bodies, and actively engaged in creating and organising Masonic bodies throughout its jurisdiction, which was claimed to extend over Cuba, St Thomas, Porto Rico, St John, St Croix, and a portion of St Domingo] ; Maine, 1879 ; and Letter from Mr Rasmus Nielsen, Grand Secretary, Denmark, dated May 10, 1886.

III. The Lesser Antilles, or Caribbee Islands.

Antigua.—The earliest Lodges in the West Indies were established in this island, which is the most important of the Leeward group, and the residence of the British Governor-in-Chief. No less than three holding English warrants were in existence in 1739, and a fourth is said to have been established in the previous year by the authority of the Prov. G.M. of New England. A little later the Freemasons in the colony built a large hall for their meetings, and applied to the Grand Lodge of England for permission to style one of their Lodges (No. 192), "the Great Lodge at St John's in Antigua," which favour was granted to them in April 1744.[1]

The Leeward Islands were constituted a Province under England[2] in 1738, and under Scotland in 1769. The first Scottish Lodge in the Lesser Antilles was erected in the latter year at St Kitts, by which name the province was designated in 1786. But in 1792 the old title—Leeward Caribbee Islands—was restored, and again altered in 1837 on the appointment of Dr Stephenson of Grenada, to be "Provincial G.M. of the Province *comprehending* the Caribbee Islands." Lieut.-General James Adolphus Oughton[3] was appointed Lieut.-Governor of Antigua, December 18, 1772, but the presence on the island of a former Grand Master of Scotland was destitute of any Masonic result, as the earliest Scottish Lodge in the colony was not established until 1787.[4] The only Lodges[5] since erected are the two now existing, both of which are on the roll of the Grand Lodge of England.[6]

The following extract from a long-forgotten work will show the exceptional difficulties against which the European residents in the West Indies had to contend, and may serve to excite our surprise—not that more Lodges were not constituted, but that any survived at all in the pestilential climate where the Lodge work had to be carried on. According to my authority, "the 68th regiment was sent to Antigua in 1805, with its ranks sadly reduced by the climate. It had arrived in the West Indies about five years before, with two battalions, each 1200 strong; and I have understood from their officers that they had buried in those five years 2400 men and 68 officers—the regiment had, of course, received repeated drafts of men from England during that period."[7]

Barbadoes.—Masonry was early established in this the chief of the Windward Islands, and the residence of the Governor-General of the group. It was constituted a Masonic province in 1740,[8] and in the same year the first of a long series of Lodges under the Grand Lodge of England[9] came into existence. None of these, however, were carried forward on the

---

[1] Lodges (Grand Lodge of England):—Nos. 191, Parham, 1737 ; 192, Courthouse, 1738 ; 193, Baker's, 1739 ; 233, Evangelists, 1753—removed to Montserrat, 1761, or earlier ; 435, 1772 ; and 447, 1782. All the above were continued in the lists until the Union, when they disappear. *Cf.* Chap. XX., p. 467.

[2] Prov. G.M.'s:—Leeward Islands, Governor Matthew, 1788 ; Antigua, Rev. F. Bryan, D.D., 1754-55 ; Antigua and Leeward Islands, W. Jarvis, 1758-62 ; succeeded provisionally by Captain J. Dunbar, 1764-67, but name again shown in Calendar, 1783, and only disappears in 1808.

[3] *Cf. ante,* p. 63, and Chap. XIX., p. 447.   [4] No. 225, St John, "cut off" in 1816.

[5] Nos. 723, 1843 ; and 967, 1856.

[6] Authorities:—Southey, vol. ii., p. 411 ; Preston, 1792, p. 291 ; Lawrie, 1804, p. 188 ; Laurie, 1859, p. 404.

[7] Lieut.-Colonel J. Leach, Rough Sketches of the Life of an Old Soldier, 1831, p. 18.

[8] Prov. G.M.'s :—Barbadoes and Windward Islands, Thomas Baxter, 1740 ; W. Maynard, 1754-55 ; Caribbee and Windward Islands, Governor Robert Melville, 1764 ; Barbadoes, John Stone, 1765-67 ; Samuel Rous, 1768-69 ; Benjamin Gettins, 1780 ; W. Bishop, 1791 ; John Straker, 1801 ; J. A. Beccles, 1818 ; and Sir R. B. Clarke, 1841.

[9] Nos. 186, 1740 ; 260-61, 1752 ; 262, 1754 ; 238, 1758 ; 434, 1772 ; and 585, 1791. *Cf.* Chap. XX., p. 467.

Union roll in 1814, though one—No. 186, St Michael's Lodge—was a few years later restored to the list, but again left out at the next change of numbers (1832), to be a second time restored (1841), and finally erased, March 5, 1862. It is a little singular that the first five Lodges established in Barbadoes bore saintly appellatives.

Three Lodges were warranted in the colony by the Grand Lodge of Ireland in the last century, and there was a Prov. Grand Lodge in existence in 1804, but this having now become a lapsed jurisdiction, its further consideration may be dispensed with. Though for the information of local antiquaries, the Lodges formerly existing are specified in a note.[1]

The Atholl or Ancient Masons obtained a footing on the island in 1790, and a Lodge constituted in that year still exists. Three others were afterwards erected, but though carried forward at the Union, were dropped out at the change of numbers in 1832.[2]

The Grand Lodge of Scotland has never been represented in the colony by more than a single Lodge, the first—Scotia, No. 267—having been chartered in 1799; and a second (of the same name) in 1844. At the present time there are only two Lodges in Barbadoes—the Scottish one last referred to, and the original "Atholl" Lodge of 1790; for although three others have been constituted since the Union by the United Grand Lodge of England,[3] all these have passed out of existence.

CURAÇOA.—Lodges under the Grand Lodge of Holland appear to have been established on the island in 1757, 1773, and 1787—L'Amitié, L'Union, and De Vergenoeging. In 1807 it was taken by the English, but restored to the Dutch in 1815. During the British occupation, Nos. 346, Union, and 627, Content and British Union, were warranted in 1810 and 1811 by the Atholl and Original Grand Lodges of England respectively. Both were carried forward at the Union, but are now extinct, the latter not surviving the closing up of numbers in 1832, and the former being struck off the roll, March 5, 1862. Curaçoa is the seat of the Dutch Masonic province of the West Indies, and there are at the present time only two Lodges on the island, one under the Grand Lodge of Holland—De Vergenoeging (*Contentment*)— established in 1787, but apparently revived after a period of abeyance in 1854;[4] the other under the Grand Lodge of England, No. 939, erected in 1855. The close resemblance between the names of the early Dutch and English Lodges might almost suggest that in some instances there was a divided or dual allegiance.

DOMINICA.—The Lodge of Good Friends was formed at Roseau by the Grand Lodge of England in 1773.[5] In the same year a warrant was granted (though not issued) for the colony by the Atholl Masons, and in 1785 a second,[6] under which a Lodge was constituted, also at the capital, Roseau. But neither of the bodies thus established survived the union of the two societies, which is not to be wondered at when we take into consideration that the island was captured by the French in 1778, restored to England in 1783, again surrendered to France in 1802, and finally received back as a British possession in 1814. A revival took place in 1823, when the Lodge of Chosen Friends, No. 777, was established, which remained on the roll until swept away—in company with eighty-eight other foreign or colonial Lodges

---

[1] Nos. 622, 1783-1858 ; 649 [granted but never issued]; 653, 1786-1856; 222, 1822-47; 259, 1822-30; 277, 1822-41; 282, 1842-45. The dates last given are those of removal from the roll.

[2] Nos. 263, 1790 ; 286, 1794 ; 308, 1797 ; and 331, 1804.   [3] Nos. 848, 1829 ; 713, 1842 ; and 1499, 1874.

[4] *Cf. ante*, pp. 337, note 1 ; and 345, note 3.   [5] No. 460.   [6] No. 229.

—by order of the Grand Lodge of England, March 5, 1862. The only Lodge at present on the island is No. 1742, under the same jurisdiction, erected in 1878.

GRENADA.—In 1763—October 8—Brigadier-General Robert Melville was appointed Governor of Dominica. Grenada, the Grenadines, St Vincent, and Tobago were included in his government—a new one—which was styled that of Grenada. This officer received three patents as Prov. G.M.—(1) for Guadeloupe—when Lieutenant-Governor of Fort Royal on that island, and Lieutenant-Colonel 38th Foot, 1759-62;[1] (2) for the Caribbee and Windward Islands, 1764; and (3) for Grenada, 1780. The year following Melville's appointment to this new government, Lodges were formed on the island by the Grand Lodges of England and France. Three in all were constituted under the former,[2] and two under the latter jurisdiction[3] in the last century; whilst the Atholl Masons, who were five years later in obtaining a footing in the colony, chartered one military and two stationary Lodges within the same period.[4]

None of the English Lodges were carried forward at the Union, and the next evidence of Masonic activity is presented by the erection of an Irish Lodge—No. 252—in 1819, which, however, surrendered its warrant in 1825, and another of later constitution—No. 224, formed 1848—has also ceased to work.

Scotland was next in the field (1820), and four Lodges[5] have been warranted under that jurisdiction, the three latest of which are in existence at this day. A year later (1821) the Masonry of England was again represented, and shortly afterwards by a second Lodge,[6] but both the bodies thus constituted are now extinct. G. G. Munro was appointed Prov. G.M. under the same sanction in 1825, and Felix Palmer in 1831.

The latest foreign jurisdiction by which the colony was invaded would appear to have been that of the Grand Orient of France, if by "Grenade" we are to understand Grenada, where a Lodge—"La Bienfaisance"—was established December 21, 1828.

GUADELOUPE.—In this, the chief West Indian possession of France, and its dependency Marie-Galante, the following Lodges are shown in the lists as having been constituted by the Grand Lodge or Grand Orient of France:—Antigue, 1766; La Vraie Fraternité (Marie-Galante) and St Jean d'Ecosse, 1768; La Bonne Amitié and L'Humanité, 1770; St Louis de la Concorde, 1772; *La Paix*, 1784; Les Philalèthes [under a warrant from the Mother Lodge of the Scots Philosophic Rite], 1806; L'Amenité, 1807; La Fraternité (Marie-Galante), 1829; *Les Disciples d'Hiram*, 1835; and *Les Elus D'Occident*, 1862. The Lodges still existing are shown in italics, the two of earliest date being at Pointe-à-Pitre, and the remaining one at Basse-Terre.

Although Guadeloupe was in the hands of the English, 1759-63, and again occupied by

---

[1] The dates of these early Patents can rarely be given with precision, as the Deputations and Provincial Commissions granted down to about 1770 are ordinarily cited—without distinction of dates—in connection with the particular G.M. during whose administration they were issued. Subsequently there is less vagueness, as the names of Prov. G.M.'s were annually published with the lists of Lodges. The official calendars, however, were very carelessly edited, some names not finding places for many years, whilst others were continued long after the appointments had lapsed, and in not a few cases for long periods after the decease of the former holders.

[2] Nos. 347, La Sagesse, 1764; 425, Lodge of Vigilance; and 426, Lodge of Discretion, 1772.

[3] La Tendre Fraternité, 1764; and Les Frères Choisis, 1781.

[4] Nos. 163, 1769; 271, 1792; and 272, 45th Foot, 1792.

[5] Nos. 356, St George, 1820; 395, Caledonia, 1827; 603, St Andrew, 1877; and 650, St George, 1880.

[6] Nos. 732, St George, 1821; and 797, Harmony, 1825.

them in 1813 and 1815, this—as already related—was attended by no other Masonic result than the grant of a Provincial Patent to Lieutenant-Colonel Melville, one of the officers of the British garrison, 1759-62.

MARTINIQUE.—Masonry, in this magnificent island, appears to have been introduced almost as early as in France itself. Thus, by the Grand Orient, or by the several Grand Bodies which preceded it, we find there were chartered—La Parfaite Union, 1738 ; St Pierre des Frères Unis, 1760 ; La Tendre Fraternité,[1] 1765 ; La Sincérité des Cœurs, 1777 ; Les Frères Choisis, 1781 ; Le Zèle et la Bienfaisance, La Parfaite Amitié, and La Paix (au Marin), 1786.

From 1794 to 1802, and again, 1809-15, the island was in the possession of the English. During the first period a Lodge was established under the Grand Lodge of Ireland—No. 690, in 1801 ; and during the second another under the (Atholl) Grand Lodge of England—No. 359, Lodge of Chosen Friends, 1813. The former of these was transferred to Trinidad, 1811, and cancelled 1858. The latter, which bore the last *number* issued by the so-called " Ancients," was carried forward on the Union roll, but died out before the year 1832.

The later Lodges constituted by the G.O. of France were L'Harmonie, 1803 ; Les Frères Choisis, 1814 ; La Concorde, 1820 ; and La Bienfaisance, 1821. At the present time, however, according to the various calendars, there is but a single Lodge at work on the island—L'Union, St Pierre—established by warrant of the (French) S.C. 33° in 1848.[2]

MONTSERRAT AND NEVIS.—Although the earliest Lodges in the West Indies sprang up with a luxuriant growth in Antigua, to Montserrat belongs the distinction of having been constituted the first Masonic Province either in the Greater or the Lesser Antilles. This occurred in 1737 during the administration of the Earl of Darnley ;[3] and thirty years later, December 2, 1767, a Prov. Grand Lodge for Montserrat and Nevis—No. 151—was set up by the Atholl (or Ancient) Masons. Up to this time, however, there appears to have been no Lodge on either island ; but in 1777 one was erected—No. 507—at Nevis by the original Grand Lodge of England ; whilst the Evangelists' Lodge, established at Antigua in 1753, shifted its place of meeting to Montserrat shortly before 1780. These two Lodges were continued in the lists of the older Society until the Union, when they disappear, and so far as my research extends, no others have since been in existence in either island.

ST BARTHOLOMEW.—A Lodge—Sudermania—under the Grand Lodge of Sweden, existed on this island from 1797 to 1820.

ST CHRISTOPHER, or ST KITTS.—Four Lodges were warranted in this colony by the Grand Lodge of England in the last century. The first in 1739, and the last in 1768.[4] The latter did not survive the change of numbers in 1770, but all the other Lodges were carried forward until the Union, and one—the Clarence, originally No. 206—only disappeared at the renumbering in 1832, though a Lodge of the same name was warranted on the island in the

---

[1] Amalgamated with the first Lodge on this list under the title La Parfaite Union et la Tendre Fraternité Réunies.

[2] Leon Hyneman (World Wide Register, p. 533) locates two Lodges—Réunion des Artes and Trigonométrie—at Martinique, which, from having been established at *Port* (not *Fort*) Royal, I have assigned to Jamaica. He also gives the name of "Sante Trinité" among those of the Lodges at Martinique. This, however, I have altogether failed to trace in the lists of Lodges warranted by the G.O. or S.C. of France.

[3] Prov. G.M.'s :—*Montserrat*—James Watson, 1737 ; Edward Daniel, 1764-67 ; William Ryan, 1777. *St Christopher and Nevis*—R. Wilkes, 1798.

[4] Nos. 194, Basseterre, 1739 ; 123, Old Road, 1742 ; 206, Sandy Point, 1750, and 428, 1768.

following year—which lived until 1865—and may have been a revival. A Prov. G.M. was appointed, January 27, 1798,[1] and a second, the Hon. John Garnett, November 23, 1808.

A Scottish Lodge was erected on the island in 1769, and others in 1786 and 1791.[2] These are now extinct; but a fourth, No. 407, Mount of Olives, 1835, still exists, and is the only Lodge in St Christopher. During the years 1786-92 the island was the seat of the Scottish West Indian Province,[3] but is now included with some others in Province No. 32.

St EUSTATIUS.—Masonry in this island appears to have increased *pari passu* with its material prosperity. Three English[4] and four Dutch[5] Lodges were at work during the last century, the earliest of the former having been erected in 1747, and of the latter in 1757. Edward Galliard was appointed Prov. G.M. of St Eustatius and the Dutch Caribbee islands by the Grand Lodge of England in 1754-55; and R. H. de Plessis held a similar commission— extending over St Eustatius, Saba, and St Martin—under the Grand Lodge of Holland in 1777.

The settlement was taken by the British, February 3, 1781. All the merchandise and stores were confiscated, the naval and military commanders—Admiral Rodney and General Vaughan—considering it their duty "to seize for the public use, all the effects of an island inhabited by rebellious Americans and their agents, disaffected British factors, who, for base and lucrative motives, were the great supporters of the American rebellion." At this time, except for warlike stores, St Eustatius had become one of the greatest auctions that ever was opened in the universe. "Invitation was given," says Southey, "and protection offered to purchasers of all nations, and of all sorts."[6]

The English Lodges continued to appear in the lists until the Union, but were probably extinct for many years before that period. In 1813, it must be added, a Lodge—No. 30— was established in the settlement by the Atholl Grand Lodge, but this, like the others, failed to secure a place on the Union roll.

At the general peace the island was finally ceded to Holland, and some of the Dutch Lodges survived until within recent memory. It is possible, also, that others may have been established, of which no record has been preserved.[7] At present there are no Lodges on the island.

St LUCIA.—Two Lodges, Le Choix Réuni and L'Harmonie Fraternelle, were established by the Grand Orient of France in 1784. In 1814 the island was ceded to England, under whose sanction a Lodge—No. 762—was formed in 1845, and erased in 1862.

St MARTIN.—There are at present no Lodges either in the settlements of the French or the Dutch, between whom the island is divided; but one was formerly in existence—Unie, No. 3, under the Grand Lodge of the Netherlands—constituted in 1800.[8]

St VINCENT.—An Irish warrant—No. 733—was granted to some brethren in this

---

[1] See the last note but one.   [2] Nos. 151, St Andrew, 1769; 217, Union, 1786; and 241, Mount of Olives, 1791.
[3] *Ante*, p. 363.   [4] Nos. 268, New Lodge, 1747; 269, No. 2, 1754; 428, Union, 1768.
[5] St Pierre and La Parfaite Union, 1757; La Parfaits Maçons, 1758; and St Jean Baptiste, 1760 (Freemasons' Calendar, 1776 and 1778).
[6] Hist. of the West Indies, vol. ii., pp. 484, 492. It is related by the same authority "that the greater part of the inhabitants of our Leeward Islands wished the expedition in 1759 against Martinique to miscarry (1.) because it interrupted their iniquitous trade with St Eustatia, of transferring French sugars, their property, in Dutch bottoms; (2.) because very many of them had plantations of their own in Martinico" (*Ibid.*, p. 329).
[7] *Cf. ante*, p. 337, note 1; and the World's Masonic Register, p. 546.
[8] The World's Masonic Register, p. 540, shows a *second* Dutch Lodge, which is incorrect

dependency in 1806, which was surrendered in 1824. Two Lodges were afterwards established by the Grand Lodge of England, but are now extinct.[1]

TOBAGO.—A Scottish Lodge—No. 488—was erected at Scarborough, the capital, in 1868.

TRINIDAD.—A charter was granted—No. 77, Les Frères Unis—by the G.L. of Pennsylvania in 1798, to some brethren at Port D'Espagne, who had formerly been members of a Lodge at St Lucia, under a warrant from France. After this, in 1811, No. 690, under the Grand Lodge of Ireland, was transferred from Martinique to Trinidad, but passed out of existence in 1858. Scottish Masonry obtained a footing in 1813, and there are now four Lodges[2] in all under that jurisdiction, which form the present province, No. 44. The first English Lodge on the island had its origin in 1831. This was followed by four other warrants from the oldest of Grand Bodies, and all five Lodges are in existence at this day.[3] Trinidad became a province under the Grand Lodge of England in 1860, but ceased to be one in 1876.

IV. THE LUCAYAS, OR BAHAMA ISLANDS.

The Masonic history of this group begins with the appointment of Governor John Tinkler[4] as Prov. G.M. in 1752, who was succeeded by James Bradford in 1759. But they had apparently no Lodges to control, neither do we hear of any having been established either before or after under the jurisdiction[5] of which they were the representatives.

In 1785, however, a warrant for the Bahamas—No. 228—was issued by the "Atholl" Grand Lodge of England. The Lodge thus established died out before the Union, but a second —No. 242—under the same jurisdiction, established at Nassau, New Providence, in 1787, survived the closing up of numbers in 1814, though its vitality was exhausted before the repetition of that process in 1832.

A Scottish Lodge was erected at Turk's Island in 1803, which is now extinct, but others formed in New Providence and Inagua in 1809 and 1856 respectively, still exist, and constitute Province No. 39,[6] under the Grand Lodge of Scotland.

Lodges under the United Grand Lodge of England were established at Nassau, 1837; Grand Turk, 1855; and Harbour Island, 1869.[7] These are still active, and the first and last together constitute the existing Province of the Bahamas, which (under this jurisdiction) dates from 1843.

V. THE BERMUDAS, OR SOMMER'S ISLANDS.

This group, like the Bahamas, was provided with a Prov. G.M. long before there were Lodges for him to supervise. Alured Popple received a patent as such from Lord Strathmore

---

[1] Nos. 730, Sussex, 1821; and 755, Victoria, 1845.

[2] Nos. 322, United Brothers, 1813; 368, Eastern Star, 1854; 438, Athole, 1864; and 596, Rosslyn, 1876.

[3] Nos. 856, Philanthrophic, 1831; 837, Trinity, 1850; 1169, Prince of Wales, 1861; 1213, Phœnix, 1862; and 1788, Hervey, 1878.

[4] *Cf.* Chap. XVII., p. 385, note 3.   [5] The original Grand Lodge of England.

[6] Nos. 275, Turk's Island; 298, Union, Nassau; and 372, St John, Inagua. The first Prov. G.M. was J. F. Cooke, appointed November 7, 1842.

[7] Nos. 649, Royal Victoria; 930, Forth; and 1277, Britannia.

in 1744, and William Popple was similarly commissioned during the administration of the Earl of Aberdour (1758-62). The first Lodge under the older (English) sanction was formed in 1761, and the second in 1792.[1] Five years later (1797) the titular "Ancients" gained a footing, and in 1801 possessed, like their rivals, two Lodges.[2] At the Union, however, the former succumbed to destiny, whilst the latter were carried forward, and still survive.

Further English Lodges were constituted in 1819 and 1880—Nos. 712 and 1890—thus making a total of four, which report direct to the Grand Lodge of England, as the succession of Prov. G.M.'s ceased with the appointment of William Popple in 1758-62.

Lodge St George—No. 266—under the Grand Lodge of Scotland was erected in 1797, and the Bermudas became a Scottish Province in 1803. This was followed, however, by no increase of Lodges until 1885, when a warrant was issued to No. 726,[3] which, with "St George," forms the thirty-fourth Province on the roll of Scotland.

Three Irish Lodges have been established at St George's Island, Nos. 220, 1856 (warrant surrendered 1860) ; 224, 1867; and 209, 1881. The last two are, singularly enough, the only Lodges now at work under the Grand Lodge of Ireland in any of the West India islands.

Under the Grand Lodge of Ireland there is no West Indian Province, but under those of England and Scotland, there is in the former case two, and in the latter five. Jamaica, with ten (exclusive of Montego Bay), and the Bahamas with two Lodges, constitute the English Provinces (or Districts), though the first named, from the death of Dr Hamilton in 1880, down to the appointment of his successor, Mr J. C. Macglashan, in 1886, might be said to have been in a condition of suspended animation. The remaining West Indian Lodges (17) under this jurisdiction are in direct communication with London.

The Scottish Provinces are five in number, Nos. 32, West India Islands—Grenada, 3 ; St Kitts, Barbadoes, and Tobago, 1 Lodge each; 33, Jamaica—Greytown, 1 ; Jamaica, 10 Lodges; 34, Bermudas, 2 Lodges; 39, Bahamas, 2 Lodges; and 44, Trinidad, 4 Lodges.

MEXICO.

The so-called "Scottish Rite" was introduced into Mexico—then the principal colony of Spain—by civil and military officers of the Monarchy about the year 1810. After this, Lodges were erected by the Grand Lodge of Louisiana at Vera Cruz and Campeachy in 1816 and 1817 respectively,[4] and the example thus set was followed by the Grand Lodge of Pennsylvania, under which body a Lodge was established at Alvarado in 1824.[5] A period of confusion next ensued, during which Masonry and politics were so closely interwoven as to render quite hopeless any attempt at their separate treatment.

Soon the entire population of the country became divided into two factions, the *Escoceses* and the *Yorkinos*. The former were in favour of moderate measures, under a central

---

[1] Nos. 266 and 507, Union and Bermuda Lodges.
[2] Nos. 307 and 324—*now* 224 and 233—St George's and Somerset Lodges.
[3] With regard to the formation of this Lodge, see the *Freemason*, March 20, 1886 (p. 171).
[4] Nos. 8, Los Amigos Reunidos ; and 9, Reunion a la Virtud.
[5] No. 191, Hermanos legitimos de la luz del Papaloapan.

government, or a constitutional monarchy. The latter were the advocates of republican institutions, and the expulsion of the "old" or native Spaniards.

The Escoceses—originally the "Scots Masons"—numbered among their members all who, under the ancient *régime*, had titles of nobility; the Catholic clergy, without exception; many military officers; together with all the native Spaniards of every class.

The republican party, according to one set of writers, viewing with dismay the progress of their opponents, resolved "to fight the devil with his own fire," and therefore organised a rival faction, on which they bestowed the name of Yorkinos, the members of which were supposed to be adherents of the York Rite.

The authorities, however, by whom the movement is described as purely Masonic in its inception, are probably right, though at this point the facts do not stand out with the clearness that might be wished, and therefore deductions are of slight value.

Mackey informs us that authority was obtained in 1825 from the Grand Lodge of New York for the establishment of three Lodges in the city of Mexico. These Lodges, according to the same writer, were formed into a Grand Lodge of the York Rite by Mr Joel R. Poinsett (American Minister), a former G.M. of South Carolina. Here there is a little confusion, as Mr E. M. L. Ehlers,[1] in kindly replying to my enquiries, expressly states that since the year 1815, no foreign Lodges have been warranted by the Grand Lodge of New York. But however established, the so-called York Rite, or, in other words, pure English Masonry, flourished, and towards the end of 1826 there were 25 Lodges, with a membership of about 700. The Escoceses, or "Scots Masons," finding their Lodges deserted, regarded the Yorkinos as renegades and traitors, and with a view to counterbalance the fast increasing power of the latter, they formed the *Novenarios*, a kind of militia, which derived its name from a regulation requiring each member to enlist nine additional adherents. These ingratiated themselves with the clergy, who, after having been the most embittered enemies of the Craft in past years, now joined the Escoceses almost in a body.

The Yorkinos, becoming aware of these proceedings, tried to outdo their rivals by recruiting their own Lodges upon the plan of receiving all applicants without distinction, provided they belonged to the *federal*, *i.e.*, the patriotic party. Thus, the system of Masonry very soon degenerated into a mere party question, and at last all the adherents of one side styled themselves Escoceses, and of the other side, Yorkinos. In 1828, the two parties resorted to open warfare, with a view to deciding the question at issue by the sword, and the civil war then commenced, lasted for more than a generation.

Somewhere about this time, whilst Dr Vincente Guerrero—G.M. under the York Rite— was President of the Republic, a law was enacted by which all Masonic Lodges were closed. The Yorkinos obeyed their Grand Master, and discontinued their meetings. The Escoceses went on working, but some of their most influential Lodges were suppressed, and the members banished. Subsequently, all native Spaniards were expelled from Mexican territory.

This internecine strife seriously affected the Fraternity in general, and gave birth, during the darkest hours of the struggle for supremacy, to an organisation called the National Mexican Rite, formed by Masons, and composed of distinguished men, but containing inno-

---

[1] Grand Secretary, New York, in a letter dated March 30, 1886.

D. MURRAY LYON

GRAND SECRETARY GRAND LODGE SCOTLAND

vations and principles so antagonistic to Masonic usage and doctrine, that it was never accorded recognition, even in Mexico, by any Masonic body of acknowledged legality.

This new school of Masonry was established by nine brethren of both rites, and who had belonged to the highest grade of either system, in 1830. To guard against the intrusion of unworthy members and the revival of political antagonism, they resolved to create a rite which should be national, in the sense of not depending upon any foreign Grand Lodge for its constitution, and to obviate by safeguards and precautions of an elaborate character, the dangers to be apprehended from the reception of either Escoceses or Yorkinos.

The National Mexican Rite consisted of nine degrees, which, omitting the first three, were —4°, Approved Master (equal to the 15° "Scots"); 5°, Knight of the Secret (equal to the 18° "Scots"); 6°, Knight of the Mexican Eagle; 7°, Perfect Architect (or Templar); 8°, Grand Judge; and 9°, Grand Inspector General. All these degrees had their equivalents in the grades of the A. and A.S.R. 33°. With the "St John's" (or purely Craft) degrees certain special signs were associated, which, however, were not required from foreigners unless they had acted as auxiliaries in any of the party contests.

A Grand Orient, composed of members of the 9°, was supreme in matters of dogma or ritual. There was also an administrative body or National Grand Lodge, whose members were elective, and met in the metropolis. The Provincial Grand Lodges had their seats in the State capitals, and were formed by the "three lights" of at least five St John's Lodges.

But although still preserving a nominal existence, the several Grand Bodies, owing to political convulsions, were virtually dormant for many years after 1833. A Lodge—St Jean d'Ulloa—was constituted at Vera Cruz, by the Supreme Council of France, in 1843; and another—Les Ecossais des Deux Mondes—at the city of Mexico, by the Grand Orient of the same country, in 1845.

The National Mexican Rite appears to have somewhat recovered from its torpor in 1863. At that date we find in the metropolis, a National Grand Lodge with six working Lodges, though of these one—belonging to the A. and A.S.R.—was constituted by the Grand Lodge of New Granada, and consisted chiefly of foreigners; in Toluca a Prov. Grand Lodge with five Lodges; in Vera Cruz and Guadalajara two Lodges each; and in five other cities single Lodges.

"In the year 1858 or 1859," according to an official report,[1] "Bro. Lafon de Ladebat went to Mexico with authority from Bro. Albert Pike [of Washington D.C.] to organise and establish Masonry on a sound basis in that country. Unfortunately Bro. Ladebat did not organise a Grand Lodge of Symbolic Masonry first, as instructed, but constituted the Supreme Council with jurisdiction over the three degrees of E.A., F.C., and M.M."

After this came the invasion of Mexican territory by a foreign foe, the establishment of the Maximilian Empire, its overthrow, and finally the war of reform. Meanwhile the Grand Lodge of the Yorkinos had ceased to exist, and the "Scots Rite," which by this time had become divested of its political colouring, had erected—December 27, 1865—a Supreme Council 33°. This, in 1868, joined, or was absorbed by, the Supreme Council of 1858-59, and in the same year the amalgamated body effected a fusion with the National Grand Lodge— one of whose highest officials at the time was Benito Juarez, President of the Republic. The latter union, however, was not of a thorough nature, but rather assumed the features of a

---

[1] Proc. Grand Lodge of Louisiana, 1884, Appendix, p. 5.

friendly pact, as it left each rite independent of the other with regard to ritual and internal government. In 1870 the National Rite numbered thirty-two Lodges, and the A. and A.S.R. twenty-four.

It would seem as if the authority of Juarez alone held these rites together, since at his death in 1872—although he was succeeded as President by his chief follower, Sebastian Lerdo de Tejeda, also a prominent Freemason—dissensions arose, and they fell asunder, Alfredo Chavero becoming G.M. of the Grand Orient, and José Maria Mateos of the National Grand Lodge. In 1876 a Lodge of Germans left the G.O. and joined the National Grand Lodge, but in the following year, with the consent of the latter, affiliated with the Grand Lodge of Hamburg—under which body there is also (1886) another Lodge at work in Vera Cruz.

From the scanty information at my disposal it seems probable—more cannot be said—that the two rites again formed a junction about 1882; whilst, on the other hand, it is quite possible that the National Mexican Rite may still exist, though its proceedings are unrecorded. So far, indeed, as evidence is forthcoming, upon the re-establishment of peace and order in Mexico, the Lodges under the jurisdiction of the Supreme Council throughout the Republic organised State Grand Lodges. A Central Grand Lodge was established in the capital, with jurisdiction over them, and though the Supreme Council made no formal abdication of its authority over Symbolism, this was interfered with very little, save by the Central Grand Lodge. In 1883 there were the following State Grand Lodges:—Vera Cruz and Jalisco, each with seven Lodges; Puebla, Yucatan, and Guanajuato, with six; and Morelos and Tlaxcala, with five; thus making a total of seven Grand and forty-two subordinate Lodges, exclusive of the Central Grand Lodge and the metropolitan Lodges.

It will be seen that at this period there existed at Vera Cruz a State Grand Lodge, but from the fact that it was subordinate to the Central Grand Lodge, it was not deemed by the Grand Lodge of Colon to exercise legitimate authority over Symbolism in that State. Indeed, the whole of Mexico was regarded by the last-named body as " unoccupied territory," and it therefore proceeded to charter three Lodges, which in January 1883 formed themselves, at the city of Vera Cruz, into the " Mexican Independent Symbolic Grand Lodge."

Two of the Lodges taking part in this movement had originally held Mexican warrants, but having quarrelled with their superiors, solicited and obtained charters from the G.L. of Colon (*now* Colon and Cuba), shortly after which the third Lodge was formed, and then, finally, the Grand Lodge, although the Supreme Council of Mexico had formally protested against the invasion of its territory. Indeed the step thus taken by their former superiors appears rather to have accelerated the action of the three Lodges, as in the record of their proceedings it is stated, " that they hasten to constitute themselves into an Independent Grand Lodge, pending the protest of the Supreme Council of Mexico, to relieve their friend and mother, the Grand Lodge of Colon, from any further unpleasant complications !"

The Supreme Council of Mexico, in a Balustre numbered XXX., and dated April 25, 1883, renounced its jurisdiction over the symbolical degrees, and promulgated a variety of regulations with regard to Grand and subordinate Lodges. This threw the Craft into the utmost confusion, and might have ended in the destruction of the greater number of Mexican Lodges, or at least in the establishment of some half dozen Grand Bodies, all claiming supremacy, had it not been for the skill and address of Carlos Pacheco, who succeeded Alfredo Chavero as Sov. G. Com. 33°.

The former Balustre was revoked, and by a new one (XXXII.), dated May 27, 1883, the Supreme Council renounced, in favour of the State Grand Lodges then existing or which might afterwards be formed, the jurisdiction over Symbolism conferred upon it by the Constitutions of the A. and A.S.R. 33°. The transmission of powers was to take effect from June 24 then ensuing. The Lodges having no Grand Lodge were to remain under the jurisdiction of the Grand Lodge nearest to them, or the oldest if two were equi-distant, until they organised their own in accordance with Masonic usage and precedent. The Lodges of the Federal District, however, were directed to form and inaugurate their Grand Lodge on June 15 then following. Balustre XXXII. was signed (*inter alios*) by Carlos Pacheco, Mariano Escobedo, Alfredo Chavero, and Porfirio Diaz.

On June 25, 1883, twelve Lodges at the capital met and established the Grand Lodge of the Federal District (or city) of Mexico, with Porfirio Diaz as the first G.M. The event was announced to the Masonic world in two circulars, the first of which is in Spanish—an immense document of 180 pages ! The second is in English, and its only noticeable feature is a declaration that the American system of State Grand Lodges, each with exclusive jurisdiction, has been adopted. Grand Lodges have since been established on the same plan—*i.e.*, in conformity with the edict of the Supreme Council, as promulgated in Balustre XXXII.—in the States of Vera Cruz, Tlaxcala, Morelos, Puebla, Campeachy, and Lower California. The complications, however, already existing in the Republic, were still further increased in 1883 by the action of the Grand Lodge of Missouri, in granting a charter to the Toltec Lodge, in the city of Mexico, which had been provisionally established at the close of the previous year under a dispensation from the Grand Master.

As these sheets are passing through the press, I learn that the recognition of the Grand Lodge of which Porfirio Diaz became the head, by the Grand Lodges of Louisiana and Florida, was duly protested against by Carlos Pacheco, Sov. G. Com. 33°, and Carlos K. Ruiz, the latter of whom claimed to be himself the legitimate G.M. It would appear from *La Gran Logia*, a bulletin published by some members of the Ruiz Grand Lodge, and denominated their official organ, that on the same day, at the same hour, and in the same hall, when and where the Diaz Grand Lodge was organised and installed, the other body was organised also. There was this difference, however, that whereas the Diaz party transacted *their* affairs within the body of the Lodge, the supporters of Ruiz were reduced to the necessity of attending to *theirs* in the ante-room—the latter brethren having withdrawn from the original convention whilst it was being organised, but not leaving the building, in the vestibule of which they afterwards conducted their own proceedings.[1]

CENTRAL AMERICA.

NICARAGUA.—The Lodge of Regularity—No. 300—St John's Hall, Black River, Mosquito Shore, was established under the Grand Lodge of England in 1763, and remained on the roll until 1813. The Mosquito Coast, or Mosquitia, is an ill-defined territory of Central America, which was under British protection from 1660 to 1859, when it was ceded to Honduras. In

---

[1] Authorities :—Masonic Calendars ; Freimaurer Zeitung, No. 25, 1866 ; Freemason's Magazine, 1865, pt. i., pp. 62, 183 ; Handbuch, vols. ii., p. 318 ; iii., p. 600 ; iv., p. 115 ; Latomia, vol. xxv., p. 120 ; Mitchell, p. 645 ; Scot, p. 25 ; Mackey, p. 500 ; Proc. G.L. Louisiana, 1884, p. 4 ; 1885, p. 15 ; Illinois, 1884, pp. 103, 106 ; 1885, p. 48 ; 1886, p. 93 ; Maine, 1884, p. 724 ; Vermont, 1886, p. 86 ; and Early Hist. G.L. Pennsyl., List of Lodges, p. 17.

1860 it was handed over to Nicaragua, and in 1877 appears to have been claimed by New Granada. Lodges at "Greytown, Mosquito," were erected by the Grand Lodge of Scotland in 1851 and 1882. These are included in the Jamaica Province, a practice first carried out under the Grand Lodge of England, by the authority of which body Thomas Marriot Perkins, who was appointed Prov. G.M. of the Mosquito Shore by Lord Aberdour *circa* 1762, had his authority extended over Jamaica in the same or following year by Earl Ferrers.

BRITISH HONDURAS.—The Lodge of Amity—No. 309—St George's Quay, Bay of Honduras, was also warranted in 1763 by the Grand Lodge of England, and, like the earlier Lodge on the Mosquito Shore, continued to appear on the lists until the Union. Subsequent English warrants were granted in 1820 to the British Constitutional Lodge No. 723, Bay of Honduras; and in 1831 to the Royal Sussex, No. 860, Belize. Both these Lodges, however, were erased, June 4, 1862.

COSTA RICA.—A Lodge was chartered at San José by the Grand Orient of New Granada, about the year 1867; and, according to the Masonic Calendars, a Grand Orient and Supreme Council 33° for Central America was established at the same town in 1870. Dr Francisco Calvo was at the head of both bodies, and appears to have been succeeded in 1879, or shortly before, by Carlos Urien. The present G.M. and Sov. G. Com. is Manuel B. Bonilla, and there are twenty-three Lodges under the jurisdiction of the Grand Orient.

GUATEMALA.—A Lodge—Constance—was established in this republic in 1881, by the Grand Orient of Colombia at Carthagena. In 1886 the members divided themselves among three new Lodges, Igualdad, Libertad, and Fraternidad—Nos. 21-23 on the roll of the Grand Orient of Central America (Costa Rica), "installed" May 22, 1886, which adhere to the A. and A.S.R.—and Union—of uncertain parentage—which is alleged to work in accordance with the "York Rite." The last-named Lodge has probably received an American or German charter, as a large number of its members are composed of these nationalities. At the present time there are about 200 Masons in the Republic of Guatemala, of whom about a moiety reside at the capital, and the remainder are distributed throughout the departments.

SAN SALVADOR.—Masonry obtained a footing and the Craft flourished for a time in this State, but in 1882 the Lodges were closed and the members dispersed. In that year, however, some zealous Masons, supported by the then President of the Republic—Rafael Zaldivar—succeeded in reuniting the scattered brethren, and founding a Lodge. Excelsior, No. 17, was established by charter of the G.O. of Central America (Costa Rica), at San Salvador, the capital, March 5, 1882, and a little later, another Lodge—No. 18, Caridad y Constancia— under the same sanction, at Tecla, a neighbouring town.

With regard to HONDURAS, I have no information, beyond the bare fact that in 1885 the G.M. of New York declined to grant a dispensation for a Lodge in the republic. Should, however, any Lodges exist there, or in the other territories of the isthmus previously referred to (beyond those that have been enumerated), they will, in all probability, prove to be offshoots of the Grand Orient of Central America at COSTA RICA.

The latest details in the preceding sketch are derived from the *Chaine D'Union.*[1] From the same source I transcribe the following remarks on the conditions under which the

---

[1] Paris, Octobre 1886, p. 422.

Craft exists in SAN SALVADOR, though it may be assumed that these are generally applicable throughout the several States of Central America:—"The Masonry of this land has to contend against ignorance, superstition, and fanaticism, fostered by an all-powerful priesthood, allied with men in authority, and assisted by the women—whom they keep under their influence and their control, to a far greater extent than prevails in any country of Europe."

SOUTH AMERICA.

The minutes of the Grand Lodge of England inform us, that Randolph Tooke, Provincial Grand Master of South America, was present at a meeting of that body held April 17, 1735. Of this worthy nothing further is known beyond the bare fact that, in 1731, his name appears on the roll of Lodge No. 19, at the Queen's Arms, Newgate Street, London, of which two persons holding similar appointments [1]—Richard Hull, and Ralph Farwinter—together with Sir William Keith, Ex-Governor of Pennsylvania, and Benjamin Cole, afterwards Engraver to the Society, were also members.

The next Prov. G.M., who received an English patent empowering him to exercise Masonic jurisdiction over any part of South America, was Colonel James Hamilton, who was placed at the head of the Province of Colombia in 1824. But as the political changes of subsequent years have left their mark on the nomenclature of the existing States of the Continent, a few preliminary words are essential, before passing in review the Masonry of the Spanish-American Republics, of the Brazilian Empire, and finally, of the European settlements in Guiana, which have politically nothing in common with the other divisions of South America.

New Granada, like all the adjacent portions of the New World, was for some centuries a colony of Spain. Upon the assertion of their independence by the provinces of Spanish America, in the early part of the present century, it formed, with Ecuador and Venezuela the Republic of Colombia.

In 1831, each of the three States became autonomous, and in 1857, New Granada assumed the title of the United States of Colombia. The other parties, however, to the Federal Union, which was dissolved in 1831—Ecuador and Venezuela—have adhered to their original appellations. This it is necessary to bear in mind, because whilst a Scottish, as well as an English, Masonic Province of Colombia was created during the existence of the earlier republic of that name, the two Lodges under these jurisdictions were established at Angostura in Venezuela.[2] The first Prov. G.M. under Scotland, Don José Gabriel Nunez, the date of whose appointment is not recorded, was succeeded—May 6, 1850—by Senor Florentino Grillet, and on February 3, 1851, the designation of the Province was changed from Colombia to that of "Guayana in Venezuela."

The evidence, therefore, so far as it extends, points to Venezuela, rather than New Granada, as having been the centre of Masonic activity—at least, in the first instance— while they were both component parts of the (older) Republic of Colombia. For this reason, I shall assign a priority of narration to the record of Venezuelan Masonry. It remains to be

---

[1] *Ante*, pp. 325, 343.

[2] *English*—No. 792, Concord, 1824 ; erased—at the great weeding-out of Lodges—March 5 (and June 4), 1862 ; *Scottish*—No. 379, Eastern Star of Colombia, 1824.

stated, that there was in existence a Grand Orient of Colombia at Bogota in New Granada, shortly after the time when the two Lodges were established at Angostura, under British warrants.

The exact date of formation of this body it is not easy to determine. One of the two Grand Orients of what was formerly New Granada, but is now Colombia, and which meets at Bogota, claims 1827 as its year of origin; while there is independent evidence of the exercise of authority in Peru, by a Grand Orient of Colombia at Bogota, in 1825. On the whole, the explanation which seems to me the most reasonable is, that the *Grand Orient* of 1827, was preceded by a *Supreme Council*, armed with, or at all events, exercising, the same authority as the Hydra-headed organisation of later date?

VENEZUELA.—Masonry is said to have been introduced into Venezuela at the commencement of the present century, when a Lodge was established by the Grand Orient of Spain. Several other Lodges are also reported to have sprung into existence under the same authority. The exercise of jurisdiction by the Grand Lodges of England and Scotland in 1824, within what was then the Republic of Colombia, has already been referred to. In 1825, Joseph Cerneau, who presided over a body which he had set up at New York in 1812, under the title of "Sovereign Grand Consistory of the United States of America," formed at Caraccas a Grand Lodge and a Supreme Council of the A. and A.S.R. 33°. This may have borne the title of, and doubtless has often been confounded with, the Grand Orient of Colombia in the sister State (New Granada). In 1827, Simon Bolivar, the Liberator, having prohibited all secret societies, the Lodges, with the exception of one at Porto Cabello, suspended their labours. In 1831, Venezuela having become independent by the disruption of the Colombian Republic, a dispensation to hold a Lodge for a year was obtained from certain dignitaries of the extinct Grand Lodge, in their capacity as members of the 33d or highest degree of the A. and A.S.R., by a few brethren, in the hope that within that period they would be able to procure a charter from some foreign Grand Lodge. Their efforts, however, were unsuccessful. The Lodge was suspended, and for several years the Craft languished. But in 1838 a revival took place. The Lodge last referred to renewed its labours, the old Lodges were resuscitated, and a National Grand Lodge of Venezuela was established. Charters were issued to the old Lodges, and new ones were erected. In conjunction with the highest members of the A. and A.S.R. 33°, it established a supreme legislative body, under the name of Grand Orient, and also constituted a Grand Lodge, on the roll of which there appear to have been 16 active and 36 dormant Lodges in 1860. At this time—but the details of its formation I am unable to supply—another Grand Orient was in the field, and each body placed the other under a ban. On January 12, 1865, however, a fusion was effected, and the National Grand Orient of Venezuela established at Caraccas. A breach occurred in 1882, but the schism was again healed in 1884. The Grand Orient is divided into a Grand Lodge, Grand Chapter, Grand Consistory, and a Supreme Council, each having its own chief, and possessing entire authority over its own degrees. The present G.M. of the Grand Orient (1886) is General Joaquin Crespo, President of the Republic, and there are about fifty Lodges on the roll of the Grand Lodge. But nothing has yet occurred to oust the jurisdiction of the Grand Lodge of Scotland, which is still represented by the Provincial Grand Lodge of "Guayana in Venezuela," and the Lodge "Eastern Star of Colombia," founded in 1824.

COLOMBIA (FORMERLY NEW GRANADA).—The Grand Orient of New Granada was formed at

Carthagena June 19, 1833. In 1860 there were 19 Lodges on its roll—among them La Mas Solida Virtud, at Jamaica. Francisco de Zubirias was Grand Master in 1865, and Juan Manuel Grau in 1871. Four years later—according to the somewhat fragmentary evidence at my disposal—the latter appears to have given way to, or to have been superseded by, Juan N. Pombo, whose name is shown in the calendars as G.M. from 1875 to 1878. In 1879, however, the name of Juan M. Grau again figures in the lists, whilst that of Juan N. Pombo disappears. Full details are given in the calendars with regard to the Masonic dignitaries of Colombia during the supremacy of either; and as Grau is not mentioned whilst Pombo was uppermost, and *vice versâ*, it is probable—considering the manner in which Masonry and politics are blended together in the Spanish Republics—that they were rival candidates for power in more ways than one.

New Constitutions seem to have been enacted in 1863, and after this a new Grand Orient of Colombia was formed at Bogota for the Southern States of the Republic. The ordinances were definitely settled December 12, 1866. At this date the Lodges were five in number, and the Grand Master, General T. C. de Mosquera—who, however, had given place in 1871 to Juan de Dios Riomalo.

The two Grand Orients practise the so-called "Scots Rite" (A. and A.S.R.), and appear to have worked together in perfect harmony. In 1879 we find Juan M. Grau at the head of both, with the title of Sov. G. Com. and Sublime G.M. of the Order. The Secretary General (or Grand Secretary) was also for a time the same for the two bodies, though there was always a separate Lieut. G. Com. (or D.G.M.) at Carthagena and Bogota. In 1883, Leon Echeverria was elected G.M. of the Order, an office which he continues to hold, according to the Calendars of 1886, where, however, his name is also shown as Sov. G. Com. of the Supreme Council at Bogota, "founded in 1827," whilst that of Juan M. Grau is similarly shown as the head of the Supreme Council of Carthagena, "founded in 1833." An English Lodge—Amistad Unida, No. 808—established in 1848, still exists at Santa Martha. Other foreign jurisdictions were formerly represented. "Les Philadelphes," No. 151, was erected at Colon-Aspinwall by the S.C. of France in 1858, and the Isthmus Lodge by the Grand Lodge of Massachusetts in (or before) 1866. Both these Lodges, however, have ceased to exist.

EcUADOR.—Masonry was introduced into this Republic in the year 1857 by the Grand Orient of Peru, which organised Lodges in Guayaquil and Quito. Three years later the Dictator, Garcia Moreno, sought admission into the Fraternity. His application was refused on account of his notoriously immoral character ; and in revenge he called in the Jesuits, and ruthlessly suppressed the Lodges. He was assassinated in 1875, but twelve months elapsed before the population were able to shake off the oppressive yoke of the priesthood. Rumours of a Grand Lodge at Guayaquil have obtained currency, but the evidence is wanting by which alone they can be substantiated.[1]

PERU.—It is traditionally asserted that Freemasonry was introduced into Peru about the year 1807, during the French invasion, and that several Lodges were at work until the resumption of Spanish authority and of Papal influence in 1813, when their existence terminated. But the authentic history of Peruvian Masonry cannot be traced any higher than 1825, when the independence of the Republic, declared in 1820, was completely achieved. In that year,

[1] Authorities—Venezuela, Colombia, and Ecuador :—Laurie, 1859, p. 406 ; Handbuch, vol. iv., p. 33 ; Latomia, vol. xxvi., p. 122 ; Mackey, pp. 154, 240, 854 ; and World-Wide Register, pp. 549-551. *Cf. post*, p. 379

General Valero, a member of the Grand Orient of Colombia at Santa Fé de Bogotá (New Granada), visited Lima, and as the representative of that body proceeded in the first instance to legitimate the Lodges and Chapters which had already been established in the new Republic, and afterwards to found and organise others. At this time there appear to have been four Lodges at the capital, and nine others were soon after erected in the provincial towns.[1]

A Supreme Council of the A. and A.S.R. 33° was instituted at Lima in 1830 by the senior (local) member of the Rite, José Maria Monson, Roman Catholic Chaplain in the Army of Independence, and afterwards a Canon in the Cathedral of Trujillo. In the following year —June 23—deputies from the Supreme Council 33°, the Consistory 32°, the Areopagus 30°, and the Chapters 18°, together with the Masters and Wardens of the Lodges, assembled in the capital under the presidency of the Sov. G. Com. of the S.C., and established a Grand Lodge, with Thomas Ripley Eldredge as G.M. The constitutions were settled on August 11, 1831, when it was unanimously resolved to substitute for the title "Grand Lodge," that of "Grand Orient of Peru." Shortly after this, owing to the political disturbances, there was an entire cessation of Masonic labour.

In 1845, after a recess of some twelve years, a few metropolitan brethren, members of the Lodge "Orden y Libertad," and of a Rose Croix Chapter, met and continued to work regularly until November 1, 1848, when a General convention of Masons was held, and the Grand Orient was revived. In 1850 the G.O. again assembled, and sanctioned a constitution for the government of the Lodges. Marshal Miguel San Roman—afterwards President of the Republic—was G.M. of this Grand Orient until 1852, but the Supreme Council 33° not only held aloof from its proceedings, but apparently ignored even its existence.

On July 13, 1852, the supreme Masonic body was reorganised under the title of Grand National Orient of Peru, and the members of the so-called high degrees recovered their supremacy. At this meeting twenty-five brethren represented the Supreme Council, Consistory, Areopagus, and the Rose Croix Chapters. There were also present the Masters and Wardens of three Lodges—Orden y Libertad, and Estrella Polar, of Lima ; and Concordia Universal of Callao. Of these, the first named was founded in 1822, the second (by the G.O. over which Marshal San Roman presided) in 1850-52, and the third (by the Supreme Council of Peru) in 1852.

In the same year (1852) a Royal Arch Chapter—Estrella Boreal—No. 74 on the roll of the Grand Chapter of Scotland, was established at Callao. This, however, was not recognised by the Supreme Council of Peru, nor was it allowed a voice in the deliberations of the Grand National Orient.

In 1855 a new Lodge under an old title—Virtud y Union—was erected at Lima by charter of the Supreme Council 33°.

New statutes were promulgated by the Grand Orient May 5, 1856. These were very defective, consisting only of some disjointed extracts from the laws of the G.O. of Venezuela, and placed the government of the Fraternity entirely in the hands of the Supreme Council

---

[1] *Lima*—Paz y Perfecta Union, 1821 ; Orden y Libertad, 1822 ; Virtud y Union, 1823 ; and Constancia Peruana, 1824 : *Cuzco*—Sol de Huayna Ccapac, 1826 : *Lambayeque*—Union Justa, 1826 : *Piura*—Constancia Heroica, 1829 : and *Ica*—Filosofia Peruana, 1829. Five other Lodges were also formed about the same time in *Arequipa*, *Trujillo*, *Cajamarca*, *Puno*, and *Huamachuco* respectively, but their names and dates of constitution have passed out of recollection.

33°. At this time there were seven Lodges holding warrants from the Supreme Council—acting on behalf of the Grand National Orient. Of these five were in Peru, and one each in Ecuador and Chilé. Additional regulations, framed with the especial object of restraining certain irregularities which—it was alleged—had penetrated into the Lodges, were enacted in May 1857. The new statutes caused the cup of indignation to overflow, and three Lodges—Concordia Universal, Estrella Polar, and Virtud y Union—on June 3, 6, and 10 respectively ensuing, declared their independence. These were joined by others to the number of fifteen, and a Grand Lodge was erected at Lima, November 20, 1859. In 1860 there was another schism in the Supreme Council, and the seceders, with the G.L., formed a G.O. and S.C. under a charter from the Grand Orient of Colombia (New Granada). In 1863, however, dissensions arose in this body, and it passed out of existence.

Irish Lodges were established at Lima in 1861 and 1863, and several foreign jurisdictions soon after became represented. Among these Scotland is entitled to the first place, having chartered no less than thirteen Lodges.[1] Under the Grand Lodge of Massachusetts a Lodge was formed by dispensation at Arica in 1866, but is now extinct. The Grand Orient of Italy and the Grand Lodge of Hamburg each possess a Lodge at Lima, the Italian Lodge bearing the name "Stella D'Italia," and the German one " Zur Eintracht " (Concord).

The Supreme Council reorganised the Grand Orient, but again suppressed it in 1875, and sentenced the opponents of this summary proceeding to " perpetual expulsion." The sentence was revoked in 1881, the G.O. once more revived, and the Lodges placed under it. This gave umbrage to the latter, who contended that even if the S.C. was justified in separating itself from the Lodges, it could not possess the right of turning them over to any other body. Ultimately, in March 1882, five Lodges met in convention at Lima, and organised the " Grand Lodge of Peru." Four out of the five Scottish Lodges at the capital are said to have given in their adhesion on May 31, and shortly after a Lodge was established at Guayaquil in Ecuador. The present G.M. is Cæsar Canevaro—General and Senator—and the Grand Lodge has a following of twenty-two Lodges.[2]

BOLIVIA.—There is no Grand Lodge in this Republic. In 1875 a Lodge was chartered by one of the competing jurisdictions in Lima, and is possibly included among the four Lodges in Bolivia under the present G.L. of Peru.

CHILÉ.—Masonry is said to have been practised in Chilé, under a French warrant, as early as 1840, but the first Lodge in the Republic which I have succeeded in tracing is L'Etoile du Pacifique, established at Valparaiso by the Grand Orient of France, September 12, 1851. The next was the Pacific Lodge, formed shortly afterwards, under a dispensation from the G.M. of California, but its existence was limited to a single year. After this came L'Union Fraternelle—under the G.O. of France—also at Valparaiso, chartered in 1854. The fourth

[1] Nos. 445, Peace and Concord, 1865, Callao ; 479, Honour and Progress, 1868—515, Kosmos, 516, Paz y Progreso, 521, Arca de Noe, and 522, Regeneracion Fraternal, 1872—545, Atahualpa, 1874—558, Virtud y Union Regenerada, and 559, La Valle de Francia, 1875—all at Lima ; 560, Independencia, 1875, Callao ; 561, Constantia y Concordia, 1875, Tacna ; 577, Paz y Caridad, 1876, Mollendo ; and 643, Pioneer, 1879, Iquique.

[2] Authorities :—Arthur M. Wholey, Freemasonry in Peru ; Handbuch, vol. iv., p. 137 ; Latomia, vols. xv., p. 230; xvi., p. 248 ; xxiii., p. 187 ; xxvi., p. 125 ; Freemasons' Magazine, May 12, 1866 ; Mackey, p. 576 ; Proc. Grand Lodge, Massachusetts, 1866, p. 96 ; Louisiana, 1877, p. 159 ; 1883, p. 163 ; Illinois, 1884, pp. 70, 106 ; and Maine, 1884, p. 118 ; 1885, p. 204 ; and 1886, p. 530.

Lodge—Aurora du Chilé—is said to have been established under the same sanction at Concepcion, and to have subsequently assumed the name of Fraternidad, but I have been unable to trace it in the French Calendars. The fifth—Estrella del Sur—which also met in Concepcion, was chartered by the G.O. of Peru, but the warrant was returned in the year 1860.

The next three Lodges, Bethesda, Southern Cross, and Hiram of Copiapo, derived their origin from the Grand Lodge of Massachusetts, the first in 1853, and the last two in 1858. Bethesda and Southern Cross met at the capital, and Hiram—as its name imports—at Copiapo in the first instance, and afterwards at Caldera. The Lodge of 1853—Bethesda—is still at work, but those established in 1858—Southern Cross and Hiram—became extinct about 1860 and 1881 respectively.

In 1861 a member of the A. and A.S.R. 33°, from Lima, Peru, established by his own authority a Lodge called Orden y Libertad in Copiapo, which forthwith addressed circulars to the other Lodges in Chilé asking for recognition. This they declined to accord, basing their refusal on the ground that the founder of the new Lodge belonged to a spurious and irregular Supreme Council 33°, and had been expelled from the Grand Orient of Peru; also that it was not within the power of even a *regular* Inspector General 33° to establish .a Lodge as it were single-handed, or, in other words, without the sanction of a Supreme Council of the Rite.

In April 1862 the news that Marshal Magnan had been appointed by the Emperor G.M. of the Grand Orient of France reached Chilé. The Lodges L'Union Fraternelle, Valparaiso, and Fraternidad, at Concepcion, immediately threw up their charters, and, it is said, were formally erased from the roll of the G.O. of France by decree dated November 10, 1863.

The two Lodges followed up their secession by asking L'Etoile du Pacifique to unite with them in forming a Grand Lodge, but their request met with a refusal. Nothing daunted, they then, in order to obtain a quorum of Lodges, formed a third, called Progreso, but to which no charter was given.

On April 20, 1862, these three Lodges met in convention, where they also found delegates from Orden y Libertad, of Copiapo, the very same Lodge to which recognition had been refused in the previous year. The delegates, however, were received, and thus four Lodges combined to form the Grand Lodge of Chilé.

Javier Villanueva was G.M. in 1872, and his address—as reported in the *Boletin Official* of that year—announced internal prosperity and good prospects; the consecration of two new Lodges; large contributions by the Craft for the erection of a Masonic Temple at Valparaiso;[1] and a satisfactory explanation of the action of the Grand Lodge of Massachusetts in her establishment of Lodges in the jurisdiction. The Grand Lodge of Chilé had then nine subordinate Lodges. Their strength is not given, but in the previous year there were seven Lodges, with a total membership of eight hundred and seven. The number of Lodges on its roll has since risen to eleven, and the Grand Master at the present date (1886) is Don José-Miguel Faez. There are also some Lodges under the A. and A.S.R. 33°, which, according to Van Dalen's Calendar, obey a Grand Orient, established in 1862; but in the *Annuaire* of the G.O. of France, are rendered subject to a Supreme Council, founded in 1870.

---

[1] This was subsequently built at a cost of nearly 80,000 dollars.

Foreign jurisdictions are numerously represented. The Grand Lodge of Massachusetts has two Lodges—Bethesda, 1853, and Aconcagua, 1869—at the capital, besides Huelen, 1876, in Santiago, and St John's Lodge, constituted in 1885 at Concepcion. These are subordinate to a District Deputy Grand Master, the Rev. David Trumbull, D.D. Under the Grand Lodge of Scotland there are Nos. 509, Star and Thistle, Valparaiso, 1871, and 616, St John, Coquimbo—both included with the Lodges of Peru in Province No. 54. The Grand Lodges of England and Hamburg have each chartered a single Lodge, No. 1411, Harmony, 1872, existing under the jurisdiction of the former, and Lodge Lessing under that of the latter. Both of these meet at Valparaiso. The Lodge of earliest date in the country, L'Etoile du Pacifique, established by the Grand Orient of France in 1851, is still active, and has never swerved from its original allegiance.[1]

ARGENTINE REPUBLIC, or CONFEDERACY OF LA PLATA.—The province of Buenos Ayres, after forming for some years a distinct State, re-entered in 1860 the General Confederacy of La Plata, or Argentine Republic, of which it constitutes the head. The Masonic history of the allied States down to the year named may be very briefly summed up. A Lodge —No. 205, Southern Star—was chartered at the city of Buenos Ayres by the Grand Lodge of Pennsylvania, September 5, 1825. This capital, as the largest town and the outlet of all the trade of the Republic, has always exercised a preponderating influence in the formation and execution of the intrigues, conspiracies, and insurrections, which constitute the political history of the Confederation. From the close connection, therefore, between Masonry and politics, which we find subsisting in all parts of South America, it will excite no surprise that, without exception, all the early Lodges in La Plata, of which any trace has come down to us, were held at Buenos Ayres. Some were in existence there in 1846, but, about that time, the political aspect becoming gloomy in the extreme, their labours were suspended.

Two Lodges bearing the same name—L'Amie des Naufragés—were established by the Grand Orient of France in Buenos Ayres and Rio-de-la-Plata respectively in 1852. The example thus set was followed by the Grand Lodge of England, under whose authority the first of a series of Lodges [2]—in what is now the Confederacy—was erected in 1853. In 1856, there seems to have been in existence a body claiming the prerogatives of a Grand Lodge. It practised the A. and A.S.R., but was never recognised by the family of Supreme Councils, and soon ceased to exist. Two years later—April 22, 1858—a Supreme Council and Grand Orient of the Argentine Republic was established at Buenos Ayres by the S.C. and G.O. of Uruguay, at Monte Video.

About this time—so at least it is gravely related—"the Roman Catholic Bishop [at Buenos Ayres] fulminated a Bull against all Masons within his bishopric, and he went the length of declaring the marriage contract dissolved, and absolving the wife *a vinculo matri- monii*, in all cases where the husband refused to renounce Masonry. Some parties, as high in temporal authority as the Bishop was in spiritual, appealed from his decree to his Holiness Pius IX. at Rome. After waiting a long time for a reply or decision upon the

---

[1] Authorities:—Proc. G.L. Mass., 1866-86 ; Freemason's Mag., 1865, pt. ii., p. 282 ; Latomia, vol. xxvi., p. 130 ; Handbuch, vol. iv., p. 80 ; and Boletin Official de la Gran Lojia de Chilé, 1872.

[2] Nos. 900, Excelsior, 1853 ; 1092, Teutonia, 1859 (*erased*, October 11, 1872) ; 1025, Star of the South, 1864,—all three at Buenos Ayres ; 1553, Light of the South, 1875, Rosario de Santa Fé ; and 1740, Southern Cross, 1878, Cordoba.

appeal, and receiving none, an inquiry was instituted as to the cause of the delay, when it was found, to the great satisfaction of the Roman Catholics of La Plata, who were unwilling to bow to the behests of the Bishop, that, during a sojourn at Monte Video in 1816, the venerable Pontiff—then a young man—received the degrees, and took upon himself the obligations of Masonry!"[1]

This story has now passed into oblivion, but its salient feature—the initiation of Pius IX.—served for a long time as the text for innumerable disquisitions, in which, however, the scene is not always laid in South America, but shifts from Uruguay to Pennsylvania, and from North America to Italy. A statement of similar character (and value) was made long before by J. L. Laurens in his *Essai Historique*, with regard to Pope Benedict XIV., of whom it is related that, being himself a Freemason, he, not unnaturally, mitigated in some slight degree the rigour of the Papal edict against the Craft, which had been launched by his immediate predecessor, Clement XII.

In 1861 a treaty was concluded between the Grand Lodge of England and the Grand Orient of the Argentine Republic. This empowered the former to establish Lodges in La Plata, and to appoint a district G.M. to rule over them. The Rev. J. Chubb Ford presided over the English District Grand Lodge until 1867, when he was succeeded by Mr R. B. Masefield.

About the year 1877, the invariable rebellion of the Lodges against the domination of the Supreme Council 33°, which is always met with in the histories of Grand Orients, occurred in Buenos Ayres. There appears to have been both a protest and secession, but without, in this case, culminating in any definite result.

There were some 13 Lodges under the Grand Orient of La Plata in 1860, 39 in 1878, and 60 in 1886. The Grand Master, who has held office for several years, and was previously the Grand Secretary, is Dr Manuel H. Langenheim. Foreign jurisdictions are represented by four Lodges under the Grand Lodge of England; by two under the Grand Orient of Italy; and by one each under the Grand Orient of France and the Grand Lodge of Hamburg. With the exception of two (English) Lodges, all these meet at Buenos Ayres. The French Lodge was established in 1852, and has already been referred to. Teutonia, under the Grand Lodge of Hamburg, appears to be of English origin, as a Lodge of the same name, working in the German language, was established at the capital by the Grand Lodge of England in 1859.[2]

PARAGUAY.—When this country proclaimed its independence of Spain, the reins of government were seized by Dr Francia, a well-meaning despot, who, during his long administration, carried into effect his ideas of advancing the material interests of the state by shutting it off from all communication with the outer world. Under his government Paraguay was for a long period as effectually closed as Japan had been before it. The same exclusive policy, though without carrying it quite so far, was pursued by his successor, Don Carlos Antonio Lopez. The latter was followed in turn by his son, Don Francisco Solano Lopez, whose action involved the country in the disastrous war of 1864-70 with Brazil, Uruguay,

---

[1] World Wide Register, p. 528.

[2] Authorities :—Rebold, Hist. Tr. G.L., p. 249; Proc. G.L. England, 1877, p. 292; Handbuch, vol. iv., p. 7; Latomia, vol. xxvi., p. 130; and Mackey, p. 132.

and the Argentine Republic. This war cost Paraguay nearly one-half of its territory, and reduced its population from nearly a million and a half to about 220,000, of whom only 29,000 were men. If, conjointly with this, we bear in mind that Paraguay is the only country in South America without any seaboard, it will occasion no surprise that the traces of Masonry in the existing Republic are so faint as to be almost indistinguishable. The population of Asuncion, the capital, had fallen after the war from nearly 50,000 to about 10,000, of whom 3000 belonged for several years—if they do not at the present time—to the Brazilian army of occupation. The Masonic calendars of 1881-82 show a Lodge under the G.O. of Brazil as existing at Paraguay, but whether composed of natives or of the Brazilian garrison, and whether it still exists, are points upon which the statistics at my command leave me wholly in the dark.[1]

URUGUAY.—Masonry—if we may credit Dr Mackey—was introduced into this Republic in 1827 by the Grand Orient of France, which in that year chartered a Lodge called the "Children of the New World." But I have failed to trace any such Lodge in the French Masonic calendars, and it is important to recollect that the independence of Uruguay, or, as it was formerly called, Banda Oriental (*Eastern Side*), as a Republic, was only definitely established by a treaty dated August 27, 1828. The country prides itself on possessing one of the finest political constitutions in South America. It sounds, therefore, almost like irony to be obliged to add that this Republic has been cursed with more frequent revolutions than any other in the New World. In one respect, however, Uruguay is decidedly in advance of the Indian Republic of Paraguay. It has a large, well-built, and pleasant capital, Monte Video, of which one-third of the residents are foreigners. A Lodge—No. 217, Asilio de la Virtud—was chartered in this city by the Grand Lodge of Pennsylvania, February 6, 1832. After this the Masonic history of Uruguay is a complete blank until the year 1841, in which year, also at Monte Video, Les Amis de la Patrie—ultimately a Lodge, Chapter, Areopagus, and Consistory—was established by the Grand Orient of France. Further Lodges are said to have been erected under warrants from Brazil, but of these no exact record is forthcoming. The next event of any importance occurred in 1855, when authority was obtained from one of the then existing Grand Orients at Rio Janeiro to establish a governing Masonic body, and the Supreme Council and Grand Orient of Uruguay were formally constituted at Monte Video. The present Sov. G. Com. and G.M. is Dr Carlos de Castro, who has held both offices for some years. The number of subordinate Lodges is thirty-four.

Besides Les Amis de la Patrie, under the G.O. of France, which still exists, foreign jurisdictions are represented at Monte Video by the following Lodges—England, No. 1178, Acacia, 1861; Spain (Becerra's Grand Lodge), No. 281, Paz y Esperanza; and Italy, I. Figli Dell' Unità Italiana, and I. Liberi Pensatori. A Lodge, Avenir et Progres, No. 182, was formed—also at the capital—under the Supreme Council of France in 1865, but is now extinct.[2]

BRAZIL.—In 1820 the solitary representative of the Craft in the then kingdom of Brazil was a Lodge at Rio Janeiro, which is said to have been established under a French warrant in 1815. In 1821 this Lodge threw off two shoots, or, more correctly speaking, divided itself

[1] Masonic Calendars; Bates, Central and South America, pp. 399, 599; and Globe Encyclopædia, *s.v.* Paraguay.
[2] Authorities :—Masonic Calendars; Rebold, p. 333; Mackey, p. 850; and Bates, pp. 404, 406.

into three parts, and these by their deputies formed the first Grand Orient of Brazil. The modern French rite of seven degrees was adopted, or rather continued, which, together with the traditional ancestry of the original Lodge, will account for the speedy recognition of the new organisation by the G.O. of France. In the same year Dom Pedro, Regent, and afterwards Emperor, of Brazil, was initiated in one of the three Lodges. This was immediately followed by his being proclaimed Grand Master, but soon convincing himself that the Masonic associations were in all but name mere political *coteries*, he ordered their meetings to be discontinued in 1822.

In the following year—November 17—Le Bouclier de l'Honneur Français was erected at Rio Janeiro by the G.O. of France, but there is no reason to suppose that it enjoyed any better fate than befel the Lodges of earlier date, all of which remained in an enforced trance until the departure for Europe of the Emperor Dom Pedro in 1831.

After the abdication of that monarch a "Grand Brazilian Orient" was established, which led to the revival of the older (or original) "Grand Orient of Brazil," under its first G.M., Jose Bonefacio de Andrada e Silva. Political enmities soon made their presence felt. The Grand Orient of 1821 was despotic, and that of 1831 democratic. Both worked the modern French Rite, but each anathematised and hurled defiance at the other.

In 1832 Montezuma, Viscount Jequitinhonha, who had served as ambassador at several European Courts, returned to Brazil, where he was empowered by the Supreme Council of Belgium to establish a branch of the A. and A.S.R. Accordingly, in November 1832, he proceeded to institute a Supreme Council 33° for Brazil. The rivalry of this new body put the two Grand Orients on their mettle. They at once commenced to warrant Chapters and Consistories, and ended by each erecting a Supreme Council. In 1835, however, further complications arose. Dissensions occurred among the constituents of Supreme Council No. 1. Some of these cast in their lot with the "G.O. of Brazil," and elected Andrada e Silva their Sov. G. Com.; another section erected a Supreme Council of its own (No. 2); whilst the remainder continued steadfast in their allegiance to their founder, Montezuma. At this period, therefore, there were in active existence two Grand Orients and four Supreme Councils. In the same year (1835) the first of a series of Lodges in the Empire was chartered by the Grand Lodge of England,[1] and the peace of the Craft was much harassed by political disturbances in the Province of Pará—the last in Brazil to declare its independence of the mother country and acknowledge the authority of the first Emperor. According to a recent writer, at this time the native party in Pará were much enraged with the Portuguese. There was a serious revolt, and the former in an evil hour called to their aid the ignorant and fanatic mongrel and Indian population. "The cry of death to the Portuguese was soon changed to that of death to the Freemasons, then a powerfully organised society, embracing the greater part of the male white inhabitants."[2]

In 1838 Viscount Albuquerque succeeded Andrada e Silva as G.M. of the Grand Orient of Brazil (G.O. No. 1), and was followed in 1850 by the Marquis d'Abrantes. Meanwhile, in 1842, the Grand Brazilian Orient (G.O. No. 2) had openly rejected the Modern French Rite, and transferred its allegiance to the A. and A.S.R. 33°. This in turn had been followed by a

---

[1] Nos. 616, Orphan, 1835, and 703, St John, 1841, Rio Janeiro (*erased* March 5, 1862); and 970, *now* 672, Southern Cross, 1856, Pernambuco.

[2] H. W. Bates, The Naturalist on the River Amazons, 1863, p. 39.

junction between the Grand Brazilian Orient and Supreme Council No. 2. Thus only three distinct and separate organisations were left in the field, viz., the two Grand Orients, each with a Supreme Council, and the Original Supreme Council (No. 1) under Montezuma.

A list of Brazilian Lodges, numbered in consecutive order from 1 to 130, is given in the *World Wide Register* for 1860. In the year last named—September 30—Grand Orient No. 2 and Supreme Council No. 1 were dissolved and suppressed by Imperial decree. This left the older (or original) G.O. of Brazil in possession of the field. Not, however, for any long period. In 1863 there was further strife, and the Grand Orient split into two parts, each of which became popularly known by the name of the street in which it assembled. One body, the G.O. of Lavradio Valley, chose as its G.M. Baron Cayru, who was followed by Dr Joachim Marcellino de Brito in 1865, and by the Visconde do Rio Branco in 1870. The other moiety, the G.O. of Benedictine Valley, elected Dr Joachim Saldanha Marinho to preside over them.

In 1872 the schism was apparently healed by the amicable fusion of the two Grand Orients, but within a year dissensions again broke out, and with undiminished virulence, each of the two opponents once more seeking recognition as the legitimate Grand Orient of Brazil.

The Lavradios were again arrayed under the standard of Rio Branco, Prime Minister of the Empire; whilst the Benedictinos renewed their fealty to Saldanha Marinho, a former Minister of State, and the head of the Liberal party. The various Lodges throughout the country once more divided their allegiance, some adhering to the Lavradio faction, but the larger number enrolling themselves on the side of the Benedictinos.

The discord passed through sundry phases. In the first instance, and to go back beyond the temporary fusion of 1872, the two Grand Orients reflected pretty accurately the prevailing opinions of the rival parties in the State. In course of time it became a recognised fact that the Lavradios were supporters of the clerical authority, whilst the Benedictinos, on the other hand, everywhere denounced the evils of priestcraft and Ultramontanism. At this period the clergy entered fully into the fray. On one party they bestowed high praise; on the other they lavished terms of opprobrium. The Lavradios, however, under the benignant rule of Rio Branco, gradually grew less bigoted and illiberal in their ideas, and in 1873 twenty-three of their Lodges went over to the enemy. This example was quickly followed by fifteen others. It is probable that the secession just referred to was also in some measure the result of proceedings which it becomes my next task to relate.

The Jesuits, driven from most of the European countries, selected Brazil as a field for their enterprise. For a long time the Church and the Freemasons had lived in peace, and the population of Pernambuco was always recognised as the type of Christian piety. But the Bishop of that diocese—a young monk, aged twenty-three—at the bidding of the Jesuits, attempted to enforce the Papal Bull against the Freemasons. The prelate had counted on the support of the people, but his high-handed measures turned the tide of popular feeling. The Bishop was mobbed in his own palace, and the military had to be called in to protect him.

Eventually the Government interfered, and the Bishop, disdaining to avail of the *locus pœnitentiæ* which had been devised for him, was sentenced to four years' imprisonment. The Archbishop of Bahia and the Bishops of Olinda, Pará, Rio Janeiro, Dramantina, and Marianna are also said—in violation of the orders of their Government—to have hurled their anathemas against the Craft.

The fickle populace then turned once more against the Freemasons, who suffered much at the hands of the mob, and were refused the sacraments of the Church, and burial for their dead in consecrated ground, by the clergy. The Benedictinos nevertheless held their own, and especially distinguished themselves in the spread of liberal ideas. Among the measures they energetically supported were acts for the abolition of slavery and for the foundation of public libraries. Instructive lectures, moreover, were delivered from time to time by members of this party. Meanwhile the Lavradios had gradually shaken off the yoke of their clerical allies, by whom they were ultimately regarded with the same aversion as their rivals, and in 1877 there were attempts at a fusion. At this time the Benedictinos under Saldanha Marinho numbered 216, and the Lavradios, under Rio Branco, 56 Lodges.

Six years later—January 18, 1883—the union was perfected, and Francisco José Cardoso proclaimed G.M. and Sov. G. Com. of the (sole) Grand Orient of Brazil. Three rites are recognised by this body—the A. and A.S.R. 33°, the Modern French (7°), and the Adonhiramite rites. Each of these is governed by a Chamber of the G.O., which is styled a Grand Lodge. In 1883 there were 139 Lodges, 48 of these meeting at the city of Rio Janeiro, and 91 in the provinces. At the present date (1886) the total number of Lodges under the G.O. is 210. Foreign jurisdictions (or Grand Lodges) are represented by the following Lodges:—ENGLAND: No. 970, Southern Cross, Pernambuco, 1856; SCOTLAND: No. 473, Progresso, Rio Grande, 1867; and HAMBURG: of the Palm of Peace, Blumenau, 1885. Among the Lodges formerly existing, but now extinct, may be named Le Bouclier de l'Honneur Français, Rio Janeiro, 1823 (G.O. of France); No. 378 [   ], Maranham, 1856 (Grand Lodge of Ireland); and "German Friend-ship of the Southern Cross," originally two Brazilian Lodges, which amalgamated in 1856, and found a place on the roll of the Grand Lodge of Hamburg in 1859.[1]

GUIANA.

I must now devote a few words to the region situated north of Brazil and east of Vene-zuela, which forms the only remaining portion of the Southern Continent still held by European Powers. Guiana, or Guayana, in its widest sense, certainly embraces the whole of the Sierra Parimé, thus including districts belonging to Venezuela and Brazil; but the term is now generally restricted to the colonial possessions of England, France, and Holland in this part of the world.

BRITISH GUIANA.—Two Lodges are known to have been in existence at the capital, George-town or Demerara, in the last century. The first—St Jean de la Re-Union—was established by the Grand Lodge of Holland in 1771, and the second, No. 887, on the roll of the Grand Lodge of Ireland, apparently very soon after the cession of a portion of Guiana—now forming the British Colony of that name—in 1796. Three years later a Dutch Lodge, bearing the

---

[1] Authorities :—Mackey, p. 125 ; Findel, p. 696 ; New England Freemason, vol. i., 1874, pp. 27, 287 [giving the admirable speech made by Visconde do Rio Branco in reply to the attack on Freemasonry in the Senate of Brazil] ; Boletim do Grande Or.˙. Unido do Brazil, 1872 ; Handbuch, vols. i., p. 127 ; iii., p. 554 ; iv., p. 20 ; Proc. G. L. Canada, 1873-74, pp. 477, 495, 671 ; Latomia, vol. xxiii., pp. 63, 226 ; and Cosm. Cal. 1886, p. 278.

somewhat singular name of Cœlum non Mutat Gesus, was formed in Berbice; and in 1801 the "Chosen Friends of Demerara" was established by the Grand Lodge of New York. The fourth Lodge at Georgetown—Union, No. 358—was constituted under an Atholl warrant, July 28, 1813; and the fifth—Mount Olive, No. 812—by the United Grand Lodge of England in 1827. Further English Lodges—Nos. 682, Lodge of Fellowship, and 1183, Phœnix—were erected at New Amsterdam in 1839 and 1867 respectively. The four earliest Lodges have long since ceased to exist; No. 682 under the Grand Lodge of England was erased June 4, 1862; but all the other Lodges above enumerated are still active. In 1858, a dispensation to open a Lodge at Demerara was refused—in my opinion, very prudently—by the Grand Lodge of Canada.

DUTCH GUIANA, or SURINAM.—In the *Freemason's Calendar*, 1776, a list is given of the Lodges in Holland and the Dutch colonies. Among these are La Vertieuse, 1769, and La Fidèle Sincèrité, 1771, at Batavia; and Concordia, 1762, La Zelée, 1767, and Le Croissant des Trois Clefs, 1768, at Surinam. Apparently the same Lodges, though with slightly varied dates of formation, and in a solitary instance a change of name, are also shown in the edition of the same publication for 1778.[1] Of these there seem to be two survivors at the present day, which in the Official Calendar of the Grand Lodge of the Netherlands (1886) are described as Nos. 8, De Ster in het Oosten, 1769, Batavia; and 13, Concordia, 1773, Parimaribo. They are included in the Masonic province of Surinam.

Other Lodges in Guiana, of which there is no complete record, have doubtless lived their span and died; but the only particulars with regard to them that I have been able to glean will be found in the note below,[2] to which, however, must be added, that there was a "Surranam Lodge" under the Prov. G.L. of New England in 1761.

FRENCH GUIANA, or CAYENNE.—Three Lodges in all appear to have been constituted at Cayenne, the capital of the colony, which is now scarcely anything more than a penal settlement of the French Government. The first, L'Anglaise, was established in 1755 by the Mother Lodge of the same name—No. 204—at Bordeaux; the second, La Parfaite Union, in 1829, by the Grand Orient of France; and the third, La France Equinoxiale, in 1844, by the Supreme Council 33° of the same country. The last named is at present the only Lodge at work in Cayenne.[3]

The only region of South America which still awaits notice is PATAGONIA, and it is almost needless to state that Masonry is as yet unknown to the various Tehuelche tribes which roam between the Rio Negro and the Strait of Magellan.

AUSTRALASIA.

Tasmania and New Zealand, together with the whole of Australia, were originally subject

---

[1] La Vertieuse, 1767, and La Fidèle Sincèrité, 1771, Batavia; La Zelée, 1707, Concordia and L'Union, 1773, Surinam.

[2] Standvastigheid, Parimaribo; La Zelée, L'Union, La Solitaire, Cura et Vigilantia, and Concordia, Surinam (World Wide Register, 1860, p. 546). *Cf. ante*, p. 337, note 1.

[3] Authorities—English, Dutch, and French Guiana :—Masonic Calendars; Daruty and Rebold's Lists; Letters from S. B. Oldham, Dep. G. Sec. Ireland, and J. P. Vaillant, G. Sec. Holland; Proc. G.L. Canada, vol. i, 1855-60, p. 192; and St John's G.L. Boston, U.S.A., 1783-92, pp. 73, 79.

to the government of New South Wales, and the following are the dates on which the former colonies became independent of the latter:—Tasmania, 1825 ; Western Australia, 1829 ; South Australia, 1834 ; New Zealand, 1841 ; Victoria, 1851 ; and Queensland, 1859.

NEW SOUTH WALES.—The Lodge of Social and Military Virtues—No. 227 on the roll of the Grand Lodge of Ireland—attached to the 46th Foot in 1752, after undergoing many vicissitudes, was at work in the same regiment at Sydney in 1816. This paved the way for the establishment of stationary Lodges, and Irish warrants were issued to Nos. 260, Australian Social, in 1820, and 266, Leinster, in 1824. The third (strictly colonial) Lodge, No. 820, Australia, was erected by the Grand Lodge of England in 1828. The last named, as well as the Irish Lodges, met at Sydney, the capital. The first established in any other part of the Colony was No. 668, St John, constituted at Paramatta in 1838, and the second, No. 697, the Lodge of Australia Felix, at Melbourne—then included in the government of New South Wales—in 1841. An Irish Lodge—No. 275—was erected at Windsor in 1843, and in the same year, No. 408, Australasian Kilwinning, at Melbourne, received a Charter from the Grand Lodge of Scotland.

From this point the statistics will be given according to the jurisdictions represented. Thus, the number of Lodges established in the Colony during the two decennial periods next ensuing was as follows:—1844-53, English, seven ; Irish and Scottish, one each : 1854-63, English, fourteen ; Irish, one ; and Scottish, seven. In the twelve years immediately following (1864-75), the additions were: English, fourteen; Irish, three; and Scottish, ten. The subsequent numbers (1876-85) are: English, thirty-three; Irish, two; and Scottish, thirty-one. The Lodges now active under the three jurisdictions, reckoning the further additions during the current year (1886), are: English, seventy-four (including one in New Caledonia); Irish, one; and Scottish, fifty (with a membership of 2242).[1] An English Provincial Grand Master was appointed in 1839, an example which was followed by the Grand Lodge of Scotland in 1855, and by that of Ireland in 1858. The present rulers of the Craft (under the jurisdiction of the mother countries) in this Colony are: District Grand Masters, Mr John Williams (E.), and Dr W. G. Sedgwick (S.). The Irish Provincial G.L. has ceased to exist.

So far as I am aware, the question of separation from the mother Grand Lodges was first formally mooted in Victoria. Still, for some years, at least, before the event which it becomes my next task to relate, "there had existed in Sydney a body styling itself 'the Grand Lodge of New South Wales,' formed from the great majority of a regular Lodge—St Andrews. It affected to make, pass, and raise Masons, grant charters, and issue certificates."[2]

On December 3, 1877, the representatives of twelve or (at most) thirteen Scottish and Irish Lodges met at Sydney, and established another Grand Lodge of New South Wales, to which, however, the pre-existing body of the same name eventually made submission, and accepted an ordinary Lodge warrant at its hands. At this time (1877) there were eighty-six regular Lodges in the Colony: English, forty-seven; Scottish, thirty; and Irish, nine. The thirteen Lodges which thus assumed to control the dissenting majority of seventy-three,

---

[1] The services of the District G.S., and the expansion of Scottish Masonry in New South Wales, which are alike phenomenal, represent cause and effect. Mr Higstrim, it may be added, has more than once declined the offer of a similar though more highly paid appointment in the Colony.

[2] Circular dated December 23, 1878, signed by "J. S. Farnell, G M., New South Wales."

sheltered themselves under a perverted principle of Masonic law [1]—applied to a wholly illusory state of facts. This was, that any three Lodges in a territory "Masonically unoccupied"—the *three* jurisdictions already existing being thus coolly and quietly ignored—could form themselves into a Grand Lodge, and that when so formed, the remaining Lodges— averse to the movement—were they one hundred or one thousand in number, would be irregular!

The leader in this "misguided and untimely movement,"—as it has been happily characterised by the present Scottish D.G. Secretary, Mr Higstrim—was Mr James S. Farnell, who had been appointed Prov. G.M. under the Grand Lodge of Ireland in 1869. In Australia, as in Canada, the Irish Lodges first raised the flag of independence, but in the former unlike the latter country, there was not the community of feeling, produced by an equal pressure of discontent, which had induced the brethren under the three British jurisdictions in North America to unite for the furtherance of a common end. The disadvantages, indeed, with which all the Australian Lodges had (and still have) to contend were considerable, but, on the other hand, there were (and are) in many minds, feelings—not wholly sentimental— opposed to working under any other warrants of Constitution than those granted by the three earliest of existing Grand Lodges. It may be taken as an axiom, that in any country where matters are ripe for the formation of an independent Grand Lodge, the movement will proceed and mature, and that the large majority of Lodges and brethren will connect themselves with it. If, however, a step in the direction of independence is taken before the Lodges are quite ready for it, the success of the movement will be mainly contingent upon the amount of influence wielded by the leaders of the agitation, or, in other words, upon the extent of their following. Mr Farnell—according to his own statement in 1881—served for twenty years as a member of the parliament of New South Wales, and was also for a time prime minister, but his influence as a Mason does not seem to have been great. When he was elected Grand Master, the affairs of the Irish Province of New South Wales were in thorough confusion,[2] and not the least of the motives which weighed with his supporters— Scotch as well as Irish—appears to have been the growing indisposition to be taxed by (or remit fees to) the mother countries.

The new organisation, at the close of 1885, had been recognised *as the only regular governing Masonic body* in the Colony by thirty-eight Grand Lodges, chiefly, however, American. There seems, indeed, in the United States a decided inclination to regard each uprising of the Lodges in a British colony, as a tribute to the efficacy of a certain doctrine which has been

---

[1] *I.e.*, of *American* Masonic law. Mr Josiah H. Drummond observes :—"The proposition, then, derived from the original principle, as expounded by universal practice in this country, is—Not less than three Lodges, comprising a majority of the Lodges in a new territory, may form a Grand Lodge, having exclusive jurisdiction in such territory." But the same distinguished writer goes on to state :—"The idea that a small minority of the Lodges may form a Grand Lodge, and force the other Lodges into it against their will, or drive them out of existence, seems to us monstrous. In almost all matters in Masonry the majority rules; and while we allow a minority in certain cases to have a decisive negative upon proposed action, in no case do we allow a minority to adopt affirmative action against the will of the majority " (Proc. G.L. Maine, 1885, p. 163). *Cf.* Proc. G.L. Tennessee, 1885 ; and Louisiana, 1886.

[2] According to the Dep. G. Sec. of Ireland (in a letter to Mr H. A. Richardson of Paramatta, dated February 1879) no returns or remittances had been received from the Prov. G.L. for a considerable time, and to clear off the arrears of the subordinate Lodges, the Grand Lodge of Ireland had consented to accept £300, or a composition of about 15s. in the £.

laid down by Dr Mackey with regard to the formation of Grand Lodges. But those American jurisdictions which have lent a willing ear to the specious representations of the Grand Lodge of New South Wales, are now running the gantlet of intelligent criticism, and the several committees by whom they have been hoodwinked or misled, may read with profit some of the reports on correspondence in the larger States, notably, Illinois, Pennsylvania, and New York, where the unaccountable delusion into which so many Grand Lodges have fallen, is discussed with equal candour and ability. It is almost needless to say that a Grand Lodge thus constituted by a small minority of the Lodges in New South Wales, has been refused recognition by the Grand Lodges of the British islands.

In December 1885 the G.M. was Dr H. J. Tarrant. There were forty-four subordinate Lodges, and the total number of initiations since the inauguration of the Grand Lodge had been 1926.

VICTORIA.—The Lodges of Australia Felix and of Australasia (*now* Nos. 474 and 530) were established at Melbourne by the Grand Lodge of England in 1841 and 1846 respectively. Scottish Masonry obtained a footing in the same city—with "Australasian Kilwinning"—in 1843; and an Irish Lodge—Hiram, No. 349—was also chartered there in 1847. In the same year a third English, and apparently the fifth Victorian, Lodge—Unity and Prudence, No. 801—was constituted at Geelong. After this the Craft advanced in prosperity by leaps and bounds. Thirty-six English Lodges were added to the list between 1847 and the close of 1862; twenty-eight during the ensuing thirteen years, and twenty within the decennial period commencing January 1, 1876. During corresponding intervals of time, the Irish warrants granted in the colony were respectively twelve, seven, and three: and the Scottish, three each in the first two periods, and two in the last.

The first Provincial G.M. of Victoria (or Australia Felix) was the Hon. J. E. Murray. The date of his appointment by the Grand Lodge of Scotland has not been recorded, but he was succeeded by Mr J. H. Ross, August 3, 1846. The present District G.M. is Sir W. J. Clarke, who received his Scottish patent in 1883. English and Irish Provinces were established in 1855 and 1856 respectively, and the following has been the succession of English Provincial (*now* District) Grand Masters:—Captain (*now* Major-General Sir Andrew) Clarke, 1855; Captain F. C. Standish, 1861; and Sir W. J. Clarke, 1883. The rulers of the Irish Province have been Mr J. T. Smith, 1856-79; and from 1880, Sir W. J. Clarke.

The Lodges now (1886) at work under the three jurisdictions, all of which, however, are in a manner united under a single Provincial G.M., are:—English, ninety-one; Irish, seventeen; and Scottish, twelve (including one in Levuka, Fiji).

The idea of forming an independent Grand Lodge of Victoria seems to have been first launched in 1863, and after encountering the opposition of the Earl of Zetland, was debated —March 2, 1864—in the Grand Lodge of England, by which body a resolution was passed declaring its "strong disapprobation" of the contemplated secession. It was observed in prescient terms by the late John Havers, that "every new Grand Lodge was the forerunner of new and conflicting degrees. It was a stone pulled away from the foundations of Masonry, and opened another door for inroads and innovations;" and he exhorted the brethren in Victoria to "remember that union was strength, and universality one of the watchwords of Masonry."

In 1876, the agitation for a local Grand Lodge was renewed, but again slumbered until

1883, when the scheme was fairly carried into effect by an insignificant minority of the Lodges.

In the latter year a meeting was held, and a Masonic Union of Victoria formed, April 27. At this time there were seventy English, fifteen Irish, and ten Scottish Lodges in the colony—total, ninety-five. On June 19 certain delegates met, and the adhesion of eighteen Lodges—twelve Irish, five Scottish, and one English—to the cause was announced. But the number has since been reduced by the subtraction of the English Lodge and one other, which were erroneously named in the proceedings. By this convention it was resolved "that the date of founding the Grand Lodge of Victoria should be July 2, 1883." Thus we find *sixteen* Lodges, with an estimated membership of about 840, calmly transforming themselves into the *governing body* of a territory containing *ninety-five* Lodges, and a membership of *five thousand !*

This organisation has a following of about twenty subordinate Lodges; and as the proceedings of some Grand Lodges baffle all reasonable conjecture, it will occasion no surprise to learn that by seventeen of these bodies the titular "Grand Lodge of Victoria" had been duly recognised at the close of 1885, as the supreme Masonic authority in this Australian colony. At the same date Mr G. Coppin entered upon the second year of his Grand Mastership, having been installed—November 4—in the presence of the Grand Masters of New South Wales and South Australia.

Meanwhile, however, the English, Irish, and Scottish Lodges, which have remained true to their former allegiance, are united in a solid phalanx under a single Provincial (or District) G.M.—Sir W. J. Clarke ; and should the day arrive when independence is constitutionally asserted by the century and m re of Lodges [1] which obey this common chief, those bodies by whom the *soi-disant* Grand Lodge has been accorded recognition, will find themselves confronted by an interesting problem, not unlike that propounded with so much dramatic effect by the late Mr Sothern in the *rôle* of Lord Dundreary, viz., "whether it is the dog that wags his tail, or the tail that wags the dog ?"

SOUTH AUSTRALIA.—The South Australian Lodge of Friendship, Adelaide, No. 613 (and later, No. 423), on the roll of the Grand Lodge of England, was constituted at the British metropolis in 1834. The founders were all in London at the time, and two persons—afterwards Sir John Morphett, President of the Legislative Council, and Sir R. D. Hanson, Chief Justice of the colony—were initiated. A second English Lodge was established at Adelaide in 1844, and in the same year, also at the capital, a Scottish one.

In 1855 the first Irish charter was received in the colony, and in 1883 the total number of Lodges formed in South Australia was as follows:—English, twenty active, one extinct; Irish, seven active, three extinct; and Scottish, six, all active.

The initiative in forming a province was taken by Scotland in 1846, a step followed by England in 1848, and Ireland in 1860.

In 1883 there were premonitory symptoms that the lamentable examples set by a minority of the Lodges in the adjacent colonies of New South Wales and Victoria, in usurping the authority and honour which should belong to the majority, would be followed in South Australia. The imminence of this danger induced Mr H. M. Addison to form a Masonic Union, whose labours resulted—April 16, 1884—in a convention of 85 delegates, representing

---

[1] The approximate number, counting Lodges under dispensations, is 125.

twenty-eight Lodges, by whom the Grand Lodge of South Australia was established. The proceedings of the executive committee of the Masonic Union, which were characterised throughout by the most scrupulous regularity, were crowned by an unprecedented unanimity of feeling on the part of the Lodges. A resolution in favour of independence was carried *nem. con.* in eighteen English, four Irish, and six Scottish Lodges, and with a single dissentient in one English, and with two dissentients in one Irish Lodge; whilst in the sole remaining Lodge under England, and in the "Mostyn" under Ireland, a majority of the members joined the Union. Thus, in effect, out of a grand total of thirty-three Lodges under the three British jurisdictions, only a single Lodge—No. 363—Duke of Leinster (I.), has adhered to its former allegiance. The new Grand Lodge (besides the usual indiscriminate recognition of American Grand Bodies) has been admitted to fraternal relations with the Grand Lodges of England, Ireland, and Scotland. The privilege, however, accorded by the last named in August 1885, was cancelled in the November following, a proceeding, there is every reason to believe, arising out of the inconsistent action of the colonial Grand Lodge in recognising the authority of the Grand Lodge of New South Wales—the irregular establishment of which, it was declared by Mr Addison, at the formation of the Masonic Union in Adelaide, July 30, 1883, would, if imitated, "bring Masonry in South Australia into disrepute throughout the world."

The Hon. S. J. Way, Chief Justice of the Colony, and Mr J. H. Cunningham, formerly District Grand Secretary (E.), have been Grand Master and Grand Secretary respectively, since the foundation of the Grand Lodge. The subordinate Lodges are thirty-six in number, with a total membership of 2277.

QUEENSLAND.—The North Australian Lodge was established at Brisbane by the Grand Lodge of England in 1859, and two others under Irish and Scottish warrants respectively, were constituted at the same town in 1864.

Each jurisdiction is represented by a Provincial (or District) G.M., and the number of Lodges is as follows:—English, twenty-six active, two extinct; Irish, eleven active, three extinct; and Scottish, twelve, all active.

WEST AUSTRALIA.—Eight Lodges in all have been formed in this colony, the first of which —St John, No. 712—was erected at Perth in 1842. Seven of these survive, and being included in no Province, report direct to the Grand Lodge of England, which in this solitary instance, has not suffered from the exercise of concurrent jurisdiction by other Grand Bodies.

TASMANIA.—Lodges under the Grand Lodge of Ireland were established at Hobart Town in 1823, 1829, 1833, and 1834, but the three earliest of the series are now extinct. A fourth Lodge under the same sanction was constituted at Launceston in 1843, and it was not until 1846 that English Masonry obtained a footing on the island. In that year Tasmanian Union, No. 781, was formed at Hobart Town, and a second English Lodge—Hope—sprang up (in the first instance under a dispensation from Sydney) in 1852. In the following year the Rev. R. K. Ewing became the Master of the latter, and in 1856 the Lodges of Faith and Charity were carved out of it—Mr Ewing then becoming, on their joint petition, Prov. G.M. The other English Lodge—Tasmanian Union—objecting to these proceedings, as having been carried on clandestinely, was suspended by the Prov. G.M., and remained closed for nine months. The strife thus engendered nearly put an end to English Masonry in Launceston. Lodge Faith became dormant, Charity was voluntarily wound up, and even in Hope the light almost went out. Soon, however, there was a revival, and in 1876 the Grand Lodge of Scotland also began to charter Lodges on the island, where there are now four in existence under its jurisdiction. These are included in the Province of New South Wales. The Grand Lodges of England and Ireland have each a roll of seven Lodges on the island,—one under the former body, and four under the latter, having surrendered their charters. The English Prov. Grand Lodge died a natural death on the removal of Mr Ewing to Victoria, but a new one was established under Mr W. S. Hammond in 1875. The Irish Lodges were constituted into a Province in 1884.

NEW ZEALAND.

The first Lodge in the Colony—Française Primitive Antipodienne—was founded at Akaroa by the Supreme Council of France, August 29, 1843; the second—Ara—at Auckland, by the Grand Lodge of Ireland in 1844; and the third—New Zealand Pacific—by the Grand Lodge of England in 1845. No further charters were issued until 1852, when English Lodges were established in Lyttelton and Christchurch, whilst others sprang up at New Plymouth and Auckland in 1856, at Wanganui in 1857, and at Nelson and Kaiapoi in 1858. In the latter year an Irish Lodge (the second in the colony) was formed at Napier, and in 1860 an English one at Dunedin—where also the first Scottish Lodge was erected in 1861. After this the diffusion of Masonry throughout New Zealand became so general, that I must content myself with giving the barest statistics, which, for convenience sake, will be classified so as to harmonise as far as possible with the Provincial systems of the three competing jurisdictions. Between 1860 and 1875 there were warranted in the colony twenty-five English, eight Irish, and twenty-one Scottish Lodges; whilst in the ten years ending January 1, 1886, the numbers were respectively forty-seven, seven, and thirty-two.

The Lodges in New Zealand are usually classified according to the Masonic Provinces of which they form a part. Of the latter there are five English and three Scottish, of late years denominated *Districts*, in order to distinguish them from bodies of a like character in Great Britain; and one Irish, to which the more familiar title of Provincial Grand Lodge is still applied. These preliminaries it will be necessary to bear in mind, because the arrangement which seems to me the simplest and best, is to group the Lodges according to their positions on the map, which in the present case will correspond very closely with the territorial classi-fication, or division into Districts, by the Grand Lodge of England.

NORTH ISLAND.

AUCKLAND DISTRICT.—The District (or Provincial) Grand Masters are Mr G. S. Graham (E.), Sir F. Whitaker (S.), and Mr G. P. Pierce (I.); whilst the number of Lodges under the several jurisdictions is eighteen under the G.L. of England, and six each under those of Scotland and Ireland, that is if taken according to locality, for all the Scottish Lodges on the North Island are comprised within the Auckland *District*, and the whole of the Irish Lodges in both islands within the Auckland *Province*.

WELLINGTON DISTRICT.—The only D.G.M. is Mr C. J. Toxward (E.); and the number of Lodges is respectively eighteen (E.), eight (S.), and four (I.).

MIDDLE, OR SOUTH ISLAND.

CANTERBURY DISTRICT.—The D.G.M.'s are Mr Henry Thomson (E.) and the Rev. James Hill (S.), who rule over nineteen and nine Lodges respectively. The seat of government is at Christchurch, where there is also an Irish Lodge, the only one in the District.

OTAGO AND SOUTHLAND DISTRICT.—Mr T. S. Graham presides over one D.G.L. (E.), and Mr G. W. Harvey over the other (S.). There are fourteen Lodges in each District, *i.e.*, according to the local arrangement, for the Scottish D.G.L. (of which there are only two in the South Island) exercises authority beyond the territorial limits of Otago and Southland. The total number of Lodges on its roll is twenty-one, and doubtless Otago has derived much of its importance as a Scottish Masonic centre, from the fact of having been originally founded by an association connected with the Free Church of Scotland. At Dunedin and Invercargill there is in each case an Irish Lodge.

WESTLAND DISTRICT.—The only D.G.M. is Mr John Bevan (E.), who rules over six Lodges; and there are three others (S.) which are comprised within the D.G.L. of Otago and Southland at Dunedin.

MARLBOROUGH AND NELSON DISTRICT.—These Provinces of the colony are exempt from any local Masonic jurisdiction, under the Grand Lodge of England, which is represented by five Lodges. There is also a Scottish Lodge (at Blenheim), which is subject to the D.G.L. of Otago and Southland.[1]

OCEANIA.

Although the various islands and archipelagoes have been treated as far as possible in connection with the continents with which they are ordinarily associated, there are some few of these, lying as it were in mid-ocean, that must be separately dealt with, and their consideration will bring this chapter to a close.

NEW CALEDONIA.—This island was taken possession of by France in 1854, and has been used for some years as a penal settlement. At Noumea, the chief town and the seat of government, there are two Lodges, L'Union Calédonienne, and No. 1864, Western Polynesia. The former was established by the Grand Orient of France in 1868, and the latter (which is included in the Masonic Province of New South Wales) by the Grand Lodge of England in 1880.

FIJI ISLANDS.—The formation of a Lodge—Polynesia—at Levuka, with the assent of the native king, was announced to the Masonic world in a circular dated March 12, 1872. The islands were annexed to Britain in 1874, and on February 1, 1875, a Scottish charter— No. 562—was granted to a Lodge bearing the same name and meeting at the same place as the self-constituted body of 1872. This is comprised in the Masonic Province of Victoria. A second British Lodge—No. 1931, Suva na Viti Levu—was established in the Archipelago by the Grand Lodge of England in 1881.

SOCIETY ISLANDS.—Masonry was introduced into Papeete, the chief town of Tahiti (or Otaheiti), the largest of the Society Group, by the Grand Orient of France in 1834. A

---

[1] Authorities—Australasia :—Proc. G.L. England, 1864, 1865, 1881, 1885 ; Scotland, 1886 ; New Brunswick, 1879, 1884 ; Pennsylvania, 1882 ; Iowa, 1883 ; Illinois, 1884-86 ; New York, 1885 ; and South Australia, 1884-86 ; Freemasons' Calendar ; Masonic Journals ; Manifestoes and Proceedings, claiming recognition as Grand Lodges, from the Associated Lodges in New South Wales and Victoria ; and G. Robertson, New Zealand Masonic Directory, 1886.

Chapter—L'Océanie Française—was established in that year, and a Lodge of the same name in 1842. The labours of these bodies were intermittent, the latter having been galvanised into fresh life in 1850, and the former in 1857. Both Lodge and Chapter are now extinct.

MARQUESAS ISLANDS.—A Lodge, which has long since ceased to exist—L'Amitié—was established at Nukahiva by the Grand Orient of France in 1850.

SANDWICH or HAWAIIAN ISLANDS.—In 1875 there were three Lodges in this group, and more recent statistics show no increase in the number:—Le Progrés de l'Océanie, erected by warrant of the Supreme Council of France in 1850; and the Hawaiian and Wailukee Lodges, under the jurisdiction of the Grand Lodge of California. The last named is at Maui; the others meet at Honolulu, the capital, where they occupy a hall in common. The earliest of the two American Lodges (Hawaiian) was formed in 1852. These three Lodges are composed of natives, Americans, Englishmen, and Germans, between whom the most friendly relations subsist. King Kalakua is an active member of Le Progrés de l'Océanie, and his brother, William Pitt Leleihoku, of the Hawaiian Lodge. The former, who has visited many foreign countries, also evinces the same interest in Masonry while on his travels. On January 7, 1874, he was entertained by Lodge Columbian of Boston (U.S.A.), and on May 22, 1881, by the National Grand Lodge of Egypt. By the latter body the King was elected an Honorary Grand Master, and afterwards delivered a lengthy oration, in which he expressed his belief in Egypt being the cradle both of Operative and Speculative Masonry, and thus may be said to have fully reciprocated the compliment which had been paid him by the meeting.[1]

---

[1] Authorities:—Masonic Calendars; Rebold, Hist. Tr. G.L., pp. 175, 195, 235, 295; Proc. G.L. Canada, 1872, p. 244; 1873, p. 390; Mackey, p. 687; Freemason, July 16, 1881; and New England Freemason, 1875, p. 44.

CHAPTER XXX.

SEA AND FIELD LODGES.

HE only Stated Lodges in ships-of-war appear to have been held under English warrants, though in Portugal and elsewhere there have been meetings of Occasional Lodges where members of the Craft, persecuted on shore, have sought a refuge in the shipping. Field Lodges have existed in numerous jurisdictions, and are variously described. The title used by me occurs in a calendar of 1763, and while sanctioned by early usage, will admit of the inquiry being restricted to the existence of Lodges in military bodies—attached to the latter both in quarters and in the field. The earliest of these Lodges was established in the 1st (British) Regiment of Foot in 1732, under the Grand Lodge of Ireland, and four other similar Lodges, making a total of five, were at work in the same jurisdiction at the close of 1734.[1] The number had risen to eight in 1743, when the first Military Warrant was issued by the Grand Lodge of Scotland, and stood at twenty-nine when the earliest Lodge of the kind was established—1755—by the Grand Lodge of England, in the 8th Foot.

The Irish jurisdiction has always included the greater number of (British) Army Lodges, and in 1813 possessed a military following of one hundred and twenty-three. At the same date, the number of Lodges in regiments under the other British Grand Lodges, and without counting the remote pendicles under Provincial Grand Lodges in foreign parts, was: England, fifteen; Ancients, sixty-two;[2] and Scotland, eighteen. This total has declined, in 1886, to fifteen Lodges, of which nine are Irish and the remainder English.[3]

A record of all the Lodges in regiments, or other movable military cadres, warranted by the British Grand Lodges or their representatives abroad, will be found—to the extent that I have succeeded in tracing them—in the present chapter.[4] The enumeration of stationary Lodges in garrisons or fortresses, even though composed exclusively of military members, lies, however, beyond the scope of my present purpose. The same may be said with regard to the

---

[1] Pocket Companion, Dublin, 1735. From this year I am mainly dependent on information supplied from the Grand Lodge of Ireland, but as *four* out of the *five* Lodges named above are not mentioned in it, and for other reasons, I think there must have been many Irish Lodges in the British army of which all traces have been lost.

[2] Fifty Lodges were carried forward at the Union. *Cf. ante*, p. 8.

[3] *Post*, p. 405.

[4] In cases where a portion of the general subject has been already dealt with, as in the instance of the Brigade Lodges in India (*ante*, p. 326 *et seq.*), the reference will be given.

distinguished roll of general officers, who have been active members of the Society. Of these I shall merely cite the names of Abercrombie, Moore, Earl Moira, and Sir Charles Napier. The task before me is to exhibit in the smallest possible compass a picture of an almost obsolete branch of Freemasonry, and neither sympathy with the subject, nor an affluence of materials collected with a larger object in view, must divert me from this imperative duty.

Of the Sea Lodges there is nothing further to be said beyond the passing allusion that the existence of all of them was probably due to the exertions of a single individual.[1] With the Field or Army Lodges it is different, and the outline of these bodies, as given in successive tables, I shall to a limited extent fill in, by prefacing each separate list with a brief introduction, commencing with the Lodges in British Regiments, and deriving the materials for my sketch in great part from their actual minutes and records.

The Gibraltar Lodge (128),[2] in the 39th Foot—" Primus in Indis "—claims to have made the first Mason in India, under a European Warrant, in 1757. It subsequently founded numerous Lodges in various parts of Hindostan. There is a stone let into the wall in Fort-William, Calcutta, commemorative of the early history of this Lodge. All its working tools and jewels fell into the hands of the enemy during the Peninsular War, but were subsequently returned to the regiment. The same fate befel the Lodge chest in the 6th Dragoon Guards (577), which was returned under a flag of truce and with a guard of honour. The 17th Foot lost its Warrant (18) in the American War, and it was courteously transmitted to them by General Parsons, with a fraternal letter. The 46th Foot (227) twice lost its chest, which was sent back on the first occasion by order of General Washington,[3] and on the second, by the French military authorities, three years after its capture at Dominica, in 1805. The historian of the 43d Foot complains, in 1758, that " the time passes very wearily " at Nova Scotia, and adds, " when the calendar does not furnish us with a loyal excuse for assembling in the evening, we have recourse to a Freemason's Lodge, where we work so hard that it is inconceivable to think what a quantity of business of great importance is transacted in a very short space of time."[4] This Lodge I have not succeeded in tracing, and the same is the case with regard to another, in the 54th Foot, attached to that corps at St John, New Brunswick, in 1786.[5] A battalion of the 9th Foot was wrecked on the French coast in 1805, and the members of the Lodge (183) solaced the weary hours of their captivity by assembling regularly at Valenciennes until the peace of 1814. The colonel of a regiment often became the first master of the Lodge attached to it. Thus in the 20th Foot, A.D. 1748, Lord George Sackville presided in the first instance over the Minden Lodge (63), though it cannot have borne that title until after his famous escapade at the battle of the same name in 1759.[6]

The following announcement appeared in the *Newcastle Courant* of January 4, 1770 :—

" This is to acquaint the public, That on Monday the first instant, being the Lodge (or monthly meeting) Night of the Free and Accepted Masons of the 22d Regiment, held at the *Crown* near Newgate (Newcastle), Mrs Bell, the landlady of the house, broke open a door (with a poker) that had not been opened for some time past, by which means she got into an adjacent room, made two holes through the wall, and, by that stratagem, discovered the secrets of Freemasonry ; and she, knowing herself to be the first woman in the world that ever

---

[1] Thomas Dunckerley.   [2] Figures within brackets in this section denote the numbers of the Lodges.
[3] *Ante*, pp. 59, 388.   [4] J. Knox, Hist. Journal, 1759, vol. i., p. 143.   [5] *Ante*, pp. 53, 54.   [6] *Ibid.*, p. 344.

found out the secret, is willing to make it known to all her sex. So any lady who is desirous of learning the secrets of Freemasonry, by applying to that well-learned woman (Mrs Bell, that lived fifteen years in and about Newgate), may be instructed in the secrets of Masonry."

"It would be interesting to know," continues my authority,[1] "how many pupils Mrs Bell obtained, and why she appealed to her own sex in particular."

The 38th Foot still possesses a Lodge (441), originally constituted in 1765, and as its proceedings have figured largely in the Masonic journals, some account of these, derived from the actual minutes and records, may be interesting to my readers. The Lodge re-opened at St Pierre, Martinique, on November 8, 1796, "the former registry, with the chest, warrant, and jewels, having been captured by the enemy at Helvoet-Sluys in January 1795." The regiment proceeded to St Lucia and Saints, 1797; Ireland, 1802; Cape Town, 1806; Buenos Ayres and Monte Video, 1806-7;[2] and after a period of home service, the Lodge, which was closed in 1811, re-opened, November 7, 1819, at Cape Town, when a letter—dated April 5 of the same year—was read from the Grand Lodge of Ireland, of which the following is an extract:—

"The Union of Ancients and Moderns in England had no particular effect in this country, as we never had any Lodges but *Ancient*, neither have we adopted any of their new ceremonies."

The working of the Royal Arch degree was resumed in the *Lodge* November 14, 1822, when a letter, dated May 15, 1820, from the Deputy Grand Secretary, was read, of which the following passage is recorded in the minutes :—"There is not any warrant issued by the Grand Lodge of Ireland other than that you hold; it has therefore always been the practice of Irish Lodges to confer the Higher Degrees under that authority."[3] The names of the members of the degree are headed, "Roll of Excellent-Super-Excellent Royal Arch Masons of Lodge No. 441."[4]

The Lodge was next opened at Berhampore, E.I., in the same year (1822), but closed in 1823, and remained dormant until 1840, when it resumed work at Limerick. At this period Lord Ebrington was the Lord-Lieutenant, on whose arrival in Ireland, the Lodge No. 473 at Enniskillen, knowing that he was Provincial Grand Master of Devon, voted him an address, but in his published reply he declared that Masonry was not suited to the condition of Ireland, and that therefore he could not countenance it. Shortly after this a paragraph appeared in the papers announcing the revival of Lodge No. 441 in the 38th Foot, and the

---

[1] Chambers's Journal, 1882, p. 400. According to Clavel (p. 34), Madame de Xaintrailles, who had been given the rank of captain for service in war, by the First Consul, was made a Mason at Paris in the Lodge "Frères-Artistes," of which many French officers were members. An incident of the late American Civil War appears to be on all-fours with the stories of Miss St Leger and Mrs Bell. The life of a young Irishman, taken red-handed as a guerilla by a party of the Iowa Regiment in 1861, was spared—so it is related—through his sister making a Masonic sign for relief, it proving on Examination that she had passed all the degrees (Weekly Budget, U.S.A., March 28, 1883).

[2] The 38th formed the storming party at the attack and capture of this city. The colonel, who was mortally wounded, after entering the breach surveyed the scene, supported by his orderly sergeant, James Matthews (a member of the Lodge), and his dying words were, "Bravo, 38th, my brave regiment."

[3] The Minden Lodge (63), in the 20th Foot, continued to work the R.A. degree under their original warrant until October 9, 1838, when a separate charter was issued by the Grand Chapter of Ireland.

[4] The following singular entry appears in the earlier R.A. record :—"1803.—T. Fallon, Ensign, was produced for entrance, but declined, and was dismissed with the usual precautions."

commander-in-chief, Sir Edward Blakeney, set in motion by the Lord-Lieutenant, peremptorily ordered the meetings to cease, and "all documents connected with the institution to be forthwith returned to the Parent Society." The warrant was therefore sent to the Grand Lodge, from whom, however, a hint was received in 1842—the 38th being then at Corfu—that "it was as much at the disposal of the members as when in their own possession;" and in the same year the box containing it, which had not been opened, was returned to the regiment.

As appears above, the Irish Lodges always worked according to the system in vogue among the so-called Ancient Masons, or perhaps it would be better to say, that the latter took their Masonry undiluted and unchanged from the former. The result, however, in America, where the influence of the Army Lodges made itself chiefly felt, was very marked. The customs of the Scottish Regimental Lodges were in no respect different to those of the Irish, and the older Grand Lodge of England was too sparsely represented among the military forces of the crown to exercise any counter-influence, if indeed her Field Lodges in foreign parts did not—as I imagine must have generally been the case—acquire the tone and character of the vast majority of these associations.

The active part played by Lodges in British regiments in the Masonic history of Massachusetts and New York will be separately narrated, but it may be incidentally observed that the predominance in North America of the "Ancients" over their rivals, the titular "Moderns," must be ascribed in great part to the influx of Regimental Lodges from the Old World, and to their subsequent dissemination of the principles and the practice of what was then termed "Ancient Masonry" throughout the length and breadth of the continent.[1]

The muster-roll of Field Lodges in the British Army has been drawn up so as to agree with the order in which the various regiments were understood to rank, before the recent abolition of numerical titles, though, for convenience sake, I shall not interrupt the regimental sequence by placing the Royal Marines and the Rifle Brigade after the 49th and 93d Foot respectively, in accordance with their regulated precedence.

During the last century so many battalions were raised and disbanded, with the resultant shuffling of numbers, as to render it impossible to be quite sure in all cases whether the numerical titles of regiments are those borne on the dates when the Lodges attached to them were erected, or at a later period. The identification of particular corps has been a laborious task. These are sometimes described by the names of their colonels, and at others by territorial or (obsolete) regimental designations. Thus we meet with Lodge No. 612 (I.) "in the First Ulster Regiment"—which is the only entry that has baffled me—and No. 277 "in the 2d Green Horse" (now 5th Dragoon Guards), 1757.

The Irish Lodges were always chiefly, and in many cases exclusively, known by their *numbers*, which, whenever practicable, were made—by exchanging the ones previously held—to correspond with those of the regiments whereunto such Lodges were attached.

When there were several Lodges existing in a regiment at the same time, this fact will ordinarily coincide with a plurality of battalions, but the possibility of two Lodges working simultaneously in a single battalion of the ordinary strength, is evidenced by the proceedings at the centenary of the Grand Lodge of Scotland, in 1836—when the members of Lodges

---

[1] Chap. XIX., p. 450.

"Hibernia" and "St Andrew," in the 42d Foot (or Black Watch), attracted admiration, alike for their martial appearance and Masonic behaviour.

The exact rank of the Hon. Artillery Company of London has never been definitely settled. According to the historian of the corps, "the members are usually classed with the Volunteers, which, properly speaking, they are not; and it is still an open question whether the officers would rank before or after militia officers, or with them according to the dates of their commissions." [1]

No Lodge has yet been established in the Indian Native Army, though the erection of one—to be called "John of Gaunt in the East"—in the 15th Madras N.I., was all but carried into effect in 1858.

SEA LODGES.[2]

On Board the Vanguard, 254, E., 1760. | On Board the Prince, 279, E., 1762.

On Board the Canceaux, at Quebec, 224, E., 1762.

BRITISH AND IRISH FIELD LODGES.[3]

CAVALRY.

1st Life Guards, Truth, 571, E., 1798.

DRAGOON GUARDS.

1st, George,	520, E.,	1780-1813.
2d,	960, I.,	1805-28.
4th, St Patrick,	295, I.,[4]	1758.
5th,	277, I.,	1757-95.
,, Charity,	570, I.,[5]	1780.
,, Salamanca,	663, E.,	1815-28.
6th,	577, I.,	1780-1858.
7th,	805, I.,[6]	1758.

DRAGOONS.

1st,	384, I.,	1799-1800.
2d,	[ ], K.,	(circa) 1747.
,, St Andrew,	158, S.,	1770-1816.

3d, R.A. Union,	211, S.,	1785-1852.
,,	197, A.,[7]	1806.
4th, Union R.A.,	260, S.,	1796.
,,	50, I.,[8]	1815.
5th,	289, I.,	1757-83.
,,	297, I.,	1758-1818.
6th,	123, I.,	1763.
,,	508, E.,	1777-1813.
,,	311, A.,	1797-1837.
,,	876, I. [ ].	
7th, Queen's,	188, S.,	1776-1816.
,,	262, A.,	1807-24.
8th,	280, I.,	1757-1815.
,,	752, E.,	1822-32.
9th,	158, I.,	1747-1815.
,,	356, I.,	1760-1818.
,,	284, A.,	1794-1813.

11th,	211, E.,	1756-82.
,,	339, A.,	1807-10.
12th,	255, I.,	1755-85.
,,	179, I.,[9]	1804.
,, Sphinx,	179, I.,	1868.
13th,	234, I.,	1752-1815.
,,	607, I.,	1782-88.
,,	400, I.,	1791-1849.
14th,	273, I.,	1756-1822.
16th,	929, I.,	1803-19.
17th,	478, I.,	1769-95.
,,	285, A.,	1794-1828.
,,	218, I.,	1873.
18th, 1st Squadron,	388, I.,	1762-1813.
,, 2d ,,	389, I.,	1762-1821.
20th,	759, I.,	1792.
23d,	873, I. [ ].	

---

[1] Raikes, vol. ii., p. xxv.   [2] *Cf.* Chaps. XVII., p. 345 ; XX., p. 482 ; and XXIII., p. 67.

[3] EXPLANATIONS.—E. denotes *English* (*i.e.*, G.L. of England until 1813, and United G.L. afterwards); A., *Ancients*; I., *Irish*; S., *Scottish*; K., *Kilwinning*; Gib., *Gibraltar*; Jam., *Jamaica*; U.C., *Upper Canada*; L.C., *Lower Canada*; N.E., *New England*; N.Y., *New York*; and N.S., *Nova Scotia.* When known, the *name* is given before the *number* of a Lodge. A second date denotes erasure or last register, but in the majority of cases dormant Lodges continued to be shown in the Lists for many years after they had virtually ceased to exist.

For previous allusions to the general subject, the reader is referred to Chaps. XVIII., pp. 418, 419 ; XIX., pp. 443, 450 ; XX., pp. 482, 493 ; XXI., p. 8 ; XXII., pp. 42-44 ; XXIII., pp. 53, 54, 58-60, 62, 63, 74 ; and XXIX., pp. 313, 326 *et seq.*, 337 ; and for articles on " Military Masonry " by the present writer, to the *Freemason's Chronicle*, January 3, July 10 and 2, and October 2, 1880, and the " Voice of Masonry," 1880, p. 748.

[4] Warrant surrendered, 1830 ; reissued, 1878.   [5] Warrant returned, 1858 ; reissued, 1863.

[6] Exchanged for No. 7, 1817 ; cancelled, 1858.   [7] Closed by order of C.O.

[8] Exchanged for No. 4, 1818 ; called in, 1821.   [9] Exchanged for No. 12, 1817 ; called in, 1827.

ROYAL ARTILLERY.[1]

1st Batt.,[2] Scotland, 134, A., 1764-74.	5th Batt., Eastbourne, 101, A., 1812-28.	Quebec, St John, 241, A.,[7] 1787.
,, Chatham, 187, A., 1774-77.	6th ,, Ceylon, 329, A., 1802-30.	Pt. Royal, Jamaica, 262, A., 1790-1805.
,, Gibraltar, 230, A.,[3] 1785.	9th ,, Gibraltar, 187, A., 1812-22.	Calcutta, 317, A.,[6] 1798.
2d ,, Perth, 148, A.,[6] 1767.	10th ,, S. Africa, 354, A., 1812-51.	Gibraltar, 2 and 5, Gib., 1802.
4th ,, New York, 213, A.,[5] 1781.	,, Gibraltar, 356, A., 1813-21.	,, 4, 5, 9, and 11, Gib., 1811.
,, 144, A., *cir.* 1804.	Rl. H. Art., Colchester, 156, A., 1809-28.	Quebec, 40, A., 1804-14.
,, Gibraltar, 209, A., 1779.	[ ], Woolwich, 86, A.,[6] 1761.	Halifax, Virgin, 2, N.S.,[9] 1782.
4th ,, Gibraltar, 345, A., 1809-27.	Capt. Webdell's Cmpy., 183, A., 1773.	,, Royal Standard, 39, N.S., 1819.

ROYAL ENGINEERS.

Div. of Artificers, Jersey, 293, A., 1795. | Rl. Mil. Artificers, do., 350, A., 1810. | 37th Cmpy. R. E., 1275, E.,[10] 1863-64.

FOOT GUARDS.

Coldstream Regiment, Perseverance, 492, E.,[11] 1776.

INFANTRY REGIMENTS.

1st,	11, I., 1732-1847.	8th,	255, E., 1755-1813.	16th,		300, I., 1758-1801.
,,	74, I., 1737[12]-1801.	9th,	246, I., 1754-70.	17th,		136, I., 1748.
,,	381, I., 1762-65.	,,	183, A., 1803-29.	,,	Unity,	168, S., 1771-1816.
,,	Unity P. and C., 574, E., 1798.	10th,	177, I., 1748-55.	,,		237, A., 1787-92.
,,	Rl. Thistle, 289, S., 1808-52.	,,	299, I., 1758-1803.	,,	Unity,	18,[18] 1779.
2d,	244, I., 1754-1825.	,,	378, I., 1761-65.	,,		921, I.,[16] 1802.
,,	390, I., 1762-1815.	11th,	72, A., 1758-67.	18th,		168, I., 1747.
3d,	170, A., 1771-92.	,,	604, I., 1782-94.	,,		351, I., 1760-84.
4th,	United, 147, S., 1769-1809.	,,	313, A., 1798-1813.	,,		335, A., 1806-13.
,,	522, I., 1785-1823.	12th,	D. of N'folk's, 58,[14] S., 1747-1809.	,,		18, Jam.,[17] 1810.
,,	91, I., 1857-65.	,,	Mt. Calpe, 1116, E., 1860.	19th,	St Andrew's, 590, E., 1802-32.
5th,	86, I., 1738-1815.	13th,	153, A., 1768-76.	20th,	Minden, 63, I., 1748-1850.
,,	St George, 353, A., 1812-62.	,,	637, I., 1784-88.	,,	Sphinx, 263, I., 1860.
6th,	643, I., 1785-1800.	,,	661, I., 1787-1819.	21st,		33, I., *cir.* 1734.
,,	646, I., 1785.	14th,	211, I., 1750-61.	,,		936, I.,[18] 1803.
,,	4, L. C., 1804.	,,	58, A., 1759-1813.	22d,	Moriah, 132, S., 1767-1809.
,,	Orthes, 689, E., 1817.	,,	Union, 338, A., 1807-30.	,,		251, I., 1791.
7th,	38, I., 1750.	,,	Officers' L., 347, A., 1810-13.	23d,		63, S.,[19] 1751-1809.
,,	231, I., 1752.	,,	Integrity, 771, E., 1846.	,,		137, S., 1767-1816.
,,	153, A.,[13] *cir.* 1804.	15th,	245, I., 1754.	,,		252, A., 1788-1822.
,,	2 and 7, L. C., 1804.	16th,	293, I., 1758-1817.	,,		738, I.,[20] 1808.

---

[1] The Lodges in the H. E. I. C. Artillery have been referred to in the last chapter (India). See also Chap. XVII., p. 350.

[2] Since 1859 the companies (R. A.) have been linked together in brigades instead of battalions.

[3] United with No. 13 in 1826. [4] Present St John's Lodge, Gibraltar.

[5] Purchased the No. 9 (A.) in 1787, *now* Albion, No. 2, under the G. L. of Quebec.

[6] Purchased the No. 7 (A.) in 1788, *now* No. 13. [7] *Now* under the G. L. of Quebec.

[8] *Now* No. 229. [9] Nos. 2 and 39 became Nos. 829 and 835 (E.) at Halifax in 1829.

[10] "Warrant withdrawn and fee returned by order of the G. M." (Note in G. L. Reg.).

[11] Now No. 7, Royal York Lodge of Perseverance.

[12] This date is given by Barker (*ante*, p. 331)—the year 1783 appears in the G. L. Records—and the Pocket Companion, Dublin, shows only thirty-seven Irish Lodges as existing in 1735.

[13] In Downe's List, Dublin, 1804, only. [14] *Ante*, p. 53.

[15] A Lodge in the 17th F. (which arrived in Boston, Jan. 1, 1776) is shown at this number on the rolls of the G. L. of England (A.) and Pennsylvania, and the warrant captured by the Americans was returned to the *Unity* Lodge, No. 18, in the 17th F., by General Parsons, in 1779. The *Scottish* Lodge (168) bore the same name, and I think must have become No. 18 on the Provincial List. *Cf. Freemasons' Chronicle*, July 10 and 24, and Oct. 2, 1880.

[16] Exchanged for No. 258, 1824 ; returned, 1847. [17] Prov. G. L.

[18] Exchanged for its old number (33), 1817 ; last register, 1822. [19] Confirmed, 1767.

[20] Cancelled, 1821 ; renewed, 1882.

24th, 426, E., 1768-1813.	39th, Gibraltar, 128, I.,[11] 1742.	52d, Oxfordshire, 853, E., 1830-62.
25th, 92, I.,[1] 1749-1815.	,, 290, I., 1758-1813.	,, 244, I., 1832-37.
,, 250, I.,[2] 1819.	40th, 42, A., N.D.	53d, 236, I., 1753-75.
26th, Cameronian, 309, I.,[3] 1758.	,, 204, I., 1810-13.	,, 950, I., 1804-24.
27th, 24, I., 1734.	,, 284, I., 1821-58.	54th,[18] 669, E., 1838-62.
,, 528, I., 1787-1815.	42d, 195, I., 1749-1815.	55th, [ ]S.,[19] 1743.
,, 692, I., 1808-18.	,, Hibernia, 42, I., 1809-40.	,, 7, N.Y.,[20] 1762.
28th, 35, I., 1734.	,, St Andrew, 310, S.,[12] 1811-48.	56th, George III., 101, S., 1760-1809.
,, [ ], N.E.,[4] 1758.	43d, St Patrick's, 156, S., 1769-1816.	,, 420, I.,[21] 1765-69.
,, Royal Arch, 510, I., 1773-1824.	44th, Rainsford, 467, E., 1784-1813.	57th, 41, A., 1755.
,, 6 and 9, Gib., 1804.	,, 788, I., 1793.	,, Zion, 3, N.Y.,[22] 1783.
,, 260, I., 1809-15.	45th, 445, I., 1766-73.	,, Albuera, 704, E., 1818-24.
29th, Glttrng. Star, 322, I.,[5] 1759.	,, 272, A., 1792-1807.	58th, 466, I., 1769-1817.
30th, 85, I., 1738.	46th, 227, I.,[13] 1752-1847.	,, 692, I., 1789.
,, 535, I.,[6] 1776.	47th, 192, I., 1748-1823.	,, 332, A.,[23] 1805-23.
31st, Fort George, 100, S., 1760-1852.	,, 147, I., 1810-23.	59th, 243, I., 1754-97.
,, St George, 108, S.,[7] 1761-1816.	48th, 218, I.,[14] 1750-1858.	,, 219, I., 1810-17.
,, 5, Gib.,[8] 1802.	,, 982, I., 1806-17.	60th,[24] 448, E.,[25] 1764.
,, Meridian, 1045, E., 1858.	49th, 354, I., 1760-1849.	,, 7, N.Y.,[26] 1783.
32d, 61, I., cir. 1747.	,, 616, I., 1783-88.	62d, 407, I., 1763-86.
,, White's, 73, S., 1754-1809.	50th, 113, I., 1763-70.	63d, 512, I.,[27] 1774-1814.
,, 617, I., 1783-85.	,, 112, A., 1763-1830.	64th, D. of York, 106, S., 1761-1816.
33d, 12, I., cir. 1732.	,, 58, I., 1857-63.	,, 686, I., 1788-1817.
,, 90, A., 1761-1813.	51st, Orange, 94, A., 1761-1805.	,, 130, I., 1817-58.
,, 681, E., 1816-29.	,, 94, I., 1763-1815.	65th, 191, A.,[28] 1774.
34th, Barry, 466, E.,[9] 1784-1813.	,, 690, I.,[15] 1788-96.	,, 631, I., 1784.
,, 340, A., 1807-32.	,, Orange, 274, S., 1801.	66th, 392, I., 1763-64.
35th, 205, I., 1749-90.	,, Minden, 677, E., 1816-43.	,, 538, I., 1777-90.
36th, 542, I., 1777-80.	52d, 370, I., 1761-1825.	,, 580, I., 1780-90.
,, 559, I.,[10] 1778.	,, 226, E., 1762-1813.	,, 656, I.,[29] N.D.
37th, 52, A., 1750-1813.	,, 309, A., 1797-1801.	67th, 175, A.,[30] 1772.
,, N. Hants, 726, E., 1844-62.	,, 170, A.,[16] 1801-13.	,, 338, I., 1815-26.
38th, 441, I., 1765.	,, 53, N.S.,[17] 1826.	68th, 714, I., 1790.

[1] The "Lodge chest" having been lost at Munster, in Germany, a new one was "consecrated" at Berwick, Dec. 2, 1763 (Minutes of St Abb Lodge, No. 70 (S.), Eyemouth).

[2] Exchanged for No. 25, 1823; warrant returned, 1859.　　　[3] Exchanged for No. 26 in 1823.

[4] Provincial warrant granted to hold a Lodge at Louisburg.　　　[5] Warrant returned, 1820; renewed, 1854.

[6] Apparently exchanged for No. 30 in 1805; last register, 1806.

[7] Charter confirmed, 1805.　　　[8] Prov. G.L.　　　[9] Previously No. 17, L.C.

[10] Exchanged for No. 36, 1781; returned, 1848.　　　[11] Warrant renewed April 1, 1819.

[12] Eighty-nine members were enrolled within nine months of its constitution; and fifty intrants were admitted in the four months immediately following the Battle of Waterloo.

[13] Lodge of Social and Military Virtues, now "Antiquity" No. 1, Quebec.　　　[14] Cf. Hayden, p. 31.

[15] Cf. ante, p. 368.

[16] The 2d Batt. 52d Foot was made the 96th Foot, 1803; the 95th, 1816; and disbanded 1818.

[17] Afterwards No. 842 on the general list, and a stationary Lodge until about 1838, when it was attached to the Rifle Brigade.

[18] A sermon was preached at St John, New Brunswick, December 26, 1786, before the members of a Lodge in this regiment. Its registry, however, I have failed to trace.

[19] The first Military Lodge under the G.L. of Scotland. Cf. ante, p. 53.　　　[20] Boston Records.

[21] 59th Foot in Downe's list, 1804.　　　[22] P.G.L. The Lodge held a dispensation from 1780.

[23] Ante, p. 308.　　　[24] "The Royal Americans," 1757-1816.

[25] Warrant originally granted in 1764, by the Prov. G.M. of New York to Lieut. J. Christie, 60th Foot, as Master, and others, to meet as Lodge No. 1 at Detroit. Became No. 62 in 1806, and later No. 3 G.L. of New York; and is now Zion Lodge No. 1 G.L. of Michigan.

[26] P.G.L. The Lodge was to be held "in H.M. Loyal American Regiment or elsewhere." Cf. ante, p. 58.

[27] Cf. Brennan, p. 377.　　　[28] Not issued.　　　[29] Cf. post, Maryland.

[30] Transferred to Rl. Cornish Miners, 1807; became a stationary Lodge, 1826; now No. 131 Truro.

DANIEL SPRY ESQ

M W GRAND MASTER, GRAND LODGE, CANADA.

Thomas C. Jack, London & Edinburgh

68th, Durham L., 348, A., 1810-44.	79th, Waterloo, 191, A., 1808-38.	91st, Argyle, 321, A., 1799-1828.
69th, 174, I., 1791-1821.	80th, St Andrew, 197, S.,1769[4]-1816.	92d, 364, I., 1761-62.
,, 983, I., 1808-26.	,, Fortitude, 724, E., 1820-37.	,, 333, A., 1805-32.
70th, Hooker, 97, S., 1759-1809.	82d, Thistle, 4, N.S.,[5] 1782.	94th, Union, 121, S.,[5]1764-1809.
,, 7, Gib.,[1] 1804.	,, 138, I., 1817-58.	,, Philanthropists, 591, E., 1802.
71st,[2] P. of W., 92, S., 1759-1809.	83d, 339, I., 1759-64.	,, George William, 328, S., 1830-60.
,, 895, I., 1801-58.	,, 435, I.,[6]1808.	95th,[9] 842, E., 1829-62.
72d, 75, A., 1759-64.	85th, 298, A., 1801-46.	96th, 170, A.[10]
,, 65, I., 1854-60.	88th, 176, I., 1821-40.	,, 176, I., 1818-19.
75th, 292, I., 1810-25.	89th, 863, I., 1798-1818.	97th, 984, I.,[11]1803.
76th, 359, I., 1760-64.	,, Hibernia, 633, E., 1836-44.	100th, 3, Gib., 1804.
,, 248, A., 1788-1828.	,, Social Friendship, 729, E., 1844.	103d,[12] 292, I., 1834-38.
77th, [8]578, I., 1780-82.	90th, 8, Gib.,[7] 1803.	108th, 4, Gib., 1804.
78th, 822, A., 1801-30.	,, 688, E., 1817-24.	112th, 815, I., N.D.

ROYAL MARINES.

Plymouth, Marine L., 237, E., 1759.	St'neh'se,Amphibi'us L.,[13]498,E.,1787.	Stonehouse, Roy. Mar.,336,A.,1808-30.
Portsmouth, 122, A., 1763-64.	Chatham, 256, A., 1789-92.	Woolwich, Roy. Mar., 328, A., 1810.
	Chatham, Roy. Mar., 260, A., 1812.	

BRITISH MILITIA.

Aberdeenshire,[14] Aboyne, 278, S.,1799.	Devon (North), Good Intention, 452, E., 1783.	Lancashire (Second), Knight of Malta, 309, A.,[15] 1803.
Antrim, 289, I., 1796-1856.	,, (North), 228, A., 1812-21.	,, (Third), Unanimity, 147, A., 1812.
Argyle, St John, 258, S., 1795-1809.	Donegal, 865, I., 1798-1821.	
Armagh, 888, I., 1800-45.	Downshire, 212, I., 1795-1808.	Leicester, 87, A., 1761-64.
Ayr and Renfrew, St Paul, 271,S., 1799.	Dublin, 62, I., 1810-21.	Leitrim, 854, I., 1797.
Berwickshire, Hirsel, 237, A., 1811-20.	Durham, St Cuthbert, 320, S., 1813-48.	Lincoln (South), 867, I., N.D.
Cambridge, 327, A., 1799-1801.	Fermanagh, 864, I., 1795-1830.	London (West), Justice, 198, A., 1801.
Carlow, 903, I., 1801-16.	Fifeshire, 311, S., 1811-37.	,, ,, Euphrates,292, A.,1812.
Cavan, 300, I., 1801-30.	Forfar and Kincardine, 292, S., 1808.	Louth, 10, I., 1809-49.
Cheshire, 541, E., 1794-1818.	Hants(Nth.), Love,197, A., 1808-38.	Mayo (South), 79, I., 1810-26.
Cork, 741, I., 1808-17.	Kerry, 66, I., 1810-56.	,, (North), 81, I., 1812-25.
,, (South), 495, I., 1794-1865.	Kildare, 847, I., 1797-1825.	Meath, 898, I., 1801-49.
Cornish Miners, Fortitude, 175 A.,1807.	Kilkenny, 855, I., 1797-1825.	Middlesex (West), 298, A., 1796-1801.
Cornwall, Royal Cornwall, 618 E., 1810.	King's County, 948, I., 1804-47.	,, (Westminster), Harmony, 583, E., 1799.
Cumberland, 215, A., 1807-38.	Lancashire (First), 197, A., 1776-1806.	
Devon (East), 216, A., 1781-1835.		

[1] P.G.L.

[2] Raised at Elgin as the 73d Foot, 1777, and became the 71st—a numerical title held by three previously extinct regiments—in 1786.

[3] *Ante*, p. 63.

[4] The first regiment numbered the 80th was disbanded in 1764. The second (Royal Edinburgh Volunteers) was raised in 1778, and disbanded in 1783. The Lodge, therefore, must really date from about 1780, which would accord with its position on the roll.

[5] A petitioner from "the Thistle Lodge, 82d Regiment, by dispensation," was relieved in 1789 by the (Atholl) Stewards' Lodge, "as a sojourner, with one guinea."

[6] Exchanged for No. 33, 1817; last register, 1846.   [7] P.G.L.

[8] In the famous Scots Brigade. This, except between 1688 and 1691, was in the Dutch service from 1586 until 1793. In 1794, it became the *fourth* English regiment numbered the 94th, and was disbanded 1818.

[9] The *fourth* regiment numbered the 95th, was raised in 1800, and in 1816 became the "Rifle Brigade," to which corps No. 842 was attached about 1838. *See* 52d Foot.

[10] *Ante*, 52d Foot.

[11] Exchanged for No. 176 in 1818. The *fifth* regiment numbered the 97th (Queen's Germans), was disbanded in 1819 as the "Queen's Own" or 96th Foot.

[12] Until 1858, "The Bombay European Regiment."

[13] Ceased to be a service Lodge in 1792; warrant reissued, 1803.

[14] *Ante*, p. 74.   [15] Exchanged for No. 120, 1804; erased 1822.

Middlesex(Westminster), 309, A., 1804.	Sligo,	837, I., 1796-1835.	Wexford,	935, I., 1803-24.
Monaghan,	552, I., 1796.	Southdown,	214, I., 1810-15.	Wicklow,	848, I., 1796-1815.
,,	200, I., 1801-26.	Staffordshire,	327, A.,² 1801.	,,	877, I., 1800.
Monmouth,	664, E., 1815-22.	Tipperary,	856, I., 1797-1825.	Wilts, Loyalty,	282, A., 1794-1834.
Queen's County,	857, I., 1797-1832.	Tyrone,	846, I., 1796-1818.	Yorkshire(First), Moriah, 176, A., 1772.
,,	398, I., 1805-10.	,,	562, I., 1797-1830.	,, (East), St George, 442, E., 1782.
Roscommon,	242, I., 1808-20.	Warwickshire, Shakespeare, 501 E.³	,, (West), Union, 626, E., 1811.
Shropshire,¹ Salopian, 153 A., 1810.	Westmeath,⁴	791, I., 1793-1826.	,, (N.), L. Dundas, 674, E., 1815.

HONOURABLE ARTILLERY COMPANY OF LONDON.

Armoury House, Finsbury, Fitzroy, 830 E., 1849.⁵

FENCIBLE REGIMENTS.

P. of Wales F. Cavalry, 312, A., 1798.	Breadalbane F.,	907, I., 1801-13.	Essex F.,	825, I., 1796-1813.
Cornwall F. Light Drags.,582, E., 1799.	Elgin F.,	860, I., 1798-1813.	
	Nova Scotia, Loyal Surrey Rangers, 587, E., 1801-13.	

GARRISON AND VETERAN BATTALIONS.

Garrison Batt.,	125, I., 1808-14.	4th Gar. Batt, Fr'dship, 343, A., 1809-32.	8th Garr. Batt.,	995, I., 1808-14.
4th ,, ,,	986, I., 1810-15.	7th ,, ,,	992, I , 1808-15.	1st Veter. ,,	351, A., 1810-33.
	4th Veteran Battalion,	988, I., 1808-15.	

AUXILIARY CORPS (FOREIGN).

Reg. of Anspach-Beyreuth, 215, A., 1781.	Recton's Hanoverian Brigade, 232, A.,⁶	Reg. of Anholt-Zerbst, 516, E., 1787.
Knyphausen, Hiram, 5, N.Y., 1783.	1786.	Turkish Contingent, 373, S., 1856-64.

FOREIGN AND COLONIAL REGIMENTS.⁷

Scots Brigade, Holland, Union, 121, S.,⁸	Pr. Edw. I., St George, 2, N.S., 1781.	Pr. Edw. I., 26, N.S., 1797.
1764.	New Jersey Volunteers, St George, 2,	1st American Regiment, 3, U.C., 1804.
Sicilian Foot, Naples, 433, E.,⁹ 1768.	N.Y., 1783.	Nova Scotia Regiment, 24, N.S., 1804.
Garrison, Halifax, Union, 1, N.S., 1781.	King's Rangers, St James, 14, L.C., 1784.	Rl. Canadians, Glengarry, 1, L.C., 1805.
	Military (under Travelling Warrant), 54 N.S., 1826.	

¹ *Ante*, p. 44.   ² Exchanged for No. 209, 1803 ; erased, 1827.

³ A Norwich Lodge, taken by the Regiment in 1796, and brought to Warwick in 1802, where it became stationary, in spite of the opposition of the military members, in 1808.

⁴ *Ante*, p. 44.

⁵ The Court of Assistants in this year sanctioned the formation of a Masonic Lodge to consist of members of the company only. A proposal to establish "the Hon. the Artillery Company's Lodge" was agreed to in 1781, but negatived at the next Court (G. A. Raikes, Hist of the Hon. Art. Company). Although the "Fitz-Roy" Lodge, now No. 569, is stationary in a sense, as having met hitherto at the Armoury House of the Company, it would, without doubt, accompany that distinguished corps should it ever change its head-quarters in time of peace, or be arrayed with the regular forces in time of war.

⁶ Probably granted to the Lodge previously named ?

⁷ The dates appended to the sixth and three following Lodges merely denote that they *existed* in those years.

⁸ See 94th Foot.   ⁹ *Ante*, p. 298.

EXISTING BRITISH[1] FIELD LODGES, 1886.[2]

4th Drag.G'rds,St Pat'k's,295,I., 1758.	12th Ft., Calpe,	824, E.,1860.	29th Ft., 322, I., 1759.
5th ,, ,, Charity, 570,I.,1780.	14th ,, Integrity,	528, E.,1846.	31st ,, Meridian, 743, E.,1853.
12th Rl.Lancers,Sphinx, 179,I., 1868.	20th ,, Sphinx,	263, I., 1860.	38th ,, 441, I., 1765.
1st Foot,Unity,P.and C.,316,E.,1798.	23d ,,	738, I., 1882.	39th ,, Gibraltar, 128, I., 1742.
6th ,, Orthes, 852, E.,1817.	26th ,, Cameronian,	26, I., 1758.	89th ,, Social Fr'ndship,497, E.,1844.

Hon. Artillery Company, London, Fitzroy, 569, E., 1849.

SWEDEN.—An ancient document in the archives of the Grand Lodge informs us that " the Lodge 'St Jean Auxilaire'—instituted in 1752—was formed by sundry brethren of the military and travelling Lodges (*loges militaires et voyageuses*) existing at that time ; " but with regard to the number of these itinerant bodies, the field of their operations, or indeed to any further particulars concerning them, we are left wholly in the dark. The next evidence in point of date—afforded by the same source of authority—relates to the formation of the " Lodge of the Swedish Army " (*Svenska Arméens*) at Greifswald, in Pomerania, January 10, 1761. According to its statutes, the seat of the Lodge was to be at the headquarters of the Swedish army during the continuance of the (Seven Years') war, and at Stockholm in time of peace. Captain (afterwards General) the Count of Salza was the first Master, and among the other founders were Barons de Beck-Trius, de Cederstrom, de Duval, and the Count de Creutz—all Swedish military officers. During the continuance of the war, the Lodge threw off shoots at Greifswald, Stralsund, and Christianstadt.[3] At the peace of 1763, it removed to Stockholm, after having received—February 17—a confirmation of its charter from the Grand Lodge of Sweden. The " Lodge of the Swedish Army " established a pension fund for wounded soldiers, and the recipients of its bounty wore silver medals, struck at the expense of the Lodge. Prince Frederick-Adolphe, Duc d'Ostrogothie, the king's brother, was its Master at the period of his decease ; but in 1781 its labours came to an end, and the members joined other Lodges at the capital.

RUSSIA.—In 1761 a Field Lodge was formed in the Russian Army, which at that time had its winter quarters in West Prussia, and its headquarters at Marienburg. A second was established at the same place in 1764, which afterwards became the stationary Lodge " of the Three Towers." The latest appears to have been " George the Victorious," constituted by Grand Lodge Astrea, March 12, 1817.

GERMANY.—Throughout the empire, Field or Camp Lodges are regarded as merely auxiliary to the regular or stationary Lodges. The former are in every case erected to serve

---

[1] Authorities :—Minutes and Records, Grand Lodge of England ; Masonic Calendars ; Army Lists ; Cannon, Historical Records of the British Army ; Regimental Histories ; Trimen, Regiments of the British Army ; Early Histories G.L. of New York and Pennsylvania ; Brennan, Standard History ; Boston (U.S.A.) Records ; Letters from the following officers of Grand Lodges—S. B. Oldham, Ireland ; D. M. Lyon, Scotland ; J. J. Mason, Canada ; W. F. Bunting, New Brunswick ; and G. H. Wakeford, Pr. Edw. I. ; W. Badgley and J. H. Isacson, Quebec (P.G.L.) ; and N.C.O. of British regiments—W. Robertson, 26th Foot ; A. Paterson, 29th ; W. Conyard, 38th ; J. Horton (and also Major J. Powell), 39th ; and Mr Edward Bacon, schoolmaster, R.A., Gibraltar.

[2] The present numbers are here given, but up to this point the various changes, except in the case of the Irish Lodges, have not been recorded. All the numbers, however, borne by the Scottish Field Lodges, will be found in the Constitutions, G. L. of Scotland, p. 166 ; whilst those of the entire body of English Lodges from 1729 down to the present date, are given by Lane in his "Masonic Records," a work of extraordinary merit, involving vast labour, which presents at a glance the skeleton history of every Lodge of English maternity.

[3] In 1762. Carl of the Three Griffins, Gustavus Adolphus of the Three Rays, and (possibly) Concord, respectively.

a temporary purpose, and before a candidate is accepted for initiation, he is required to name one of the latter as the Lodge he will repair to for admission, when the warrant of the movable and transitory body is surrendered or withdrawn. They only exist in time of war, or when an appeal to arms is believed to be impending. In the last century there were Military (which sometimes became Field) Lodges. These were constituted in garrisons and fortresses during peace as well as war. Examples are afforded by the three Lodges which head the subjoined table. The first was founded by Frederick the Great,[1] the second by French prisoners of war,[2] and the third by military officers in Potsdam. The Flaming Star, originally a Military Lodge, was established February 24, 1770, it being thought desirable by Krüger [3] " to take the brethren of Military rank out of all the Lodges, and to erect a separate Lodge for them, which, in the case of war, might follow the camp, and exemplify the benefits of Masonry in the field." From this time all military candidates were sent to the Flaming Star for initiation.

In 1778, there was a concentration of troops both in Saxony and Silesia, and the military duties of the Master—Marschall von Bieberstein—taking him in the former direction, he was accompanied by the Flaming Star, whilst a branch or " Dispensation " Lodge—duly constituted by the G.M.—under Major von Kleist proceeded to diffuse Masonic light in the other. On August 23, 1779, the brethren were reunited in a single Lodge, which is still in existence at Berlin.

Nos. 12-14 on the list were also erected in Saxony and Silesia in the commencement of the Bavarian War of Succession—the most important being the Golden Goblet, of which Zinnendorff was a member. No. 16 was established by Count von Lottom, in furtherance of his resolution to found a Lodge " on hearing that General Blücher was to command the Army Corps on the Prussian coast of the Baltic." The latter was a member of Field Lodge No. I., in 1812. The particulars with regard to No. 8 are a little confusing, and it is not clear that it ever received a warrant, or if so, at whose hands. The general in command appears to have arrested its development at a very early stage, and the same thing occurred in 1816, when an attempt was made by thirty military brethren to establish a Lodge in Sedan.[4]

1. Court L.,	Rhenisberg, 1739.	9. Blucher,	Luxemburg, 1820.	15.	At Hanover, 1797.
2. Parfaite Union, Magdeburg, 1761.		10. Victorious Eagle, Potsdam, 1850-51.		16. Field L. No. I.,	1811-14.
3. Minerva,	Potsdam, 1768.	11. William of the Black		17. ,, No. II.,	In France, 1818.
4. Flaming Star,	Berlin, 1770.	Forest,	Rastadt, 1861-67.	18. ,, No. III., ,,	1815-16.
5. ,, ,, (Deputy L.), 1778-79.		12. Golden Goblet, Field Hos-		19. F. W. of the Iron Cross,	1818.
6. Frederick of Patriotism,	1812.	pital,	Silesia, 1778-79.	20. Iron Cross,	Mayence, 1813-15.
7. Of the Iron Cross,	1815.	13. Army L. No. I., Silesia,	1778-79.	21. John of the Sword,	1797-99.
8.	At Bar-le-Duc, 1816.	14. The Guide-Post, Saxony, 1778.		22. Adolphus of German Unity, 1817-24.

Two Lodges in Frankfort—of which mention has already been made [5]—are not shown in the foregoing table. One of these (consisting chiefly of foreigners) was founded by Count

---

[1] *Ante*, p. 242.

[2] *Ibid.*, p. 244 ; Chap. XVIII., p. 418; and Freemason, vol. xix., pp. 496, 511, 524, 533, 556, 613, 627.

[3] *Ante*, pp. 244, 245.

[4] The first Lodge in the list was founded by Frederick II. ; Nos. 2-7, and 9-11, by the Three Globes ; 8, and 12-19, by the National Grand Lodge (Zinnendorff's) ; 20, by the Royal York ; and 21, 22, by the Prov. Grand Lodge of Hanover. Most of them are extinct, and the few survivors have ceased to possess any military character.

[5] *Ante*, p. 231.

Schmettau in 1743, and the other would appear to date from about the year 1760. The latter, in the Royal Deux Ponts[1] Regiment, affiliated in 1762 with Lodge Union of Frankfort, receiving at the same time a local warrant empowering it to resume work as a " Field " (and *daughter*) Lodge on quitting that city. The Royal Deux Ponts Lodge joined the Strict Observance in 1771, but we again meet with one—Les Dragons Unis des Deux-Ponts—in the same Regiment, which was taken on the roll of the G.O. of France in 1783, with precedence from the previous year. This *Regiment*, and possibly the *Lodge*—which may have only shaken off the fetters of the S.O. in 1782—accompanied the expedition of General Rochambeau to North America in 1780, and was commanded by the Marquis de Deux Ponts.

HOLLAND.—The following Military Lodges (all of which are now extinct) were constituted by the Grand Lodge of the Netherlands:—

La Loge Militaire,	Maastricht,	1745.	St Andreas,	Sluis,	1786.	L'Union Constante Militaire,		
L'Harmonie,	Sluis,	1749.	L'Union Helvétique,	Maastricht,	1788.		Alkmaar,	1799.
La Concorda,	Venlo,	1757.	Biedertreu,	Heusden,	1788.	De Harten door Vriendschap		
L'Esprit du Corps,	Leeuwarden,	1777.	De Opgaande Oranjezon,	Sluis,	1789.		Zaamverbonden,	Amersfoort, 1800.
Curâ et Vigilantiâ,	Suriname,	1777.	La Réunion Neufchatelloise,			Fidelitas,		's Gravenhage, 1807.
L'Union Militaire,	Zwolle,	1778.		Ceylon,	1790.	De Toevallige Vereeniging,		
L'Unanimité,	Brielle,	1783.	Pax Inimica Malis, 's Heerenberg, 1793.				Bergen op Zoom, 1808.	
Le Temple de la Vertu,			La Fraternité Militaire,			St Napoleon,	Amsterdam,	1810.
	Tholen,	1783.		Leeuwarden,	1795.	La Paix,	Amsterdam,	1810.
			De Militaire Broederschap, Alkmaar, 1814.					

BELGIUM.—The subjoined list of Field and Garrison Lodges (none of which are in existence at this day) has been compiled from official and other sources:—

Friends of Order, 1st Army Div., 1832.	Defenders of Leopold, Namur,	1834.	United Brethren, 3d Army Div., 1835.		
Scots Camp, 4th Army Div., 1833.	Shield of Belgium, 4th Foot, 1834.		Military Union, Beverloo,	1836.	

No warrants for Field or Army Lodges have been granted at any time under the jurisdictions of Switzerland, Greece, Denmark, Hamburg, and Darmstadt. In the Austro-Hungarian empire, the members of both the sea and land services are forbidden to become Freemasons, " for which reason," writes the Grand Secretary of Hungary (1880), " there are no Military Lodges in existence, nor any military brethren among us." [2]

FRANCE.—Entombed in the archives of the Grand Orient are the records (*dossiers*) of about two hundred Regimental Lodges, together with a number of documents formerly belonging to the Lodges established in England by French prisoners of war, and which subsequently came under the G.O. These books and papers, according to their official custodian, " contain very valuable information (*renseignments précieux*)," which, however, considerations of time and space would have prevented my making any use of, even had I not been effectually barred from any such endeavour by the consciousness of already possessing what, for the purposes of

[1] German, *Zweibrücken ;* French, *Deux Ponts ;* —a town of Rhenish Bavaria, which, passing to Charles XI. of Sweden, became French territory in 1718, and is now again Bavarian. The fortunes of the Regiment doubtless followed those of the town.

[2] Authorities—Continental Field Lodges—to this point :—Handbuch, vols. i., p. 326 ; iv., p. 75 ; C. Schulze, Prussian Field Lodges (Zirkel Corr., iv., 1880, pp. 324-39) ; F. Q. Rev., 1846, p. 48 ; Letters from the late Carl Bergmann, P.M., Pilgrim Lodge ; and the following officers of Grand Lodges :—E. E. Wendt, England ; C. L. Thulstrup and R. Dickson, Sweden ; T. Fürst, Hamburg ; F. Feustel, Bayreuth ; J. J. F. Noorziek and J. P. Vaillant, Holland ; A. Uhl, Hungary ; A. Hugel, Darmstadt ; and G. Jottrand (Supreme Council), Belgium.

this sketch, may be termed a superfluity of materials. The Lodges in the following table are shown, as nearly as possible, in the order of their appearance in any official list. They are seventy-six in number, and while some were founded by the *Grand Lodge*, all such Lodges were afterwards newly constituted by the *Grand Orient*. The roll extends to 1787, and an asterisk in each instance is placed before the names of the fifty-two Lodges which in that year were represented at the G.O. by their deputies. The dates of origin given are those from which the Lodges were allowed to rank. Some of the regiments named in the table—as holding warrants for long periods—served in America during the War of Independence ; and the stability, or tenacity of existence, of the older French Army Lodges, as contrasted with the ephemeral character of their successors under the Consulate and Empire, has induced me to describe the former with a minuteness of detail, which would be altogether out of keeping with the importance of the latter in a general history of Freemasonry.

The Lodge Montmorenci-Luxembourg, constituted June 1, 1762, in the Regiment of Hainault Infantry, of which the Duke of Luxemburg was the Colonel, was accorded—April 18, 1772—by the Grand Lodge of France, the privilege of attendance at all its meetings. This Lodge has been styled, with great show of reason, the stem or trunk from which the Grand Orient budded forth in December 1773. The list of its members in 1772 is certainly a remarkable one. The Duke of Luxemburg was the Master, the wardens were his son and the Prince de Rohan-Guéménée, and among the members—who were all, with one exception, noblemen—may be named the Princes of Condé, Ligne, Tarente, Montbazon, Nassau, and Pignatelli ;[1] the Dukes of Lauzun, Coigny, and Fronsac; and many others of lesser rank. Of the first officers of the Grand Orient, the five highest in rank (after the Duc de Chartres, G.M.), and nearly the whole of the honorary grand officers, were members of this Lodge.[2]

The last Lodge on the list was constituted March 16, 1787, and its first Master was André Masséna — afterwards Marshal of France — at that time Adjutant of the Royal Italian Regiment.

The abbreviations, Inf., Cav., Drag., Art., Chass., and Huss., denote Infantry, Cavalry, Dragoons, Artillery, Chasseurs, and Hussars, respectively.

FRENCH FIELD LODGES DOWN TO THE YEAR 1787.

Parfaite Egalité,[3]	*Walsh*, Inf.,	1688.	*Union Frat.,	*Rl. Roussillon*, Inf.,	1765.
Parfaite Union,	*Vivarais*, Inf.,	1759.	Union Parfaite,	*Corps Rl. du Génie*,	1765.
„ „	*Dauphin*, Drag.,	1760.	S. Alexandre,	*Mousquetaires, Ière. Cie.*,	1766.
Tendre Fraternité,	*Rl. Marine*, Inf.,	1760.	*Henri IV.,	*Corps Rl.*, Art.,[5]	1766.
*Union Parfaite,	*Vigier, Suisse*, Inf.,	1761.	*Parfait Union,	*Flandre*, Inf.,	1766.
*Montmorenci-Luxembourg, *Hainault*, Inf.,		1762.	*Paix et Union,	*Lyonnois*, Inf.,	1767.
*Sigismond-Luxembourg, *Hainault*, Inf.,		1763.	*Pureté,	*La Sarre*, Inf.,	1767.
*St Charles des Amis Réunis, *Saintonge*, Inf.,		1763.	*Concorde,	*Auvergne*, Inf.,	1769.
*Parfaite Harmonie,	*Corps Rl. Marine*,	1764.	Amis Réunis,[6]	*Lyonnois*, Inf.,	1769.
*Militaire du Bourb.,[4]	*Bourbonnois*, Inf.,	1764.	*S. Louis,	*Guyenne*, Inf.,	1771.

[1] *Ante*, p. 298, note 2.   [2] *Ibid.*, pp. 148, 151.

[3] This Lodge, in the "Regiment Irlandais de Walsh," was legitimated by the G.L. of France in 1772, and by the G.O. in 1777. According to an (English) Army List of 1743, the earliest Irish regiment existing at that time in the French service was only "formed" in 1690 ! *Cf. ante*, pp. 53, 157, 160.

[4] In 1787, Les Vrais Amis.   [5] Described as the "Toul Regiment," at La Fère, in 1776.

[6] In 1805, Les Amis Réunis de la Victoire, and the only Lodge on the above list shown in the official calendar for that year.

*S. Louis de l'Union,[1]	*Chass. des Cévennes,*	1771.	*Dragons Unis,	*Deux-Ponts, Drag.,*	1782.
*Parfaite Union,	*Rl. Champagne, Cav.,*	1773.	*Heureux Hasard,	*Foix, Inf.,*	1783.
Tendre Fraternité,	*Rl. Pologne, Cav.,*	1773.	*Maréchal Saxe,	*Septimanie, Cav.,*	1783.
*Heureux Hazard,	*Rl. Vaisseaux, Inf.,*	1772.	*Bonne Intelligence,	*Languedoc, Inf.,*	1781.
Parfaite Union,	*Vermandois, Inf.,*	1774.	S. Jean,	*Gendarmerie de Fr.,*	1783.
Union désirée,	*Mousquetaires, 2e. Cic.,*	1774.	*Élèves de Mars et Neptune, *Marine,*		1783.
Parfait Union,	*Rl. Roussillon, Cav.,*	1774.	*Réunion Parfaite,	*Pyrennées, Chass.,*	1783.
*Triple Alliance,	*Beaujollois, Inf.,*	1774.	*Frères Unis,	*Maréchal Turenne,*	1784.
*Trois Frères Unis,	*La Cour* [ ],	1775.	*Bons Amis,	*M. de Camp. Gén., Cav.,*	1784.
S. Louis,	*Du Roi, Inf.,*	1775.	*Modeste,	*Col. Général, Inf.,*	1784.
Marine,	*Marine (Corps Rl.),*	1775.	*Nouvelle Harmonie,	*Marine,*	1784.
Double Amitié,	*Navarre, Inf.,*	1775.	*Amitié,	*Brie, Inf.,*	1785.
Famille Unie,	*Condé, Inf.,*	1776.	*Amitié Frat.	*Segur, Drag.,*	1782.
Parfait Amitié,	*Conti, Drag.,*	1776.	*Parfaite Alliance,	*Bretagne, Inf.,*	1785.
*Sully,	*Toul., Art.,*	1777.	*Réunion,	*Rl. Roussillon, Inf.,*	1785.
*Intimité,	*Orléans, Inf.,*	1777.	Amis Intimes,	*Perche, Inf.,*	1785.
*Fabert,	*Du Roi, Inf.,*	1777.	*Valeur,	*Touraine, Inf.,*	1785.
Parfaite Union,	*Rohan Soubise, Inf.,*	1777.	*Amis Réunis,	*Marine,*	1785.
Parfaite Union,	*Angoumois, Inf.,*	1777.	*Amis Réunis,	*Armagnac, Inf.,*	1786.
Amitié,	*Strasbourg, Art.,*	1778.	*Frères d'Armes,	*Berri, Cav.,*	1785.
*Amitié,	*Salm-Salm, Inf.,*	1778.	*Franchise,	*Picardie, Inf.,*	1786.
*Franchise Helvétique,	*Ernest, Suisse, Inf.,*	1778.	Vigilance,	*Bercheny, Huss.,*	1786.
*Guill. Tell,	*Sonnenberg Suisse, Inf.,*	1778.	*Vrais Soutiens,	*Gaudeloupe,*	1784.
*Amitié,	*Dauphiné, Inf.,*	1778.	Bellone,	*Penthievre, Inf.,*	1786.
*Amitié à l'Epreuve,	*Orleans, Drag.,*	1779.	*S. Louis de Palestine,	*Boufflers, Drag.,*	1787.
*Héroisme,	*Gardes du Roi, Cie. Écoss.,*	1779.	*Régularité,	*Gardes, Corps du Roi,*	1786.
*Vrais Amis,	*Médoc, Inf.,*	1780.	*Constance,	*Béarn, Inf.,*	1787.
*Maréchal Coigny,	*Col. Gén., Drag.,*	1781.	Parfaite Amitié,	*Rl. Italian, Inf.,*	1787.

No Field Lodges were constituted in 1788 or 1789, and only eight between 1790 and 1801. The next seven years, however, witnessed an addition of sixty-four; but at the close of this period nearly all the Lodges established under the old Monarchy had ceased to exist. The Calendar of 1805 shows a total of forty-three, of which one only was of earlier date than the Revolution, the next in point of age being a Lodge of 1790, whilst no less than thirty-five had been warranted in 1802-4. In 1809, sixty-seven regiments had Lodges attached to them, and three years later the number had risen to sixty-nine. At this time the Lodges were both opened and closed with a cry of "Vive l'Empereur!" In 1811-13, six further Lodges were established, but, as already related, no less than four hundred and twenty-nine on the general roll became dormant in 1814. Two new Lodges were formed in 1817-19, but only three regiments in all are shown as possessed of Masonic warrants in 1820. Three Lodges were constituted between 1821 and 1834; and ten years later, "Cirnus" (1821), in the 10th Regiment of the line, the last of the long roll of French Military Lodges, disappeared from the scene. It may be added, that a confidential circular from the Minister of War—Marshal Soult—to the colonels of regiments, in 1845, declared "that it was contrary to the rules of the service for any of the military to become even members of the institution." Soult himself was a Freemason, as were also many other Marshals of France—for example, Serrurier, Beurnonville, Kellerman, Masséna, Lefebvre, Mortier, Perignon, Bernadotte, Murat, Macdonald, Lauriston, Magnan, and (it is alleged) Augereau, Brune, and Sebastiani.[2]

[1] The subsequent Lodges on the list are shown in the order in which they were constituted or legitimated by the G.O., and with the rank (or precedency) assigned to them by that body.

[2] Authorities:—Thory, Acta Lat., and Hist. G.O.; Daruty, Recherches, etc.; Rebold, Hist. Tr. G.L.; Isis on L'Initiation Maçonnique, p. 308; F. Q. Rev., 1845, p. 490; 1846, p. 48; 1851, p. 183; and Letters from MM. Thévenot (G.O. of Fr.), and J. E. Daruty (Mauritius). *Cf. ante*, pp. 157, 160, 164, 169.

AMERICA.—The general history of Masonry in the United States may be divided into three periods—the first extending to the year 1755, the second to the Peace of Versailles in 1783, and the third until the present date. Of these, the first and last will be hereafter considered, but the second—so far, at least, as the details are capable of being treated as a whole—I shall, to the best of my ability, deal with in the current section, premising, however, that in the next chapter the story will be duly brought up to the point thus reached by anticipation, and continued after a smooth and methodical fashion.

According to a talented writer, " all warranted American Lodges, previous to the French War [1755], had worked the rituals and acknowledged the authority of the Grand Lodge of England only (sometimes denominated the Grand Lodge of Moderns); but during this war Lodges holding warrants from the Grand Lodges of Scotland, Ireland, and the Ancients of London, were working in America. They probably owed their introduction to the Military brethren." [1]

Here it may be convenient to explain, that while the members of Lodges under all the jurisdictions of the British Islands, with the exception of the Original Grand Lodge of England, were generically classified as " Ancient Masons," the terms " Ancient York Masons " and " Ancient York Masonry " were at first only employed by the English Schismatics, and did not come into common use—in America—until towards the close of the century.

A list of the stationary Lodges established in North America by the authority of European Grand Lodges, other than that of the earliest of such bodies, will be found in Chapter XXXI.,[2] but the influences which conduced to their formation, and to their subsequent predominance over the original Lodges of the Continent, I shall now proceed to narrate.

It will, however, in some degree clear the ground for our inquiry to mention that prior to the French War the only Lodge of a military character known to have been established in America was one at Annapolis Royal, in Nova Scotia, formed in 1738 by Erasmus James Phillips—Fort-Major of that garrison—as D.G.M. under an authority from Boston.

1755.—General Braddock arrived in America with two thousand regular troops, and was defeated by the French and mortally wounded, July 8. Other regiments were despatched from Britain in this and later years. The movements of these battalions can be easily traced in a number of well-known books. A list of the British regiments to which Lodges were attached has already been given.

1756.—In this year there were six battalions and eight independent companies of King's troops in America, the whole being under the Earl of Loudoun. Richard Gridley was authorised—May 13—by the Prov. G.M. of North America, " to congregate all Free and Accepted Masons in the Expedition against Crown Point, and form them into one or more Lodges." For military reasons, however, the proposed movement against Ticonderoga and Crown Point was not attempted.

Richard Gridley—the younger brother of Jeremy Gridley, Prov. G.M. of North America —was born in 1711, and after seeing much active service, was appointed Chief Engineer and

---

[1] Sidney Hayden, Washington, and his Masonic Compeers, 1866, p. 31.

[2] Where will be found the *general* history of Freemasonry in the United States. " Ancient Masonry," however, in the conventional acceptation of that term, is so closely associated with the proceedings of the numerous Field Lodges in America, that its consideration becomes indispensable to the present narrative, and will, it is to be hoped, enable the reader to grasp the subject more firmly than if the entire history of American Masonry were to be presented in Chapter XXXI.

Colonel of Infantry in 1755. For his distinguished services at the siege of Quebec he received a pension and grant of land from the British Government. Appointed Major-General by the Provincial Congress, September 20, 1775. D.G.M., St John's Grand Lodge, Boston, January 22, 1768, and continued to hold that office until the Union of the two Grand Lodges in Massachusetts (1792), though his presence in Grand Lodge is last recorded under the year 1787. It is probable that the connection of this veteran soldier and Craftsman with the older Grand Lodge was not without influence in preventing its total collapse pending the happy amalgamation of the two Grand Lodges in 1792. Scottish charters for Lodges in Blandford (Virginia) and Boston were granted March 9 and November 30 respectively.

1757.—Lodge at Lake George named in the Boston Records[1] April 8. Colonel John Young, 60th Foot, appointed Scottish Provincial G.M. in America, November 14. Three Ancient warrants sent by Laurence Dermott to Halifax, in one of which Erasmus James Philips was named as Prov. G.M. About this year "several persons in Philadelphia, active in political and private life, were made Masons according to the practice of the Ancients."[2]

1758.—Capitulation of Louisbourg, July 26 : a Lodge formed there in the 28th Foot by Richard Gridley, November 13. A warrant—No. 69—granted by the Ancient or Schismatic G.L. of England to Philadelphia. After this year there were only—in that city—one or two notices of any Lodges under the older (English) sanction. Scottish charters were issued by the Grand Lodge and "Mother Kilwinning" respectively to brethren at Fredericksburg[3] and Tappahannock[4] (Virginia).

1759.—Abraham Savage was authorised by Jeremy Gridley, Prov. G.M. of North America, to "Congregate all Free and Accepted Masons in the Expedition against Canada into one or more Lodges," April 13. Crown Point surrendered, August 4; and twelve officers of the 1st Foot were made Masons in the Lodge there by the Master, Abraham Savage. Capitulation of Quebec, September 18. "The anniversary of St John the Evangelist was duly observed by the several Lodges of Freemasons in the Garrison,"[5] where, at the time, Colonel Young, Provincial Grand Master of North America, under Scotland, was present with his regiment, the 60th Foot or "Royal Americans."

1760.—Quebec invested by the French, May 11. Commodore Swanton, with the Vanguard[6] and two frigates, arrived and raised the siege, May 16. Charter of St Andrew's Lodge —granted[7] in 1756—received at Boston, September 4. No. 98 (S.) erected at Charleston, South Carolina.

1761.—The members of the "Boston Regular Lodges" were forbidden to visit St Andrews. Charter—No. 89—appointing William Ball Prov. G.M. of Pennsylvania, granted by the Ancients, but not received. No. 92 (A.) erected at Charleston, S.C.

---

[1] *I.e.*, The Early Proceedings of the "St John's" and Massachusetts Grand Lodges (at Boston), recently published, and a copy of which—from Mr S. D. Nickerson—has reached me as these sheets are passing through the press.

[2] Early Hist. G.L. Pennsyl., p. xxxiii.

[3] Washington's "Mother Lodge," originally established by warrant from New England, but which shifted its allegiance in 1758.

[4] Or Rappahannock. Both are Virginian names, but Wylie gives one and Lyon the other.

[5] Knox, Campaigns in North America, 1769, vol. ii., p. 235.   [6] *Ante*, p. 400, and Chap. XX., p. 482.

[7] By the G.L. of Scotland, to certain persons who, having been irregularly initiated, were refused admission into the Boston Lodges.

1762.—A Lodge in the 55th Foot[1]—No. 7 from New York—petitioned Jeremy Gridley to grant a charter to the Provincial troops at Crown Point (March 5), and a Deputation was issued to Colonel Ingersoll to hold a Lodge there.

1763.—Nos. 117 (S.) erected at Norfolk, Virginia, and 399 (I.) at New York.

Owing to the loss of a great part of its records by the Grand Lodge of Ireland, the number of stationary Lodges warranted in America from that jurisdiction must remain a matter of uncertainty. Lodge No. 74, in the 1st Foot, as we have already seen,[2] gave an exact copy of its warrant to a set of brethren at Albany (N.Y.) in 1759, and it is unreasonable to believe that it was a solitary instance of the kind. Schultz[3] mentions three Lodges of unknown origin in Maryland, as having existed in 1759, 1761, and 1763, and it is possible, to say the least, that one or more of them may have derived their authority either directly or indirectly from Ireland? Dove, also, in his account of the early Lodges in Virginia, names the Irish as one of the *five* jurisdictions by which that State was Masonically "occupied" in 1777.[4]

1764.—Provincial warrant—No. 89—received in Philadelphia from the Ancient or Schismatic G.L. of England. "From the time of the establishing of these Lodges of the four degrees by the Ancients, such records as we can find," says a careful writer, "show the speedy decline of the Moderns."[5] A Lodge at Quebec—probably constituted by Richard Gridley or Abraham Savage—is first named in the Boston Records of this year.

1765.—No. 346, at Joppa, Maryland, under the *Original* Grand Lodge of England, was inaugurated November 21; and the 14th by-law, passed the same day, enacts :—"That none who hath been Admitted in any *Modern* Lodge, shall be Admitted as a Member of this Lodge, without taking the respective Obligations Peculiar to *Ancient* Masons."[6]

1766.—In this year bickerings occurred between the St Andrew's and the "Boston Regular Lodges," and "a Union of Love and Friendship," to which the members of both jurisdictions should be parties, was proposed by the former.

1767.—The funeral of Jeremy Gridley, Prov. G.M., North America, took place September 12, and the members of St Andrew's Lodge—sixty-four in number (Joseph Warren being the S.W.)—walked in the procession. After this, however, when every generous effort on the part of St Andrew's had completely failed, and when it became evident that no "Union of Love and Friendship" could be effected, the members of that Lodge changed their ground. Men like Warren, Revere, Hancock, and others of illustrious name, felt their patience exhausted, and determined not to quietly submit to be any longer denounced as clandestine Masons and impostors. The early proceedings of St Andrew's were indeed as irregular as it is possible to conceive. Originating in the association of nine Masons who had been made clandestinely, it was chartered by the G.L. of Scotland in 1756, and then numbered twenty-one members, exclusive of the original nine, who had left Boston in the interval. Its charter did not arrive until 1760, at which time the Lodge had been increased by eighteen additional members, so that in all thirty-one candidates were initiated before the Lodge received its charter, and thirteen before the charter was signed. At a conference—held April 28, 1766—between committees of St John's G.L. and St Andrew's Lodge (Richard Gridley being a

---

[1] This may have been the Scottish Lodge in this regiment, and if so, like the one in the 17th Foot, it must have accepted a Provincial number. *Cf. ante*, pp. 401, 402.

[2] *Ante*, p. 331.   [3] *Op. cit.*, pp. 25, 30, 68.   [4] *Cf. post*, under the year 1778.

[5] C. E. Meyer, Hist. of Jerusalem R. A. Chapter, p. 10.   [6] Schultz, Freemasonry in Maryland, p. 39.

member of one and Joseph Warren of the other), the representatives of the latter fully admitted the illegality of their early proceedings, but contended that it was in the power of the G.M. of Scotland to "make irregular Masons, Regular." Against this, the other committee formulated their belief that "the Language of the Constitutions for irregularities was SUBMISSION."[1] The older Society forgot for a moment its animosity over the grave of its Grand Master, and, as already related, the brethren of both jurisdictions walked together in the procession. Subsequently, however—and this brings us to the point reached above—the spirit of manliness prompted the leading members of St Andrew's to vindicate their own characters as Masons, and to stand forth in defence of the Lodge which made them. It was therefore voted unanimously on St Andrew's Day (November 30), that during the continuance of the interdict against Masonic intercourse imposed by the English Prov. G.L., the brethren under that jurisdiction, unless also members of, or raised Masters in, St Andrew's, were not to be admitted as visitors.

In this year there were three Lodges at work under the Provincial Grand Lodge of Pennsylvania (Ancients), the last of which—Royal Arch Lodge—was constituted October 20.

From the earlier records of this Lodge, it appears "that they received and acted upon the petitions of at least one hundred Modern Masons, who petitioned to be made Ancient Masons, and upon their petitions taking the same course as the profane, they were, after approval by ballot, regularly initiated."[2] No. 3 maintained a close intercourse with a Lodge in the 18th Foot—No. 351 (I.)—and the Royal Arch furniture of the two bodies became in a measure common property.

1768.—The Grand Lodge of Scotland erected a Lodge—No. 143—at East Florida, and appointed Governor James Grant, Prov. G.M. for North America, southern district. In this year a standing army was quartered in Boston. The 14th, 29th, and a part of the 59th Regiments, with a train of Artillery, arrived October 1, and a short time after, the 64th and 65th Regiments, direct from Ireland. In these regiments were three Lodges, all working under what was then commonly known as the "Ancient System"—Nos. 58 (A.), 14th Foot; 322 (I.), 29th; and 106 (S.), 64th. The presence of these troops created an intense excitement, and the members of St Andrew's, particularly Joseph Warren, participated in the universal feeling of opposition to the continuance of this strong force in Boston. Nevertheless, the members of the Lodge saw the opportunity before them of forming a Grand Lodge under the authority of the Grand Master of Scotland, and with this end in view, did not scruple to enter into fraternal communion with, and to make use of, their brethren in the obnoxious regiments.[3]

None of these Field Lodges were present at the installation of John Rowe—the Prov. G.M. under England—on November 23, but all of them joined St Andrew's, in December, in a petition to the G.L. of Scotland, requesting the appointment of "a Grand Master of Ancient Masons in America," and nominating Joseph Warren for that office.

1769.—The Earl of Dalhousie, G.M., Scotland, appointed Joseph Warren, "G.M. of Masons in Boston, New England, and within one hundred miles of the same," May 30. The commission was received in September, but in the interval the 64th Regiment had been removed from Boston. Little notice was taken of the Lodges in the other regiments in the arrangements for the installation, and they were merely informed of the approaching event. The

---

[1] *Sic,* in Boston Records, p. 107.   [2] Moyer, p. 11.   [3] Proc. G.L. Mass., 1869, p. 162.

Grand Lodge was formally inaugurated on December 27, in the presence of St Andrew's and of Lodges Nos. 58 and 322, in the 14th and 29th Regiments respectively. Although for convenience sake this body will be henceforth referred to as the " Massachusetts Grand Lodge," it may be observed that it did not adopt that title until December 6, 1782.

1771.—No. 169 (A.), established in Battery Marsh, Boston. This Lodge, which is only once named in the records of the Massachusetts G.L., accompanied the British army to New York on the evacuation of Boston in 1776.

1772.—By a further Scottish patent, signed by the Earl of Dumfries, Joseph Warren was appointed Grand Master for the Continent of America, March 3. The strife between the rival systems of Masonry is thus pleasantly alluded to in the records of a Lodge at Falmouth,[1] Massachusetts, under the date of December 16 in this year :—

In order to establish harmony amongst the Freemasons in this town, it is *Voted*, That (for the future) the Lodge be opened one evening in the Modern form and the next evening in the Ancient form, which is to be continued till the Lodge vote to the contrary.[2]

" N.B.—The makings to be as usual in this Lodge."

1773.—A resolution was passed *nem. con.* that the members of St Andrew's and of the Lodges under the "Massachusetts" Grand Lodge should be admitted as visiting Brothers in the Lodges under the older (Boston) jurisdiction, January 29. John Rowe, "G.M.," and Henry Price, " P.G.M.," attended the meeting of the English Prov. G.L. on Boston Neck, June 24; and among the visitors was Joseph Warren, also described as " G.M." Meetings of both Grand Lodges took place, December 27, on which date Warren was installed under his patent of the previous year, and at a fixed hour each G.L. drank the health of the other.

In this year certain ships laden with tea were boarded in Boston Harbour by Paul Revere and others, disguised as Mohawk Indians, and their cargoes, consisting of 342 chests of tea, valued at £18,000, thrown into the sea, December 16.

1774.—Nos. 177 (S.) and 190 (A.) were established at Philadelphia and Charleston, S.C., respectively. No. 243 (I.), in the 59th Foot, placed itself " under the Protection and Direction" of the Massachusetts G.L. The British Government shut up the port of Boston, repealed the charter of the State of Massachusetts, and sent a body of troops to Boston under General Gage. The other colonies took the part of the people of Boston, and deputies from each Province were sent to Philadelphia, where they assembled in Congress for the first time, December 5.

1775.—On April 18, the day before the battle of Lexington, Dr Joseph Warren, hearing of the intended approach of the British, under General Gage, to Concord and Lexington, despatched Paul Revere to the latter town, *via* Charlestown, to announce the British expedition of the following day.[3]

Paul Revere was an active member of St Andrew's Lodge, and after filling both Wardens' chairs, and twice holding the office of D.G.M. in the " Massachusetts G.L.," served as G.M. of the (United) G.L. of Massachusetts, 1795-97.

[1] Warrant granted by Gridley, 1762 ; renewed by Rowe, 1769 ; *now* Portland Lodge, No. 1, Maine.
[2] Proc. G.L. Mass., 1877, p. 118.
[3] An account of the "Midnight Ride of Paul Revere" will be found in the "Tales of a Wayside Inn," by Longfellow.

Hostilities commenced between Great Britain and America, April 19. The town of Boston became a garrison, and was abandoned by many of its inhabitants, so that the regular meetings of the stationary Lodges were suspended.[1] Joseph Warren appointed Major-General, June 14. Battle of Bunker's Hill, and death of Warren, June 17. Colonel Richard Gridley, D.G.M., St John's G.L, the engineer who planned the works that Warren laid down his life to defend, was also wounded in the fight. The war was carried into Canada, and Major-General Montgomery fell at the assault of Quebec, December 31.

Prince Hall, and fourteen other free coloured citizens of Boston, were initiated in "a travelling Lodge attached to one of the British Regiments in the army of General Gage,"[2] March 6. St John's Regimental Lodge, No. 1, New York,[3] organised July 24; and a "Kilwinning" charter granted to brethren at Falmouth, Virginia, December 20.

1776.—American Union Lodge, established February 15, by a warrant issued in the name of John Rowe, G.M. (St John's G.L.), and bearing the signature of Richard Gridley, his Deputy. Boston evacuated by the British, March 17. Funeral of Joseph Warren, April 8. Richard Gridley was a pall-bearer, but John Rowe, though present by invitation of Joseph Webb (D.G.M., Mass. G.L.)—according to his own diary—"was very much insulted," and retired.[4] Declaration of Independence, July 4. It is said that all but three of those that signed it were Freemasons. British occupation of New York, September 15, and introduction of so-called "Ancient Masonry" into that State. Little or no intercourse was held between the Army and the Provincial Lodges. Of the latter, those in the city of New York virtually ceased to meet, while the others, with the exception of St Patrick's—which met at Johnson Hall, the family seat of the Prov. G.M.—continued their labours, and were subjected to but little interruption during the war. Of the Prov. G.L. under Sir John Johnson, there are no records after this year. St Patrick's Lodge was constituted in 1766, Sir William Johnson serving as Master until 1770, when his son-in-law, Colonel Guy Johnson, took his place. Sir John (the Prov. G.M. and second Baronet) was a regular attendant from 1767 to 1773. Sir William, late in life, took to his home as his wife Mary Brant, or "Miss Molly," as she was called; and her brother, Joseph Brant, or Thayendanegea, was afterwards secretary to Colonel Guy Johnson, who succeeded his father-in-law as General Superintendent of the Indian Department. Joseph Brant was a Freemason, and during the fierce struggle for independence, many military brethren owed their lives to his protection, one of whom, Captain John M'Kinstry, at the period of Brant's interposition on his behalf, after the battle of the Cedars, near Montreal, in 1776, was actually bound to a tree, and surrounded by the faggots intended for his immolation.[5] Similar tales are related of Tecumseh, the famous Shawnee warrior and orator, in connection with the war of 1812.

1777.—The authority granted to Joseph Warren by the G.L. of Scotland having died with him, the Master and Wardens of the subordinate Lodges were summoned to attend and elect

---

[1] There are no records of the St John's and Massachusetts Grand Lodges, in the former case between January 27, 1775, and February 17, 1787 ; and in the latter, between April 19, 1775, and December 27, 1776.

[2] Grand Master Gardner, Mass., *ut supra.*

[3] *I.e.*, under the *Original* Prov. G.L., which, as we shall presently see, was supplanted by the *Ancients* in 1781.

[4] Rowe was elected a member of St Andrew's Lodge in 1766, and of the Boston Committee of Safety, November 30 1773, though with regard to the latter, his diary records, "was Chose a Committee Man much against my Will."

[5] W. L. Stone, Life of Joseph Brant, 1838, vols. i., pp. 18, 33 ; ii., p. 156.

a Grand Master by Joseph Webb, his late Deputy. Accordingly, eleven brethren[1] met as a Grand Lodge, and elected Joseph Webb Grand Master, March 8. This, if we leave out of present consideration the Lodge (and Grand Lodge) at Philadelphia, in 1731, which will be referred to at some length in the next chapter, was the first Independent or self-created Grand Lodge on the Continent. Philadelphia was occupied by the British, September 27. At that time the Provincial Grand Lodge (A.) had eighteen Lodges on its register. The American army took post at Valley Forge, twenty-six miles from Philadelphia, and traditions affirm that Lodges were held in this camp, which Washington often attended. There can hardly be a doubt that such was the case, but unfortunately no records of the Continental Field Lodges, for this year, are in existence.

1778.—Philadelphia evacuated by the British, June 18. The Grand Lodge of Virginia, the *second* Independent organisation of the kind, formed October 13. The Lodges in this State had derived their charters from the Grand Lodges of England and Scotland, " Mother Kilwinning," the Prov. G. Lodges of New England and Pennsylvania, and (according to Dove[2]) the G.L. of Ireland. At the close of this year, the city of New York, the town of Newport, Rhode Island, and Savannah, Georgia (captured December 29), were alone held by the British.

1779.—No. 210 (A.), constituted at New York—making with No. 169 (A.)—removed from Boston in 1776—two " Ancient " Lodges in that city. Three Lodges in the Continental Army were chartered by the Prov. G.L. (A.) of Pennsylvania.[3] " The membership of the Lodges subordinate to the two Grand Lodges in Philadelphia gradually became merged, the Ancients receiving and remaking the Moderns. The records of the Grand Lodge contain the names of many Modern Masons who were subsequently identified with the Ancients."[4] A notable instance of this is the case of Dr William Smith, Provost of the University, who was a so-called " Modern " in 1755, and became Grand Secretary of the Ancients (in Pennsylvania), October 22, 1779.

1780.—Washington nominated as General Grand Master by the G.L. of Pennsylvania, January 13 ; Convention of American Field Lodges at Morristown, February 7. A French force,[5] under General Rochambeau, arrived at Newport, R.I., July 12. Among the subordinate officers employed with this expedition were the Dukes de Laval Montmorency, de Castries, and de Lauzun, Prince de Broglio, the Marquis and the Count de Deux Ponts, Count de Segur, and many other noblemen. The Baron de Kalb, a Major-General in the American army—mortally wounded at the battle of Camden, August 17—was buried with military and Masonic honours by his victorious enemies. In this year No. 212 (A.) was established at New York ; and three further warrants were granted in the Continental army by the G.L. of Pennsylvania, on the roll of which body there were now thirty-one subordinate Lodges.

1781.—The " Ancient " and Field Lodges in New York met as a Grand Lodge, and elected Grand Officers, January 23 ; and a warrant for a Prov. Grand Lodge—No. 219—was granted

---

[1] Ten of these, including Webb and Paul Revere—as D.G.M. and S.G.W. respectively—acted as Grand Officers, the proceedings virtually resulting in the wheels of the old machinery being again set in motion.
[2] Virginia Text Book, p. 129.　　[3] All the American Field Lodges will be found in a subsequent table.
[4] Early Hist. G.L. Pennsyl., p. xlix.
[5] Including the regiments of Agenais, Saintonge, Bourbonnais, Soissonnais, Touraine, Neustrie, Anhalt, Royal Deux Ponts, de Lauzun, and Gatinais. The last named came from St Domingo with the Marquis de Saint-Simon, and for its gallantry at York Town was allowed to resume its former name of " Royal Auvergne." *Cf. ante*, pp. 407, 408.

by the (Atholl) G.L. of England, September 5. A Lodge in the Continental army was established in this year under a Pennsylvanian charter.

1782.—Provincial Grand Lodge of New York (A.) inaugurated by the following Lodges:—Stationary—Nos. 169, 210, 212 (A.); and Nos. 132 (S.), 52 (A.), 441 (L), 213 (A.), and 215 (A.), together with a Lodge under dispensation—in the 22d, 37th, and 38th Regiments, the 4th Battalion Royal Artillery, the Regiment of Anspach-Beyreuth, and the 57th Foot respectively, December 5. The title of "Massachusetts Grand Lodge of Ancient Masons" was assumed by the G.L. at Boston under Joseph Webb, December 6, and from the official records of the same date we learn that three subordinate Lodges were constituted before the death of Joseph Warren, and fourteen subsequently.

1783.—Peace of Versailles, April 19. The *third* Independent Grand Lodge, that of Maryland, organised July 31. A majority of the Grand Officers, being about to leave New York with the British army, commended the "Grand Warrant" to the care of their successors, September 19. At this date seven Lodges had received charters from the Prov. G.L., four of which were attached to the New Jersey Volunteers, the 57th Foot, the Regiment de Knyphausen, and the Loyal American Regiment; also two Irish Lodges, Nos. 478, in the 17th Dragoons, and 90, in the 33d Foot, had at different dates ranged themselves under its banner. In this year there were forty Lodges on the roll of the G.L. of Pennsylvania, and eighteen under the Grand Body of which Webb was the head, in Massachusetts. Of the former, ten were established in Maryland (before the close of 1782), five in New Jersey, four in Delaware, three each in Virginia and South Carolina, and single Lodges in North Carolina and Georgia.[1] Of the latter, six were outside the State of Massachusetts, viz., in Connecticut three, and in New Hampshire, Vermont, and New York one each. Thus making a grand total of thirty-three Lodges from these two sources only—whose members gloried in the title of "Ancients," and believed that they were walking in the old paths, from which the older Grand Lodge of England and her daughter Lodges had lamentably strayed.

Ten Lodges in all were at work in the American army during the Revolution, the earliest of which was—

ST JOHN'S REGIMENTAL LODGE, warranted by the Prov. G.L. of New York, July 24, 1775, *i.e.*, before the military occupation of that city by the British. There are no records, and we only learn that it was attached to the United States battalion during the war.

AMERICAN UNION, though of later date, was the first Lodge organised in the Continental army, and may be justly regarded as the eldest Masonic daughter of the Federation. It was formed—February 15, 1776—by warrant of the English Prov. G.M. of North America—John Rowe—in the Connecticut Line of the army, wherever stationed, provided no other G.M. held authority. Shortly after, the Lodge having removed to New York, asked for a confirmation of their charter from the D.G.M., Dr Middleton; but a new warrant was granted to the members under the name of Military Union, No. I. The Lodge is described as having "moved with the army as a pillar of light in parts of Connecticut, New York, and New Jersey." Joel Clark, the first Master, was taken prisoner August 27, and died in captivity. He was succeeded by S. H. Parsons (the first treasurer), and the latter by Jonathan Heart (the first Secretary).

---

[1] This is inclusive of Lodges in the Military Lines other than that of Pennsylvania.

The original warrant was taken by Heart to Marietta, Ohio, and the Lodge is now No. I. on the roll of that State.

WASHINGTON LODGE, No. 10, was constituted at West Point—November 11, 1779—by Jonathan Heart, as representative of Joseph Webb, G.M. Massachusetts G.L. The first Master was Brigadier-General J. Paterson, and the Wardens, Colonels Benjamin Tupper and John Greaton. At this and the previous Lodge (American Union) General Washington was a frequent visitor.

ARMY LODGE, No. 27, in the Maryland Line, was warranted by the G.L. of Pennsylvania in April 1780. The first Master was Brigadier-General Mordecai Gist, and the Wardens, Colonel Otho Williams and Major Archibald Anderson. All three greatly distinguished themselves at the battle of Camden, August 17, 1780, Gist in command of a brigade, and Williams as Adjutant-General; while after the defeat of the Americans Major Anderson was the only infantry officer who kept together any number of men.

No records of the American Field Lodges of the Revolution have been preserved, except a portion of the minutes of American Union, and some returns of the Washington Lodge. The latter merely inform us that in 1782 two hundred and forty-five names had—up to that date —been borne on the roll of the Lodge.[1] The former are of a more interesting character. The principal officers of the army, and the general in command, are frequently named as visitors, and at all the banquets, while the first toast was "Washington" or "Congress," the second was invariably—"Warren, Montgomery, and Wooster," followed by the Dead March.[2]

Dr Warren was the first man of distinction to lay down his life in the cause of American liberty. "At Boston," says a famous writer, "Joseph Warren, a young man whom nature had endowed with grace and manly beauty, and a courage that bordered on rash audacity, uttered the new war-cry of the world, FREEDOM AND EQUALITY." .·. .·. "The good judgment and daring of Warren singled him out above all others then in the province as the leader of rebellion."[3] He presided over the Provincial Congress the day before the battle of Bunker's Hill—where, though holding the commission of Major-General, he fought as a volunteer. It was ordered by Congress, that a monument should be erected at Boston in remembrance of him, and—having left behind him very little of this world's substance—that his son should be considered as the child of the public, and be educated at the expense of the United States.

Warren was initiated in St Andrew's Lodge, Boston, in 1761, and became its Master in 1768. During his Grand Mastership there were thirty-seven meetings of the Grand Lodge, thirty-four of which were held in "ample form."

Montgomery was of Irish birth, and after serving with distinction in the French war, settled in America. The commission of Brigadier-General in the Continental Army was bestowed upon him early in the war, and he was killed at the attack on Quebec, December 31, 1775. No man that ever fell in battle during a civil contest was more universally regretted, and his untimely fate was as much deplored in England as in the country of his adoption. He was among the Masonic friends who gathered around Washington at Cambridge in the beginning of the war.

David Wooster, who was born in 1711, served as a Captain in the expedition against

---

[1] Proc. G. L. Mass., 1877, pp. 63-67. [2] E. G. Storer, Freemasonry in Connecticut, 1859, pp. 14-48.
[3] Bancroft, Centenary edit., 1876, vol. iii., p. 598.

Louisburg in 1745. In the French war he commanded a regiment, and subsequently became a Brigadier-General. In 1776 he was appointed Major-General in the American Army, and was mortally wounded while leading an attack on the British troops at Ridgefield, April 27, 1777. General (then Captain) Wooster was the first Master of the first chartered Lodge in Connecticut, instituted in 1750—now Hiram No. 1.

According to the late C. W. Moore, all the American Generals of the Revolution, with the exception of Benedict Arnold, were Freemasons. The Marquis de Lafayette was among the number, and it is believed that he was initiated in American Union Lodge at Morristown, the jewels and furniture used on the occasion being lent by St John's Lodge at Newark, N.J.

In nearly all cases the Army Lodges, in the event of removal from one State to another, were authorised to continue working, unless there was in existence a Grand or Provincial Grand Lodge, when the sanction of the presiding officer had to be obtained. In this we may possibly discern the first germ of the principle of Exclusive (State) Jurisdiction.

It is supported by evidence, that the asperities which characterised the rivalry of the two Masonic systems, found no place in the Army Lodges. To quote the words of a somewhat . impassioned orator, " the ' Ancient and Modern ' contest turned to ashes in the red-hot furnace of liberty," and it is on record, that at the constitution of Washington Lodge, Jonathan Heart of " American Union," under the titular " Moderns," was appointed by Joseph Webb, G.M. of the Boston " Ancients," his Special Deputy Grand Master, to open and inaugurate the new Lodge.

On December 27, 1779—the headquarters of the Army being then at Morristown, New Jersey—the American Union Lodge met to celebrate the festival of St John. At this meeting " a petition was read, representing the present state of Freemasonry to the several Deputy Grand Masters in the United States of America, desiring them to adopt some measures for appointing a Grand Master over said States ; " and it was ordered " that the petition be circulated through the different Lines in the Army ; " also, " that a committee be appointed from the different Lodges in the Army, from each Line, and from the Staff of the Army, to convene on the 1st of February, at Morristown, to take it into consideration." There were present on this occasion thirty-six members of the Lodge, and sixty-eight visitors, one of whom was General Washington.

Before, however, these proceedings ripened into action, the Grand Lodge of Pennsylvania, at a special meeting—held January 13, 1780—passed three resolutions ; the first, affirming the principle that it would be for the benefit of Masonry " that a Grand Master of Masons throughout the United States " should be nominated on the part of that Grand Lodge ; the second, unanimously electing General Washington to the office ; and the third, directing " that the minutes of the election and appointment should be transmitted to the different Grand Lodges in the United States, and their concurrence therein should be requested."

At the same meeting a committee was nominated " to inform themselves of the number of Grand Lodges in America, and the names of their officers "—a point upon which a good deal of ignorance prevailed throughout the country at large, as I shall hereafter have occasion to show.

On February 7, 1780, " according to the recommendation of the *Convention* Lodge," held December 27, a committee of ten met at Morristown, delegated by the Masons in the Military Lines of Massachusetts, Connecticut, New York, and Maryland ; St John's Regimental Lodge, the Staff of the Army, and the Artillery. The representatives of the Massachusetts and Connecticut Military Lines—John Pierce and Jonathan Heart—also acting on behalf of Washington and American Union Lodges respectively. Mordecai Gist was chosen President, and Otho Williams, Secretary of the Committee. An address was then drawn up to " the Grand Masters of the several Lodges in the respective United States of America." In this— to avert " the impending dangers of Schisms and Apostacy "—the expediency was maintained of " establishing one Grand Lodge in America, to preside over and govern all other Lodges, licensed or to be licensed, upon the Continent ; " and the Grand Masters, or a majority of their number, were requested to nominate as M.W.G.M., a brother whose merit and capacity might be adequate to a station so important, and to submit his name, together with that of the Lodge to be established, " to our Grand Mother Lodge in Europe for approbation and confirmation." This " address " being read and unanimously agreed to, was " *signed in convention*, and the committee adjourned without delay."

A " Convention Lodge " from the different Lines of the Army and departments, was held— March 6—under the authority of the American Union Lodge, at which the proceedings of the committee were unanimously approved.

At this period the only Grand Lodges (in the contemplation of the Committee) were those in Massachusetts, Pennsylvania, and Virginia ; and although the name of Washington as Grand Master designate does not appear in the address from the Masonic Convention in the army, yet it was formally signified to these Grand Lodges that he was their choice. It will be observed that the Masons of the various Military Lines met three times in convention—on the first occasion to propound a scheme, on the second to arrange the details, and on the third to ratify the proceedings of the executive committee. Washington, therefore, whose name is recorded among those of the visitors on St John's Day, 1779, was as much a party to the proceedings of that date as were the actual members present of the American Union Lodge. This doubtless led to the project being taken up so warmly by the Grand Lodge of Pennsylvania, by which body it was communicated to other jurisdictions ; but they did not view it with favour, and no action resulted. It is a little singular that in Philadelphia—then the metropolis of North America—the governing Masonic body were only " informed " on July 27, 1780, that there was a Grand Lodge in Virginia, and the records from which this is gleaned [1] give—under the same date— the following :—" It is reported that there is a Grand Lodge in Boston." In the same year —September 4—Joseph Webb (Massachusetts) knew of but two American Grand Lodges, that of Pennsylvania and his own, and had heard of no increase in the number beyond the G.L. of New York so late as March 8, 1787.

The idea of a General Grand Master or Superintending Grand Lodge was revived in 1790, when it was taken up by Georgia, and at various other times (and ways), some seventeen in all, the last occasion being in 1862. It is somewhat curious that the project, though constantly revived by a number of American Grand Lodges *after* 1780, has since that date encountered the determined opposition of the Masonic community in Pennsylvania. The belief that General Washington was Grand Master of the United States—at one time a very prevalent one [2]—was strengthened by a Masonic medal, struck in 1797, having on one

---

[1] Early Hist. G.L. Pennsyl., p. 17.   "June 20, 1785.—Received the names of the Gr⁴. Officers of the State of Virginia. The Gr⁴. Secy. is requested to make enquiry as to their antiquity " (*Ibid.*, p. 55).

[2] *Ante*, p. 353.

side the initials, " G.W., G.G.M." [1] The following, however, is his Masonic record briefly told :
—He was initiated in the Fredericksburg Lodge, Virginia, November 4, 1752, and became a
Master Mason, August 4, 1753. This Lodge derived its authority from Boston, but obtained
a Scottish charter in 1758, which seems on the whole to fortify a conjecture which has been
advanced by Hayden,[2] that Washington was " *healed* and re-obligated " in No. 227 (46th Foot)
in order to qualify him for admission into a Lodge held under a warrant from the Grand
Lodge of Ireland. In 1779 he declined the office of G.M. of Virginia, but accepted that of
Master of Alexandria Lodge, No. 22, in his native State, in 1788. As President of the United
States he was sworn in—April 30, 1789—on the Bible of St John's Lodge, New York, by
Chancellor Livingstone, G.M. of that State. In 1793—September 18—he laid the corner-
stone of the Capitol, and is described in the official proceedings as " Grand Master *pro tem.*,
and Worshipful Master of No. 22, of Virginia." Washington died in 1799, and was buried
with Masonic honours on December 18 of that year.

It is a curious circumstance, and deserves to be recorded, that with the exception of Major-
General Richard Gridley, who attended two meetings of the St John's Grand Lodge, Boston,
in 1787, Washington appears to have been the only man of mark, who, graduating under the
older system of Masonry before its popularity was on the wane, associated himself at all
closely with the proceedings of the Craft, either during the war with England or at any
later date. Before the political troubles—as will be hereafter narrated—no one figured more
prominently on the Masonic stage than Benjamin Franklin ; but we nowhere read of his
participating in Masonic fellowship, in the country of his birth, after his return from England
in 1762. According to a publication of great weight and authority, " the ' Moderns ' numbered
among their prominent members many who were opposed to the independence of the colonies,
while the Ancients were mostly in favour thereof." [3] In 1776 the earliest Provincial Grand
Lodge of Pennsylvania was practically extinct, its members having been sharply divided in
political sentiment at the era of the Revolution, and their Grand Master, Chief Justice
Allen, having placed himself under the protection of General Howe. At the same date the
condition of affairs was very similar in New York, the Prov. G.M. of which State, Sir John
Johnson, was commissioned as a colonel by the British, and (according to an unfriendly
biographer) " directed the movements of as bloody a band of savages and outlaws as existed
during the Revolution ; " [4] while at Boston the influence of Joseph Warren, both in Masonry
and politics, has already been narrated.

At the termination of hostilities in 1783, we find, therefore, that in Pennsylvania the
Ancients were not only supreme but unchallenged. In Massachusetts about an equal number
of Lodges held charters from each of the two Grand Lodges, and at the Union of these bodies
in 1792 the only allusion to the diversity of rites was the single proviso that " All distinctions
between Ancient and Modern Masons shall be abolished as far as practicable." [5] In New
York many of the Lodges under the older sanction gradually attached themselves to the predominant system, and beyond the fact that their members were understood to have shifted
their allegiance, and to have become " Ancients," very little more seems to have been required
of them. In South Carolina the strife lingered for some years, and this I imagine to have

[1] See Plate, fig. 9.   [2] P. 31 ; *cf. ante*, p. 59.   [3] Early Hist. G.L. Pennsyl., p. xxxix.
[4] Hayden, p. 257.   [5] Proc. G.L. Mass., 1877, p. 45.

been mainly the result of the presence of a large British garrison in that State during the closing years of the struggle for independence.

Gradually, however, all distinctions between the two systems were removed throughout the Continent, and the prudent course adopted by the Grand Lodge of New Jersey, in 1807, must be commended, by which body the difficulties of reconciling any discrepancies were at once surmounted by the appointment of a committee "to consider of and introduce an uniform system of working to be observed throughout the several Lodges of the State." [1]

AMERICAN FIELD LODGES.[2]

U.S. Battalion, St John's,	1 N.Y.,	1775.	Pennsylvania Line,	29 P.,	1780.
Connecticut Line, American Union,	[ ] N.E.,	1776.	New Jersey Line,	31 P.,	1781.
1st Reg. Pennsyl. Artillery,	19 P.,	1779.	„ „	36 P.,	1782.
Massachusetts Line, Washington,	13 M.,	1779.	Legion of the U.S.A.,	58 P.,	1793.
North Carolina Regiment,	20 P.,	1779.	2d Div. Northern Army,	[ ] N.Y.,	1814.
Maryland Line,	27 P.,	1780.	United States Army,	140 P.,	1814.
Pennsylvania Line,	28 P.,	1780.	Missouri Military,	86 Mo.,	1847.
		Vera Cruz, Quitman, 96 Miss., 1848.			

The first ten Lodges on this list were in existence during the Revolution. The third in order, now "Montgomery," No. 19, Philadelphia, is traditionally asserted to have been "originally a Military Lodge, with a travelling warrant from the G.L. of England." All warrants issued to military bodies were recalled by the Grand Lodge of Pennsylvania in 1784, and from that date the Army Lodges either ceased to exist or assumed a new character.

An application for "a warrant to hold a Travelling Lodge in the armies of the United States" was refused by the G.L. of New Jersey in 1791; and in the same year a "Travelling Warrant" was granted by the G.L. of New York to some non-military brethren desirous of erecting a Lodge in the Island of Curaçoa.

The first Field Lodge, after the peace—No. 58 (P.)—was established in the "Legion of the United States," commanded by General Anthony Wayne, in 1793; and it is said that nearly all the members were killed in the Indian War. After this, in the G.L. of New York— March 2, 1814—"a petition from a number of officers of the second division of the Northern Army, at Plattsburgh, praying for a 'marching warrant,' to be called Northern Light Lodge, was read and referred to the Grand Officers." Whether the charter solicited was granted or not, I am unable to state; but later in the same year a Field Lodge—No. 140—was erected by the G.L. of Pennsylvania, to be held wherever the Master for the time being should be stationed in the Army of the United States.

The last two Lodges on the list were established during the Mexican war, and it is quite possible that there were others, though the particulars with regard to them have not fallen in my way.

Field Lodges sprang up with rather a luxuriant growth during the late civil war, and were freely established on both sides. But the experience of the war was decidedly unfavourable to their utility, and we find the Grand Lodge of Pennsylvania, in 1865, congratulated on having "kept herself free from the difficulties, embarrassments, and entanglements, which the

---

[1] J. H. Hough, Origin of Masonry in New Jersey, p. 125.

[2] The letters N.Y. denote *New York*; N.E., *New England* (St John's G.L.); P., *Pennsylvania*; M., *Massachusetts G.L.*; Mo., *Missouri*; and Miss., *Mississippi*.

issuing of warrants for Army Lodges could not but have led to." The practice was, to issue dispensations, and when the Regiments in which they were held were mustered out of the service, or the individuals to whom they were granted returned to civil life, the Lodges ceased to exist.

The following statistics have been supplied to me with regard to the number of dispensations issued in the different jurisdictions:—Alabama, nineteen; Arkansas, thirteen; New York, eight; New Hampshire, five; Massachusetts, Virginia, Louisiana, and North Carolina, several each; and both in Connecticut and Nebraska, single dispensations. None whatever were granted in Kentucky, Tennessee, California, Kansas, Oregon, and Pennsylvania, and the general verdict passed upon such Lodges by all the American Grand Secretaries with whom I have been in correspondence, is strikingly in accord with the remarks of Past Grand Master Perkins of the last-named State, in 1865, to which I have already referred. There are no Lodges in the Standing Army of the United States, and for this a very sufficient reason will be found, in the fact that the few Regiments of the Regular Army are generally—if not always—divided into small fractions, separated at widely different posts.[1]

---

[1] Authorities—besides those already cited—Bancroft, Hist. U.S.; Ramsay, The Revolution of South Carolina, 1785; Andrews, Hist. of the Wars, 1786; Steadman, Hist. Amer. War, 1794; Carmichael-Smyth, Precis of the Wars in Canada, 1862; Léon Chotteau, Les Français En Amerique, 1876; Barker, Early Hist. G.L. New York; Proc. G.L. Pennsylvania and Michigan, 1865; Massachusetts and Connecticut, 1866; Letters from Grand Secretaries Frizzle (Tenn.), Barber (Ark.), Abell (Cal.), Cheever (Mass.), Austin (N.Y.), Pain (N.C.), Bowen (Neb.), Wheeler (Conn.), Brown (Kan.), Babcock (Ore.), Isaacs (Va.), Batchelor (La.), and Cleaver (N.H.). I am also very greatly indebted to Mr Sereno D. Nickerson of Boston, who has drawn my attention to many entries in the Proceedings of American Grand Lodges, which would otherwise have escaped my observation, as well as to the Deputy G.M. (Clifford P. MacCalla) and the Chairman of the Library Committee (C. E. Meyer), G.L. of Pennsylvania; also to Hughan, whose store of facts, placed ungrudgingly at my disposal, has vastly added to the materials out of which this and the next chapter have been constructed.

CHAPTER XXXI.

FREEMASONRY IN THE UNITED STATES OF AMERICA.

OCUMENTARY evidence and tradition are alike silent with regard to the introduction of Masonry into America. Lord Alexander, Viscount Canada, who in company with his brother Anthony—Master of Work to the King—became a member of the Lodge of Edinburgh in 1634, shortly afterwards founded a colony on the river St Lawrence.[1] But if any Lodges were established by early explorers of the continent, they perished before the dawn of accredited Masonic history, leaving behind them no traces of their existence. It has indeed been related that in 1658 the three degrees of Masonry were introduced by some Dutch Jews into Newport, Rhode Island,[2] but the statement is unworthy of serious refutation.

Governor Belcher, as mentioned at an earlier page,[3] was admitted (according to his own testimony) into the Craft in 1704, and must have carried back with him some slight acquaintance with its principles on his return to the New World in 1705. Ten years later—March 10, 1715—a letter is said to have been written by John Moore, the King's Collector at the port of Philadelphia, in which he alludes to a few evenings spent in festivity with his Masonic brethren.[4] There is also a tradition that a Lodge under the jurisdiction of the Grand Lodge of England was duly warranted at Boston in 1720, but died out shortly afterwards owing to the violent opposition it encountered.[5] After this we are brought down without a break to the year 1730, when the real history of Masonry in the United States may be said to have its commencement, and we find ourselves fairly launched upon an inquiry of great interest and singular complexity.

It is not so difficult a task to plant new truths as to root out old errors, and therefore the practice of Timotheus, an ancient teacher of rhetoric, must be commended, who always demanded a double fee from those pupils who had been instructed by others, since in that case he had not only to plant in, but also to root out.

So long, indeed, as specious probabilities are placed on the same footing with well-attested facts, so long will Masonic history be a misleading guide, and the misfortune is—to

---

[1] Chaps. VIII., p. 408; XXIII., p. 47; Lyon, p. 86.   [2] F. Peterson, Hist. of Rhode Island.
[3] Chap. XVI., p. 269.   [4] Proc. G.L. Pennsyl., 1882, p. 152.   [5] Proc. G.L. Mass., 1883, p. 155.

quote Hobbes, who considered all books to be merely extracts and copies—" that most authors are like sheep, never deviating from the beaten path."

Of late years, it is true, many new facts have been brought to light, and the materials for an exhaustive sketch of the early Masonry of America have been vastly extended. Nevertheless the story continues to be told in the old way, and there has hitherto been no attempt to deal with the subject as a whole, divested of the incrustations of error which have been laid over it by successive narrators.

To those who love to ride at anchor, it may be a disquieting reflection that no Statute of Limitations is recognised in our courts of literary jurisdiction. But this fact notwithstanding, the student of our antiquities cannot always hold his opinions in solution, expecting that fresh discoveries will keep pace with the search for them.

In historical inquiry—as observed at the outset of this work—finality can have no place, but while I readily admit that the conclusions to which I am about to give expression may be overturned by additional facts, I shall cherish the hope that no evidence available at the time of writing will be found to have been neglected, nor that I have anywhere failed to indicate with sufficient fulness the points on which differences of opinion may rationally exist.

With the names of Daniel Coxe and Henry Price the generality of Masonic students will be familiar. The former received a deputation as Provincial Grand Master, but there is hardly a *scintilla* of evidence to show that he ever exercised any authority under it. The latter, on the other hand, exercised all the authority of a Prov. G.M., though no absolute proof is forthcoming that he was at any time in lawful possession of a deputation.

The various questions arising, directly or indirectly, out of the authority granted or exercised by Coxe and Price respectively, have been largely debated in the journals of the Craft. By one set of writers the Masonic precedency of Philadelphia, and by another that of Boston (Massachusetts), has been affirmed. But it seems to me equally impossible to side completely with the former or the latter, and the examination upon which we are about to enter will, I think, necessitate our following the example of Lord Keeper Bridgman, of whom it is related " that if a case admitted of divers doubts, what the lawyers call points, he would never give all on one side, but either party should have somewhat to go away with." [1]

In the earliest minute-book of the Grand Lodge of England there is a list of Lodges, with the names of their members, as registered in 1731-32. Although there are some omissions— in the absence, doubtless, of returns—a roll is given of by far a majority of the Lodges, the total silence of the records with regard to the membership of the " Old Horn Lodge," being perhaps of all the *lacunæ* the loss that will be chiefly deplored. The last Lodge on the list is No. 104, at the Virgin's Inn, Derby, constituted September 14, 1732. With the exception of the dates of constitution, which I have taken from the Engraved Lists, and the publication of Dr Anderson (1738 edition), the following are extracts from this register. The names shown are in each case a selection from the actual list of members.[2]

---

[1] Roger North, *Lives of the Norths*, edit. 1826, vol. i., p. 179.

[2] In dealing with the *early* history of American Masonry, I have looked through the small end of the telescope, while in the latter—or comparatively modern—portion, the instrument has been reversed, and by treating the subject in broader outline, I have endeavoured to bring it within the limits of a general history.

No.	Description.	Date of Constitution.
8	DEVIL TAVERN, WITHIN TEMPLE BAR. Claude Crespigny (Master), Edw. Ravenell (S.W.), John Houghton, and Daniel Coxe.	April 25, 1722.
75	RAINBOW COFFEE-HOUSE, IN YORK BUILDINGS. John Pitt (Master), Edward Ravenell, John Houghton, "*Senr.*"; John Houghton, "*Junr.*"; and Henry Price.	July 17, 1730.
79	CASTLE, IN HIGHGATE. Thos. Moore (Master), A. Chocke (D.G.M., 1727), W. Blackerby (G. Treas., 1730-37); and Claude Crespigny.	1731.

In the Lodge at the "Devil" there were twenty-eight members, and the name of Daniel Coxe appears as the eighteenth on the list. The Lodge at the "Rainbow" boasted a much larger membership, no less than sixty-three names figuring in the roll, of which the fifty-third in order was that of Henry Price.

At about the middle of the last-named list there is an apparent break, and then follows a further series of names, belonging in all probability to brethren who had become members in 1732. There can hardly be a doubt as to the Daniel Coxe and Henry Price of the Lodges Nos. 8 and 75, being the American worthies bearing the same names. The former was certainly in England in the early part of 1731, and the latter refers on more than one occasion to having been personally acquainted with some of the leading Masons of London about 1733. Moreover, his patent as Prov. G.M., which he always stated was delivered to him in person, bears the date (according to records, the authority of which will be presently examined) of April 30 of that year.

It will be seen that three persons—Claude Crespigny, Edward Ravenell, and John Houghton—belonged at the same time to more than one Lodge, while in the case of two of them, the dual membership was of an identical character. These points may be usefully noted, as a good deal of speculation has arisen with regard both to Coxe and Price, which the details here given may assist in placing on a sounder basis. Thus, to slightly anticipate, Claude Crespigny, the Master of the Lodge to which Coxe belonged, was also a member of No. 79, then meeting at the Castle in Highgate, but shortly to become vacant, and later still to be arbitrarily assigned in a publication of 1735, to a Lodge within Coxe's jurisdiction. To this may be added, that Edward Ravenell and John Houghton apparently enjoyed Masonic fellowship both with Coxe and Price.

Among the members of other English Lodges at the same period, as shown in the register of Grand Lodge, were governors Burrington and Tinker, Sir W. Keith, Bart., Richard Hull, Randall Took, Ralph Farwinter, Captain William Douglas, and Alexander Pope. The last name, though an illustrious one, is not connected in any way with the spread of Masonry beyond the seas, but the others are those of well-known characters, who were all either Colonial Governors or Provincial Grand Masters abroad.

Daniel Coxe was the son of Dr Daniel Coxe of London, who from the year 1687 to 1690 was the largest landed proprietor and also the Governor of the Province of West Jersey. The father was a man of large wealth, and before his arrival in America had been in succession the physician to the Consort of Charles II., and to Queen Anne. The younger Coxe, who was born about the year 1674, arrived in England in November 1716, and six years later published "A Description of the English Province of CAROLANA." This was written in support of a claim, which he had inherited from his father, to the extensive region then called "Carolana." It included the present States of Virginia, North and South Carolina, Georgia, Florida, Louisiana, and all the country north on both sides of the Mississippi, up as high as Kentucky. In the preface the author suggests that all the North American colonies should be UNITED, and it has been maintained "that the celebrated 'Albany plan of Union,' recommended by Dr Franklin in 1754, is little more than a transcript of the design sketched by Daniel Coxe many years before."

A letter written by Coxe from Trenton, Falls of Delaware, dated April 28, 1728, shows that he must have returned to America, in the interval preceding the Masonic occurrences which it becomes my next task to relate.

On June 5, 1730, he was appointed by the Duke of Norfolk, Provincial Grand Master of New York, New Jersey, and Pennsylvania—his deputation or commission differing, it may be observed, in some important particulars from those of any similar instrument of this class. The term of office of Daniel Coxe was limited to two years, from June 24, 1730, "after which time," the brethren "in all or any" of the three colonies aforesaid, were "empowered every other year on the feast of St John the Baptist to elect a Provincial Grand Master," who, with the concurrence of his Deputy and Wardens, might establish Lodges at his discretion. An account in writing of the number of Lodges so constituted, with the names of the members, was to be furnished annually, but there is no allusion whatever to the payment of a *fee* for registration or for any other purpose. The deputation was granted, it may be added, on the petition of Coxe himself "and several other brethren residing and about to reside" in the Provinces over which his authority was made to extend.

In 1731—January 29—Coxe attended a meeting of the Grand Lodge of England, on which occasion his health was drunk "as Provincial Grand Master of North America."

In the same year, according to the records already referred to, we again meet with his name as a member of Lodge No. 8, meeting at the Devil Tavern, within Temple Bar.

The date of his final return to New Jersey, I am unable to supply, but it is on record that he was appointed Associate Justice of that Province in 1734, an office held by him until his death, which is thus announced in Franklin's *Pennsylvania Gazette* of April 26, 1739:—

"Yesterday morning, died at Trenton, the Hon. Daniel Cox, Esq., one of the Justices of the Supreme Court of the Province of New Jersey."

The archives of the Grand Lodge of England contain no further allusion to the subject of this memoir, and a thorough inquiry among his descendants for letters and papers bearing upon the subject has failed to disclose any testimony whatever of the exercise by him, or by any one acting under his authority, of the prerogatives conferred by his deputation.[1]

If, however, we accept without demur the statements in the following letter, which is said to have been written—November 17, 1754—by Henry Bell,[2] at that time residing in

---

[1] J. H. Hough, Origin of Masonry in New Jersey, 1870, p. 9.

[2] The name of Henry Bell appears on the Tax Lists of Derry Township, Lancaster County, Pennsylvania, for the years 1750-59 (Early Hist. G.L. Pennsyl., Introduction, p. x.).

Lancaster, to Dr Thomas Cadwallader,[1] of Philadelphia, there can remain no doubt as to the first Grand Master in America having constituted a Lodge at Philadelphia:—

"As you well know, I was one of the originators of the first Masonic Lodge in Philadelphia. A party of us used to meet at the Tun Tavern, in Water Street, and sometimes opened a Lodge there. Once, in the fall of 1730, we formed a design of obtaining a Charter for a regular Lodge, and made application to the Grand Lodge of England for one, but before receiving it, we heard that Daniel Coxe, of New Jersey, had been appointed by that Grand Lodge as Provincial Grand Master of New York, New Jersey, and Pennsylvania. We therefore made application to him, and our request was granted."

The documentary evidence last presented rests on the authority of the Library Committee, Grand Lodge of Pennsylvania, who state, "The letter was exhibited in the Grand Secretary's office [Philadelphia], in 1872. It bore all the marks of being genuine, and we have no doubt of its being correct." But, it has been pertinently observed,[2] "Where has the letter been for one hundred and twenty years? In whose custody? Why has it never been brought to light before? What is the full text? These, and numerous other questions, must be satisfactorily answered before we can admit this piece of evidence. For an item that has been waited for almost one hundred and fifty years, it comes remarkably pat. If not a swift witness in one sense, it is in another, for it certainly covers the whole ground."

Again, the opening words of the letter, addressed to Cadwallader, who was only initiated —in a Lodge of which Bell was at no time a member—in 1737, are somewhat enigmatical. Moreover, we are led to believe that in the fall of 1730, there was but a single body of Masons in Philadelphia, whereas the existence of at least a plurality of Lodges, on December 8 of that year, is distinctly stated in Franklin's newspaper.

What is new is not necessarily true, and indications are not wanting that, even in Philadelphia itself, among those by whom the authenticity of the letter was formerly upheld, there are some persons who begin to doubt the validity of the proofs, and it is, at least, a significant fact, that since the discovery by MacCalla of some genuine records dating from 1731, the document has been as far as possible withdrawn from the arena of discussion.

The letter, indeed, though inadmissible as evidence in any court of justice, has derived a factitious importance from its appearance in two official publications,[3] though it may be well doubted whether we should have heard of it at all, had the early ledger of St John's Lodge (*liber* B.)—with which it clashes—been discovered ten years earlier than it actually was?

The only other evidence that I have met with relating to the possible exercise of jurisdiction by Coxe, occurs in a letter of July 28, 1762, written from Elizabeth Town, New Jersey, claiming a deputation, which Jeremy Gridley, Prov. G.M. at Boston, had promised to send, on the receipt of satisfactory proof that Daniel Coxe had died before 1754.[4]

The *Pennsylvania Gazette* of December 8, 1730, contains the earliest printed notice of the Craft in America:—

---

[1] An eminent physician, born 1707; a member of St John's Lodge, Philadelphia, 1737; died 1779.

[2] By Mr Sereno D. Nickerson, in the "New England Freemason," vol. i., 1874, p. 380; and Proc. G.L. of Mass., 1883, p. 187. This distinguished Mason was G.M. of Massachusetts in 1874, and Grand Secretary in 1883.

[3] Dedication Memorial, Masonic Temple, Philadelphia, 1875, p. 21; Early Hist. Grand Lodge of Pennsylvania, Introduction, 1877, p. xl.

[4] E. T. Schultz, Freemasonry in Maryland, 1884, p. 24; Boston Records, 1886, p. 78.

"As there are several Lodges of Freemasons erected in this Province, and people have lately been much amused with conjecture concerning them, we think the following account of Freemasonry from London will not be unacceptable to our readers."

Then follows a recital, that "By the death of a gentleman who was one of the Brotherhood of Freemasons, there has lately happened a discovery of abundance of their secret signs and wonders, with the mysterious manner of their admission into that Fraternity, contained in a manuscript found among his papers."

Although Franklin here deposes to the existence of *several* Lodges in 1730, there is no further evidence that will enable us to identify more than one of them—St John's Lodge, Philadelphia—in which that remarkable man is believed, with good reason, to have himself received the light of Masonry in February 1731. The date of Franklin's initiation remained for a long time uncertain, although it was rightly assumed that the insertion by him in his newspaper of a so-called "exposure of Masonry" must have necessarily preceded his own membership of the Society.

The discovery by Mr Clifford P. MacCalla, in 1884, of an original Masonic record, dating from 1731, has thrown much light on the early history of the Craft in Pennsylvania. The book in question is bound in parchment or vellum, and bears on the front cover the words—

"PHILADELPHIA CITY,

"ST JOHN'S LODGE, LIBRE B."

The title with which it is labelled, suggests a "Liber A.," or earlier record of the Lodge. This, however, has not yet been found, and it would be idle to speculate upon its contents. Liber B. is the Secretary's ledger account with all the members of the Lodge from June 24, 1731, to June 24, 1738. Altogether, the names are given of fifty members between 1731 and 1737. The initiation or entrance fee was £3, until 1734, when it was raised to £5. The monthly dues (also styled "quota" and "omition") were 6d. per member, and there was a fine of 1s. for absence. The lodge met on the *first Monday* of each month, and (in the opinion of local antiquaries) was constituted (with thirteen members) at the close of 1730, or the beginning of 1731. Among the names—June 24, 1731—we find those of "W^m. Button, late Mast.; W^m. Allen, Esq., Grand Mast.; and William Pringle, Deputy Mast.:" the last two brethren being continued in their respective offices in the following year, as we shall see by an extract from Franklin's newspaper to be presently quoted. The name of one Warden is given for the year 1735, and of both for 1736, 1737, and 1738. These are identical with those of the *Grand* Wardens for the same years, and in every case the brethren named as Grand Officers in the period covered by Liber B., were members of the private Lodge. If, indeed, any lingering doubt remained as to the *Lodge* and the *Grand Lodge* being one and the same body, this would be dispelled by a printed notice of June 16, 1737, signed by "Thomas Hopkinson, Grand Master," and his officers, "on behalf of all the members of St John's Lodge at Philadelphia."[1]

Dr Thomas Cadwallader, whose name is first given under the year 1737, was a (Grand) Warden in 1738. Of Henry Bell there is no mention. Benjamin Franklin is charged— June 24, 1731—"To remainder of your £3 entrance is £2, 0s.," and had apparently paid the

[1] Early Hist. G.L. Pennsyl., p. 79. *Cf. post*, p. 434.

sum of £1, five months before, or some time during that period, as he is charged with five months previous dues. This will tend to prove that he was made a Mason in February 1731. The last entries in the records or accounts, were made by Franklin, and an interesting report, drawn up—June 5, 1732—by a committee of the members, is pronounced on good authority to be in his handwriting.

This report is distinct from the Ledger, but both these ancient documents fulfil the legal requirement "of coming from the proper custody," having been inherited by Mr G. T. Ingham, together with other old writings and papers, formerly the property of David Hall, for many years Franklin's partner in the printing business.[1] Two of the "Resolutions" agreed to by Franklin and the other members of the committee, are so quaintly expressed, and withal so admirable in their tenor, that I am induced to transcribe them:—

> "1. That since the excellent Science of Geometry and Architecture is so much recommended in our ancient Constitutions, Masonry being first instituted with this Design, among others, to distinguish the true and skilful Architect from unskilful Pretenders; total ignorance of this art is very unbecoming a Man who bears the worthy Name and Character of MASON:
>
> "We therefore conclude, that it is the Duty of every Member to make himself, in some Measure, acquainted therewith, as he would honour the Society he belongs to, and conform to the Constitutions.
>
> "2. That every Member may have an Opportunity of so doing, the present Cash to be laid out in the best Books of Architecture, suitable Mathematical Instruments, &c."

It will be remembered, that by the terms of his Patent, Daniel Coxe was to hold office until June 24, 1732, when a new Grand Master was to be elected, and the following notice which appeared in the *Pennsylvania Gazette* of June 26, in that year, has been relied upon, as proving to demonstration that a successor to Coxe was duly chosen in strict accordance with the terms of the Deputation.

"Philadelphia, June 26.

"Saturday last being St John's day, a Grand Lodge of the ancient and honorable Society of FREE and ACCEPTED MASONS was held at the Sun Tavern in Water Street, when, after a handsome entertainment, the Worshipful W. Allen, Esq., was unanimously chosen *Grand Master* of this Province for the year ensuing, who was pleased to appoint *Mr William Pringle* Deputy Master. Wardens chosen for the ensuing year were *Thomas Boude* and *Benjamin Franklin*."

But as Allen and Pringle were already Grand Master and Deputy, respectively, in 1731, this piece of evidence will only become consistent with the supposition that Coxe's mantle really fell on Allen, by indulging very largely in conjecture. If, then, a loose rein is given to the imagination, it may be possible to conceive that Coxe obtained permission to resign in favour of Allen in 1731, or that the entries in the ledger of St John's Lodge were not made during the actual years under which they appear?

---

[1] Keystone, September 5, 1885. *Cf. ante*, Chap. XIV., p. 195.

Allen was succeeded in the chair of St John's (and the Grand) Lodge by Humphrey Murray, in 1733, and the latter by Benjamin Franklin, in 1734. Before attaining this distinction, however, the printer and editor of the *Pennsylvania Gazette* had visited Boston, where he seems to have made the acquaintance of Henry Price, in the autumn of 1733.[1] The election of the journalist of that era, but who was afterwards destined to take high rank as a philosopher, diplomatist, and statesman, is thus announced in the columns of his own newspaper :—

"Philadelphia, June 27 [1734].

"Monday last a Grand Lodge of the Ancient and Honorable Society of Free and Accepted Masons in this Province, was held at the *Tun Tavern* in Water Street, when BENJAMIN FRANKLIN being elected Grand Master for the year ensuing, appointed Mr John Crap to be his Deputy : and James Hamilton, Esq., and Thomas Hopkinson, Gent., were chosen Wardens. After which a very elegant entertainment was provided, and the Proprietor [Thomas Penn], the Governor, and several other persons of distinction, honored the Society with their presence."

This paragraph was reprinted in several of the London papers,[2] a circumstance which we shall do well to bear in mind, when the appearance of a Philadelphian Lodge in a list given by a Dublin Calendar as the roll of the Grand Lodge of England for 1734, has to be considered, and if possible accounted for.

In the same year, Franklin reprinted Dr Anderson's Book of Constitutions, and wrote two important letters, one an official communication to the Provincial Grand Lodge at Boston, the other a private note to Henry Price the G.M. They are thus worded :—

"RIGHT WORSHIPFUL GRAND MASTER AND MOST WORTHY AND DEAR BRETHREN,—We acknowledge your favor of the 23d of October past, and rejoice that the Grand Master (whom God bless) hath so happily recovered from his late indisposition ; and we now, glass in hand, drink to the establishment of his health, and the prosperity of your whole Lodge.

"We have seen in the Boston prints an article of news from London, importing that at a Grand Lodge held there in August last, Mr Price's deputation and power was extended over all America, which advice we hope is true, and we heartily congratulate him thereupon, and though this has not been as yet regularly signified to us by you, yet, giving credit thereto, we think it our duty to lay before your Lodge what we apprehend needful to be done for us, in order to promote and strengthen the interest of Masonry in this Province (which seems to want the sanction of some authority derived from home, to give the proceedings and determinations of our Lodge their due weight), to wit, a Deputation or Charter granted by the Right Worshipful Mr Price, by virtue of his commission from Britain, confirming the Brethren of Pennsylvania in the privileges they at present enjoy of holding annually their Grand Lodge, choosing their Grand Master, Wardens, and other officers, who may manage all affairs relating to the Brethren here with full power and authority, according to the customs and usages of Masons, the said Grand Master of Pennsylvania only yielding his chair when the Grand Master of all America shall be in place. This, if it seem good and reasonable to you to grant, will not only be extremely agreeable to us, but will also, we are confident, conduce much to the welfare, establishment, and reputation of Masonry in these parts. We therefore submit it for your consideration, and, as we hope our request will be complied with, we desire that it may be done as soon as possible, and also accompanied with a

---

[1] According to his autobiography, Franklin, who left his home in October 1723, *after ten years' absence from Boston*, made a journey there, to visit his relatives (Works, edit. by Jared Sparks, 1840, vol. i., p. 128).

[2] The *St James' Evening Post*, Sept. 3, *Read's Weekly Journal*, Sept. 7, 1734, and doubtless others.

copy of the R. W. Grand Master's first Deputation, and of the instrument by which it appears to be enlarged as above mentioned, witnessed by your Wardens, and signed by the Secretary ; for which favors this Lodge doubt not of being able to behave so as not to be thought ungrateful.

"We are, Right Worshipful Grand Master and Most Worthy Brethren, Your Affectionate Brethren and obliged humble Servts.,

"Signed at the request of the Lodge,

"B. FRANKLIN, G.M.

"PHILADELPHIA, Nov. 28, 1734."

"DEAR BROTHER PRICE,—I am glad to hear of your recovery. I hope to have seen you here this Fall, agreeable to the expectation you were so good as to give me ; but since sickness has prevented your coming while the weather was moderate, I have no room to flatter myself with a visit from you before the Spring, when a deputation of the Brethren here will have an opportunity of showing how much they esteem you. I beg leave to recommend their request to you, and to inform you that some false and rebel Brethren, who are foreigners, being about to set up a distinct Lodge in opposition to the old and true Brethren here, pretending to make Masons for a bowl of punch, and the Craft is like to come into disesteem among us unless the true Brethren are countenanced and distinguished by some such special authority as herein desired. I entreat, therefore, that whatever you shall think proper to do therein may be sent by the next post, if possible, or the next following.

"I am, Your Affectionate Brother & humb. Servt.,

"B. FRANKLIN, *G.M.*

"*Pennsylvania.*

"PHILADELPHIA, Nov. 28, 1734.

"P.S.—If more of the Constitutions are wanted among you, please hint it to me."

From these letters it may be inferred that a rumour of Price having received an extension of authority had reached Philadelphia ; also, that *at the time of their being written*, the Masonic body over which Franklin presided, had not received a warrant from either Coxe or Price, since in each of these cases "the sanction of some authority derived from home" would not have been required. It will be observed, moreover, that a confirmation of privileges already existing is all that is solicited. Some analogy between the Masonic and the political dependence of a colony upon the mother country was doubtless present to Franklin's mind. But that he considered his own position as being one whit inferior to that of Price, under the latter's first deputation, is negatived by the stipulation providing for "the Grand Master of Pennsylvania only yielding his chair when the Grand Master of All America [should] be in place."

According to a long series of authorities, a Lodge was warranted at Philadelphia by Henry Price in 1734; but this exercise of jurisdiction, if it took place at all, cannot have occurred until after the two letters of November 28 in that year were written. This point, however, we shall approach later, and I pass to a curious entry in the *Pocket Companion for Free-Masons*, printed at Dublin in 1735. At the end of the book a list is given of the warranted Lodges in Ireland, Great Britain, etc. The Irish Lodges head the roll, and absorb thirty-seven *numbers*, the first English Lodge being therefore shown as No. 38. At the 116th place on this compound list, or, if we deduct the 37 Irish Lodges, at the No. 79, there appears : "The Hoop in Water Street in Philadelphia, 1st Monday." The work quoted from is a reprint of a London publication of the same name and date; and except with regard to one particular, the list of English Lodges given in the latter has been reproduced with scrupulous fidelity in the former. The *Pocket Companion*, London, shows a vacant niche at the No. 79, which, as we have seen, is filled, in its Dublin namesake, by a Lodge at Water Street, Philadelphia, meeting on the *first Monday* in the month.

The judicial office to which Daniel Coxe was appointed in 1734, together with his death in 1739, have already been recorded. During the period covered by these years, the "Earliest Grand Master in America" resided within twenty miles of Philadelphia. Neither the letters written by Franklin in 1734, however, nor his obituary notice of Coxe in the *Pennsylvania Gazette*, betray the slightest knowledge by the former, of the latter being even a member of the Society. This silence with regard to the grant of a deputation to Coxe it is now impossible to explain. Yet if we put on one side the letters of 1734, and the newspaper entry of 1739, the remaining evidence affords good reason for supposing that Franklin was aware of Coxe's appointment in the former year, and still stronger ground for believing that it could not have been absent from his knowledge in the latter.

The proceedings of the Grand Lodge of England were circulated far and wide—by the newspapers and in private letters, as well as by oral communication. But, passing over the earlier date, there is scarcely any room for doubt that in 1739 Franklin must have read—or, at the very least, have had his attention called to—the positive statement in the Constitutions of 1738, that Coxe was appointed a Provincial Grand Master during the administration of the Duke of Norfolk?

Why, then, it may be asked, if the grant of a patent to Coxe may be reasonably assumed to have come to the knowledge of Franklin, do we meet with no allusion to the fact in the newspaper of the latter? Towards the solution of this problem I shall merely offer a conjecture. If Daniel Coxe never exercised the authority conferred upon him by his deputation, or, in more homely language, withdrew from Masonry on his return to America, this would afford some ground for supposing that his brethren of the Craft entertained a very natural disinclination to claim as a member of the Society one who, so to speak, had plainly but unmistakably turned his back upon it. I may also add, with special reference to the obituary notice of 1739 that, as far as we can now discern, between the years 1737 and 1749, Masonry in Pennsylvania was under a cloud, and courted not the light.

We may, however, assume with some confidence—and on this point the Franklin letters of 1734 seem to me conclusive—that the brethren at Philadelphia would not have applied to Henry Price for a deputation or charter, *confirming* their privileges of holding a Grand Lodge annually and regulating their own affairs, if they had received at any previous date "an authority from home," under the hand of Daniel Coxe.

Franklin was succeeded as Grand Master by James Hamilton, who in turn gave place to Thomas Hopkinson, the latter being, at the time of his election, the Admiralty Judge in the province, and the former subsequently becoming the first native Governor of Pennsylvania. Each year there was a new occupant of the chair, which in 1737 was filled by William Plumsted, a member of the Common Council, whose tenure of office was preceded by a lamentable event, that was fraught with much evil to the Society. On June 13, 1737, an apprentice to an apothecary at Philadelphia sustained such injuries from his master and two others, whilst receiving at their hands what he believed to be a Masonic degree, that death was the result.[1] This incident, as might be expected, was turned to the disadvantage of the Fraternity by the anti-Masons of that period; and the *Weekly Mercury*—a rival sheet to the *Pennsylvania Gazette*—falsely accused Franklin of conniving at the transaction. The parties concerned in this tragical occurrence were not Masons; and the Grand Officers, in a public notice (dated June 16), to which I have already in part alluded,[2] expressed, after reciting the facts of the outrage, "in Behalf of all the Members of St John's Lodge, at Philad'a, the Abhorrence of all true Brethren to such Practices in general, and their Innocence of this Fact in particular." Nevertheless, the growth of Masonry in the province was arrested, and its progress retarded, by the catastrophe. Grand Officers were apparently chosen in 1738 and 1741; but after the latter year the fount becomes dried up whence particulars of the annual elections have hitherto been derived, so we can only conclude, from the silence of Franklin's newspaper with regard to St John's Lodge, that it vegetated in obscurity until 1749.

In the year last-named—July 10—Franklin was appointed Provincial Grand Master by Thomas Oxnard, whose jurisdiction extended over the whole of North America—from which it seems to follow, as a logical deduction, that he eventually obtained in 1749 what he had vainly applied for in 1734.

At the first Grand Lodge held under this deputation—September 5, 1749—Franklin appointed his Grand Officers, and "at the same meeting a warrant was granted to James *Pogreen* and others to hold a Lodge in Philadelphia." So far Dr Mease,[3] whose sketch of the "Society of Masons" is given in full in the official history of the Grand Lodge of Pennsylvania,[4] and the latter informs us (on a later page) that the charter in question was granted to "St John's Lodge," of which, however, the first Master is stated to have been James *Pogrew*. The same name apparently, though again we meet with a slight variation of spelling, occurs in an original document showing the debts due for quarterage by members of the "First Lodge" in June 1752. In this the name of "Jas. *Polgreen*" is given, his liabilities extending to December 1751, beyond which the record does not go.[5]

The Lodge of 1749 seems therefore not to have been a new creation, but a revival of the body over which Allen presided in 1731, and if such was the case, Franklin himself, in both instances, Grand Lodge and Lodge, served as the conduit pipe through which his anxiously sought "authority from home" was derived.

Meetings of the Prov. Grand Lodge were regularly held until March 13, 1750, when William Allen, Recorder of Philadelphia, presented a patent signed by Lord Byron, G.M. of England, appointing him Provincial Grand Master, which was duly recognised, and he then nominated Benjamin Franklin as his Deputy.

The first Masonic Hall in America was erected at Philadelphia in 1754, and in the following year—the same Grand and Deputy Grand Masters holding office as in 1750—we find that three subordinate Lodges were represented at the Feast of St John the Baptist. In the official publication [6] upon which I am mainly relying at this part of the narrative, it is

---

[1] June 16, 1737.—"We hear that on Monday night last, some people, pretending to be *Free Masons*, got together in a cellar with a young man, who was desirous of being made one, and in the ceremonies, 'tis said, they threw some burning spirits upon him, either accidentally or to terrify him, which burnt him so that he was obliged to take his bed, and died this morning" (*Pennsylvania Gazette*).

[2] *Ante*, p. 429.   [3] The Picture of Philadelphia, 1811, p. 288 *et seq.*   [4] Introduction, p. xxv.
[5] *Ibid.*, p. xxxii.   [6] Early Hist. G.L. Pennsyl.

PLATE I.

Thomas C. Jack, London & Edinburgh

assumed that two of these were the First and Second "St John's" Lodges, or in other words, the unchartered and the chartered bodies of 1731 and 1749 respectively. But the evidence with which we are presented by no means justifies this conclusion, nor can we be quite certain that more than a single Lodge was in existence before 1754.[1]

In 1758 Pennsylvania was invaded by the "Ancients" or Schismatics, and from that time the Lodges under the older sanction declined, and gradually faded into obscurity. The last printed notice of any of them occurred in 1760, and in the same year—November 17— Franklin was present at a meeting of the Grand Lodge of England, in the minutes of which body he is described as "Prov. G.M. of Philadelphia," a title that may suggest the possibility of his having been elected to the office previously held by Allen?

Afterwards, during his diplomatic career, and while a resident in France, Franklin joined the Lodge of the Nine Muses, of which Lalande and other literary celebrities were also members.[2] He took a prominent part in the initiation of Voltaire, and on the death of that philosopher, acted as S.W. of the Lodge of Sorrow held to celebrate his memory.

The Lodge of the "Nine Muses" regarded Franklin with such veneration, that it struck a medal in his honour, and he was greeted with much cordiality by a Lodge at Rouen as late as 1785.

The last official act of the First Lodge in Philadelphia occurred in 1782, at which date it still existed, but in a state of suspended animation, and with but few members. About eleven years later all the Lodges in that city under the original Grand Lodge of England[3] ceased to exist. Their hall was sold, and a part of the proceeds, amounting to nearly £600, was handed over to the civic authorities to aid in forming a fund for supplying the poor inhabitants with fuel in the winter season.

At this point, and before proceeding with a memoir of Henry Price, and a review of the evidence which is closely associated with his name, it will be convenient if we pause to examine a little in detail some of the leading features of the early Masonry of Pennsylvania.

In the first place, the documentary evidence showing the existence of a Lodge reaches back to 1731, and as we then only commence with "Liber B.," the actual date at which the brethren who are named in it (or those they may have succeeded) associated together as a body, must remain a pure matter of conjecture. "Liber A.," if produced, might indeed bring us within measurable distance of this period, but on the other hand it is equally possible— not to say probable—that it would point to an uninterrupted succession of Philadelphian Masons meeting at St John's Lodge, to use a familiar expression, "from time immemorial," which, as we all know, signifies in Masonic phrase, an era more or less remote from the existence of actual records, but at all events going beyond, or as it were, behind them.

But without going back any further than the year 1731, we shall do well to reflect that

---

[1] All the subordinate Grand Officers appointed by Franklin on September 5, 1749, belonged to the First or St John's Lodge, which body (it is said) in concert with the *Grand Lodge* erected the hall in 1754. But I strongly suspect that the subscribers were all members of the Lodge. The fact, moreover, that no other Lodges contributed to the expenses, affords a strong argument against the possibility of there being any such in existence at that time.

[2] Chap. XXV., p. 156.   [3] None of them, however, obtained a footing on its roll.

the sovereignty of Grand Lodges was then only on its trial. Such bodies had been formed, it is true, at London, York, and Dublin, though we should be careful to remember that the latter towns were as much under *English* government as Philadelphia. But in Scotland—the most ancient home of Masonic precedent—there were as yet no chartered Lodges, and assemblies of brethren, formed as in Philadelphia, were the only Masonic associations existing in that country. Brethren united to form Lodges in neighbourhoods where there were fair chances of their continuance, and such assemblies, though without any other sanction, were not styled irregular when the Grand Lodge of Scotland was erected in 1736, the old Lodges, whether offshoots of "Mother Kilwinning," of other ancient courts of Operative Masonry, or simply the results of local combinations, uniting to form that organisation which has happily continued to this day.

It is evident that brethren who had left the old World, and brought to their new homes a knowledge of the Craft, were as much within their rights in holding Lodges in Philadelphia, Portsmouth (New Hampshire), and elsewhere in America, as those who assembled in like manner in England and Scotland; and just as in the latter countries the members of such Lodges were accepted as petitioners for written Constitutions without their legal status as Masons being demurred to, so we shall find that the Boston authorities raised no objection to the Masonic regularity of the Portsmouth brethren, but granted their request for a warrant in 1736. We have already seen that in 1734 the Prov. G.M. of New England was requested to *confirm* Dr Franklin and others in their privileges in Pennsylvania—thus completing the parallel.

In those early days a piece of paper or parchment, containing a written or printed authority for certain brethren and their successors to meet as a Lodge, was not held in the superstitious reverence with which it afterwards became regarded.[1] The old customs were gradually being supplanted by the new, but the former evinced great tenacity of existence in some instances, especially in the British colonies, where they appear to have remained for the longest period of time unmodified. The modern doctrine with respect to the formation of Grand Lodges it is not my purpose to examine at any length. Every case should, I think, be judged on its own merits, and the hard and fast rule laid down that three Lodges must be represented on such an occasion[2] seems to me as inconvenient in practice as it certainly is deficient in authority. But even if the rule in question were now regarded as sound Masonic law throughout the universe, we could hardly, by any feat of *ex post facto* legislation, so strain its application as to embrace the proceedings of the brethren at Philadelphia in 1731. The Fraternity there must be held to have been as much and as legally a Grand Lodge as that of "*All* England at York." Their meetings, for all we know to the contrary, may have been held before the era of Grand Lodges, and they

---

[1] Later in the century, both in England and America (and the practice was not unknown in France), the existence as well as the regularity of a Lodge was deemed to be bound up with its Charter. Thus the succession of members might come to an end, but after any interval, no matter of what duration, the issue of the old warrant to an entirely new set of brethren, was viewed as a reinstatement or revival of the original Lodge. The absurdity of this custom is self-evident, and its unfairness becomes apparent, when we reflect that under the G.L. of England the only Lodges that would necessarily become extinct on the death or dispersion of their members, were the memorable Four by whose act that body came into existence! *Cf.* Chap. XVII., p. 340.

[2] Mackey, p. 320.

certainly were before the influence of the earliest of these bodies had made itself felt across the seas.[1]

Henry Price—as we learn from the epitaph upon his tombstone—was born about 1697, and came to New England about 1723. No trace of him can be found in Boston until 1732, when he is described in some legal proceedings as a tailor, from the nature of which, however, it has been conjectured that he must have been established in his business a year or two earlier. So far his fullest biographer, but other authorities who have worked their way through the same materials which he used for the compilation of his memoir, are of opinion that there is no evidence whatever to support the statement that Henry Price was known in Boston before 1733. The discrepancy is immaterial. If the name shown on the roll of the Lodge at the Rainbow, No. 75, was his, he must have been in London—judging from its position on the list—in 1732. That he was also there in the following year we may infer from his own written statements in 1755 and 1768, and it was then, as he tells us, that he received a deputation appointing him Provincial Grand Master of New England. The visit, therefore, was in all probability a continuous one. In the spring of 1733 he seems to have returned to Boston, and in the same year Governor Jonathan Belcher appointed him Cornet in his troop of Guards, with the rank of Major, and from that time—at least so it is averred—he was known as Major Price.

In 1736 he entered into partnership with Francis Beteille, who was a shopkeeper, while Price himself carried on the tailoring department. The latter branch of the business appears to have been given up about 1739, as after that date both partners are described as shop-keepers. Price became the sole partner in 1741, and as a merchant or shopkeeper carried on the business alone until 1750, when he retired.

About May 14, 1780, while using an axe in splitting rails, it glanced and struck him in the abdomen, inflicting a severe and fatal wound. His will was executed on the following day, and in the words of the authority upon which I am relying for the preliminaries of this sketch,[2] "it especially shows what his religious character was; the possession of three pews in meeting-houses not of his faith and of his Church evince the strong sympathy he had for religious instruction, and the aid he afforded for its support."

Price lingered until May 20, when he died at his homestead in Townsend, aged eighty-three years. He left an estate of great value, but which was afterwards much reduced by lawsuits, insecurity of his titles to real estate, and by the general depression resulting from the war of the Revolution upon all property in the new States.

We have it on the authority of Price himself that he received one deputation from Viscount Montague in 1733, appointing him Provincial Grand Master of New England, and another from the Earl of Crawford in 1734, extending his powers over all North America. No record, however, has been preserved in the archives of the Grand Lodge of England of the issue of any such documents; neither does Price's name appear in the lists of Provincial

---

[1] Authorities up to this point :—Records, G.L. of England ; Hayden, Washington and his Masonic Compeers, 1866 ; Hough, Masonry in New Jersey, 1870 ; Mitchell, Hist. of Masonry, 1871 ; Mackey, 1874, *s.v.* Franklin ; Early Hist. G.L. of Pennsylvania, 1877-84 ; MacCalla, Philadelphia, the Mother City of Freemasonry in America, 1876, and Hist. of St John's Lodge, 1884 ; Phototypes of Liber B. of St John's Lodge, 1884 ; Schultz, Masonry in Maryland, 1884 ; World Wide Register, 1860 ; and the *Keystone* (Philadelphia), *passim.*

[2] W. S. Gardner, Address upon Henry Price, 1872, p. 12.

Grand Masters given in the Constitutions of 1738, 1756, and 1767. It is shown, indeed, in the Engraved List for 1770 as Prov. G.M. of North America—an appointment then actually held by John Rowe, whose name never appears at all in the English Calendars, though that of Price, having once gained a footing, was continued annually until 1804—twenty-four years after his decease !

The tangled web of Masonic history in Massachusetts is not to be easily unravelled ; but as every writer may hope to profit by the labours of those who have preceded him—to some extent, at least—I shall indulge in this consolatory reflection while engaged in the examination of a subject which has been so largely canvassed in the journals of the Craft.[1]

According to the stream of Masonic writers, a Provincial Grand Lodge, and also a private Lodge, were established at Boston by Henry Price in 1733. It is important, however, to recognise, at the outset of our inquiry, the very precarious foundation of authority on which the early Masonic history of Massachusetts reposes. The actual records of the Provincial Grand Lodge—by which I mean a contemporaneous account of its proceedings—date from 1751. There are also "what appear to be transcripts of brief memoranda describing the important incidents in the history of that body between 1733 and 1750 ; or they may have been made up from the recollection of brethren who had been active among the Craft during these seventeen years." [2]

From the documents of the latter class we learn that on July 30, 1733 (Old Style), Henry Price gathered round him ten brethren, and opened the Provincial Grand Lodge. Eight persons were then made Masons, and the whole eighteen brethren joined in a petition, asking that they might be formed into a constituted and regular Lodge, which prayer was granted on the same day.

A copy is given of the deputation granted to Price by Lord Montague, but the original petition signed by the eighteen and addressed to the former has been preserved. Of the latter Charles Pelham made a transcript, which—after a close comparison—Mr Jacob Norton says "contains many ideas that are not in the original ; " and adds : "If he took liberties with one document, he may have done so with the others." [3] This remark is incontrovertible, but even a sullied stream is a blessing compared to a total drought, and in the present case I do not think much benefit will arise from too minute a verbal criticism of the evidence. Even if the text of the missing deputation had been supplied by Pelham from conjecture, this would not invalidate the fact—if such it be—that Price was at one time the lawful owner of an English patent. Not, indeed, that there is reason for supposing any such thing. For my own part, I altogether fail to trace the clumsy hand of the forger in the alleged transcript ; and unless we bid Henry Price stand aside as a witness wholly unworthy of credit, the text of the deputation actually granted in 1733 comes down to us duly attested by the original holder.

---

[1] Freemason, vol. iii., 1870, pp. 68, 358 ; vol. v., 1872, pp. 483, 495 ; Masonic Magazine, vol. i., 1873-74, p. 322 ; vol. ii., 1874-75, pp. 275, 304 ; Freemason's Chronicle, Nov. 10, 1877 ; Nov. 6, 13, and 20 ; Dec. 18 and 25, 1880 ; Jan. 1 and 29, 1881 ; March 1, 1884 ; Keystone, July 3, 1880 ; etc., etc.

[2] Mr Sereno D. Nickerson, G.S., in Proc. G.L. Mass., 1883, p. 157. Mr Jacob Norton states : "In 1751, Charles Pelham was appointed G.S. ; but instead of beginning his record with June 1751, he thought best to manufacture first a record from 1733. That part of the record is therefore unreliable ; but yet certain facts therein are corroborated by original MSS. of that period, and some statements we may take for granted. The Lodge record, as well as that of the Master Masons' Lodge, were also the handiwork of Bro. Pelham " (Freemason's Chronicle, Nov. 10, 1877).

[3] Review of Grand Master Gardner's Address on Henry Price (Freemason, vol. v., 1872, p. 483).

This document bears date April 30, 1733, and the text, like that of the Coxe deputation, of which it is almost a counterpart, is without any allusion to fees ; but there is no proviso for the election of a successor, and the Prov. G.M. was empowered to constitute Lodges without the concurrence of his Deputy and Grand Wardens.

Price's memory has suffered more at the hands of panegyrists than calumniators ; but I shall endeavour to steer equally clear of the "special pleading" of the one, or the "historical pyrrhonism" of the other.

The "First Lodge in Boston," or "Holy Lodge of St John," was really constituted August 31, 1733. This is placed beyond dispute by two letters of 1736, in which brethren are recommended (by that body) to the favourable notice of the Grand Lodge of England and of Lodge Glasgow Kilwinning respectively. These are severally dated June 23 and September 1. Both documents are signed by Price (as G.M.) and his Deputy, and the later one by the Master (Robert Tomlinson) and officers of the Lodge. Each letter recites that the Lodge was constituted August 31, 1733, by Henry Price, Provincial Grand Master.[1] Copies of both are among the Boston records; but the letter of September 1, 1736, has also been transcribed into the minutes of Lodge Glasgow Kilwinning of November 2 in the same year, from which a certified extract has been published by Lyon.[2]

In 1734, as we have already seen, a rumour was afloat that Price's deputation and power had been extended over all America. From Franklin's letter of November 28 in that year, we may, I think, infer that the belief in Price's *earlier* patent was at least a prevalent one; while the subsequent action of the G.M. of Pennsylvania goes far to prove that the *alleged* later commission empowering Price to dispense grace beyond the limits of New England had no real existence.

Among the documentary evidence, however, of the inferior class still preserved at Boston, there is a singular memorandum which merits our attention :—

"June 24, 1734.—About this time our Worsh¹⋅ Bro⋅, M⋅ Benj⋅ Franklin from Philadelphia, became acquainted with Our R¹⋅ Wors¹⋅ Grand Master, M⋅ Price, who further Instructed him in the Royal Art, and said Franklin on his Return to Philadelphia call'd the Brethren there together, who pettition'd Our R¹⋅ Worsh¹⋅ Grand Master for a Constitution to hold a Lodge, and Our R¹⋅ Worsh¹⋅ Grand Master having this Year Rec⁴⋅ Orders from the Grand Lodge in England to Establish Masonry in all North America, did send a Deputation to Philadelphia, appointing the R¹⋅ Worsh¹⋅ M⋅ Benj⋅ Franklin first Master ; which is the beginning of Masonry there."[3]

This was first printed, I believe, in 1792,[4] and I am not aware that its accuracy was ever called in question until 1869.[5] There are persons still living who took part in a solemn centennial celebration by the Grand Lodge of Pennsylvania in 1834! At the present date, however,

---

[1] Unless these letters are wholly devoid of meaning—and it will be sufficient if we rely on that of September 1, 1736, of which a copy is preserved by Lodge Glasgow Kilwinning—Henry Price, at the date from which they speak, had for three years filled the office of Prov. G.M.

[2] A transcript of the *reply* of the Glasgow Lodge, dated February 23, 1737, in the handwriting of Benjamin Franklin, and bound up with one of his reprints of the 1723 Constitutions, was recently acquired by Mr S. D. Nickerson, who announced his discovery in the *Keystone* of June 24, 1880.

[3] Boston Records, p. 4.   [4] Constitutions, G.L. Mass.

[5] By Mr Jacob Norton.

it is only of service in assisting us to gauge with greater precision the historical value of the collection, of which it forms a part. There is a *substratum* of truth in the memorandum. Undoubtedly Franklin asked Price for a warrant, which, it is almost as equally demonstrable, was never granted,—or, to vary the expression, never *accepted*. In legal phraseology, there was no attournment (or acknowledgment of Price's authority over him) by Franklin. But this was, nevertheless, confidently assumed to have taken place by Pelham, or the Boston archivist for the time being. The facts, it is true, do not altogether square with the hypothesis. Franklin's visit to Boston occurred in 1733, and his letters to Price were written towards the close of 1734. Still, it is not necessary to impeach the good faith of the annalist. The Lodge at Philadelphia applied, without doubt—through Franklin—to Henry Price for a Charter, and if any excuse is needed for the conclusion which was arrived at in 1751, or earlier, by the Provincial Grand Officers, we find it in a recent review of the evidence, by the Grand Master for the time being of Massachusetts, where it is stoutly maintained "that Franklin received what he asked for." [1]

The date, however, of the application from Philadelphia seems to have been passed over very lightly. It is, at all events, free from doubt, that Franklin and the others could not have received *before* November 28, 1734, what they only solicited on that date. Then there is the rebutting evidence of the year 1749, which, in the opinion of most people, will be decisive of the whole point at issue, and justify the inference that the entire proofs were not forthcoming with which Franklin very properly asked to be supplied. [2]

The "first Lodge in Boston"—constituted by Price, August 31, 1733—obtained a place on the roll of the Grand Lodge of England in 1734. The Engraved (or official) Lists for 1731-33 are missing, which is to be regretted, as a curious problem presents itself in connection with an unofficial [3] list of Lodges really dating from 1734, from which the Lodge at Boston is excluded, while, to make up for the omission, one at Philadelphia finds a place.

In 1731, as we have already seen, [4] the sign of the house, where the seventy-ninth Lodge on the general list met, was the Castle at Highgate. The place or number occupied by the Lodge in question was vacant in 1733, [5] and 1734, [6] but in 1735 we find it again filled, and on this occasion the sign of the house is the Crown and Angel, Little St Martin's Lane, [7] which is also given in the official list for 1736.

In the Engraved List for 1734 there are 128 numbers in all (the 79th being vacant), and the last three are thus shown:—

126, Boston, in New England [*no date*]; 127, Valenciennes, in French Flanders [*no date*]; and 128, Duke of Marlborough, Petticoate Lane, White Chapell, November 5, 1734.

In a list of the following year, evidently taken by Picart from an official one published after February 24, and before June 24, 1735, there are no vacant numbers (the 79th being again filled). Nos. 126-128 are occupied in the same way as narrated in the last paragraph,

---

[1] Mr Sereno D. Nickerson in the "New England Freemason," vol. i., 1874, p. 382.

[2] It is evident, from his requiring copies of both patents, that the earlier one of 1733 had not been shown to Franklin by Price during their intercourse in that year.

[3] I.e., as regards the *English* Lodges. The publication was "approved of, and recommended by," the Grand Lodge of Ireland.

[4] *Ante*, p. 426. [5] Rawlinson MS., Bodleian Library. [6] Engraved List.

[7] *Supra. Cf. ante*, Chap. XVI., p. 276, note 4.

and it contains an additional Lodge—No. 129—at the Mason's Arms, Plymouth, constituted January 26, 1735.

Next comes the evidence of the *Pocket Companion for Freemasons*, of which editions bearing the imprint "MDCCXXXV.," were published both in London[1] and Dublin.[2]

The earlier of the two was, without doubt, the English publication; and in this we find a roll of Lodges, of which there are 126 in all, agreeing exactly (including the vacancy at the 79th place) with that given in the official list for 1734, down to the No. 125, but at the following and last number—126—we meet with the Duke of Marlborough's Head, which, in the Engraved Series, appears at the No. 128. Thus, the Lodges at Boston and Valenciennes are omitted from the *Pocket Companion*, which must have been printed *after* November 5, 1734, the date of constitution of the Lodge at the Duke of Marlborough's Head, and apparently *before* the admission on the roll of the two foreign Lodges above named.

In the *Pocket Companion*, Dublin, the 79th place—which in the English or earlier edition is vacant—is filled by the Lodge at the Hoop, Water Street, Philadelphia. In other respects the Lodges on the roll of the Grand Lodge of England are given in the same order, and described in the same words, as in the *Pocket Companion*, London.

The appearance of a Philadelphian Lodge in the Irish edition is consistent with the theory that the notice of Franklin's election in 1734, must have been seen and read in Dublin, where, it seems at least a reasonable conjecture, in the interval between the two publications, intelligence may also have been received from London of the constitution of an *American* Lodge? Here we have, what I shall venture to term, a natural explanation of the mystery. It is quite clear that the existence of the "First Lodge at Boston," as a unit on the Grand Lodge roll, must have become commonly known almost immediately *after* the appearance of the *Pocket Companion*, Dublin. Therefore we have only to hazard the supposition, that shortly *before* the publication of the work in question, the bare fact of a new Lodge in British North America, having been taken on the general list, had in some way obtained currency—and that this addition to the roll was assumed in Dublin to be identical with the Lodge at Philadelphia?

A theory, however, has been advanced that the *first* Lodge borne at the No. 79 on the English roll was the one at the Hoop (or other tavern) in Water Street, Philadelphia, in which case it must have been placed on the general list in 1730 or 1731. In support of this view it is argued that the date on which the Lodge at the Castle, Highgate, paid its fee for constitution—November 21, 1732—was unusually late for a Lodge formed in 1731, and fairly warrants the inference that an earlier Lodge must have previously occupied the same number. The position of the Lodge at Philadelphia, on the Dublin list, it is then contended, among other Lodges of 1730 or 1731, altogether squares with this hypothesis.

Yet although the Engraved Lists for 1731-33 are missing, we learn from the official Calendar for 1736 and the Constitutions of 1738, that Nos. 77 and 81 were constituted on January 11 and November 1, 1731, respectively. The three intermediate Lodges were erected in the same *year*, but the *months* are not given. We can therefore only assume that as the centre of the group, the position of No. 79 on the list indicates that it was warranted about June 1731. At all events we may conclude that the *number* was allotted after March 25, as

---

[1] Printed and sold by E. Rider in Blackmore Street, near Clare Market.

[2] Printed by E. Rider, and sold at the *Printing Office* in *George's Lane*; T. Jones in *Clarendon Street*; and J. Pennel at the *Hercules* in *St Patrick Street*.

Anderson has not in this instance added the date of the *historical* to that of the *legal* year, which he appears to have invariably done when describing any day between January 1 and March 25.

This will harmonise perfectly with the list of Lodges as shown in the Grand Lodge Register for 1731-32. Next, the payment by No. 79 of the fee for its constitution on November 21, 1732, proves that it had a continuous existence down to nearly the close of that year. Nor would such a payment import a proximate dissolution. All we know with certainty is, that according to a list drawn up by Dr Rawlinson, apparently between March and July 1733, the Lodge at the Castle, Highgate, was extinct, and the No. 79 a vacant one —remaining so until after November 5, 1734, the date borne by the last Lodge on the Engraved List for that year.

St John's Lodge, Philadelphia, of which Franklin was "Grand Master" in 1734, assembled on the first Monday in the month, which was also the day of meeting of the Lodge at the "Hoop" in the same city, as described by the *Pocket Companion*.

There was a "Sun" as well as a "Tun" tavern in Water Street, Philadelphia. According to Franklin's *Gazette*, the "Grand Lodge" in 1732 met at the former, and in the two following years at the latter. All three designations, Sun, Tun, or Hoop, are believed by MacCalla to apply to one public-house at different dates not far apart.[1]

I shall now pass from the consideration of No. 79 to that of No. 126 on the same list.

It is a well-established fact that more than one edition of the Engraved Series was often published in the same year. This may serve to explain why the Lodges at Boston and Valenciennes are not shown in the *Pocket Companion*, London,[2] but which includes nevertheless a London Lodge—No. 126, at the sign of the Duke of Marlborough—subsequently placed below them on the list. The first Lodge at this number, then, was constituted November 5, 1734, and the date is of importance as assisting us to determine about what period the First Lodge at Boston obtained a footing on our roll. This apparently occurred in November or December 1734, or to speak roundly, about fifteen months after its original constitution. The delay in registration is a material point, since it forms one of the aggregate of minor circumstances upon which I think we shall do well to base our final judgment of Henry Price. It has been nowhere doubted that the Lodge was regularly established, but it has been urged that the deputation granted to Price was simply an authority to open a Lodge, or in other words, a warrant of constitution—not a patent as Provincial Grand Master. Had this been so, the Lodge at Boston would have appeared on the roll in 1733, at (about) the No. 113, as the roll was arranged according to "seniority of constitution," an expression, the meaning of which has now become obsolete, but in use at that time to indicate that the precedency of Lodges was to be regulated by the priority of the written instruments severally possessed by them. In plainer words, the "constitution" of a Lodge was its warrant or authority to assemble, and the columns headed "constituted" in the Engraved Lists merely gave the dates when the various Lodges were chartered by the Grand Master or his Deputy. Thus, the days of meeting of the Boston Lodge, with the year and month of its formation, would have been duly entered in the register of Grand Lodge, and thence transferred in the ordinary course to the published list, had the deputation granted to Price been of the limited character which has been suggested. But the Lodge did not even secure a footing on the general list until

---

[1] Keystone, November 7, 1885.　　　　　　　　　[2] *C.*, Chap. XVII., p. 390.

some fifteen months after its establishment, while the days of meeting—"2d and 4th Sat.'
—appear for the first time in the Engraved List for 1738, and the *year* of constitution, though
without the *month*, through the same channel of publication in 1740. Yet, there is no
room for doubt that the Lodge was regarded as having been properly constituted by some
competent authority, which in the case before us could only have emanated from Price. In
other words, the admission of the First Lodge of Boston on the roll of the Grand Lodge of
England, involved as a necessary corollary, a recognition of the Provincial commission under
which it was called into being.

Great stress has been laid on the absence of Price's name from the lists of Provincial
Grand Masters published in the successive editions of the Constitutions. But with regard to
this purely negative evidence there are some considerations which have not as yet received
their due weight. The preservation or destruction of historical materials is as providential as
the guidance of events.[1] Of this aphorism the existing records of the Grand Lodge of England
afford a good illustration. The first minute-book of that body relates the proceedings of the
Grand Lodge from June 24, 1723, to March 17, 1731. In the same volume are contained
several lists of Lodges, with the names of their members, and copies of various deputations
granted to brethren in foreign parts—and among them the exact text of the patent issued
to Daniel Coxe.

The second minute-book begins with the proceedings of March 27, 1731, and ends with
those of April 26, 1771. Volume II., however, was not used like its predecessor, as a recep-
tacle for documentary waifs and strays, which, by transcription into the actual minute-book
of Grand Lodge, were happily preserved from destruction. From the date, therefore, at which
the earliest minute-book ends, many occurrences not actually forming a part of the proceedings in Grand Lodge, must have been recorded on loose papers or in books that have
now perished. Dr Anderson, in preparing the second edition of his Constitutions, had the
minutes of Grand Lodge to refer to; but with regard to what other records were placed at his
disposal, it is now, of course, impossible to speak with precision. Still, judging by results,
there is very little in the Constitutions of 1738, which betrays a deeper fount of information
than the recorded proceedings of the Grand Lodge.

The deputation granted to Daniel Coxe necessarily came under observation, but not so the
later patent to Henry Price, the date of which precluded its being entered in the first volume
of minutes, and, as already related, documents of that class found no place in the second.
William Read, moreover, who had been Grand Secretary from December 27, 1727, was succeeded—March 30, 1734—by John Revis; and it was not until February 24, 1735, that
Anderson sought the permission of Grand Lodge to bring out a new edition of his Constitutions. Above all, we must not forget that the latest contribution to the literature of the
Craft by the "Father of Masonic History" has come down to us without any great weight of
authority.[2] Bearing all this in mind, we need attach less importance to the omission of Price's
name in the successive editions of the Constitutions. The case of his successor, Robert
Tomlinson, whose appointment is duly recorded, stands on quite another footing. It is but
natural to suppose that Anderson obtained from John Revis a list of Provincial Grand
Masters in foreign parts appointed during his own tenure of office. For the same reason, I
am inclined to regard the claim advanced by Price to have had his authority extended over

[1] *Cf.* Chap. XVI., p. 258.　　　　　　　　　　[2] *Ibid.*, p. 291.

VOL. III.　　　　　　　　3 L

all America by Lord Crawford, in 1734, as an hallucination arising out of circumstances which are only dimly shadowed in Franklin's letter of that year.[1] The files of Boston newspapers for 1734 are incomplete, and the "article of news from London" referred to by the "Grand Master" of Pennsylvania cannot be found. A search by me in the library of the British Museum has been equally fruitless. But the accuracy of Franklin was such[2] as to leave no room for doubt that a statement, importing the extension of Price's "deputation and power over all North America," duly appeared in some Boston print.

On February 5, 1736, a petition (the original of which has been preserved) was addressed by six brethren at Portsmouth, New Hampshire, to Henry Price, whom they style "Grand Master of the Society of Free and Accepted Masons held in Boston." The petitioners described themselves as " *of the holy and exquisite Lodge of St John,*" and asked for power to hold a Lodge "According to order as is and has been granted to faithfull Brothers in all parts of the World," and they declared that they had their "Constitutions both in print and *manuscript* as good and as ancient as any that England can afford." The favour was asked because they had heard "there is a Superiour Lodge held in Boston." Be it noted, this was early in 1736, when no Lodge had been warranted at Portsmouth; and as the brethren stated they possessed "Constitutions" in *manuscript*—which it is hardly possible could have been anything else than a copy of the "Old Charges"—as well as in print, the evidence is consistent with the supposition that while at the date named the Lodge must have been some years in existence, its origin may have reached back even to the seventeenth century.

I am anxious not to lay too much stress on the precise meaning attached by me to the mention of manuscript Constitutions; nevertheless I think the petition may be taken as fair evidence that in 1736 there were brethren in New Hampshire (meeting as Masons in a Lodge) who possessed a copy (or reprint) of the English Constitutions published in 1723, as well as a version of an older set of laws in MS., thus pointing to the possible existence of the Lodge at even an earlier period than the Grand Lodge era of 1716-17.

In the same year (1736) Price is alluded to in the two letters of recommendation from the First Lodge of Boston, which have been previously referred to, as "Provincial Grand Master." The later of these is dated September 1, 1736, and three months afterwards—December 7— the charge of the province of New England was committed by patent to Robert Tomlinson. Whether Price resigned or was superseded, there is no evidence to show; but it is not unreasonable to suppose that, with the influx of many new members of higher social standing, there may have arisen a feeling that his occupation in life was incompatible with the appointment. Therefore, choice was made of Tomlinson, "a gentleman of means and distinction." The deputation to Price's successor recites that it was granted in response to the prayer of a petition that a *new* Prov. G.M. for New England might be nominated. To the word "new" great importance has been attached by some commentators, but I think without reason, as the more we rely upon the early Boston records as independent authorities, the greater becomes the necessity of critically appraising the *weight* and thereby the value of their testimony.

---

[1] *Ante,* p. 431.

[2] "Through the press, no one was so active as Benjamin Franklin. His newspaper defended freedom of speech and of the press, for he held that falsehood alone dreads attack and cries out for auxiliaries, while truth scorns the aid of the secular arm, and triumphs by her innate strength" (Bancroft, Hist. U.S.A., vol. ii., 1885, p. 260).

The deputation requires the sum of two guineas, in respect of every new Lodge constituted by the Prov. G.M., "to be paid into the Stock of General Charity." This fee, it may be remarked, gradually increased in amount, becoming, as we learn from subsequent patents, two guineas and a-half, in Oxnard's time, and three guineas under later administrations.

In 1738, Tomlinson went to England, *vid* Antigua, "where," says the Rev. T. M. Harris,[1] "finding some old Boston Masons, he went to work and made the Governor, and sundry other gentlemen of distinction, Masons, whereby from our Lodge sprung Masonry in the West Indies." Soon after his arrival in London, he was present at a meeting of the Grand Lodge— which was also attended by John Hammerton, Prov. G.M. of Carolina—January 31, 1739.

His death in 1740 left the province without a head, and an interregnum of some duration ensued, during which—so the Boston records tell us—Price presided and acted as Provincial Grand Master.

The vacancy was filled up, September 23, 1743, by the appointment of Thomas Oxnard, a merchant of character and influence. The deputation contains a recital, that "a Provincial Grand Master for North America, in the room of Robert Tomlinson," had been asked for, so it is highly probable, that the enlarged patent conferred on Oxnard—wherein the jurisdiction craved is duly granted to him—simply originated in a mistake, either on the part of the Grand Secretary, or on that of Governor Belcher, at whose instance the appointment is said to have been made. Nor can the error, if such it were, be styled an uncommon one, for the same comprehensive title was bestowed on Daniel Coxe, when the Deputy Grand Master proposed his health in 1731.[2]

The "Second Lodge in Boston" was constituted in the usual manner, on February 15, 1750. In the previous year, as we have already seen, Franklin received a Provincial Commission from Oxnard, and it will be convenient, therefore, if at this point, the narrative is interrupted, while we pause to consider some of the more striking features in the system of Masonry which for nearly twenty years had existed side by side in the two Colonies of Massachusetts and Pennsylvania.

At each capital, Boston and Philadelphia, there was a Society of Masons, meeting sometimes as a Grand, and at other times as a Private Lodge. That the same characteristics were common to the two brotherhoods, we may fairly assume, which is so far an advantage, inasmuch as while our stock of information is but small regarding the one, we know absolutely nothing of the inner life of the other. To the extent possible, an outline has been already given of the early Masonry of Pennsylvania, and I shall now proceed to supplement that sketch, by some remarks of a kindred character.

Whether Henry Price was the first Master of the Lodge founded by him in 1733, is a matter of uncertainty, but he appears to have filled that position at the establishment of the Lodge of Masters, and Second Lodge of Boston, in 1738 and 1750 respectively. In the First Lodge only two degrees were conferred, the third not being given in it until 1794.

A separate set of minutes was kept of the *Master Masons' Lodge,* or, in other words, of the "Lodge of Masters." Independent records of the Third Degree were frequently kept in

---

[1] Constitutions, G. L. Mass., 1792. A biographical sketch of the compiler will be found in the "Proceedings" of the same body, 1874, pp. 185-98.

[2] *Ante*, p. 427.

this country also.   Mr Norton estimates that between 1733 and January 2, 1739, the number of Masons identified with the "First Lodge in Boston" was 105, 15 of whom, he thinks, founded the Master Masons' Lodge, and 6 only were subsequently raised therein. From the latter period to September 1751, 238 joined the Lodge, of whom 84 became Master Masons, so that many appear to have been content with the First and Second Degrees, just as we find was formerly the case in Scotland—where the practice was a very general one until late in the last century—and is still so in Germany.   Thomas Oxnard (afterwards Prov. G.M.), who was Master of the Lodge in 1736, and again in 1737, was not raised to the degree of Master Mason until 1739.

The "Lodge" and the "Grand Lodge" at Boston, appear to have been regarded—at least during the first decade of their existence—as one and the same body, both at home and abroad.   The letter of September 1, 1736, despatched in the lesser capacity, to Lodge Glasgow Kilwinning, is signed by Price as G.M., while a communication dated June 27, 1739, "from the Grand Lodge at the Court-house in St John's," Antigua,—written by command of Governor Mathew, the Prov. G.M.,—was addressed, not to the G.L. of New England, but to the First Lodge of Boston.   The latter body was styled the Mother Lodge of New England, and of America, by a committee of its members in 1741, the two titles being used in a correspondence with Governor Belcher and his successor Governor Shirley.   Jonathan Belcher was Governor of Massachusetts and New Hampshire from 1730 to 1741, and it was in the latter year, when thanked for his protection by the First Lodge of Boston, that he placed on record his long connection with the Society, to which I have adverted on an earlier page.[1]   Governor Shirley was not a Mason, nor did he avail of the sufficiently broad hint that he should become one, thrown out by the "MOTHER LODGE OF AMERICA," [2] through their committee in 1741—"As it has been the Custom for men in the most exalted Station to have the Door of our Society's Constitution always, opened to them (when desired), we think it our Duty to acquaint your Excellency with that Custom, and assure you, that we shall chearfully attend your Excellency's Pleasure therein."

It is probable that at Boston, as well as in Philadelphia, the brethren assembled as a *Lodge* at all meetings except (on St John's Days, and) when officers were elected (or appointed).   This was evidently the practice in the latter city, where, indeed, the possibility may be conceived of the expression "Grand Lodge" bearing in the first instance only the restricted signification of the *adjective*, without the meaning which is now conventionally ascribed to it in conjunction with the *noun?*   Besides, we must not lose sight of the fact, that for half a century and more after the occurrences I am relating, there was nothing at all unusual in the assumption by a private Lodge, of a prefix now only met with in connection with a governing body.   So late as 1786, the Grand Lodge of Scotland found it necessary to ordain, that no Master should be addressed by the style or title of *Grand*, except the Grand Master Mason of that country.[3]   The expression, "Mother Lodge of America," used in 1741 by a committee of the first Lodge in Boston, forcibly reminds us of the maternal title assumed under closely analogous circumstances by the Lodge of Kilwinning, the "Three Globes" at Berlin, and other European Lodges.   The members of the Prov. Grand Lodge of New England, so long as there was only one Lodge in the province, must have belonged to it,

---

[1] *Ante*, p. 424 ; Chap. XVI., p. 269.   [2] *Sic*, in Boston Records, p. 390.

[3] Laurie, 1859, p. 139 ; Lyon, p. 331 ; Constitution and Laws of the Grand Lodge of Scotland, 1881, p. 6.

but they formed after all but a single brotherhood, though meeting at times in different capacities.

Oxnard went to England in the summer of 1751, and on October 7 of the same year, a "Humble Remonstrance" signed by the Masters and Wardens of the First, Second, Third, and Masters' Lodges of Boston, was addressed to the G.M. of England, in which it was requested that a "Full and Plenary Commission to act as Grand Master in and over all the Lodges in North America" might be granted to him and his successors. On January 20, 1752, the D.G.M. (McDaniel) convened a meeting of the Prov. Grand Lodge, to decide who should take the chair under Old Regulation XXI. It was moved that the right belonged to Henry Price, but on a vote being taken whether two of the Brethren should be sent to desire him "to come and resume his office, it passed in the negative." Whether the movement, or the opposition thereto, grew out of any ill feeling, or whether Oxnard's appointment had any connection with it, cannot now be determined. Price did not resent the vote, for he was present at the next meeting, and at the Festival, at each of which McDaniel presided.

On June 26, 1754, Oxnard died after a lingering illness, his funeral, attended by the Prov. Grand Lodge, taking place on the 29th; and on the 12th of the following month two brethren were appointed by the Deputy Grand Master to wait upon Price and request him to resume his office as G.M.,—which he did on the same day.

On October 11, 1754, a Committee was elected to obtain the appointment of "Jeremy Gridley, Esqr., Counsellor at Law." The petition to the G.M. of England, signed by McDaniel (D.G.M. under Oxnard), and six others, recites that on the decease of Oxnard, Henry Price, "formerly G. Master, reassumed the chair *pro tempore*," and expresses the desire of the members that "all future Grand Masters should be deputed for three years only," this being clogged, however, with a proviso for the continuance in office of the Prov. G.M. at the will · of the P.G.L. Mention is also made in the petition of the origin of Masonry "here" (*i.e.*, Boston) in 1733, "and in the year following" (it continues), "our then G.M., Price, received orders from G.M. Crawford to establish masonry *in all North America*, in pursuance of which the several Lodges hereafter mentioned have rec'd Constitutions from us."[1] They likewise craved "due precedency, and that in order thereunto our G.M. elect may in his deputation be styled G.M. of all North America."

Price wrote—August 6, 1755—in support of the petition, describing his services as Prov. G.M., and how he was succeeded by Tomlinson, and the latter by Oxnard, when the chair reverted to him again, "according to the Constitutions." He declared, that with his consent, all the Brethren in North America had made Choice of their Bro^r., Jeremy Gridley; after which he mentions the payment of the fee of three guineas, per Capt. Phillips, to the Rev. John Entick, and expresses surprise at receiving no acknowledgment.

Price, with pardonable pride, records the great success of Masonry in America since his settling there. "No less than forty Lodges," he says, have "sprung from my first Lodge in Boston." "Therefore," he proceeds, "we desire that our deputation may be made out for, or over, *all North America*."[2]

---

[1] The Lodges referred to are the first twelve—omitting the *second* Lodge at Philadelphia—of those outside Massachusetts, shown in the table of Lodges (on the next page), warranted by Henry Price or his successors.

[2] The italics are mine. In the same letter, Price states that he received a deputation for *North America* from Lord Montague in April 1733, and held it for *four* years; that he was succeeded in his office by Tomlinson and Oxnard; and that he has "some remote thoughts of once more seeing London with all Brethren in the Grand Lodge after twenty-two years' absence."

At this point it may be convenient if the narrative is interrupted by a list of the Lodges warranted at any time by Price or his successors, so far at least as their names have been preserved in documents now extant. The following table has been compiled from the "Boston Records," and an asterisk denotes in each case that the Lodge is mentioned *for the first time* among those represented or otherwise at a meeting of the Grand Lodge. Thus, the Lodge in Virginia, which appears under the year 1766, was probably that in which Washington received the light of Masonry at Fredericksburg in 1752; and it is scarcely possible that such a cluster of Lodges could have been formed in a single year (1766) without some allusion to their charters or fees of Constitution, appearing in the proceedings of the Grand Lodge. There was certainly one other Lodge—American Union—which received a warrant from the same source of authority, but as explained above, the list has been made up from actual entries in the official records of the G.L. of Massachusetts.

LODGES UNDER THE ENGLISH PROV. G.L. AT BOSTON.

Philadelphia, Pennsylvania,	. .	1734.	Marblehead, Massachusetts, . .	1760.
Portsmouth, New Hampshire,.	.	1735.	Surranam,* [Dutch Guiana], .	1761.
Charleston, South Carolina,	. .	1735.	Hartford, Connecticut, . .	1762.
Boston, Master's Lodge, .	. .	1738.	Falmouth,[3] Massachusetts, .	1762.
Antigua, West Indies,	. .	1738.	Elizabeth Town, New Jersey, .	1762.
Annapolis, Nova Scotia, .	.	1738.	Quebec,*	1764.
Newfoundland,	. . .	1746.	Crown Point, Provincial Troops,	1764.
Newport,[1] Rhode Island,.	. .	1749.	Waterbury, Connecticut, .	1765.
Boston, Second Lodge of,	. .	1750.	Prince Town, New Jersey, .	1765.
„ Third Lodge of, .	. .	1750.	Norwich,* [Connecticut ?], .	1766.
Annapolis, Maryland,	. . .	1750.	Virginia,*	1766.
Halifax, Nova Scotia,	. .	1750.	Salem,*	1766.
Newhaven, Connecticut, .	.	1750.	St Christopher,* West Indies, .	1766.
Philadelphia,[2] Pennsylvania, .	.	1752.	Barbadoes,* „ .	1766.
New London, Connecticut,	. .	1753.	Pitt County,* North Carolina,	1766.
Middletown, „	. .	1754.	Newbury,* [Massachusetts ?], .	1766.
Lake George,* Canada, .	. .	1757.	Newfoundland,* Second Lodge of, .	1766.
Louisburgh, 28th Foot, .	. .	1758.	Wallingford, Connecticut, .	1769.
Crown Point, Canada, .	. .	1758.	Sherburne, Massachusetts, .	1771.
Providence, Rhode Island,	. .	1757.	Guildford, Connecticut, . .	1771.
Newport (Master's Lodge),	. .	1759.	Boston, 4th Lodge of (Rising Sun), .	1772.

Gridley's deputation, dated April 4, 1755, was granted prior to the receipt of Price' letter. It conferred authority over "all Such Provinces and Places in North America and the Territories thereof, *of which no Provincial Grand Master is at present appointed.*" The commission winds up with an exhortation to the holder to remit the sum of three guineas to the Grand Treasurer, in London, for every Lodge he should constitute.

It will be observed that the deputation of 1755 to Gridley was a qualified one, in respect to his appointment for "all America." Not so, however, the one sent to Oxnard of 1743, which simply specifies his title to be "Provincial Grand Master of North America." I assume,

---

[1] Warrant of Confirmation, 1753.

[2] "Aprill 10th, 1752.—For the Lodge att Philadelphia Bro^r. McDaniel appeared and paid for their Constitution £31 „ 10 „," (Boston Records, p. 20). This payment, amounting to about two guineas and a half actual money, must have been made on behalf of the Lodge chartered at the meeting presided over by Franklin in 1749.

[3] *Ante*, p. 414.

nevertheless, that in reality Oxnard possessed no further powers than were bestowed on Gridley, viz., to act as Prov. G.M. in North America, in districts or territories for which no Prov. G.M. had been appointed; for we may rest assured that neither of these two representatives of the Grand Lodge of England in the Western Hemisphere, had any authority over the Prov. G.M.'s of Pennsylvania, New York, and South Carolina, who had been appointed from home during their respective tenures of office.[1]

Attorney-General Gridley—an initiate of the St John's Lodge, May 11, 1748—was installed as Prov. G.M. by Henry Price on October 1, 1755, with great pomp and ceremony, the two brethren, "clothed with their jewels and badges, walking together" in the procession to Trinity Church, after the Masonic meeting held in the Concert Hall, Boston.

Jeremy Gridley, who at the time of his decease was Attorney-General, a member of the General Court, and a Justice of the Province, Colonel of the First Regiment of Militia, and President of the Marine Society, died September 10, 1767. The Provincial Grand Lodge in the following month requested Price to reassume his old office, and in October 23, he was invested with the Jewel of Grand Master by John Rowe, D.G.M., who addressed him in the following words :—"You, (to the Satisfaction of all the Lodges[2]) have had the Honour of first introducing Masonry into these Parts of the World, and intentionally, for the good of Masonry, have resign'd the Chair of Grand Master to three Successors, whom Providence has deprived us of."

The Feast of St John the Evangelist was observed December 30, 1767, Henry Price presiding. The same day, as Grand Master, he executed a commission to Thomas Cooper as D.G.M. of North Carolina, "by virtue of the power and authority committed to [him] by Lord Viscount Montague, Grand Master of Masons."

At an adjourned Grand Lodge held January, 22, 1768, on the nomination of the Grand Master (*pro tem.*), John Rowe (D.G.M. and Treasurer) was elected to the office of "Grand Master of Masons for North America," 12 out of 16 votes being recorded in his favour, whereupon he was saluted as G.M. elect.

A committee of nine was appointed to write to England for the patent, and, having settled the text of the communication on January 25, 1768, signed the petition accordingly. The appointment was solicited for three years only, but with certain reservations, which, as in the former instance, would have rendered nugatory the provision for a restricted term of office.

The petition winds up with the following clause :—

"Whereas Masonry in America originated in this Place Anno 5733, and in the year following, our then Grand Master Price received Orders from Grand Master Craufurd to establish Masonry in all North America, in Pursuance of which the several Lodges hereafter mentioned have received Constitutions from us.[3] We therefore crave due Precedency, and

---

[1] Of this there is distinct evidence in the case of Gridley, who, in 1762, only consented to warrant a Lodge at Elizabeth-town, New Jersey, on receiving information that Daniel Coxe had died before the grant of his own deputation. *Cf. ante*, p. 428.

[2] The words within parenthesis may either be a merely complimentary phrase, or they may import that Price had made good a *disputed title* to the "Honour" upon which he was congratulated ?

[3] Hugh McDaniel, chairman of the Committee, was made a Mason in the First Lodge, January 30, 1735, less than eighteen months after the organisation of the Grand Lodge by Price. In June 1736, he was elected Senior Warden of the First Lodge, which constituted him a member of the Grand Lodge, and continued to represent that Lodge as Warden or Master until 1744, when he was appointed Deputy Grand Master. Thus (it is contended), he must have been thoroughly informed of the early history of Masonry in New England and of the Provincial Grand Lodge.

that in Order thereunto, Our Grand Master Elect may, in his Deputation, be styled Grand Master of all North America."

Then follow the signatures of the petitioners (or Committee), and after these, there is a postscript or memorandum which reads :—

"2d Lodge, or No. 2 in Boston, Constituted Feb. 15, 1749[O.S.], meets the 3d Wednesday in every month at the British Coffee House, in King Street."

"New Haven Lodge, in Connecticut, Constituted in November.1750, kept at the Golden Lion in that Town."

"Providence Lodge, in Rhode Island Government, Constituted Jan. 18, 1757, meets the first and third Wednesday of every month."

"Marblehead Lodge, in this Government, Constituted March 25, 1760."

A letter, dated January 27, 1768, was forwarded at the same time by Price, addressed to the G.M., Grand Officers, and Brethren, "in Grand Lodge assembled," stating that "the money now sent to you is for the Constitution of four Lodges in America, which I pray may be Registered in the Grand Lodge Books; the money would have been paid long before, but some unforeseen accidents prevented." It will be seen that no explanation is really given with regard to the delay in remitting to England fees which, on the writer's own showing, had been in arrear from 1750. Virtually, indeed, it was the first "return" made by the Prov. Grand Lodge since 1733; but Price expresses a hope that "the said Lodges will not be denied their Rank, according to the Time of their Constitution, notwithstanding the above Omission;" and for particulars the Grand Master is referred to "the Letter from the Grand Committee of the Grand Lodge here, which goes by the same hand that presents this to you."

Price then goes on to say that "several other Lodges have been Constituted by the Grand Lodge here in different parts of America, who have not yet Transmitted to us the Stated Fees for their Constitution." Payment, however, was promised on the amounts being received, so that such Lodges might "likewise be Registered." He next recites the oft-told tale of his having been appointed Prov. G.M. of New England by Lord Montacute in 1733, and that in the year 1735 [1734] his commission was extended over all North America by Lord Crauford. On inquiry, however, he found that "said Deputations were never Registered, though [he himself] paid three Guineas therefor to Thomas Batson, Esqr., then Deputy Grand Master, who, with the Grand Wardens then in being, signed [his] said Deputation." He then proceeds with the claim that his own patent was the first ever issued "to any part of America"—here, as we see, plainly ignoring the earlier appointment of Daniel Coxe, as officially stated in the editions of the Constitutions for 1738, 1756, and 1767. "So," he continues, "would submit it to your Wisdom and Justice whether said Deputations should not be Registered in their proper Place, without any further Consideration therefor, and the Grand Lodge here have Rank according to Date, as it has (by Virtue of said Deputations) been the foundation of Masonry in America, and I [Henry Price] the Founder." The letter concludes with the following :—

"P.S.—Rt Worshipful, I herewith send you an Attested Copy of my said Deputation in the Grand Lodge Book of this Place, under the Hand of our Grand Secretary, whose Signature you may depend upon as genuine. H. P."

The copy of this epistle in the Boston Records, contains two misstatements, which have been much criticised—one, the name (Montacute), wrongly assigned by Price to Lord Montague; and the other, his assertion with regard to the extension of his powers, in 1735. But the first is easily explained on the supposition that his clerk (or amanuensis) must have followed the spelling given by Entick (Constitutions, 1756), and both are to a great extent neutralised by the fact that the petition which accompanied the letter states the name of Lord Montague correctly, and dates the extension of powers at 1734.[1]

But the letter has other features which demand our attention. It is, for instance, a curious circumstance that the attested copy of Price's deputation was made from a *transcript*, and not from the original; while the alleged payment to D.G.M. Batson stands in need of some further explanation, as it is doubtful whether any fee was paid at that time by a Prov. G.M. for his deputation, and the sum of three guineas does not represent the ordinary amount which he was required to contribute at a subsequent period.

William Jackson, who took the petition and letter to England, carried also with him a recommendation from the Grand Lodge in Boston, dated January 22, 1768—signed by Henry Price, G.M., and his Grand Wardens—to their "Mother Lodge" in England. He returned to Boston with a deputation for John Rowe, who is styled "Provincial Grand Master for all North America, and the Territories thereunto belonging, where no other Provincial Grand Master is in being," issued by order of the Duke of Beaufort, G.M., and dated May 12, 1768.

We are told that "the Deputation of Rowe contains a complete and thorough vindication of Price."[2] It recites that he was "constituted Provincial Grand Master for North America" by Viscount Montague, April 13, 1733, and that "He Resigning, Recommends John Rowe."

From this, according to the same commentator, there is no appeal; but putting aside the notorious fact that the historical value of recitals in Masonic charters is very much in keeping with that of the preambles of ancient statutes,[3] the misstatements with regard to locality, date, and the resignation of Price, seem to me to carry with them their own condemnation.

John Rowe outlived Henry Price—who died in 1780—and continued to hold the office of Prov. G.M. until his own decease in 1787. But from about the date of the *former's* appointment until 1804, the name of the *latter* was annually shown in the Calendar of the Grand

---

[1] Another copy of the letter is preserved in the archives of the Grand Lodge of England. In this the name of Lord Montague is correctly spelt, while the words ascribed to Price with regard to his Grand Lodge are, that it had been "the Foundations of Masonry in America." Four original letters from Henry Price to the Grand Secretary of England are in the same custody. These are dated June 3 and December 20, 1769, and January 29 and May 16, 1770. The letter of June 3, 1769, is in duplicate. Each of the others is endorsed "Lʳ. from the P.G.M. for America." With one unimportant exception (December 20, 1769), copies of the letters are given by Gardner. In every case Price's own handwriting is limited to his signature.

[2] Gardner, p. 53—in a review of whose "Address," however, Mr Jacob Norton observes—"The petition for the First Lodge of Boston stated that Price's deputation was dated April 13, 1732, and in the year of Masonry 5732, but both dates were altered several years afterwards into 1733 and 5733" (Freemason, vol. v., 1872, p. 483). The final 3 in each case certainly appears—from a *facsimile* of the petition—to have been originally a 2. As a motive for the alteration, the tardy discovery by Price of the fact that Viscount Montague only became Grand Master on the *nineteenth* day of April 1732, has been suggested !

[3] *Cf.* Chaps. VII., p. 373 ; XIX., p. 439.

Lodge of England as "Provincial G.M. for North America." Why it was persistently kept there throughout this long period—and there is distinct evidence that in 1792, if not before, the Grand Secretary in London was informed of Price's death—is, in my opinion, only another example of the gross carelessness of the executive of the Grand Lodge of England with regard to the foreign and Colonial Lodges on the roll of that body. The explanation given by Gardner is, that the Grand Officers, desirous of repairing "the injury which had been done to the fame of Henry Price, purposely retained his name upon the Official Calendar for thirty-six years, a period of time equal to that which had elapsed from the time of his appointment in 1733 to the date of his recognition in 1768!"

This far-fetched scheme of reparation need not be seriously discussed. It will be wiser to balance one error of the Grand Lodge publications against the other. From this we may safely arrive at the conclusion, that the omission of Price's name in the Constitutions of 1738, 1756, and 1767, is of no greater historical value than its insertion in the Calendars of 1770-1804.

It remains to be stated that Rowe's name does not appear in any English Calendar as Prov. G.M., also that there are no communications in the archives at Boston addressed to him in such capacity.

In reply to Price's letter of January 27, 1768, Grand Secretary French wrote a long letter, dated November 29, in the same year. French succeeded Samuel Spencer, whose protracted illness was the cause of the delay. The Grand Secretary consented to register the four Lodges as desired, but requested that in future an account might be forwarded immediately of every Lodge, when constituted, as otherwise it could not be expected that they should rank in their order of precedency. Why Price's name was not to be found in the list of Prov. G.M.'s he expressed himself unable to explain, but his letter goes on to state, "These mistakes might have been long since rectified, if you had kept up, according to your Charter, a regular annual correspondence with the Grand Lodge. However, as it appears by some loose papers [1] in my possession that you had resigned in favour of John Rowe, [the Grand Master] desires you will forward a letter to me relating to this point, per first opportunity, that the Provincialship may be properly settled, with an account of the date of his warrant. No deputation which has been granted since your appointment for any part of America, can affect you, as their authority can only extend over those provinces where no other Provincial Grand Master is appointed." Here we find French asking for the date of Rowe's patent, evidently not being aware of its having been signed earlier in the same year by his predecessor (deceased). This shows what little interest was taken at that time in Masonry beyond the seas. The Grand Secretary also informs Price that no deputation granted since his own could affect his status. This assertion was simply ridiculous,

---

[1] A copy of this letter is to be found in the MS. volume of records (p. 120), to which I have already referred. In the same book (p. 3) are the following curious entries in the handwriting of Grand Secretary French :—

"N.B.—The Deputation of Bror. H. Price has never come to my hand, but among other loose papers I have found the following memorandum.   [Signed] THOˢ. FRENCH.

"Viscount Montague, G.M.

"Henry Price, Esq., P.G.M. for all North America and the territories thereunto belonging, Dated April 13th, 1733, desire the favour to resign his Provincialship in favour of John Rowe, Esq., to be Provincial G.M. over North America where no other Provincial is appointed.   BEAUFORT, G.M.

"He resigning recommends John Rowe, Esq. We therefore do hereby con— . . . . . ."

as the later deputations to Oxnard, Gridley, and Rowe gave them authority over all parts of North America, for which no Prov. G.M. was appointed, consequently Price's position was wholly ignored, and indeed was not officially recognised (except indirectly) until 1768, in Rowe's patent, by which, however, Price himself was superseded.

To the request of the Duke of Beaufort, G.M., as communicated through Thomas French, Price replied—June 3, 1769—in the following words:—"It would be tedious to explain the matter of my resigning as Provincial Grand Master; I recommended our Right Worshipful Brother John Rowe to be Provincial Grand Master of New England, but you cannot find that I ever gave up my own Appointment over all North America: this ∴ ∴. I shall explain to you ∴ ∴. face to face in London, some time in the Fall ∴ ∴. then we may settle the Provincial Grand Masters and Rank the Lodges properly."

Yet the writer of this letter had himself particularly requested that the deputation to Gridley might be "made out for all North America," and on the decease of that Brother, nominated John Rowe for the vacant appointment. Price, it is quite evident, was not possessed of a very retentive memory, but it is only fair to recollect that his age at that time exceeded the three score and ten, which, the Scripture informs us, is the ordinary span of man's activity.

The letter last cited was acknowledged by James Heseltine—appointed Grand Secretary April 28, 1769—who in a communication dated September 6, 1769, requests Price to forward certain proceedings of the Grand Lodge of England "to the Lodges in America, except those in Canada, North and South Carolina, to which Lodges [he had] forwarded the same [himself]." This letter was addressed to "Henry Price, P.G.M. for America," and it indicates clearly that —Canada and the Carolinas alone excepted—his authority was understood in England to extend over the whole Continent. With one further allusion I shall bring to a close my extracts from this correspondence. On January 29, 1770, Price wrote to Heseltine, and once more expresses an intention of soon visiting London, when he purposes to "Give the Grand Lodge a true State of Masonry in America."

Price attended the Prov. Grand Lodge for the last time on January 28, 1774. There were but three Communications held after this prior to the siege of Boston, when the meetings of all the Lodges were suspended. At the last of these—January 27, 1775—Richard Gridley presided as D.G.M., and was again *nominated* to that office, but at his own request a ballot was taken, which resulted in his being unanimously *elected.*

In 1776, the diary of John Rowe records, under June 25, "dined with the Brethren of the Lodges under my direction." The next evidence brings us to 1783, in which year—February 7—the First and Second Lodges of Boston amalgamated; the Third Lodge seems to have passed quietly out of existence, but the Fourth, which was originally an offshoot of St John's, rejoined its parent Lodge in 1791. In 1784, according to a local almanack, there were thirty Lodges under the St John's and twenty under the Massachusetts, Grand Lodges. In the same year, the African Lodge—No. 459—Boston, received an English charter, and St Andrew's split into two parts, one (with the warrant) separating from, and the other adhering to, the Massachusetts Grand Lodge. The latter became the "Rising States Lodge," with the rank of No. 1, and in 1809, united—under the old name—with the former, which in that year was readmitted within the fold.

John Rowe died in 1787, and meetings of the St John's Grand Lodge were held on

February 7 and August 4 of that year under the presidency of Richard Gridley, D.G.M., with John Cutler (a former grand officer [1]) as S.G.W.   The latter—after whose name again appear the letters "S.G.W."—took the chair "as Grand Master" on July 29, 1790, when a Grand Lodge was held for "the Choice of new G. Officers," and a Grand *Junior* Warden, Treasurer, and Secretary were elected.   Further meetings took place November 25, 1791, January 13, and March 2 and 5, 1792, at all of which Cutler presided, and on the last occasion is described as "D.G.M."   This date—March 5—is that of the Union of the two Grand Lodges in Boston, the initiative with regard to which was taken by the junior body in 1787, though nothing came of it until 1792, when seven electors from each of the Grand Lodges, under the chairmanship of Paul Revere, D.G.M. of the younger Society, made choice of John Cutler as the first Grand Master of the "Grand Lodge of Free and Accepted Masons for the Commonwealth of Massachusetts." [2]

The following American Lodges were placed on the English Register, and without excep; tion continued to figure annually in the official lists until 1813.   The first date in each case is that from which the Lodge was allowed to rank, but the second denotes the actual year of its original appearance in the published Calendar.

LODGES ON THE ROLL OF THE GRAND LODGE OF ENGLAND, 1733-89.

No.			No.		
126,	St John's, Boston, Massachusetts, . .	1733-34.	141,	2d Lodge, Boston, Massachusetts, . .	1750-69.
139,	Solomon's, Savannah, Georgia, .	1735-36.	142,	Marblehead Lodge, Massachusetts, . .	1760-69.
236,	Royal Exchange, Norfolk, Virginia, .	1753-54.	143,	New Haven, Connecticut, . . .	1750-69.
205,	Swan, Yorktown, Virginia, . .	1755-56.	224,	Providence Lodge, Rhode Island, . .	1757-69.
213,	Wilmington, North Carolina, .	1754-56.	448,	Zion Lodge, Detroit [*Michigan* [3]], .	1764-73.
247,	Prince George, Winyaw, S.C.,	1743-60.	457,	Williamsburg Lodge, Virginia, .	1773-74.
248,	Union, Charleston, S.C., . .	1755-60.	458,	Botetourt Lodge, ,, . .	1773-74.
249,	Masters Lodge, Charleston, S.C., .	1756-60.	465,	Unity, Savannah, Georgia, . .	1774-74.
250,	Port Royal Lodge, Beaufort, S.C., .	1756-60.	481,	Grenadiers, ,, . .	1775-75.
251,	Solomon's, Charleston, S.C., .	1735-60.	488,	Union, Detroit [*Michigan*], . .	1775-78.
272,	St John's, No. 2, New York, .	1757-62.	459,	African Lodge, Boston, Massachusetts, .	1784-85.
299,	St Mark's Lodge, S.C., . . .	1763-63.	465,	St John's [*Michigan*], . .	1784-86.
346,	Joppa Lodge, Maryland, . .	1765-66.	517,[4]	Fort William Henry [*N.Y.*], . .	1787-89.
*03,	White Hart, Halifax, N.C., . .	1767-67.	520,	New Oswegatchie [*N.Y.*], . .	1787-89.

Returning to Pennsylvania, it has been already shown that this was the first of the American States in which a stationary Lodge was established by the Ancients or Schismatics. We have also seen how the older system of Masonry was completely swept away in this part

---

[1] J.G.W., 1767 ; S.G.W., 1771.

[2] The same works quoted as my authorities for the sketch of Masonry in Pennsylvania, have also been used in the section just concluded.   In addition I have consulted the Pocket Companions (London and Dublin), 1785 ; E. G. Storer, Early Records of Freemasonry in Connecticut, 1859 ; W. S. Gardner, Address upon Henry Price, 1872 ; New England Freemason, vol. i., 1874, pp. 57, 281, 312, 380 ; Proc. G.L. Mass., 1883, pp. 150-193 ; and the Boston Records, 1886.   Throughout the remainder of the chapter, the works already cited, must also be regarded as my authorities, as in order to avoid a multiplicity of references, no book or author will be cited *for the second time* in a note, unless there is some special reason for so doing.

[3] The territory forming the present State of Michigan was retained (as a part of Canada) by Great Britain after the War of Independence, and in 1796 ceded to the United States.

[4] The localities in which Nos. 517 and 520 were originally constituted, only ceased to be Canadian territory about the year 1796.

of the continent by the preference accorded to the Lodges working *four* degrees. The Grand Lodge of Pennsylvania, " acting by virtue of a warrant from the [Schismatic] Grand Lodge of England, was closed for ever," September 25, 1786, and on the following day, " at a Grand Convention of thirteen Lodges," was established as an independent Grand Lodge.

The annexed table gives a list of the Lodges formed in the United States by warrants from the British Islands, other than those issued by the original G.L. of England. A solitary Lodge, formed in Virginia by the G.O. of France, has also been included.

LODGES OF EUROPEAN ORIGIN, EXCLUDING THOSE UNDER THE G.L. OF ENGLAND.[1]

Boston (St Andrew's),	Mass., 81 S.,	1756.	East Florida (Grant's),	Fla., 143 S.,	1768.
Blandford,	Va., 82 S.,	1756.	Boston,	Mass., 169 A.,	1771.
Fredericksburgh,	Va., [ ] S.,	1758.	Philadelphia (St John's),	Pa., 177 S.,	1774.
Tappahannock,	Va., [ ] K.,	1758.	Charleston,	S.C., 190 A.,	1774.
Philadelphia,	Pa., 69 A.,	1758.	Falmouth,	Va., [ ] K.,	1775.
Charleston (Union Klwng),	S.C., 98 S.,	1760.	New York,	N.Y., 210 A.,	1779.
Philadelphia (P.G.L.),	Pa., 89 A.,	1761.	,,	,, 212 A.,	1780.
Charleston,	S.C., 92 A.,	1761.	,, (P.G.L.),	,, 219 A.,	1781.
New York,	N.Y., 399 I.,	1763.	Portsmouth (Sagesse),	Va., [ ] Fr.,	1785.
Norfolk (St John),	Va., 117 S.,	1763.	Charleston,	S.C., 236 A.,	1786.

Baltimore. Md., 656 I., N.D.

I shall now pass to the remainder of the thirteen or original States of the Union, taking them in the order of their connection with Freemasonry. The statistics of all the American Grand Lodges, so far as these can be conveniently grouped, it may be observed, will be found at the close of the chapter.

NEW YORK.—The first Provincial G.M. was Daniel Coxe (1730), after whom came Richard Riggs, 1737; Francis Goelet, 1751; George Harrison, 1753; and Sir John Johnson, 1767. The earliest Lodge of which any record has been preserved was in full working order, and had probably existed for some time, on January 24, 1738. During his long administration Harrison warranted at least eleven Lodges, and five others, meeting at New York City, are also supposed to have been constituted by him. Sir John Johnson, who was not installed until 1771, appointed Dr Peter Middleton his D.G.M., and the authority of the latter continued during the war. A Lodge at Schenectady, St John's Regimental, and Military Union, were warranted by the last-named Prov. G.M. or his Deputy.

The military occupation of New York by the British in 1776, and the erection of a Masonic Province by the " Ancients " in 1781, has already been related. After the war the body so established abandoned its provincial character, and assumed the title of Grand Lodge of New York. The " Grand Cheque Word " is mentioned in the proceedings of December 3, 1794, as having " continued in use for a longer time than was at first intended, and it was resolved to change it." In 1823 there was a schism, but the two Grand Lodges united in

---

[1] *Ante*, p. 410. The first entry in each line gives the locality, after which (when known) the name of the Lodge is shown within a parenthesis. With the abbreviations used to distinguish the various States American readers will be familiar, but for the information of others, it may be stated, that Mass. denotes *Massachusetts*; Va., *Virginia*; Pa., *Pennsylvania*; S.C., *South Carolina*; N.Y., *New York*; Fla., *Florida*; and Md., *Maryland*. The letters placed between the numbers of the Lodges and the dates of their constitution represent, as in the last chapter, the different sources of origin. There is only one addition to the previous list, viz., "Fr.," which here signifies *Grand Orient of France*, by which body a Lodge was established in Portsmouth, Virginia, in 1785.

1827. A few years later, however, further dissensions occurred, and the "St John's Grand Lodge" was established September 11, 1837. In 1848 a law was passed by the G.L. of New York depriving Past Masters—except each "immediate" P.M.—of their votes. This was repealed in a highly irregular fashion in March 1849, and on June 5 following, the G.M.—Willard—declaring the law of 1848 to be a part of the constitution, on the motion of the acting J.G.W.—Isaac Philips—and amid great uproar, a Provisional Grand Master and other Grand Officers were elected in dumb show. After this there were three Grand Lodges, and it will be sufficient to state that two earliest in point of date amalgamated in 1850, and were joined by the "Philips" Grand Lodge in 1858.

Lodge Pythagoras of New York—instituted June 24, 1841—at first sided with the Philips party, but afterwards joined the "Willard" Grand Lodge, having in the interim applied to the G.L. of Hamburg for a charter, which was granted in 1851, and in the same year the Lodge returned its original warrant to the G.L of New York. Eventually, however, it resumed its old place under the jurisdiction of origin, and thus happily terminated a suspension of intercourse between the Grand Lodges of Hamburg and New York. Two further Lodges were warranted in the same way[1] by the former body, but have died out or joined the latter, which has now on its roll twenty-eight Lodges working in the German language, with a membership of 3208.

NEW JERSEY.—Although the "earliest Grand Master in America" resided in this colony, there is no record of a Lodge having been chartered by him, or of his having performed any official act as the owner of a Deputation. Neither of the Grand Lodges of England were directly, though both were indirectly, represented in this territory. The first Lodge was warranted at Newark from New York in 1761; and two others sprang up under charters from Boston in the next and following years. A similar number of Lodges was then established by the Prov. G. Lodge of Pennsylvania (*Ancients*), in 1767, 1779, and 1781. The Grand Lodge of New Jersey was organised by a convention of Master Masons on December 18, 1786, and in the following year—April 2—the Lodge of 1767 was given the first place on the roll, the others balloting for their numbers, which resulted in the Lodge at Newark drawing the No. 2.

GEORGIA.—The Charity of the Society was solicited in the Grand Lodge of England—December 31, 1733—to enable the trustees of the new colony "to send Distressed Brethren to Georgia, where they may be comfortably provided for." In 1735, a deputation to Mr Roger Lacy, for constituting a Lodge at Savannah, was granted by Lord Weymouth. This —the *second* American Lodge on the English roll—was doubtless the body referred to by Whitfield in his diary, where he records under June 24, 1738 (Savannah), "was enabled to read prayer and preach with power before the Freemasons, with whom I afterwards dined." In all, three English warrants were issued for Savannah. Grey Elliot was appointed Prov. G.M. by Lord Aberdour (1757-61), and he was succeeded by the Hon. Noble Jones about the year 1772.

In 1784, a Lodge was chartered by the G.L. of Pennsylvania at Savannah, and on December 16, 1786, the Grand Lodge of Georgia was organised. The details are wanting, but according to Mackey, "Samuel Elbert, the last Prov. G.M. [whose name I have elsewhere

---

[1] *Ante*, p. 230.

failed to trace], resigned in favour of William Stephens, who was elected the first Grand Master."

SOUTH CAROLINA.—The first Provincial Grand Master was John Hammerton, appointed by the Earl of Loudoun in 1736. After this the office appears to have become elective, as James Graeme—Chief Justice of the colony in later days—who held it on December 27, 1737, was again chosen Grand Master for the ensuing year. Chief Justice Leigh succeeded to the charge of the Province in 1754, and was succeeded by Benjamin Smith under a patent dating between 1758 and 1762.

Five Lodges are shown in the Engraved List of 1760, the earliest of which was probably identical with the Lodge at Charleston constituted by Henry Price in 1735. A sixth Lodge was placed on the English roll in 1763, and about the year 1768, Egerton Leigh became Prov. G.M. This worthy, it is stated, was in England in 1777, in which year the Prov. G. Lodge elected the Hon. Barnard Elliot "Grand Master of Masons in the State." The new ruler died in the following year, and no meetings of the "Grand Lodge" took place in 1779 and 1780. In 1781, on the death of Leigh, the Provincial G. Lodge—wholly ignoring its own proceedings of 1777—met and elected John Deas, Prov. G.M.[1] Elliot's election is open to some doubt, but there is none with regard to the Provincial Grand Lodge awaking from its slumber, and continuing to assemble until after the peace. Indeed, the English patent granted to Deas was dated November 26, 1788, which will harmonise with the supposition that without any formal act beyond a mere change of title, the body over which he presided became what was ultimately styled the "Grand Lodge of Moderns" in the State.

The rival system was represented by eight Lodges, warranted between 1760 and 1786—one by the G.L. of Scotland, and three and four respectively by those of Pennsylvania and England (*Ancients*). Some of these combined, and on March 24, 1787, erected a "Grand Lodge of Ancient York Masons." In 1808 the two Grand Lodges united, but again separated in the following year, and a permanent union did not take place until 1817, when the two bodies were merged into one, under the name of "The Grand Lodge of Ancient Freemasons."

NEW HAMPSHIRE.—One Lodge was warranted in this State by Henry Price (1736), and four by the Massachusetts G. Lodge—the latter in 1780, 1784, and (two) in 1788 respectively. The G.L. of New Hampshire was organised on July 8, 1789—there being at the time only three Lodges in the State—by one Deputy from the Lodge of 1736, and four from that of 1784—five Deputies from two Lodges.[2]

RHODE ISLAND.—The two Lodges, established under warrants from Boston in 1749 and 1757, met and formed the Grand Lodge on June 25, 1791. The early history of Masonry in this State has only one feature of interest, namely, the decision of the Grand Master of North America in 1759, that the warrant granted by Oxnard to the Newport Lodge in 1749 was an insufficient authority to confer more than the first two degrees of the Craft.

MARYLAND.—Lord Baltimore, who was proprietary Governor from 1715 to 1751, resided in the Province from 1732 to 1734. This nobleman was made a Mason in 1730, and seven years later assisted in forming the "Occasional Lodge," at which Frederick, Prince of Wales,

---

[1] Mackey, Hist. of Masonry in South Carolina, and Encyclopædia of F. ; Proc. G.L. Mass., 1877, p. 29 ; and Keystone, December 5, 1885.

[2] W. S. Gardner, Address, March 8, 1870.

was initiated;[1] but with these exceptions his Masonic record is a blank, and it is altogether unknown whether or not he was a supporter of the Craft in America. Lodges were warranted from Boston in 1750, England in 1765,[2] and three—in 1759, 1761, and 1763—of uncertain origin. Ten more—the first dating from 1766, and the last from 1782, derived their existence from the Prov. G.L. of Pennsylvania. A Lodge at Baltimore (without date) is shown on an Irish list, and it is traditionally asserted that there were two others of foreign origin—besides a Lodge near Newmarket, in 1776. The former are assigned to Georgetown and New Bremen, with the dates of 1737 and (before) 1789 respectively. The earlier of these —supposed to have been composed of Scottish Masons—is believed to have opened a branch Lodge at Joppa in 1751. The Lodge at New Bremen is said to have derived its constitution from Germany. Robert Molleson was Prov. G.M. under England in 1776, and Henry Harford in 1783; but there is no evidence to show that either of them exercised any authority under the appointment.

The Grand Lodge of Maryland was organised July 31, 1783, by a convention of five Lodges, there being eight in the State at the time, all of which were on the roll of the G.L. of Pennsylvania. Four years later—April 17, 1787—actuated by a laudable desire not to err, but if at all, on the side of caution, the same number of Lodges again met in convention and *re-organised* the Grand Lodge, choosing the same Grand Master and Grand Secretary as on the previous occasion.[3]

CONNECTICUT.—Seven Lodges were chartered in this State by Oxnard and his successors at Boston—the first in 1750, the last in 1771; three by the Prov. G.M. of New York—in 1762, 1765, and 1766; and six by the Massachusetts Grand Lodge. A seventeenth Lodge, King Solomon's, at Woodbury, of unknown registry, was in existence when, "in pursuance of a recommendation of a committee of thirteen Lodges of the State, holden at New Haven on March 18, 1783," delegates from twelve Lodges met in convention, and formed what was virtually a Grand Lodge, though in lieu of the usual Grand Officers they elected a Moderator and Clerk. Of these Lodges, four held warrants from Boston and three from New York— under the older sanction; four from the Massachusetts G.L. (*Ancients*); and one (King Solomon's) has left behind it no trace of its origin. From this time it was arranged that General Conventions should be held half-yearly; but on July 8, 1789, a Grand Lodge was duly formed with the usual solemnities, the same number of Lodges being represented as in 1783.[4] The delay receives some explanation from the Early Proceedings of the G.L. of New York, the officers of which body were appointed—February 4, 1784—"a committee to deter- mine the most eligible mode for the Grand Officers Elect of the State of Connecticut obtaining a Grand Warrant from the Grand Lodge in England."[5]

VIRGINIA.—From lists already given in this chapter, it will be seen that four Lodges were established by the G.L. of England, and two each by the Grand Lodge and Lodge Kilwinning of Scotland. One Lodge received a charter from Boston, and the jurisdiction of Ireland is

[1] Chaps. XII., p. 10; XVI., p. 288.   [2] No. 346, afterwards (1782) No. 35, Pennsyl.   *Cf. ante*, p. 412.
[3] Schultz, *passim.* The G.L. of Pennsylvania, in 1783, doubted the regularity of the G.L. of Maryland, as being formed without a warrant, though at the same time they frankly confessed their inability to decide "from what authority a warrant could be issued."
[4] Storer, Freemasonry in Connecticut, pp. 57-63.
[5] Barker, Early Hist. G.L. of New York, p. 22.   *Cf.* the last note but one.

also supposed to have been represented in the State. The Prov. G.L. of Pennsylvania (*Ancients*) established Lodges at Winchester, 1768; Alexandria, 1783; and Portsmouth, 1784. H. P. Thornton was Prov. G.M. under the original G.L. of England about the year 1764, and Peyton Randolph in 1774. In this State it was customary, in the absence of a warrant from any Grand Lodge, for a competent number of Master Masons to obtain a written authority to assemble, which document operated as their warrant. It has also been inferred that in many instances the degrees of Masonry were imparted to non-military persons in Field (or travelling) Lodges, who received a warrant to confer these degrees on others in lieu of a certificate of enrolment.[1]

The Grand Lodge of Virginia was established, October 13, 1778, by a Convention at which four Lodges were represented. This assumed, however, the form of a Lodge, and the Master and Wardens of Williamsburg Lodge presided. John Blair, Past Master of the same Lodge, was elected Grand Master, and duly installed. There was an invasion of the jurisdiction by the Grand Orient of France in 1785, in which year a warrant was issued to some brethren in Portsmouth, and again in 1849, when a new Lodge was established at Richmond; but on the latter occasion the charter was recalled at the request of the G.L. of Virginia, and the Lodge advised to apply for one to the local authorities, which was done.

NORTH CAROLINA.—Lodges in this State appear in the English Lists of 1756 and 1767, and under the year 1766 in the Boston Records. In 1767—December 30—Thomas Cooper was appointed by the Prov. G.M. of North America D.G.M. of North Carolina, with power to congregate the brethren into one or more Lodges. A year or two later, Joseph Montford became Prov. G.M. under the G.L. of England, and, it is said, constituted St John's Lodge at Newbern in 1771. According to Mackey there were nine (and to another authority, ten[2]) Lodges in the State in 1787, all of which were represented at the organisation of the Grand Lodge on December 9 of that year.

DELAWARE.—Five Lodges in this State received warrants from Pennsylvania, the first in 1765 and the last in 1802. There was also, if we may believe some authorities,[3] the Union Lodge, which is said to have been erected by the G.L. of Scotland about the middle of the last century. Of this, however, there is no trace in the official lists of that body. Four Lodges combined to organise the Grand Lodge on June 6, 1806; but it was refused recognition for some time by the G.L. of Pennsylvania on the ground that less than *five* Lodges having been represented the brethren had not "formed themselves in that regular way pointed out by the ancient Constitutions."

The remaining States and the territories of the Union will now be noticed according to the order in which Grand Lodges have been established in them, and after they have all been passed in review, a table will be given showing the number of Lodges and the aggregate of members (or Master Masons) under the several jurisdictions.

VERMONT.—Lodges were established in this State by the "Massachusetts G.L." in 1781 and 1785, the first of which was authorised to meet at Cornish, Vermont, but appears to have been held at Charlestown, New Hampshire. For a period of four years, ending in February 1782, both sides of the Connecticut river were to some extent common territory; but after that date, when the boundaries were better defined, the Lodge moved to Windsor, Vermont, and

---

[1] Dove, Hist. G.L. Virginia, and Virginia Text Book. *Cf. ante*, pp. 416, 448, 454.
[2] Proc. G.L. Illinois, 1884.   [3] *Cf.* Macoy, Masonic Directory.

took the name of Vermont Lodge, No. I.   The third Lodge was erected by Sir John Johnson, Prov. G.M. Lower Canada, who granted a warrant to Thomas Chittenden, Governor of the State, and others in 1791.   This is a little remarkable as showing that neither the Provincial G.M. of a part of Canada (and who had held a similar position in New York), or the Chief Magistrate of an American commonwealth, then believed that the War of Independence had severed the Masonic connection between the parent power and the newly created States on the northern continent.   Two further Lodges were established by the G.L. of Connecticut in 1793 and 1794.

The representatives of these five Lodges met in Convention, October 10; a Grand Lodge was organised October 14; and that body duly held a meeting, October 15, 1794.   In no State of the Union did the anti-Masonic party, as a political power, exercise so much influence as it did in Vermont.   The Grand Lodge was compelled to suspend its labours in 1833 (or 1836), and all the Lodges under its jurisdiction surrendered their charters.   The Grand Lodge resumed work in 1846.[1]

KENTUCKY.—Five Lodges were established under warrants from the G.L. of Virginia, the earliest of which—erected in 1788—was the first Lodge instituted west of the Alleghany Mountains.   These Lodges met in Convention, and—October 16, 1800—organised the Grand Lodge, by which body warrants were shortly after issued for parts of Tennessee, Mississippi, Indiana, Ohio, and Missouri.[2]

OHIO.—" American Union " met for the last time as an Army Lodge, April 23, 1783, and was ordered " to stand closed until the W. Master should call them together." [3]   This occurred in 1790, when a colony from New England having become established north-west of the Ohio, the Lodge was reopened at Marietta by Jonathan Heart, the Master, with Benjamin Tupper and Rufus Putnam officiating as Wardens.[4]   In the same year " Nova Cæsarea " was chartered at Cincinnati by the G.L. of New Jersey ; but the warrant, which was not received until 1795, was returned in a somewhat irregular manner in 1805, and some of the members obtained in lieu thereof an authorisation to meet as the " Cincinnati " Lodge, No. 13, from the G.L. of Kentucky.   These two Lodges, however, for all practicable purposes, must be regarded as one, since the members were reconciled in 1812, and all irregularities condoned.   The third Lodge —Scioto—was erected by the G.L. of Massachusetts, also in 1805, and the fourth (for which I am able to assign a date and jurisdiction)—Amity—by that of Pennsylvania, in 1806.   There were also in 1808, two others—" Erie," No. 47, and " New England," No. 48—and all the Lodges enumerated, or a total of six—Cincinnati, No. 13, being named, and Nova Cæsarea, No. 10, not—are stated to have been represented at the organisation of the Grand Lodge on January 6 of that year.[5]   By other authorities the number of Lodges participating in this movement has been reduced to five [6] by the omission of " New England, No. 48," which agrees

---

[1] Records G.L. Vermont, 1794-1846 (printed 1879) ; Proc. G.L. Canada, 1857, p. 125 ; and J. H. Drummond, Hist. and Bibl. Memoranda (New England Freemason, vol. i., 1874, p. 131).

[2] R. Morris, Masonry in Kentucky, 1859.   [3] Storer, p. 48 ; cf. ante, pp. 417, 418.

[4] Jonathan Heart was appointed, April 29, 1783, by the " Grand Convention " of Connecticut, " to visit each of the Lodges in that State, in order that there might be uniformity in the mode of working."   He retained the position of Master, on the revival of " American Union," until August 1791, when he joined the army of St Clair, and was killed in the following November at the battle of Fort Recovery.

[5] J. H. Sutor, Hist. L. of Amity, No. 5, Ohio, 1879.   [6] Mackey, p. 543 ; Mitchell, p. 605.

PLATE II.

.

with the official version,[1] though as this includes "Nova Cæsarea," and leaves out "Cincinnati," while, as a matter of fact, it is certain that the former had been superseded by the latter,[2] I am inclined to discredit it.

DISTRICT OF COLUMBIA.—This territory—the seat of the Federal Government—is enclosed by the States of Maryland and Virginia, from which jurisdictions it received in all five warrants of constitution. The Grand Lodge was organised, December 11, 1810, by four Lodges, one only standing aloof from the movement. This was "Alexandria Washington," No. 22,[3] which is at the present time both within the Masonic and the territorial jurisdiction of Virginia.

LOUISIANA.—A Lodge—La Consolante Maçonne—was established at New Orleans by the Lodge Anglaise de Bordeaux, in 1764. After a long interval, in 1793-94, refugees chiefly from the island of Guadaloupe established the Lodges, Perfect Union and Polar Star, the former working the "York," and the latter the French or Modern Rite, and holding warrants from the G.L. of South Carolina and the Mother Lodge "la Parfaite Sincérité" of Marseilles respectively. Polar Star, it may be observed, was reconstituted by the G.O. of France in 1804, and the G.L. of Pennsylvania in 1811. The first Lodge under a warrant from Philadelphia was erected in 1801, and the last—Polar Star—making nine in all, in 1811, but in several instances the charters issued were virtually warrants of confirmation, authorising brethren who had previously met in Lodges beyond the limits of Louisiana, or under other Masonic jurisdictions, to work in subordination to the G.L. of Pennsylvania. In 1804, many fugitives arrived from San Domingo, and among them the members of La Reunion Desirée (Port au Prince), who obtained a duplicate charter from the G.O. of France in 1806, but being desirous of working according to the "York Rite," changed it in 1808 for a warrant empowering them to meet under their original title, as a daughter Lodge of Pennsylvania.

The first Lodge that worked in the English language was "Louisiana," established by the G.L. of New York in 1807; and the second, "Harmony"—the latest but one of the Philadelphian Lodges—warranted in 1810. Nor were there any others until 1826, when both of these had ceased to exist.

In 1811, Polar Star obtained a Philadelphian warrant, and a new Lodge—Bienfaisance—was erected by the Grand Consistory of Jamaica; the latter, however, soon after affiliated with Lodge Concord, under the G.L. of Pennsylvania.

In 1812, there were seven Lodges in full activity at New Orleans—Perfect Union (S.C.), Louisiana (N.Y.), Charity, Concord, Perseverance, Harmony, and Polar Star (Pennsylvania). Of these all but Louisiana and Harmony—the two English-speaking Lodges—took part in the organisation of the Grand Lodge, June 20, 1812. Afterwards the French novelties obtained the upper hand, and there was much confusion. Seven Lodges were chartered in the State by the G.L. of Mississippi, February 21, 1848; and on March 8, next ensuing, these formed a second Grand Lodge. The Schism lasted until March 4, 1850, when a Union was effected.[4]

TENNESSEE.—The Lodges in this State, with the exception of one that derived its origin from Kentucky, were all held under warrants from North Carolina until the close of 1813. In that year—December 27—by order of the G.M. of North Carolina, a convention was held, at which eight Lodges were represented, and the Grand Lodge of Tennessee was organised.

---

[1] Proc. G.L. Ohio, 1880, p. 128. [3] Hough, pp. 110, 116, 132, 143.
[2] *Ante*, p. 421. [4] Daruty, p. 89 ; Scot., *passim. Cf. ante*, pp. 348, 353, 359.

INDIANA.—The Grand Lodge was formed, January 12, 1818, at which date there were eight Lodges in the State—one under Ohio, the remainder deriving their authority from Kentucky. Five of these were represented on the occasion.[1]

MISSISSIPPI.—Three Lodges were established by the G.L. of Kentucky—the first in 1801 —and two by that of Tennessee. The Grand Lodge of the State was organised by the representatives of three of these Lodges, July 27, 1818.

MAINE.—This became an independent State in 1820, and a Grand Lodge was organised by twenty-four Lodges on June 1 of that year. Maine had previously been within the territorial as well as the Masonic jurisdiction of Massachusetts, and the Grand Lodge of the latter State very gracefully consented to an equitable division of the Charity and other funds, when so large a cluster of daughter Lodges separated amicably from her.

MISSOURI.—Lodges were erected in this State by the Grand Lodges of Pennsylvania in 1807 and 1808; Tennessee, in 1816 and 1819 (2); and Indiana, in 1820. Three of these met in convention, April 23, 1821, and organised the G.L. of Missouri.[2]

ALABAMA.—The Grand Lodge was organised June 14, 1821, by seven[3] or nine[4] Lodges, the latter being the number then existing in the State. These are said to have been warranted by the Grand Lodges of Tennessee and North Carolina,[5] but the only point with regard to their origin that seems quite clear from the authorities is, that *one* was chartered by the G L. of South Carolina in 1819.

MICHIGAN.—Three Lodges at Detroit received warrants from the Grand Lodge of England. The earliest of these, Zion, affiliated with the Prov. G.L. of Lower Canada in 1794, and the G.L. of New York in 1806, remaining on the roll of the latter until the formation of the G.L. of Michigan in 1826. The last-named body became dormant in 1829, and was revived in 1841; but this step being deemed irregular by the other American jurisdictions, a majority of the Lodges again met in Convention, and organised the present Grand Lodge in 1844. The G.L. of Michigan is stated to have been formed by four out of five Lodges in the State.

FLORIDA.—This peninsula was ceded to Britain in 1763, and Masonry obtained a footing from Scotland in 1768. The 14th Foot, in garrison at St Augustine, 1776, was ordered a renewal of its charter—No. 58—by the Ancients in 1777; and a second warrant for the same place was granted by them—which failed to reach its destination—in 1778. After the war Florida again became Spanish territory, and, July 12, 1783, a warrant was issued from Pennsylvania " to St Andrew's Lodge, No. 1, *late* of West Florida," and then at Charleston, S.C. A Lodge was next established at St Augustine from Georgia in 1806, but suppressed by the Spaniards in 1811. The country was sold to the United States in 1819, and in 1820 and 1824 warrants not fated to endure were granted from South Carolina. In 1826, however, three Lodges—from Tennessee and Georgia—were established and took root, all uniting in the organisation of the Grand Lodge on July 5, 1830.

TEXAS.—Three Lodges were erected in this territory by the G.L. of Louisiana, the first in 1835. These united to form the Grand Lodge of Texas, December 20, 1837.[6] By one writer, however, it is affirmed that two additional Lodges, holding warrants from the G.L. of Mississippi, participated in this movement.[7]

[1] Proc. G.L. Indiana, 1886, p. cxii.   [3] World Wide Register, p. 242.
[2] Proc. G.L. Illinois, 1884, p. iv.   [4] Mackey, p. 52 ; Macoy, p. 17.   [5] Mitchell, p. 630.
[6] W. W. Reg., p. 405 ; Mackey, p. 811.   [7] Mitchell, p. 649.

ARKANSAS.—Owing to the loss of its early records there is much confusion with regard to the formation of a Grand Lodge. Mackey and Hyneman [1] date the event in 1832, and three Lodges are said to have united for the purpose; but, according to a Committee of the G.L., it is traditional that Masonry was introduced into Arkansas by the Spanish more than a century ago, and that the present Grand Lodge was formed in 1838 by four Lodges, two holding warrants from Louisiana, and one each from Alabama and Tennessee. [2]

ILLINOIS.—A Grand Lodge was established in 1823, which became extinct in 1828, but was reorganised, April 6, 1840, by six chartered Lodges, an equal number not being represented, one of which was dormant, and three held dispensations only.

The remaining Grand Lodges, which I am compelled by exigencies of space to pass over very briefly, were organised by a majority [3] of the Lodges in the respective States or territories as follows, the actual number of Lodges represented on each occasion being shown between the name of the Grand Lodge and the year of its formation :—

Wisconsin, three, 1843 ; Iowa, four, 1844 ; California, three, 1850 ; Oregon, three, 1851 ; Minnesota, three, 1853 ; Kansas, three, 1856 ; Nebraska, three, 1857 ; Washington, four, 1858 ; Colorado, three, 1861 ; Nevada, eight, 1865 ; West Virginia, nine, 1865 ; Montana, three, 1866 ; Idaho, four, 1867 ; Utah, three, 1872 ; Indian Territory, three, 1874 ; Wyoming, four, 1874 ; Dakota, six, 1875 ; New Mexico, three, 1877 ; and Arizona, four, 1881.

STATISTICAL TABLE.

Grand Lodges.	Number of Lodges.	Number of Members.	Grand Lodges.	Number of Lodges.	Number of Members.
Alabama,	280	7,726	Mississippi,	293	8,422
Arizona,	5	353	Missouri,	522	25,821
Arkansas,	368	10,452	Montana,	24	1,234
California,	218	14,260	Nebraska,	107	5,979
Colorado,	49	3,756	Nevada,	22	1,095
Connecticut,	110	14,904	New Hampshire,	76	8,144
Dakota,	50	2,644	New Jersey,	154	12,403
Delaware,	21	1,457	New Mexico,	10	553
Dist. of Columbia,	21	3,032	New York,	715	72,318
Florida,	80	2,802	North Carolina,	207	8,211
Georgia,	277	11,024	Ohio,	469	29,345
Idaho,	11	495	Oregon,	70	3,261
Illinois,	691	40,015	Pennsylvania,	380	37,175
Indiana,	505	22,548	Rhode Island,	35	8,597
Indian Territory,	17	653	South Carolina,	172	5,477
Iowa,	394	21,309	Tennessee,	411	14,755
Kansas,	236	13,277	Texas,	486	18,690
Kentucky,	496	14,823	Utah,	8	474
Louisiana,	129	3,826	Vermont,	101	7,940
Maine,	182	20,077	Virginia,	240	9,013
Maryland,	82	4,896	Washington,	39	1,708
Massachusetts,	227	27,590	West Virginia,	83	3,542
Michigan,	351	27,045	Wisconsin,	200	12,968
Minnesota,	145	8,677	Wyoming,	6	43

Totals :—48 Grand Lodges ; 9775 Lodges ; and 569,304 Members.

---

[1] Encycl., p. 915 ; W. W. Reg., p. 62. [2] Cited in Proc. G.L. Canada, 1873, p. 421.

[3] In the Indian Territory and New Mexico, however, there were six and seven Lodges respectively, and in each case the Grand Lodge is said to have been " legalised " by an additional Lodge joining shortly after its formation.

The Black Masons, whose initiation in 1775 has been recorded under that year in the preceding chapter, applied to England for a charter—their Lodge having then existed for eight years—in 1784. Their request was granted, September 29, 1784, but the warrant did not arrive in Boston until 1787. It bore the number 459, and the title, "African Lodge." Prince Hall—born 1748, died 1807—who was the first Master, established a Lodge by his own authority at Philadelphia in 1797, and a second at Providence R.I. shortly afterwards. The three Lodges formed a Grand Lodge in 1808. The "African Lodge" was not shown in the English lists after 1813, but it did not formally declare its independence of foreign control until 1827. In 1847 there were three coloured Grand Lodges, one at Boston and two in Pennsylvania. These met in convention and organised a National G.L., which has since met triennially. Thirty-one Grand Lodges in different States of the Union are mentioned in the statistics before me, which show a total of 694 Lodges, and 17,909 members. These coloured or "lesser Grand Lodges," have been more or less recognised as legally constituted bodies, in France, Italy, Germany, Hungary, Peru, and Liberia; and in Ohio, a resolution by the White, acknowledging the regularity of the Black Grand Lodge, in that State, was only lost by fifty-eight votes—the numbers being 332 to 390—in 1875. The case of the "Negro Mason in America" has been ably stated by Mr Samuel Clark, "G.M. of Coloured Masons of the State of Ohio," from whose pamphlet and the other authorities at my disposal, I am inclined to think that the claim of the Black Mason to be placed on a footing of equality with the White one, is destined to pass through a somewhat similar ordeal in America, to that which has been (in part) undergone by the famous Jewish question in Germany.[1]

Negro Masonry.

In August 1826, it became noised abroad, that William Morgan, then residing near Batavia in the State of New York, was about to publish a work in which the secrets of Masonry were to be revealed. Morgan was arrested on a charge of theft in September and lodged in jail for a night. The next day he was released, placed in a coach, and (with his own consent) taken to Fort Niagara, a distance of 115 miles. There he was confined for a few days by his abductors in a room formerly used as a powder magazine, after which all traces of him disappear, and what was his real fate has never been ascertained. The indignation of the community was aroused, the excitement spread, and the public did not pause to discriminate. Finally the whole fraternity were regarded as in some measure implicated in the transaction. A current of feeling so strong and so deep was soon turned to political purposes. An anti-masonic party was at once formed, and before long had converts in every part of the Union. Several of the Grand Lodges suspended their labours, and in the State of Vermont all the Lodges made a voluntary surrender of their charters. For ten years the Craft languished, but the era of persecution was brought to a close about the year 1836.

Anti-Masonry.

Congresses or Conventions have been held, by Delegates from Grand Lodges, in Washington, 1842, 1855; Baltimore, 1843, 1847; Lexington, Kentucky, 1853; and Chicago, 1859. Their Proceedings were published.

National Conventions.

Grand Chapters exist, I believe, in all the States or Territories, in which there are Grand Lodges. There is also a General Grand Chapter—organised in 1798—and to this the greater number of Grand Chapters are in nominal subjection.

Grand Chapters.

[1] Mas. Mag., vol. iv., p. 503 ; Clark, The Negro Mason in Equity, 1886 [the letters " R. W.," were prefixed to the Master's title in *all* Lodges under the Original G. L. of England, and Prince Hall was at no time vested with any higher authority, or the existing records would attest it] ; Lewis Hayden, Caste among Masons, 1866 ; War of Races, 1868 ; and Masonry among coloured Men in America, 1871 ; Proc. (*Coloured*) G. L. Boston, 1875 ; 1883-84 Ontario, 1883.

CHAPTER XXXII.

THE DOMINION OF CANADA, AND NEWFOUNDLAND.

ILLIAM DOUGLAS was appointed Prov. G.M. for the coast of Africa and the islands of America in 1737, and Robert Commins for Cape Breton and Louisbourg in 1746. The earliest Lodges, however, in the vast territory to which the name of Canada has at any time been applied, were established by warrants from New England. The Merchant's Lodge, Quebec, was shown in the Engraved List for 1762, and in the later issue of 1770, appears at the head of seven Lodges—Nos. 220-26 —one of which was at Montreal, and the remainder—including a Sea and a Field Lodge, in H.M.S. Canceaux, and the 52d Foot respectively—at Quebec. All these, though six are first shown in the list for 1770, were allowed to rank from 1762. About the same year,[1] the Hon. Colonel Simon Frazer was appointed Prov. G.M. of Canada, and his successors were— Milborne West, 1763-64; John Collins, 1768-69; Colonel Carleton, 29th Foot (provisionally), 1786; and Sir John Johnson, 1788.

Further Lodges in Lower Canada (Montreal) were erected by the Original G.L. of England in 1787 (2), and 1793; and four in all in Upper Canada, by the same body, the first in 1787 and the last in 1793. In 1791, the country was divided into the territorial provinces of Upper and Lower Canada. A single stationary Lodge—No. 265 Quebec, 1791—was established directly by the "Ancient" (or Schismatic) G.L. of England, but by the issue of Provincial warrants for Upper as well as Lower Canada in 1792, its influence and authority in British North America gradually increased, to the detriment and finally to the utter extinction of the Lodges under the older sanction. In 1794, as we have already seen,[2] the brethren under the two systems cordially united in an address to Prince Edward, afterwards Duke of Kent. In 1799, the number of Provincial Lodges in Canada, under the Ancient (or Atholl) banner was—Upper Canada (Niagara), fourteen; Lower Canada (Quebec), sixteen. None of the Lodges erected by the older G.L. of England, were carried forward at the Union; nor were any on the local lists, brought on the roll of the United G.L. until 1822, in which year a batch of twenty-one—Nos. 754-774—is shown in the Calendar, as being held in Upper Canada. Nine Lodges meeting in Lower Canada—Nos. 780-788—appear in the same way in the list for 1824. These results were due to the action of the Duke of Sussex, in applying the *new* laws to the *old* "Atholl" Provinces, by the appointment from home of Provincial Grand Masters for Upper Canada, Quebec, and Montreal.

[1] *Ante*, p. 365, note 1.   [2] Chap. XIX., p. 463.

Forty-one additional Lodges were warranted from England in the former Province—1843-57—and eight in the latter—1823-55. A Scottish Lodge was established at Quebec in 1819, another at Montreal in 1847, and a second at Quebec in 1851. Sixteen Lodges were warranted by the G.L. of Ireland, the first (at Kingstown, U.C.) in 1821, the last in 1855.

From 1791 to 1840, there were two distinct British Provinces, styled respectively, Upper and Lower Canada. In the latter year, a legislative union was effected, but the distinction between the Provinces was preserved, one (U.C.) being called "Canada West," and the other (L.C.) "Canada East."

The evils of a divided control, a diversity of working, and an imposition of rulers, not of their own selection, were endured for many years, if not with contentment, at least with equanimity, by the Canadian Craft. But in 1855, the cup of indignation overflowed, and their communications and remittances to the G.L. of England, eliciting neither response nor acknowledgment, the brethren hoisted the standard of revolt. At this time there were eighty-three Lodges in Canada—fifty English and fourteen Irish, in Canada West; and twelve English, two Irish, and two Scottish, in Canada East. Forty-one of these Lodges, fifteen Irish, one Scottish, and twenty-five English (fifteen in Canada West, and ten in Canada East), were represented by their delegates on October 10, 1855, when the Grand Lodge of Canada was organised. The English Prov. G.L. of Canada West at first discountenanced the movement; but on July 8, 1857, committees of the Grand and Prov. Grand Lodges met, and endeavoured to effect a fusion of the two bodies. This, however, fell through, and on September 9 following, the Prov. G.L. declared its independence, assuming the title of "Ancient Grand Lodge of Canada." After this, there were two Grand Lodges, until July 14, 1858, when articles of Union having been agreed to, the junior association was dissolved—its Grand Officers and Lodges being accorded their relative rank and seniority in the Grand Lodge of Canada. The united body was formally recognised by the G.L. of England in December of the same year, and on March 23, 1859, the Earl of Zetland, in a letter to Grand Master Wilson, acknowledged the jurisdiction of the G.L. of Canada, over all Canada, claiming, however, for the Lodges, still adhering to their original allegiance in Quebec and Montreal, their full privileges as individual Lodges, together with the rights and privileges of their Provincial Grand Lodges, which stipulation was agreed to, without the slightest demur, by the G.M. of Canada in his reply, dated April 23.

The Dominion of Canada was formed in 1867. Canada West became "Ontario," and Canada East, "Quebec." The federal union also included Nova Scotia and New Brunswick, and to these was added in 1869, the vast territory of the Hudson's Bay Company—now the Province of Manitoba. In 1871, the league was augmented by the addition of British Columbia, and in 1873, by that of Prince Edward's Island. The only portion of British North America not yet included in the confederation is Newfoundland, but as it is certain in time to throw in its lot with the Dominion, provision was made for its admission in the Act of Union of 1867.

It is somewhat confusing that the jurisdiction of the "G.L. of Canada," only extends over what is now the Province of Ontario, and the more so, since two other bodies—not admitted within the family of Grand Lodges—one composed of white and the other of coloured Masons, have taken the title of "Grand Lodge of Ontario."

QUEBEC.—For some little time after the political changes of 1867, the formation of a Grand Lodge for the Dominion was "in the air." But the idea having become impracticable through the action of the Masons in Nova Scotia and New Brunswick, in forming Grand Lodges for those Provinces, the example thus set was followed in Quebec—October 20, 1869—by the representatives of twenty-one out of thirty-seven Lodges meeting within its territorial limits. The first Lodge on the roll was originally in the 46th Foot (227, I.); and the two next in the Royal Artillery (Nos. 213 and 241, A.). Three English Lodges, at Montreal, under a D.G.M., appointed in 1849, have hitherto declined to affiliate with the Grand Lodge, and the G.L. of England, while interposing no obstacle to a transfer of their allegiance, wisely holds that the point is one which those Lodges are entitled to settle according to their own judgment, without pressure of any kind.

NOVA SCOTIA.—Lodges at Annapolis Royal and Halifax are said to have been formed from Boston in 1738 and 1750. The later of the two is probably identical with No. 109 on the Engraved List for 1770—where it appears for the first time—with the date of 1749 ?

Erasmus James Phillips was appointed Prov. G.M., and two Lodges were warranted by the Schismatic G.L. of England in 1757. Three others—Nos. 155, 156, and 211—sprang up under the same sanction—the first two in 1768, and the third in 1781. In the year last named three out of these five Lodges were extinct, and the "Ancients" were only represented by Nos. 155 and 211—St Andrew's and St John's,[1] by whose joint act four dispensations were granted, thus bringing up the number to six. A Prov. G.L. was organised under a renewed (but virtually a new) warrant in 1784—its subordinates numbering nineteen in 1789 and thirty-two in 1807. In 1813 the only Lodges carried forward on the Union roll were Nos. 155 and 211 (now 1 and 2, N.S.), and the Prov. G.L. continued to exist as before, electing its G.M. yearly, paying tribute to none, and exacting the respect due to any independent Grand Lodge, until 1822, when its proceedings were styled irregular by the G.M. of England. John Albro, the Prov. G.M. at that time, was annually re-elected until 1829, when he received a Patent from England, and in the same year seventeen Lodges—Nos. 828-44—were removed from the local to the general list. Nineteen others were added to the English roll between 1840 and 1868. Scotland entered the field in 1827, and Ireland in 1845. From the latter country only two warrants were received, but under the former a Province was erected, by ten of whose daughter Lodges a Grand Lodge was established, June 21, 1866. This, on June 24, 1869, formed a Union with the Prov. G.L. under England—twenty-five Lodges on each side (and one Scottish one, or fifty-one in all), taking part in the *regular* organisation of the G.L. of Nova Scotia. A single (English) Lodge adhered to its original allegiance, of which the G.M. of Nova Scotia remarks (1880)—"working side by side with us, a healthy emulation is produced, and both parties are the better for it."

In CAPE BRETON—now a dependency of Nova Scotia—a warrant was granted by Richard Gridley in 1758 (Louisbourg); and Lodges were afterwards erected by the "Atholl" G.L., 1801; three by the G.L. of England, 1844-68; and one under a Scottish warrant in 1858.

NEW BRUNSWICK.—Two Military Lodges were brought with them by the Loyalists in 1783,[2] but the first stationary Lodge was established by dispensation of Nos. 155 and 211 (A.) in 1784. Warrants of the P.G.L. of Nova Scotia were issued to the latter, and one of the former (No. 2, N.Y.) in 1786 and 1789 respectively. An English warrant (from the

---

[1] Captain (afterwards Sir John) Moore was initiated in St John's, March 12, 1781.

[2] Held in the New Jersey Volunteers (No. 2, N.Y.), and The Prince of Wales' American Regiment, respectively. The Lodge in the latter claimed to work under an Irish warrant—No. 535—really granted to the 30th Foot (but from whom they may have received a copy), and to have been "installed" in Lodge No. 512, 63rd Foot, in South Carolina.

Original G.L.) was also granted in 1789. Six further Lodges were added to the Provincial roll, 1792-1809; and eight, 1814-25. About the year 1827 a Grand Lodge was formed, independent of both Nova Scotia and England, but in 1829 the Grand Lodge at home asserted its supremacy, which was followed by submission. Between the latter year and 1865, twenty-two English Lodges were erected in the colony. Within the same period six Irish and three Scottish charters were granted. The Grand Lodge was organised October 10, 1867, by sixteen Lodges—twelve English, three Irish, and one Scottish; there being at the time twenty-six, viz., twenty English, three Irish, and three Scottish, in the Province.

PRINCE EDWARD'S ISLAND.—Military Lodges were formed under Nova Scotian warrants in 1781 and 1797. The last became a stationary Lodge, and with seven others was placed on the English roll, 1828-69. A solitary Scottish charter was issued in 1858, and the Lodge so formed, with seven on the registry of England, organised the Grand Lodge, February 24, and June 23, 1875.

BRITISH COLUMBIA.—In this territory and Vancouver's Island four Lodges were established under warrants from England, 1859-67; and five from Scotland, 1862-69. Eight of these organised the Grand Lodge, September 21, 1871.

MANITOBA.—Three Lodges were established in this Province by the G.L. of Canada (the first in 1870), and they united to form the G.L. of Manitoba, May 12, 1875. There was a schism in 1877, during which year and a part of the next there were two Grand Lodges in the Province, but a union was effected in 1879.

NEWFOUNDLAND.—The two earliest Lodges on this island were established under warrants from Boston. Others were erected by the G.L. of England in 1784 and 1785, and five by its Schismatic rival, 1774-88. Eight English Lodges have been formed since the Union and two Scottish (1866-67). Each jurisdiction has its District Grand Master, with, in one case, six, and in the other two, Lodges, to supervise. At MIQUELON, a little island on the southern coast, a Lodge was erected by the G.O. of France in 1867, but is now extinct.[1]

STATISTICAL TABLE.

	Lodges.	Members.		Lodges.	Members.
Canada,	356	18,983	Prince Edward's Island,	14	428
Quebec,	68	2,822	British Columbia,	10	312
Nova Scotia,	67	2,966	Manitoba,	31	1,350
New Brunswick,	32	1,910	Newfoundland,	8	[ ]

[1] Authorities :—Brennan, Standard Hist., p. 359 et seq. ; Weekly Telegraph, St John, N.B., July 9, 1884 ; and the Proceedings of the various Grand Lodges of the Dominion, notably those of Canada, New Brunswick, and Prince Edward's Island—which having been kindly sent me by Messrs J. J. Mason, W. F. Bunting, and G. W. Wakeford, respectively, I was enabled to peruse at leisure, and have derived much assistance from, in preceding chapters.

L'ENVOI.

" VERY considerable claim to candour may be advanced in favour of this work. The number and difficulty of the subjects treated of—the compass of reading necessary to obtain materials to elucidate them—the singular felicity of avoiding undue prolixity or unsatisfactory conciseness—and the perplexity arising from the jarring opinions of learned men on many of these subjects, render it an arduous task for an individual to accomplish."—This plea was advanced by Samuel Burder, in the preface to his " Oriental Customs," and I shall adopt it as my own, on presenting my readers with the final volume of this History of Freemasonry. Not, indeed, that in strictness I am entitled to do so, for the assistance I have received from others, to whose names I gladly turn, has alone enabled me to *complete* a general history of the Craft, an undertaking alleged on high authority to be of so formidable a character, that the span of ten men's lives was deemed too short a period for its execution.[1]

To Mr C. G. C. Rennie, I am indebted for many valuable notes, which have been of general utility, and for his assistance in Chapters I., VI., X., and XII. The proofs of the entire work have been perused by Hughan, to whose judicious counsel I owe much, and who, besides rendering assistance of a general character throughout, undertook the main preparation of Chapters II., VIII., XVIII., and XXII. For the pictures of the German Steinmetzen, of the Companionage, and of Continental Masonry—Chapters III.-V., and XXIV.-XXVIII.—I am indebted to Speth, whose co-operation, moreover, was not circumscribed within these limits, but extended to other chapters, and to the perusal of the latter half of the proofs. To this friend I stand under a peculiar weight of obligation, from his familiarity with several modern languages, which, in the absence of his assistance, I must have personally acquired in order to consult the foreign literature of the Craft with the minuteness that was essential. The earlier proofs were read by Rylands, to whom I am indebted for the plates of arms and seals, and their description; also for many valuable suggestions and useful notes, especially in Chapters IX., XI. (§ vi.), XIV., and XV. Nor must I omit to record the benefit I have derived from his special knowledge of manuscript literature. All the friends named (with the exception of Mr Rennie, who is not a Freemason) are members of my own Lodge (Quatuor Coronati, No. 2076). So also is Woodford, the *Doyen* of British Masonic students, whose wise counsel, so often sought, has never been withheld, and whose ample library was placed freely at my disposal.

The Grand Secretaries of England, Ireland, and Scotland merit my most grateful acknowledgment of their invariable courtesy in replying to my frequent inquiries. To the informa-

[1] Chap. I., p. 2.

tion so amply supplied by the officers of foreign Grand Lodges I have borne testimony on earlier pages. Messrs Wyatt Papworth, William Officer, H. D. Sandeman, T. B. Whytehead, Cæsar Kupferschmidt, Joseph Todd, Wilhelm Begemann, W. F. Vernon, and Henry Sadler (whose unwearied attention to my requirements I cannot too warmly recognise), have also in various ways rendered me great assistance. Many others have likewise contributed to my store of facts, whose names have already been gratefully referred to in footnotes. Nor in candour should I omit to state how deeply I have benefited from the robust criticisms—*de omnibus rebus et quibusdam aliis*—of a few writers, who, like Messrs W. P. Buchan and Jacob Norton, "consider rather what is said, than who says it, and the consequence of the argument, rather than the consequence of him that delivers it," and would have great names bow to the authority of truth, not truth to the authority of great names. Lane's "Masonic Records," I regret to say, was published too late to be of any service to me; but had the work appeared a year earlier, my toil would have been much lessened.

My labours are brought to a conclusion, but without the feeling of satisfaction that I had fondly anticipated, on the completion of my task. Where the friend and brother, whose approval I should have most valued, once sat, there is now a vacant chair. A worthy Mason and a good man has been called to his rest. Throughout the fleeting shadows of the past five years, I look back, with gratitude, upon the kindness and encouragement which I always received at the hands of Mr THOMAS CHISHOLM JACK, the publisher of this work, with whom, indeed, it was a great privilege to be associated in any common undertaking. But the design of a General History of the Craft will, I hope—however faulty the execution—be for ever associated with his memory. More I cannot trust myself to say, and with this brief allusion to a devoted husband, a loving father, and a true man, who

> "Never made a brow look dark,
> Nor caused a tear, but when he died,"

I bid the reader heartily farewell.

APPENDIX.

INTRODUCTORY NOTE.

THE demands upon the Text have been so great, that I am compelled to bring the Appendix within much narrower limits than I had intended. This will necessitate the omission of some original matter; of a quantity of extracts from ancient records; and lastly, of many explanatory references. These, however, I hope, may be given in due season in a further or supplementary volume.

In the course of the History, the reader has been referred to the Appendix in vols. i., 382, note 5; ii., 260, 339, 467, 493; and iii., 26, 39, 46, and 256; but having to choose between the omission of matter already printed in works that are generally accessible, or of that lying comparatively in the dark, I have decided, under these limitations, to adopt the former alternative, and in the "Grand Mystery" and "Mason's Examination" my readers will at least have specimens of what I should have proceeded with on a far larger scale had there been the requisite space at my command.

Two plates of Medals are given in Vol. III., and those who are desirous of investigating a subject of so much interest, will find their studies very pleasantly directed by Hughan in his "Masonic Register" (1878), and by Marvin in his ampler work, "The Medals of the Masonic Fraternity" (1880).

ADDENDA AND CORRIGENDA.

VOLUME I.

Page 11, note 3, *add*, Lubbock, Origin of Civilization, 1870, p. 337; and Bancroft, Hist. U.S.A., 1885, vol. ii., p. 131.

Page 16, note 3, *to read*, Epigenes de Poesi Orph. Norimb., 1702, pp. 21, 22; note 5, *to read*, De Triplici Theologiâ Mysteriisque Commentatis, Paris, 1784.

Page 17, note 4, *to read*, Ad. Dion Perieg., 524 (Geogr. Graec. Min., p. 664).

Page 22, line 27, *for* will, *read* shall.

Page 72, line 2, *for* No. 18, *read* No. 19.

Page 75, line 3, *read*, MDCCXXII.

Page 86, line 17, *for* Burano, *read* Murano.

Page 105, line 11, *for* 56, *read* 88; line 31, *delete* "the" before *facile princeps*.

Page 106, line 16, *for* p. 45, *read* p. 77.

Page 147, line 27, *for* Heinsch, *read* Heimsch.

Page 148, note 1, *add*, *cf.* Browne, Hist. of the Met. Church of St Peter, York, 1847, p. 50, note 2.

Page 166, note 3, *add*, *cf. post*, vol. ii., p. 28; and Disraeli, Cur. of Lit., 1859, iii., p. 153.

Page 177, line 9, *to read*, The cradle of German architectural skill, but not the organization of the Steinmetz Guild, is to be found in the convents.

Page 178, last line, 1829.

Page 224, Howling. *See* Brand, Pop. Antiq., 1870, ii., pp. 188, 189.

Page 231, line 8, *to read*, Between 1651 and 1648.

Page 251, line 27, *factor*.

Page 272, note 3, line 3, *read* hagiographer.

Page 275, line 22, *for* savages, *read* ravages.

Page 351, line 14, *for* "of," *read* "de."

Page 355, note 6, line 3, *read* (xxiii.); last line *to read*, See *post*, p. 266, note 2.

Page 366, note 2, line 5, *after* "Illustrations of Masonry, p. 191," *add*, copying from Scott's Pocket Companion, 1754, p. 109.

Page 382, The St Clair Charters. These have been already printed by Lawrie and Lyon in their respective Histories.

Page 396, line 27, "prejudicially."

Page 440, line 1, *for* speaking pynt, *read* founding pynt; line 26, *to read*, admitted a freeman.

Page 456, note 2, "Apprentice Steinmetz."

Page 465, note 1, Dr Birch.

Page 482, line 20, *for* there are, *read* these are.

Page 489, note 2, *add*, Disraeli, Cur. of Lit., 1858, i. 135, 136.

Page 492, line 34, *for* antiquity, *read* mysticism.

Page 497, line 2, *for* on, *read* or; line 36, *delete* it.

VOLUME II.

Page 22, Papal Bulls.

" A monk of the abbey of St Medard being on his death-bed, confessed with great contrition and repentance, that he had forged numerous Bulls of exemption in favour of various monasteries,—the abbey of St Ouen in Normandy, and of St Augustine's, Canterbury, being amongst the number, to the prejudice of the rights of their ordinaries " (Palgrave, Rise and Progress of the English Commonwealth, ii., p. ccxi.). See also, Walpoliana, ii., p. 63.

Page 153, note 1, There are also Free miners of the Forest of Dean. | Page 194, Descriptive List of the Old Charges.

Three additional MSS. have recently been discovered, which I have incorporated with the pre-existing list at the following numbers:—24a, " Dauntesy," 1690 ; 31b, " Probity," 1736 ; and 31c, " Crane," 1781. The dates given are approximate only. All are written on paper, the last named consisting of two fragments, and the others being in book form. 24a was published by Mr W. H. Rylands in the *Keystone*, Philadelphia, March 20, 1886 ; and as it possesses many common features with the " Supreme Council" MS. (24), I have placed it after that document in the numerical list. 31b has been transcribed by Hughan, and printed in the *Freemason*, January 30 and February 13, 1886. It consists of ten pages of MS., bound up with a copy of " The Book M., or Masonry Triumphant," 1736, in the possession of the Probity Lodge, No. 61, Halifax, Yorkshire. As the age of the MS. appears to correspond pretty closely with that of the printed book, its value is not great. The text is similar to that of the Lansdowne (3) and Antiquity (23) MSS. 31c, consisting of two fragments or loose sheets, was discovered by Mr J. C. Robinson, of Chester, among the papers of the Rev. T. Crane, deceased, in 1884, and by him published in the *Freemason* of that year (pp. 476, 486, 497, 507, 522), to which I refer my readers for the reasons which appear to justify the classification of the " Wren " (37) and the " Crane " (31c) MSS. as separate and distinct authorities.

Page 260, Alnwick Records. The works in which an abstract of these has appeared, are indicated in the 3d note. Page 286, note 8. This is qualified by the fuller argument in the next chapter at p. 358 *q. v.* Page 339, General Regulations and Members of Lodges in | 1724-25. The former are given in most histories of Masonry, and reprints of the Constitutions of A.D. 1723 have been issued in both England and America. The names of the latter I am simply unable to find room for in the present work.

Page 355, Dr Anderson.

The Rev. Mr Craven, of Kirkwall, Orkney, informs me that on the fly leaf of a copy of the " Royal Genealogies," in the University of Aberdeen, he has found, apparently in the handwriting of the author, the following :—" Almam Matrem Academiam *Mareschallanam* hoc libro donavit ejusdem auctor.—Jacobus Anderson, D.D."

Page 356, Masonic Catechisms.

These may be conveniently divided into three groups—all of which have their especial points of interest—the first extending over the period 1717-27, the second having its first exemplar in 1730, and the third beginning with the year 1760. The earliest collection comprises Sloane MS. 3329 (*temp. incert.*) ; the Mason's Examination, 1723 ; the Grand Mystery and the Briscoe MS., 1724 ; and the Mason's Confession (*temp. incert.*, but supposed to date from 1727, though only printed in 1755). Of these the only two not accessible to the general reader are given at a later page—the Mason's Examination, transcribed by myself from the *Flying Post or Post Master*, No. 4712, April 11 to April 13, 1723, and the Grand Mystery, 2d edition—really printed in 1724, though dated 1725—containing an interesting account of the Gormogons, which is reprinted from *the only known copy in existence*, at present in the Dresden Royal Library, through the courteous assistance of Dr W. Begemann, of Rostock. The second group commences with "The Mystery of Freemasonry," published in the *Daily Journal*, August 15, 1730 (of which the salient features were given by Franklin, under the same name, in his *Pennsylvania Gazette*); after this came Masonry Dissected, by Samuel Prichard, of which four editions were published in the same year—the first on October 20; and the *Daily Journal* of December 16 has, "This day is published—'A defence of Masonry, occasioned by a Pamphlet call'd *Masonry dissected*'" (*ante*, ii., p. 356, note 2). Passing to the third group, in 1760—February—we meet with "A Master Key to Freemasonry;" and—April—"The Three Distinct Knocks;" 1762—March—Jachin and Boaz; 1764, Hiram, or the Grand Master Key; 1765, Shibboleth, or Every Man a Freemason; and, 1766, Solomon in all his Glory, and "Mahabone, or the Grand Lodge Door Open'd." Dr W. Begemann, of Rostock, to whom I am indebted for many of the preceding details, will shortly bring out a work entitled "Catechisms and Usages of English Freemasons of the Eighteenth Century," to which the curious reader is referred.

Page 365, Hiram Abif.

This name is given in the Inigo Jones MS. (i., 63; ii., 244, 365), which document—in the opinion of Dr Begemann—was manufactured *after* 1723, "as its chronology is taken from Anderson's Constitutions of that year, while the letters of Solomon and Hiram were copied *verbatim et literatim* from an English translation of Josephus, dated 1670." The same critic assigns no higher antiquity than (at the utmost) the year 1722, to Sloane MS. 3329 (ii., 279, 316, 356), and considers that both the demand and the supply of such writings, could have had no earlier beginning than 1720.

In these conclusions I hesitate to concur, at least without further consideration, for they appear to me to suggest a qualification of my previous judgment of Harleian MS. 1942 (ii., 210), in the *simulated antiquity* of which document—like that of the Leland-Locke (i., 489), the Inigo Jones, and the Sloane MSS.—we may possibly find (if Dr Begemann's views will bear investigation) an explanation of what has hitherto appeared insoluble, when associated with the remote date, which, by experts in writing, has been somewhat arbitrarily assigned to it.

Page 372, note 10.

A curious superstition is recorded of the fishermen of the Daii—a river in Tongking. If a fish jumps into the boat, it is a very bad omen; and to avert impending evil, it is necessary to cut the fish into two and throw it into the water again (J. G. Scott, France and Tongking, 1885, p. 207).

Page 438, Early Atholl Records.

Further documentary evidence has recently been brought to light by Mr Henry Sadler, and published by Lane, who at once identified a long-missing register ("Masonic Records," preface, p. xii.). A series of articles arising out of the same discovery, from the pen of Mr G.

B. Abbott, appeared in the *Freemason*, commencing in vol. xix., p. 196 ; and Mr Sadler is now preparing for the press his own views with regard to the origin of the " Ancients."

Page 201, note 4, last line, *to read*, p. 152.
Page 242, line 13, *to read*, traditional history ; line 31, *for* aphorism, *read* aphanism.
Page 243, note 1, line 4, Sir G. Lewis.
Page 251, line 11, *for* respect, *read* repeat.
Page 255, line 22, last word *to read* he.
Page 269, line 7, Domaskins.
Page 345, line 17, 1767-73.
Page 398, line 29, 1789. This was the date of Preston's restoration to his Masonic privileges.
Page 415, note 2, *for* York, *read* Eboracum Lodge, No. 1610.

Page 423, line 9, a period after " (No. 134) ; " *and to continue*, On May 21, 1772, he instituted, etc.
Page 434, heading of Chapter, "According to *the* Old Institutions."
Page 436, line 21, inform us.
Page 467, note 1. *See* Introductory Note.
Page 493 Foreign Deputations. *See* Introductory Note.
Page 501, Articles of Union. These are given in Preston's " Illustrations of Masonry," also in Hughan's " Masonic Memorials" and " Masonic Register."

VOLUME III.

Page 14, line 13, The Emulation Lodge of Improvement was founded October 2, 1823.
Page 26, Statistics of English Masonry. *See* Introductory Note.
Page 39, The Grand Masters of Ireland. *See* Introductory Note.

Page 46, note 4. *See* Introductory Note.
Page 53, line 29, *for* 44th, *read* 55th.
Page 82, line 21, *to read*, "entered" at Kilwinning or some other Scottish Lodge previous to the era of Grand Lodges.
Page 113, line 87, *to read*, "Observantia Lata."

Page 195, C. F. Scheffer.

The name of this nobleman is shown in the Engraved List for 1770 as Prov. G.M. for Sweden, and is continued in the "Freemason's Calendar" until 1794. In a letter dated April 10, 1886, Mr Robert Dickson, G.S., Sweden, informs me—" The Grand Lodge of Sweden was constituted December 25, 1759. Its first Grand Master was Carl Frederick von Eckleff till 1777. Baron Carl Frederick Scheffer was S.P. and Deputy G. Master 1761-77." The authorities are hopelessly at variance, and we can only assume that in all probability Scheffer succeeded Fullman, as *English* Prov. G.M. in 1769 ?

Page 224, Dr Jaenisch.

Here I was misled by Nettelbladt, see p. 226.

Page 249, note 1, *to read*, *Post*, p. 284. | Page 256, note 5. *See* Introductory Note.

Page 285, Union of German Freemasons.

Out of this sprang " the Lessing Union of German Freemasons," founded in 1884. Its organ is the *Bauhütte*, and its Corypheus, Herr Findel. The aims and tendencies of the new " bund " are not regarded with favour by the Diet of German Grand Lodges.

Page 360, Porto Rico. "In 1821, authority was given by the G. L. of Massachusetts for a French Lodge at Mayaguez " (Proc. G. L., 1869).

Page 363, The Lesser Antilles. *See* pp. 422 and 488.
Page 380, Chilé.

Page 387, Dutch Guiana. *See* p. 448.

THE
Grand MYSTERY

OF THE

FREE MASONS
DISCOVER'D.

WHEREIN

Are the several QUESTIONS put to them at their
Meetings and *Installations*.

As also, Their OATH, HEALTH, SIGNS, and POINTS,
to know each other by.

As they were found in the Custody of a FREE-MASON
who Dyed suddenly.

And now publish'd for the Information of the PUBLICK.

The SECOND EDITION.

To which are ANNEXED,

Two LETTERS to a FRIEND;
The *First*, Concerning the Society of *FREE-MASONS.*

The *SECOND*,

Giving an Account of the Most Ancient Society of *GORMOGONS,*
in its *Original, Institution, Excellency,* and *Design :* Its *Rules* and *Orders,*
and the Manner of its Introduction into *Great Britain.* With an intire
Collection of all that has been made Publick on that Occasion. Together with the supposed Reason of their *Excluding the Free-Masons,*
without they previously undergo the Form of *Degradation, &c.* Now
first set forth for the *Satisfaction* and *Emolument* of the *Publick.*

Ambubajarum collegia, Pharmacapolæ,
Mendici, Medici, balatrones, hoc genus omne. HOR.
———— Mulus scabit Mulum. ————

LONDON:
Printed for A. MOORE, near St. *Paul's.*   1725.   [Pr. 1*s.*]

THE

Grand Mystery *of FREE-MASONS*

D I S C O V E R' D.

INTRODUCTION.

THIS Piece having been found in the Custody of a FREE-MASON, who died suddenly, it was thought proper to publish it in the very Words of the Copy, that the Publick may, at last, have something Genuine concerning the Grand Mystery of *Free-Masons.*

There was a Man at *Louvain*, who publish'd, That he had, with great Toil and Difficulty, found out, overcome, and tamed, and was now ready at his Booth, to shew, at the Rate of Six Stivers a-piece, the most hideous and voracious Monster, the Common Disturber of Mankind, especially in their Adversity.

Peopled flock'd from all Parts to see this Monster : They went in at the Fore-Door; and after they had seen the Creature, went out at the Back-Door, where they were ask'd, Whether the Monster was worth seeing? And as they had, at their Admittance into the Booth, promised to keep the Secret, they answer'd, It was a very wonderful Creature ; which the Man found his Account in. But, by some Accident, it was divulged, that this wonderful Creature prov'd to be a LOUSE.

But to proceed to the Subject in Hand ; we shall first present our Readers with

THE FREE-MASON'S SIGNS.

A GUTTERAL ⟩   A PEDESTAL ╱   A MANUAL ⌐   A PECTORAL ✕

EXAMINATION UPON ENTRANCE INTO THE LODGE.

PEACE be here.

Answer. I hope there is.

Q. What a-Clock is it?

A. It's going to Six, or going to Twelve.

Q. Are you very busy?

A. No.

Q. Will you give, or take?

A. Both ; or which you please.

Q. How go Squares?

A. Straight.

Q. Are you Rich, or Poor?

A. Neither.

Q. Change me that?

A. I will.

Q. In the Name of, &c. are you a Mason?

What is a Mason?

A. A Man begot of a Man, born of a Woman, Brother to a King.

Q. What is a Fellow?

A. A Companion of a Prince.

Q. How shall I know you are a Free Mason?

A. By Signs, Tokens, and Points of my Entry.

Q. Which is the Point of your Entry?

A. I Hear and Conceal, under the Penalty of having my Throat cut, or my Tongue pull'd out of my Head.

Q. Where was you made a Free-Mason?

A. In a just and perfect Lodge.

Q. How many make a Lodge?

A. God and the Square, with Five or Seven right and perfect Masons, on the highest Mountains, or the lowest Valleys in the World.

Q. Why do Odds make a Lodge?

A. Because all Odds are Mens Advantage.

Q. What Lodge are you of?

A. The Lodge of St. *John.* △

Q. How does it stand?   ✠

A. Perfect East and West, as all Temples do.

Q. Where is the Mason's Point?
A. At the East-Window, waiting at the Rising of the Sun, to set his Men at Work.
Q. Where is the Warden's Point?
A. At the West-Window, waiting the Setting of the Sun, to dismiss the Entred Apprentices.
Q. Who rules and governs the Lodge, and is Master of it?
A. Irah,
⟨ or the Right Pillar.
Iachin,
Q. How is it govern'd?
A. Of Square and Rule.
Q. Have you the Key of the Lodge?
A. Yes, I have.
Q. What is its Virtue?
A. To open and shut, and shut and open.
Q. Where do you keep it?
A. In an Ivory Box, between my Tongue and my Teeth, or within my Heart, where all my Secrets are kept.
Q. Have you the Chain to the Key?
A. Yes, I have.
Q. How long is it?
A. As long as from my Tongue to my Heart.
Q. How many precious Jewels?
A. Three ; a square Asher, a Diamond, and a Square.
Q. How many Lights?
A. Three ; a Right East, South, and West.
Q. What do they represent?
A. The Three Persons, Father, Son, and Holy Ghost.
Q. How many Pillars?
A. Two ; *Iachin* and *Boaz.*
Q. What do they represent?
A. A Strength and Stability of the Church in all Ages.
Q. How many Angles in St. *John's* Lodge?

A. Four, bordering on Squares.
Q. How is the Meridian found out?
A. When the Sun leaves the South, and breaks in at the West-End of the Lodge.
Q. In what Part of the Temple was the Lodge kept?
A. In *Solomon's* Porch, at the West-End of the Temple, where the two Pillars were set up.
Q. How many Steps belong to a right Mason?
A. Three.
Q. Give me the Solution?
A. I will. - - - The Right Worshipful, Worshipful Masters, and Worshipful Fellows, of the Right Worshipful Lodge from whence I came, greet you well.
Response. That Great God to us greeting, be at this our Meeting, and with the Right Worshipful Lodge from whence you came, and you are.
Q. Give me the *Jerusalem* Word?
A. *Giblin.*
Q. Give me the Universal Word?
A. *Boaz.*
Q. Right Brother of ours, your Name?
A. *N.* or *M.*
Response. Welcome, Brother *M.* or *N.* to our Society.
Q. How many particular Points pertain to a Free-Mason?
A. Three ; Fraternity, Fidelity, and Taciturnity.
Q. What do they represent?
A. Brotherly Love, Relief, and Truth, among all Right Masons ; for which all Masons were ordain'd at the Building of the Tower of *Babel,* and at the Temple of *Jerusalem.*
Q. How many proper Points?
A. Five ; Foot to Foot, Knee to Knee, Hand to Hand, Heart to Heart, and Ear to Ear.
Q. Whence is an Arch deriv'd?
A. From Architecture.
Q. How many Orders in Architecture?
A. Five ; the *Tuscan, Dorick, Ionick, Corinthian,* and *Composit.*
Q. What do they answer?
A. They answer to the Base, Perpendicular, Diameter, Circumference, and Square.
Q. What is the right Word, or right Point of a Mason?
A. Adieu.

THE FREE-MASON'S OATH.

You must serve God according to the best of your Knowledge and Institution, and be a true Liege Man to the King, and help and assist any Brother as far as your Ability will allow : By the Contents of the Sacred Writ you will perform this Oath. So help you God.

A FREE-MASON'S HEALTH.

HERE's a Health to our Society, and to every faithful Brother that keeps his Oath of Secrecy. As we are sworn to love each other, the World no Order knows like this our Noble and Antient Fraternity : Let them wonder at the Mystery.

Here, Brother, I drink to thee.

SIGNS TO KNOW A TRUE MASON.

1. To put off the Hat with two Fingers and a Thumb.
2. To strike with the Right-Hand, on the Inside of the Little-Finger of the Left three Times, as if hewing.
3. By making a Square, *viz.* by setting your Heels together, and the Toes of both Feet straight, at a Distance, or by any other Way of Triangle.
4. To take Hand in Hand, with Left and Right Thumb close, and touch each Wrist three Times with the Fore-Finger each Pulse.
5. You must Whisper, saying thus, The Masters and Fellows of the Worshipful Company from whence I came, greet you all well.
The Other will answer, God greet well the Masters and Fellows of the Worshipful Company from whence you came.
6. Stroke two of your Fore-Fingers over your Eye-Lids three Times.
7. Turn a Glass, or any other Thing that is hollow, downwards, after you have drank out of it.
8. Ask how you do ; and your Brothers drink to each other.
9. Ask what Lodge they were made Free-Masons at.

N.B. In the Third of King *Henry* VI. an Act of Parliament was pass'd, 𝔚hereby it 𝔴as 𝔪a𝔡e 𝔉elony, to cause MASONS to confederate themselves in 𝔠hapters and 𝔄ssemblies. 𝔗he 𝔓unishment is 𝔌mprisonment of 𝔅ody, and to make 𝔉ine and 𝔕ansom at the 𝔎ing's 𝔚ill.

TWO

LETTERS

TO A

FRIEND.

The *FIRST*, Concerning

The Society of FREE-MASONS.

The *SECOND*, Giving an Account of

The Most Ancient Order of *GORMOGONS*,

I N

Its *Original, Institution, Excellency*, and *Design :* Its *Rules* and *Orders*, and the Manner of its Introduction into *Great Britain.*

With an intire Collection of all that has been made Publick, on that Occasion. Together with the supposed Reason of their *Excluding the Free-Masons*, without they previously undergo the Form of *Degradation, &c.*

Now first set forth for the *Satisfaction* and *Emolument* of the *Publick.*

————*Nullo penetrabilis astro,*
Lucus erat.————   VIRG.

LONDON :
Printed for A. MOORE, near St. *Paul*'s.   *M.DCC.XXV.*

A

LETTER to a FRIEND,

CONCERNING

The Society of FREE-MASONS.

SIR,

THE Command, you have been pleas'd to lay upon me, is not to be discharged in a few Words : You require of me, To give you an Account of the *Fraternity* (as you are pleas'd to term it) which call themselves FREE-MASONS ; together with my Opinion about *them*, and their *Tenets*.

This, *SIR*, will cause some little Time to be spent ; first, In Enquiry after their *Tenets* ; and then, in maturely judging, and reasoning upon 'em : for rash and unpremeditated Determinations, in *such* Matters, will only expose their Authors ; and give Strength and Reputation to the opposite Parties.

As for their *Tenets*, they seem to be all Riddle and Mystery, to every Body but themselves ; and I make a Doubt, whether or no, they be able to give any fair and satisfactory Account of 'em. By what I can learn, they are under an *Oath*, or some solemn obligatory *Tie*, not to make known, or divulge their *Arcana* to any, except to the Members of their own Society. This, I presume, is because they are either so nonsensically *ludicrous*, and *foolish*, or else so horribly *lewd*, and *blasphemous*, that they will not endure a Publick Censure.

They set an huge Value upon themselves, in regard of being *Free Masons* : entertaining strange, aukward Notions of the Word *Mason* ; such as it never had belonging to it, in *Hebrew, Greek, Latin, English*, or, I believe, in any Language under Heaven. They seem to be listed under the Patronage of *Hiram*, the King of *Tyre*, who was doubtless an *Heathen* ; unless converted to *Judaism* after his Acquaintance with *Solomon* : Which is, at best, but a groundless *Chimæra*, and *Supposition* ; for the *Scriptures*, which are the only Authentick Records of those Matters, have taken no notice at all of it.

They tell strange foppish Stories of a *Tree*, which grew out of *Hiram's Tomb*, with wonderful *Leaves*, and *Fruit* of a *monstrous Quality* ; although, at the same Time, they know neither where, nor when he dy'd ; nor any thing more of his Tomb, than they do of *Pompey's*. But, to stop the Mouths of their ignorant, crackbrain'd Disciples (such as *Ale-house-keepers, Botchers, Corn-cutters*, &c.) some of their principal θαυματεργοι, lugg 'em by the Ears with a bombast Gypsie-like Jargon, which they call *Arabick* : although I am morally certain, That not one of the Society knows any more of the *Arabick* Language, than I do of the CHINESE.

Upon the Account, SIR, of this stupendous *Bocardo*, they assume to themselves the August Title of *Kabalists ;* or rather, as I submissively conjecture, *Cabal-lists* : *i.e.* A Knot of whimsical, delirious Wretches, who are caballing together, to extirpate all manner of *Science, Reason*, and *Religion* out of the World.

To explain the senseless and irrational Mode of their Proceedings, I shall ask you, or them, or all the World ; Whether 'twas ever known, that Men of common Sense and Discretion, did profess themselves to be of an Imployment or Occupation, which they know nothing at all of ? As for Instance, SIR, would you not take that Man to be qualified for *Bedlam*, that should call himself a *Gold-Smith*, when his Business is to *mend Shoes ?* and would it not make you laugh, to hear a Fellow call himself a *Lapidary*, when he gets his Living by *sweeping of Chimneys ?* Yet this is exactly the Case of *Free Masons ;* Every Member, forsooth, is a *Free Mason ;* although there be some *Divines*, or rather, if they were perfectly understood, *Dry-Vines*, some *Petti-foggers*, some *Clyster-pipe Men, Thread-makers, Taylors* and *Weavers*, and an huge Bead-roll besides, of Men calling themselves *Masons*, who know no more how to lay a Brick, or a Stone, as it should be laid, than they know how to make a *Hog* play upon a *Flute*, or a *Horse* understand *Algebra*.

There are several amongst 'em, who write themselves *S. T. P.* which some are apt to imagine, stands for *Sacrofanctæ Trinitatis Persecutores ;* for it is observable, That the Creed of St. *Athanasius* is treated very scurvily and opprobriously amongst divers of their Principals ; and the Divinity (nay, even the Divine Accomplishments of our Saviour) are handled by some of those Wretches, with a most shameful Buffoonry and Contempt. Remarkably eminent for this, is a certain *Renegado Papist ;* who has formerly wrote a nonsensical *Farrago* about the Plague : and makes the World believe, That he'll undertake to translate the Works of a certain *Classick ;* and, no doubt, in that Case, will render them nine time more ridiculous and unintelligible than any Man alive is able to do.

That, SIR, which gives the greatest Gloss, and Lustre to their Cabal, is this, *viz.* That they have artfully drawn some Great Names, into their wild, latitudinarian Measures : This I cannot in the least wonder at ; for Great Men, are but *Men*, and as apt to run into giddy, whimsical Schemes, as their Inferiors. Excellent was the Observation of the *Buzite, Job* xxxii. 9. where he says, *Great Men are not always Wise:* and I really look upon some certain Gentlemen among them, however otherwise dignified and distinguished, to be just such another Decoration to the *Free Masons*, as *Julian* and *Mazentius* were to *Atheism;* or *Constantius* and *Valens*, to the *Arian Heresy.*

I protest, SIR, I had like to have forgotten one Man, who makes a most Il-Lustrious Figure amongst 'em ; and stiles himself R.S.S. and L.L.D. He makes wonderful Brags of being of the *Fifth Order:* I presume (as he is a *Mason*) he means the *Fifth Order* of *Architecture;* which is otherwise call'd, The *Compound Order:* and by it one would be tempted to imagine, that the Doctor is a *Composition* of all sorts of *Maggots* and *Enthusiasm.* One thing there is, which makes me more bold in affirming this ; and this is it——The Doctor pretends, he has found out a Mysterious, *Hocus-pocus* Word, which belongs to the *Anathema* pronounc'd against *Ananias* and *Saphira*, in the 5th Chapter of the *Acts;* and he farther pretends, That against whomsoever he (as a Member of the *Fifth Order*) shall pronounce this terrible Word, the Person shall instantly drop down dead, as they did. I cannot imagine how the Doctor came by this powerful Word ; unless he found it in *Rablais's Pantagruel;* or in Dr. *Fuller's Dispensatory;* which are two great Repositories of incomprehensible Nonsense. I'll take all the Care I can, to keep out of the Doctor's Way ; for I am sure if he meets me, and knows me, out comes the great MILLESYLLABICUM, and I'm as dead as *William the Conqueror.*

But now, SIR, to draw towards a Conclusion ; and to give my Opinion seriously, concerning these prodigious *Virtuosi;*——My Belief is, That if they fall under any Denomination at all, or belong to any Sect of Men, which has hitherto appear'd in the World, they may be rank'd among the GNOSTICKS ; who took their Original from *Simon Magus:* These were a Set of Men, which ridicul'd not only *Christianity*, but even *Rational Morality;* teaching, That they should be *sav'd* by their *capacious Knowledge*, and *Understanding* of no Mortal Man could tell what. They babbled of an *amazing Intelligence* they had, from no-body knows whence : They amus'd, and puzzled the hare-brain'd, unwary Crowd, that follow'd 'em, with *Superstitious Interpretations*, of *extravagant Talismanical Characters*, and *abstruse Significations*, of uncommon *Kabalistick Words;* which exactly agrees with the Proceedings of our *Modern Free Masons.*

I am inclinable to believe, That by the Word MASON, they mean a *Builder*, and they take the Word BUILD, in a *Figurative* and *Metaphorick* Sense ; as it is us'd *Acts* xx. 32. and in many other Places of the New Testament : in which Places the Word *Build*, is us'd to signify the *Founding* and *Establishing* of the *Christian Church.* If this be their Meaning, 'tis no Breach of Charity to presume, that these Gentlemen are *Masoning* and *Building up* something, that it were heartily to be wish'd they would let alone ; for I must take the Freedom to say, That there are *Schisms* and *Fractions*, more than enough already, in our most Excellent Religion.

SIR, I shall trouble you with nothing more at present, than just to observe, That if the *Tenets* of these Men, do contain any thing that is conducive to the *Improvement* of *Manners*, the *Honour of God*, or the *real Advantage of Mankind* ; they are guilty of an unpardonable piece of Injustice, to conceal such beneficial *Dogmata* from the World. But if, contrariwise, they advance any thing, which is, or may be *Detrimental* and *Pernicious*, it is great Pity, it is not made Publick ; that it might be expos'd, censur'd, and taken care of, for *Diu crescentes nugæ, floreant in miserias.*

I am, SIR,

Your most Humble Servant,

VERUS COMMODUS.

P.S. SINCE my writing this, I have seen a little Tract call'd, *The Grand Mystery of the Free Masons Discover'd;* which, as I take it, gives us a Genuine Account of the Questions severally put to the Members of that Society, at their *Admission*, *Meetings*, &c. As also of their *Oath*, *Health*, *Signs*, *Points*, &c. and this I inclose, that you may have a farther Light into this pretended *Mysterious* Fraternity. Whereby, also, you will perceive what an unintelligible *Jargon* these People make a Mystery of.

LETTER II.

Giving an ACCOUNT of the

Most Ancient ORDER of *GORMOGONS,*

IN

Its *Original, Institution, Excellency,* and *Design :* Its *Rules* and *Orders,* and the Manner of its Introduction into *Great Britain.*

With an intire Collection of all that has been made Publick on that Occasion. Together with the supposed Reason of their *Excluding the Free-Masons,* without they previously undergo the Form of *Degradation, &c.*

SIR,

SINCE my last, the Venerable Order of GORMOGONS having been brought into *England,* by a *Chinese Mandarin,* of great Dignity and Note in his own Country, I could not deny my-self the Pleasure to give you as particular an Account as has come to my Knowledge, of what has been done and publish'd since his Arrival, relating to the Establishing that Society in this Island.

You, Sir, are not to be informed, That the *Chinese* pretend to have Accounts of Time and Transactions, many Thousand Years before *Adam ;* And I am now to acquaint you, That their first Chief Monarch, or Emperor, as he has since been called, who, tho' *European* Historians frequently call him by another Name, was commonly in *China,* known by that of CHIN-QUAW-KY-PO, is the Institutor of this Order, for the Reward of Merit, and Encouragement of Science, into that *Kingdom of Philosophers,* many Centuries before *Adam.* And I must needs confess, That as their only Boast is not their *Antiquity,* but that they chiefly aim to establish their Order on the MERIT of their Members ; they bid fair totally to eclipse the other Society, which, without any other Regards than the Entrance-Fine, and consequential Gluttony, and Ebriety, promiscuously, and without Distinction, admits the Worthy and the Unworthy.

This Order, it seems, as well as the other, has a SECRET, and, as I am inform'd, it is of a very extra-ordinary Nature ; but what, I am well assur'd, is neither shocking to *Decency,* to *Humanity,* or to *Morals,* tho' I cannot penetrate into the Nature of it. As the Cultivating of Arts and Sciences is the principal End of its Institution, Gentlemen of Wit and Parts, who are Members of it, entertain the Society with such Productions, either of their own, or others, as are truly Curious, whether in Prose or Verse, in every Science, as well Mechanical as Liberal. And for this Reason, ingenious Mechanicks are far from being excluded, each being encouraged, in his own particular Way, to excel. Nor do they, it seems, disdain to divert and entertain one another with a pleasant Song, so as it is not contrary to Decency and good Manners, and turns not upon Party or Politicks.

And this leads me to tell you, That the only Point of Conversation which is expresly prohibited, is that of the Politicks of their own Country ; which is a most excellent and necessary Rule, because, as the Society consists of ingenious Men of all Persuasions, and no body is excluded for his private Opinion, Disputes might otherwise arise, which would create Feuds and Animosities among them : The propagating the contrary of which, is, it seems, a fundamental Article among them.

After the Qualifications of the Person are examin'd into (which, I am told, is extremely strict) and approv'd, the Terms of Entrance are very easy : Instead of Three, Four, or Five Guineas, which the Masons require for Admission, they only deposite such a Sum as they shall think proper above so many * *Rupees.*

FRUGALITY is one extraordinary Injunction with them, that so they may avoid the Rocks on which others too frequently split : And the little easy Forfeitures and Fines of Entrance, are deposited in the Hands of a HUPU, or Treasurer, to be disposed of either to Charitable Uses, whenever any calamitous Case offers, or for the Encouragement of Arts and Sciences ; Reserving a Proportion thereof towards a General Feast, whether Quarterly, Half-Yearly, or Yearly, I cannot say, in order to cement and consolidate the Union of the several Chapters.

The Officer who presides in Chief over the whole Body or Order, must be a Man of Quality and Learning, and is called, as I am told, *Sub-Oecumenical Volgee.* He is represented by another Great Officer, stiled *Deputy Volgee,* who under him governs the Society. There is a Third Great Officer who acts as *Præses* over each par-

* *Rupee* is a *Chinese* Coin about the Value of 2s. 6d. Sterling.

ticular *Chapter*, and governs all Affairs therein, conformable to the *General Statutes* of the *Order*. But the Name of this Officer (for 'tis not made a *Secret*) I have forgot; only that it is, as all the rest, of *Chinese* Extraction.

By this Knowledge, which I have been able to come at, tho' I have not the Honour to be a GORMOGON, you will observe, Sir, the Excellency of the Order; and that they are not *asham'd* to let People know, in some Measure, the laudable *Ends* and *Purposes* of their *Institution*. I say, *In some Measure*, because it must be confess'd, they are very tenacious of the Great and Important SECRET of their Society, into which it is morally impossible, that any-body but a thoroughly-graduated GORMOGON can penetrate. You will also have the greater Opinion even of their SECRET, tho' 'tis past the Comprehension of the *Vulgar World*, inasmuch as you will observe, that they put on no affected Grimaces, in order to palm upon the Publick, the most *insignificant Trifles* for the *profoundest Mysteries*; nor do they treat *real* and *venerable Mysteries* as *Trifles*.

Having thus given you an Account of what I have been able to collect, relating to this Society, I come now to entertain you with the several Pieces that have been publish'd relating thereto. The first of which is from the *Daily Post* of the 3d of *September* last; tho' I am informed, that this Order was begun in *England* long before, and several Worthy Gentlemen had form'd themselves into a Body, under the *Auspices* of the *Mandarin* HANG CHI; and did not intend to make Publick their Institution. But, it seems, some *over-busy* Persons having got a Knowledge of a few Particulars, which were made no *Secret* of, and that the Assembly was held at the *Castle Tavern* in *Fleetstreet*, they, being minded to rally the *Free-Masons* at the same time, published the following Advertisement.

WHEREAS the truly Ancient and Noble Order of the GORMOGONS, Instituted by CHIN-QUAW-KY-PO, the first Emperor of *China* (according to their Account) many Thousand Years before *Adam*, of which Order the great Philosopher CONFUCIUS, was *Oecumenical Volgee*, has lately been brought into *England* by a *Mandarin*, and he having admitted several Gentlemen of Honour into the Mystery of that most illustrious Order, they have determin'd to hold a Chapter at the *Castle-Tavern* in *Fleetstreet*, at the particular Request of several Persons of Quality. This is to inform the Publick, that there will be no *drawn Sword at the Door*, nor *Ladder in a Dark Room*, nor will any *Mason* be received as a Member, till he has renounced his *Novel Order*, and been *properly degraded*. *N.B.* The *Great Mogul*, the *Czar* of *Muscovy*, and Prince *Tochmas*, are enter'd into this Honourable Society, but it has been refus'd to the Rebel *Meriweys*, to his great Mortification. The *Mandarin* will shortly set out for *Rome*, having a particular Commission to make a Present of this Antient Order to his *Holiness*; and it is believ'd the whole *Sacred College* of *Cardinals* will commence GORMOGONS. Notice will be given in the Public Papers the Day the *Chapter* will be held.

After this, several Gentlemen, who before had not heard of this Order, came to the *Castle-Tavern* to inquire into the Fact; and among the rest the Author of the PLAIN DEALER (a Gentleman of great Sagacity and Genius, as may be gather'd from the Excellent Papers wherewith he obliges the curious World every *Monday* and *Friday*) having in Person come to inquire concerning it, and meeting with the *Mandarin*'s Secretary and Interpreter, received from him so satisfactory an Account of the Matter, and was so pleased with the Institution, that he desir'd to be admitted a Member. But *unhappily* for the *Gentleman*, and to the *great Regret* of the Interpreter also, he happen'd to be a *Free-Mason*, and so could not be admitted without being solemnly *Degraded*, and formally renouncing that Society. Tho' that Gentleman was much mortified hereupon, not being able to persuade himself to be the *first* to give the Example of *Degradation*, yet he departed with such a favourable Idea of the Institution, that in his very next *Plain Dealer*, he began with a fine Dissertation on the Effects of *Credulity* and *Imposture*; for which I refer to his Excellent Paper, and then addressed himself to his Brethren of the *Apron* and *Trowel*, in a very Pathetick Manner. In the mean Time, the Interpreter being no less pleased with the Conversation, Curiosity, and Frankness of this Gentleman, gave the *Mandarin* an Account of it; Whereupon the illustrious HANG CHI (as he is call'd) being pleas'd with his Interpreter's Description of the Gentleman, vouchsafed to write him a Letter, to persuade him to be *degraded*, and offering to him, in that Case, the Honours of the Order, in a Manner so concise, and so polite, as seems to be peculiar to the Chiefs of the *Eastern Nations*, and at the same time communicated to him a Letter from another *Great Mandarin* named SHIN SHAW, at *Rome*; giving an Account of the good Reception the Order meets with in that once Imperial City. The *pathetick Expostulations* of the *Plain Dealer*, to his *Guilty Brethren*, as he calls 'em; The Letter of HANG CHI, that of SHIN SHAW, and the *Plain Dealer's* Answer, are all as follows, taken from that Paper of the 14th of *September*, Nº LI.

I WILL not be so partial to my own *Brotherhood*, I mean the Worshipful Society of FREE and ACCEPTED MASONS, as to forbear rebuking them, on this Occasion, for the unaccountable Pother and Noise they have lately made in the World. What Stories have been told to amuse, delude, and engage the *Credulous?* And how many have been drawn into the *Fraternity*, that have no Business there, to the manifest Detriment of their own Affairs, and Disadvantage of the Publick? What Reflections, what Reproach, have we brought upon Ourselves, and upon our *Ancient Order*, by making so many Proselytes, in so cheap and prostituted a Manner? It afflicts me sensibly, when I see so many idle, vain, and empty Coxcombs introduced into our *Lodges*, and made privy to our *Secrets*. I have often enter'd my Protest against this Abuse, in private Society; and must use the Freedom to offer this Memorial, in the Publick Character I bear. 'Tis my Opinion, that the late Prostitution of our *Order*, is next to the betraying of it. The weak Head of *Vintners, Drawers, Wigmakers, Weavers*, &c. admitted into our *Fraternity*, have not only brought Contempt upon the Institution, but do very much endanger it. Complaints have been made against the Abuse, even by Strangers and indifferent Persons: And I have heard it ask'd, Why we don't admit *Women*, as well as *Taylors*, into our *Lodges?* I profess, I have met with as *sufficient* Heads among the *Fair Sex*, as I have in the *Brotherhood*: And I have some Reasons to fear, that our *Secrets* are in Danger of being expos'd. There is, in the Conduct of too many, since their Admission, the

> ————————*Cæcus amor sui,*
> *Et tollens vacuum plus nimio Gloria verticem*
> *Arcanique Fides prodiga, perlucidior vitro ;*

which is expresaly prohibited by our Excellent *Rules* and *Constitutions ;* and which is the very Characteristick of the Fools, that were received into the *Lodges* at *Rome*, in the Days of *Augustus Cæsar ;* and whereof our Brother *Horace* complained vehemently, in an Ode to *Varus*, who was then the *Grand Master*. But whatever Freedoms others may imagine they may lawfully and discreetly use, my Conscience cannot brook them.

> —————————*NON EGO TE* . . . . .
> *INVITUM QUATIAM: NEC* . . . . .
> *SUB DIVUM RAPIAM* . . . . .

My Female Readers, and, I'm afraid, some of the *Brotherhood* too, may stop here, and stare, as if I had blabb'd out the whole *Mystery* in these Lines. My Friend *Tony Jyngle*, happening to cast his Eye upon this Paper, when I was writing it, ask'd me, Whether the above Words, and Dashes, wou'd not be *decypher'd* into the famous *Mason Word ?* But I must leave Folks, that know no better, to their *Wonder ;* and proceed to assure my guilty *Brethren*, that they have promoted *Superstition and Babbling*, contrary to the Peace of our Sovereign Lord the King, by their late Practices and Condescentions. Alarming Reports, and Stories of raising the DEVIL, of WITCHES, LADDERS, HALTERS, DRAWN SWORDS, and DARK ROOMS, have spread Confusion and Teror. Trade and Business, and *Family Duty*, have been shamefully neglected : And, if the Government does not put the Laws against us in Execution, it will be an extraordinary Favour, or *Oversight*. For my own Part, I am so faithful a Subject, and have the Weal of the good People of *England*, and of *Our Ancient Order*, so much at Heart, that I have resolv'd never to countenance a *Lodge* again, unless the *Grand Master* puts a Stop to these Proceedings, by a speedy and peremptory Charge to all the *Brotherhood*. I do not say, I will utterly forsake, far less divulge the tremendous *Secrets* of our *Society :* But I wish I could honourably enter into *Another*, that seems to be *better* establish'd, and regulated.

And, now that I have hinted at *another Society*, or *Order*, I must entertain my Readers with Two Letters ; the first is address'd to myself, and the last, written from *Rome*, to the Author of the first.

HANG CHI *to the* British PLAIN DEALER : *Health.*

Sage SIR,

BY the Help of my *Secretary* and *Interpreter* I peruse all your Lucubrations ; and write this Epistle, to assure you of my Esteem.

I am inform'd, that you have taken Notice of the *Advertisement* publish'd in the News Papers ; and that you call'd at the *Castle Tavern* in *Fleetstreet*, to be satisfy'd of the Truth of my Arrival in this Place. Your Enquiry, and the Conversation you had with my Secretary, give me Occasion to gratify you farther ; and I am proud to distinguish one of your Merit, in the Manner I intend.

The *Laws* and *Constitutions* of the most ancient and illustrious *Order* of *GORMOGONS* oblige us to be very *cautious* and *frugal*, in admitting *new Members*. Remarkable *Virtues* have always recommended the Candidates. No Rank, Station, or Condition of Life, intitles a Person to be of our *Fraternity*. We know no *Prejudice*, nor *Partiality*, in conferring this Honour ; and all the *Interest* in the World to procure it, would be fruitless, without *Merit*.

My Residence here will be but short. It cannot therefore be expected, that I should invite many worthy Persons to enter into our *Order ;* nor dare I render it cheap and contemptible, by admitting every Pretender : But I know several Persons of Quality and Fashion in this Place, who truly deserve to be received, and to whom I have promis'd the Distinction.

I shall consider it as an Honour and Ornament to our *most* ancient and illustrious *Order*, which is the Ornament of all its Members, if you, *Sage Sir*, will be pleas'd to accept the Privileges, that I am empower'd to bestow on the *Deserving*. I confess, you must be DEGRADED, as our Laws require, and renounce, and abandon, the Society of *Masons*, in the first Place : But, as your great Judgment must distinguish the Excellence of our *Order* above *that other*, I hope you will prefer being a *Fellow* with *Us*. Nothing wou'd more sensibly concern me, when I leave *London*, than not to be able to transmit your Name in the List, that I must send to the OECUMENICAL VOLGEE in *China*.

> *I am, Sage SIR,*
>
> *Your Affectionate Friend,*
>
> HANG CHI.

SHIN SHAW *to* HANG CHI *in* London: *Health.*

Most Illustrious Brother and Friend,

I Congratulate you on the speedy Progress you have made from the Court of the *Young Sophy* in *Persia,* and your safe Arrival in the Isle of *Britain.* Your Presence is earnestly expected at *Rome.* His *Holiness* is fond of our *Order,* and the *Cardinals* have an Emulation to be first distinguish'd. Our Excellent Brother GOR-MOGON and Brother *Mandarin,* CHAN FUE, is well, and salutes you. Since my last, I had Advices from *Pekin,* which confirm former Accounts, that our Emperor is an open Enemy to the *Missionary Jesuits:* But I pray, their Disgrace in *China,* may not provoke the *Europeans* to use *Us* ill. Take Care of your Health. Farewell.

SHIN SHAW.

I thankfully acknowledge the Honour done me, by the illustrious *Mandarin* HANG CHI; and, tho' I cannot prevail with myself to be DEGRADED, in the *Manner* required by the *Laws* and *Constitutions* of the Order of GORMOGONS, I approve, and applaud, their judicious and strict Virtue, in admitting none, but whom *Merit* recommends, into the Fellowship of the OECUMENICAL VOLGEE. Moreover, I propose the good Conduct, and Regularity of the GORMOGONS, as a Pattern to the *Free* and *Accepted Masons,* for the Future: And, if I shall be enabled to make any useful Discoveries for the Service of the *Brotherhood,* they may depend on my watchful Fidelity.

[*Thus far the Author of the* Plain-Dealer.]

I cannot guess why so excellent and laudable a Society as this of the GORMOGONS, should think it worth their while to make it an Article to exclude the *Free-Masons,* or that they should condescend to take so much Notice of them: Except there be any Truth in what I have heard reported, and to which I cannot give intire Credit, having never heard it from a *Graduated Gormogon.* The Report is this, That the *Mandarin* has declared, that many Years since, Two unhappy busy Persons, who were *Masons,* having obtruded their idle Notions among the *Vulgar Chinese,* of *Adam,* and *Solomon,* and *Hiram,* and I can't tell who besides, being Crafts-men of their Order, and offering to assert, that *Adam* was the first Man, which in *China,* is, it seems, received as a *Heterodox Notion,* and that the great *Chin-Quaw-Ky-Po,* the Institutor of the Order of *Gormogons,* was of *later* Date, many Centuries, than that Patriarch; and having, besides, deflower'd a venerable OLD Gentlewoman, under the Notion of making her an *European* HIRAMITE (as they called it) they were taken up, and obliged to recant, in Publick, their Absurdities, and afterwards, with Characters on their Breasts, denoting their Offence, and their Violence on the *Old Woman,* were hang'd Back to Back, on a Gibbet, erected for that Purpose, 60 Foot high, in the middle of a spacious Plain, some Miles from the great City *Nangking,* where their Bodies were left to be Food to the Fowls of the Air; And ever since, it has been an Article among the *Gormogons,* to exclude the Members of that Society, without they first undergo a solemn *Degradation, &c.* But this Story I leave as I find, for you to believe or reject as you please; having never heard it, as I have said, from the Mouth of a *Gormogon.* Tho' methinks, the Business of the OLD Gentlewoman affords, as our Weekly Politicians say, Mater of Speculation; and, at the worst, I hope the inraged Matron went too far in her Evidence, and was rather *saluted* than *violated.*

But however this be; the good Order and Regulations of the Society of *Gormogons,* have so much alarm'd the *Masons,* and convinc'd them of the Necessity of correcting the Abuses which have crept into their Fraternity, that we soon after had the Pleasure to read the following Advertisement, suppos'd to be publish'd by them, in the *Daily Journal,* on which I shall leave it to you, Sir, to make what Remarks you think fit.

On *Michaelmas Day,* being the 29th of this Instant *September,* a *New Lodge* will be open'd, at the *St. Alban's Tavern,* in *St. Alban's Street,* for regulating the *Modern Abuses,* which have crept into the *Ancient Fraternity* of *Free-Masons;* where 'tis desired, that all the *old real Masons* will be present, to accompany their Founders, viz. *Jabel, Jubel, Tubal Cain,* and their Sister *Nahama,* also *Nineveh, Marcus, Gracchus, Euclid, Hierom, Charles Martin, Athelstone,* and their good Friend St. *Alban,* who loved Masonry well.

'Tis desired, that all *Fathers, Masters,* and *Wardens* of Lodges, who have discover'd no *Secrets* but to the *Brotherhood,* will be present. None under *Seven* will be admitted, and such as come, are to enter the *Lodge,* on the bare Hand and *Knee,* as usual.

Thus, Sir, have I given you all I know, or can collect, relating to this Affair; and if ever you hear from me again on this Subject, it will be in a few REMARKS on that empty Book called, *The Constitutions, &c. of the Free-Masons,* written, as I am told, by a *Presbyterian Teacher,* and pompously recommended by a certain Reverend *Orthodox,* tho' *Mathematical* Divine. In the mean time, I remain,

SIR,

Your very Humble Servant,

VERUS COMMODUS.

POSTSCRIPT.

SINCE the closing this Letter, I have had the Pleasure to receive an Account, which I much desir'd, of the *Derivation* of the Word GORMOGON ; and, as it is very Curious and Significant, and is not made a Secret of, I could not but inform you of it. It is, it seems, a *Compound Word* in the *Chinese* Tongue, signifying, A Person made Illustrious by *Social Love*, by the *Excellency* of his *Genius*, and by the *Antiquity* of his *Descent :* For GOR, in that most expressive Language, signifies *Brother*, or *Friend*, the most valuable Title on Earth ; MO is a Word of Eminence, prefix'd to a Name or Thing, to distinguish its *Excellency ;* and GON, signifies *Antiquity* or *Length of Continuance :* And it is observable, That the Province of MO-GON in *China*, which was formerly the Residence, Birth-place, and Paternal Inheritance of the Great *Chin-Quaw-Ky-Po* (as its Name [MO-GON] denotes *The most Excellent and most Ancient Kingdom*) is one of the most plentiful and flourishing Provinces of that vast Empire.

In short, Sir, I am so pleas'd with this excellent Society, that I shall only wait for your Return from the Country, not doubting but you will join your Interest with me, that we may be recommended as Members (however otherwise unworthy I may be !) of this Ancient Order.

By this Time you will Laugh with me at the Pretensions of the *poor Masons* (who, I am told, now sculk about, and meet in Corners) since, as they pretend to derive their Ancientry from *Babel*, they seem to confess, that they found their *Order* on *Confusion ;* And indeed, I am much pleased, with what I heard an ingenious GORMOGON express on this Occasion, with which I shall conclude. " We are not displeas'd, said he, That " these *Hewers* of *Stone*, and *Drawers* of *Water*, these *mere Pretenders* to nothing more than *Labour* and *Mechanicks*, " who boast so much of their *Hod-man-ship*, should pretend to derive their Originals from any Place, where " they have *happen'd to read* of *Buildings* or *Monuments* of *Antiquity*, or from *Babel*, from *Noah*, or even from " *Adam :* We could even permit them to go still *higher*, and deduce their *Rise* before the Earth itself was created, " among the *Infernal Founders* of PANDEMONIUM, for the Erecting of which they might quote the Authority " of the Great *Milton ;* and, as a *far-fetch'd Antiquity* is their *only Pride*, so might they, with *equal Justice*, and " *equal Reputation* to themselves, derive their Original from that *Infernal Capital*, as from *Babel*. But let them, " said he, shew us once, That *Merit*, in the First Place, or ought tending to *Edification*, to *Morals*, to *Improve-* " *ment* of those *Arts* and *Sciences*, which they lay so proud a Claim to, are any Part of their Consideration ; or, " Secondly, That any *Free-Mason*, after his Commencement, became either a *wiser* or a *better Man ;* or, Thirdly, " That *Cain*, *Nimrod*, *Semiramis*, and the Founders of *Babel*, are not rather the Examples which they follow ; " and I'll give my Vote, that they shall be admitted *Gormogons* without *Degradation*, and be no longer the " *standing Jest* of the *Vulgar*, and the *Derision* of *Men of Sense*."

He concluded with a severe Sting, " That those Persons who saw the Masons go reeling Home, at unseason- " able Hours, after a *Meeting* or a *Lodge-Night*, would not question their following the Example of *Noah*, in " that Instance, at least, of his *getting drunk* with the Fruits of his own *Plantation*, and discovering his " *Nakedness*, to *Shem, Ham*, and *Japhet*."

FINIS.

A MASON'S EXAMINATION.

The earliest of the "so-called" exposures of Freemasonry appeared in the *Flying Post* or *Post Master*, No. 4712, from Thursday, April 11, to Saturday, April 13, 1723. From 1723 to the present era, hundreds of these "Examinations" and "Catechisms" have seen the light, and it may be stated generally, that they bear a strong "family likeness" to the original "revelation," which is subjoined.

The (so-called) "exposure" of 1723 professes, of course, to have been compiled from the papers of a "deceased brother"—a "formula" with which readers of more recent "Catechisms" will be familiar, and which implies that our Masonic ancestors of 150 years ago had, even then, forestalled our German brethren of to-day in the use of printed or written rituals; students will, however, find several points of interest presented in the "Examination" under notice, *e.g.*:

The allusions to the Second Degree (though this was then only conferred *in* Grand Lodge), to the *Mark* of a Master Mason, and to the *Pattern of an Arch*—the first mention of the word "Arch" in connection with Freemasonry, it may be here observed—occur in the Constitutions of 1723, at the close of Dr Anderson's exordium.

[FROM THE FLYING POST, No. 4712.—A.D. 1723.]

To the Author of the Flying Post.

The Ancient Fraternity of *Free and Accepted Masons*, has thro' all Ages been justly esteemed the only One Society, which hath inviolably observed and kept those two essential and fundamental *Pillars* of all good Fellowship, *Taciturnity* and *Concord*; there being but one single instance since the Beginning of Time, that a *Free Mason* betray'd the *Grand Arcanum* of the Society; namely, *Samson*, who indeed proved a mere *Judas*, and was punished accordingly.[1]

This has been a Matter of much Speculation to the rest of Mankind, and hath occasioned various Reasonings and Disputes.

It is indeed agreed on all hands, that *Masonry*, the most *Substantial* Part of *Architecture*, is of singular Use and Ornament: that *Free Masons* are no prying inquisitive Busie-bodies, but honest industrious Persons, who desire only to excel in their own Profession; that the *Worshipful Society* are no Innovators in Religious Affairs, no perjured Plotters or Conspirators against the established Government: that they in no way interfere or clash with any other Society or Corporation, however dignify'd or distinguish'd; for all which excellent Qualifications, a reasonable Person would be willing to pay their *Persons*, their *Lodges*, their *Constitutions*, all due Respect and Honour.

But so it is, there are Men of Shallow Capacities, Blabbers of Secrets, who, because they have lost or misused their own retentive Faculties, envy and hate those who retain the Gift of *Secrecy* and *Fidelity*; these mean Wretches have of late Studied a Thousand Practices to bring this *Worshipful Society* into Contempt and Obloquy, and are egg'd on by some silly Women, who (because for good Reasons their Sex are by the Constitutions judged incapable of *Fellowship*) are, therefore, nettled and seek Revenge. These are the Persons who trump up many foolish and idle Signs, Gestures, and Practices, and vouch them for the very *Basis* and *Ground-plot* of *Free-Masonry*. The enclosed is a sample of their Malice, and which they pretend was left in Writing by a *Fellow Mason* lately deceased; but, in very Truth, is a Senseless Pasquinade, highly derogatory to the Honour of the whole *Body*, and each *Worshipful Fellow*, many of whom daily stand in Presence of Kings, and are Cloathed with Titles, Dignities, and Honours.

I shall not take upon me to vindicate the high Reputation of the *Fraternity*, their numerous *Lodges* stand in no need of *Props* and *Buttresses* for their support; neither will their *Members*, by any Arts or Contrivances, be induced like Fools and Children to divulge the Lessons and Instructions given by their Masters and Wardens; but will have a constant Eye to that memorable Saying of Wise King *Solomon* in his Time *Grand Master of Masonry* and *Architecture*, and which pointed to *Samson's* Fate aforementioned—*A prating Fool shall fall.—I am*, &c.

When a Free-Mason is enter'd, after having given to all present of the Fraternity a Pair of Men and Women's Gloves and Leathern Apron, he is to hear the . . . belonging to the Society read to him by the Master of the Lodge. Then a Warden leads him to the Master and Fellows; to each of whom he is to say—

> I fain would a Fellow-Mason be,
> As all your Worships may plainly see.

After this, he Swears to reveal no Secrets of the Worshipful Fraternity, on Pain of having his Throat cut, and having a double Porrion (Portion?) of Hell and Damnation hereafter. Then he is blind-folded, and the ceremony of —— is performed. After which he is to behold a Thousand different Postures and Grimaces, all of which he must exactly imitate, or undergo the Discipline till he does.

After this the word *Maughbin* is whispered by the youngest Mason to the next, and so on, till it comes to the Master, who whispers it to the entered Mason, who must have his Face in due order to receive it. Then the entered Mason says what follows:

> An enter'd Mason I have been,
> *Boaz* and *Jachin* I have seen;
> A Fellow I was sworn most rare,
> And know the Astler, Diamond, and Square:
> I know the Master's Part full well,
> As honest *Maughbin* will you tell.

Then the Master says:

> If a Master-Mason you would be,
> Observe you well the *Rule of Three*;
> And what you want in Masonry,
> Thy *Mark* and *Maughbin* makes thee free.

[1] *Hence comes the saying on One who blabs all he knows*, He'll bring an old House on his Head.

When you would enter a Lodge you must knook three times at the Door, and they'll challenge you.

Q. Are you a Free-Mason?

A. Yes, indeed, I am.

Q. How shall I know it?

A. By Signs and Tokens— ☐ ☐ ☐ —from my Entrance into the Kitchen, and from thence to the Hall.

Q. What is the first Point of your Entrance?

A. Hear and conceal, on Pain of having my Throat cut or Tongue pull'd out.

Then one of the Wardens will say—God's greeting be at this Meeting; and with the Right Worshipful the Master, and the Worshipful Fellows, who keep the Keys of the Lodge from whence you came; and you are also welcome, Worshipful Brother, into this Worshipful Society.

Then you salute as follows—

The Right Worshipful the Master and the Worshipful Fellows of the Lodge from whence I came greet you abundantly.

Q. What Lodge are you of?

A. I am of the Lodge of St. Stephen's.

Q. What makes a just and Perfect Lodge?

A. A Master, two Wardens, four Fellows, five Apprentices, with Square, Compass, and Common Gudge.

Q. Where was you made?

A. In the Valley of *Jehosophet*, behind a Rush-bush, where a Dog was never heard to bark, or Cock crow, or elsewhere.

Q. Where was the first Lodge Kept?

A. In *Solomon's* Porch; the two Pillars were called *Jachin* and *Boaz.*

Q. How many Orders be there in Architecture?

A. Five; Tuscan, Doric, Ionic, Corinthian, and Composite, or Roman.

Q. How many Points be there in Fellowship?

A. Six: Foot to Foot, Knee to Knee, Hand to Hand, Ear to Ear, Tongue to Tongue, Heart to Heart.

Q. How do Masons take Place in Work?

A. The Master S.E., the Wardens, N.E., and the Fellows Eastern Passage.

Q. How many precious Jewels are there in Masonry?

A. Four: Square, Astler, Diamond, and Common Square.

Q. How many Lights be there in a Lodge?

A. Three: The Master, Warden, and Fellows.

Q. Whence comes the Pattern of an Arch?

A. From the Rainbow.

Q. Is there a Key to your Lodge?

A. Yes.

Q. What is't?

A. A well hung Tongue.

Q. Where is it Kept?

A. In an Ivory Box between my Teeth, or under the Lap of my Liver, where the Secrets of my Heart are not.

Q. Is there a Chain to it?

A. Yes.

Q. How long is it?

A. As long as from my Tongue to my Heart.

Q. Where does the Key of the working Lodge lie?

A. It lies on the Right Hand from the Door two Foot and a-half under a Green Turf, and one Square.

Q. Where does the Master place his Mark on the Work?

A. Upon the S.E. Corner.

To know an Entred Apprentice, you must ask him whether he has been in the Kitchen, and he'll answer, Yes.

To know an Entred Fellow, you must ask whether he has been in the Hall, and he'll say, Yes.

To know a Mason in the Dark, you must say, there is no Darkness without Absence of Light; and he'll answer, There is no Light without Absence of Darkness.

To compliment a Brother Mason, you put your Right Hand to the right side of your Hat, and bring your Hat under your Chin; then the Brother will clap his Right Hand to the right side of his Hat, and bring it to the Left Side under his Heart.

To meet a Brother, you must make the first Step with your Right Foot, the Second with your Left; and at the third you must advance with your Right Heel to your Brother's Right Instep; then lay your Right Hand to his Left Wrist, and draw the other Hand from your Right Ear to the Left under your Chin; and then he'll put his Right Hand to his Left Side under his Heart.

To Gripe, is when you take a Brother by the Right Hand, and put your middle Finger to his Wrist, and he'll do so to you.

To know a Mason privately, you place your Right Heel to his Right Instep, put your Right Arm over his Left, and your left under his Right, and then make a Square with your middle Finger, from his Left Shoulder to the Middle of his Back, and so down to his Breeches.

When a Mason alights from his Horse, he lays the Stirrup over the Horse's Neck.

To call a Mason out from among company, you must cough three times, or knock against any thing three times.

A Mason, to show his Necessity, throws down a round Piece of Slate, and says, Can you change this Coin?

GENERAL INDEX.

THE END.

M'Farlane & Erskine, Printers, Edinburgh.

Milton Keynes UK
Ingram Content Group UK Ltd.
UKHW022217070923
428268UK00005B/108